America's Middlemen

Throughout American political history, the US government formed alliances with militias, tribes, and rebels. Sometimes, these alliances have been successful, dramatically reshaping the battlefield. But these alliances have also risked creating larger wars in regions where the United States had no real interest. Understanding these alliances – and much of American political history – requires moving beyond our normal focus on traditional diplomats or social elites. The architects of these alliances were traders, missionaries, former slaves, and low-level government employees. These intermediaries used their ties across borders to reshape security politics, affecting American and thereby world history. Skillfully integrating political science with history and sociology, Eric Grynaviski provides a novel account of who matters and why in international politics. By developing broader views about political agency – how people come to make a difference in world politics – he brings into focus new histories of world politics and how they matter for scholars and the public.

Eric Grynaviski is an Associate Professor of Political Science and International Affairs at George Washington University. His first book, *Constructive Illusions* (2014), won the American Political Science Association's Robert L. Jervis and Paul W. Schroeder Best Book Award for International History and Politics. His work has appeared in *International Organization*, *International Theory*, *Security Studies*, the *European Journal of International Relations*, and the *Review of International Studies*.

America's Middlemen

Power at the Edge of Empire

ERIC GRYNAVISKI

George Washington University

CAMBRIDGE
UNIVERSITY PRESS

University Printing House, Cambridge CB2 8BS, United Kingdom

One Liberty Plaza, 20th Floor, New York, NY 10006, USA

477 Williamstown Road, Port Melbourne, VIC 3207, Australia

314–321, 3rd Floor, Plot 3, Splendor Forum, Jasola District Centre, New Delhi – 110025, India

79 Anson Road, #06-04/06, Singapore 079906

Cambridge University Press is part of the University of Cambridge.

It furthers the University's mission by disseminating knowledge in the pursuit of education, learning, and research at the highest international levels of excellence.

www.cambridge.org
Information on this title: www.cambridge.org/9781107162150
DOI: 10.1017/9781316676950

© Eric Grynaviski 2018

First published 2018

Printed in the United States of America by Sheridan Books, Inc.

A catalogue record for this publication is available from the British Library.

ISBN 978-1-107-16215-0 Hardback
ISBN 978-1-316-61472-3 Paperback

For my Parents

Contents

Figures

Tables

Acknowledgements

This book relied on many people. It would not have been possible without the assistance of helpful archivists. Some people who work in archives are as difficult to negotiate with as the characters in this book. This means when people are helpful and friendly, it really stands out. There are too many to thank. In particular, I wanted to thank Katherine Collett (Hamilton Archives), Alex Johnston (University of Delaware), Bailey Romaine (Newberry Library in Chicago), Rodney Ross (Center for Legislative Archives), and Jack Lufkin (Iowa State Historical Society). Other archivists made this project a delight to work on, especially the excellent staff at the US Army Heritage and Education Center in Carlisle, Pennsylvania.

Conversations with people in the American Civil War and Indian history communities were crucial to several parts of this book. Chuck Lott generously provided me with his private research and material on Edwin Andress. Raymond Herek helped talk through issues related to Indian records in the Civil War related to Michigan. Eric Hemenway, the Director of Repatriation, Records, and Archives for the Little Traverse Bay Bands of Odawa Indians was also helpful. Malinda Maynor Lowery (UNC-Chapel Hill) spent part of an afternoon on the telephone discussing Lumbee Civil War-era experiences, which proved essential to one part of this book, as was a discussion with Alex Baker of the Lumbee Tribe of North Carolina about their historical traditions.

Eugene Shestakov, a student in the Honor's Program at George Washington University, helped me process files related to the Spanish–American War. Miles Evers, Brett Heiney, Erinn Larkin, and Daisuke Minami provided research assistance along the way as well. Konstantinos

Tsimonis provided valuable assistance with missionary archives in London. I also gratefully acknowledge the support and funding received during a fellowship at the Käte Hamburger Kollege / Centre for Global Cooperation Research, University of Duisburg-Essen.

The Institute for Security and Conflict Studies at George Washington University was kind enough to host a book workshop. I wanted to thank Bentley Allan, Michael Barnett, Stacie Goddard, John Hall, Daisuke Minami, and Dan Nexon for their participation, as well as John Owen, who closely read part of the book and sent his comments. Michael Barnett and Alexander Wendt also provided a lot of help in considering titles, covers, and the like. Parts of this book were presented at McGill University, William and Mary, and the University of Ottawa, as well as at several conferences. I appreciate the comments from everyone along the way. Conversations with Evgeny Finkel also helped me steer my way through some thickets. My colleagues at George Washington University, especially the lunch bunch, were treated to perhaps one too many stories of what happened in Samoa or Nebraska more than a century ago. I would appreciate it if they feigned more interest in the future.

Mara and Ethan deserve the most thanks. Ethan was about one year old when I started this book, and now he is finishing first grade. Watching a child grow up is the most amazing distraction. He is clearly old enough now to shoulder the blame for any mistakes in this book. Mara read every draft of this book, edited the whole, and provided running commentary on when I became too "cheesy." She shouldered burdens that helped me have time to write, especially the burden of being my best friend. This book is dedicated to my parents, Jane and Dan Grynaviski.

Abbreviations

AHEC	US Army Heritage and Education Center
ARCIA	Annual Report of the Commissioner of Indian Affairs
CD	Consular Dispatch
CWM	Council for World Mission
LC	Library of Congress
LMS	London Missionary Society
LR	Letters Received
LS	Letters Sent
NARA	National Archives and Record Administration, Washington, DC
NARA II	National Archives and Record Administration II, College Park
NDSW	*Naval Documents of the Barbary Wars*
R	Roll
RG	Record Group

Introduction

In his biography of Amhad Chalabi, Aram Roston writes that "without Chalabi there would have been no war." In the lead up to the Iraq War, Chalabi shaped information across borders. The limited information coming from Iraq before the war meant the United States was groping in the dark for military and political intelligence. Chalabi took advantage. He gave intelligence to the media and politicians about Hussein's weapons of mass destruction, claimed insider knowledge of resistance movements who would support the United States, and used his "personal magnetism, lobbying skills, and tactical abilities" to convince legislators to support his schemes. As Roston explains, some hated him and others loved him, but "most are in awe at the tangled plots he weaves around him."[1] Chalabi was not an obvious candidate to influence the war. He had left Iraq in 1958 and was a mathematician by training. He founded a bank in Jordan in 1977, but after accusations of corruption he fled Jordan as the bank failed. His Iraqi National Congress, founded in London in the 1990s, had few connections to Baghdad and served primarily as a platform to pursue his own parochial interests. Yet, the Bush administration turned to him to make its case and plans for war.

This book helps us make sense of the influence of figures like Chalabi. The Bush administration did not have the political or military intelligence necessary to make the case for or fight the war. Situations like this, in

---

[1] Aram Roston, *The Man Who Pushed American to War: The Extraordinary Life, Adventures, and Obsessions of Ahmad Chalabi* (New York: Nation Books, 2008), xi–xiii. See also Richard Bonin, *Arrows of the Night: Ahmad Chalabi and the Selling of the Iraq War* (New York: Anchor Books, 2011).

I

which there is little direct contact between a state and a foreign people, create opportunities for intermediaries to exercise outsized influence on world affairs. Although Chalabi's ties proved ineffective in the end (he could not make reconstruction smooth), the Bush administration's search for someone to broker information across borders led a corrupt Jordanian banker to be a crucial part of the country's post-war reconstruction plans. Chalabi's position between Washington and Baghdad was the source of his influence.

Chalabi provides an example of what this book will refer to as the power of betweenness. People who live in the breach between societies often have access to forms of influence that people who live at centers of power do not. They can serve as conduits of information between societies or manipulate information as it crosses borders. Chalabi is special only because he was so unsuccessful. This book shows that at the heart of US national security politics, from the founding until today, is the power of betweenness. Agents working between societies have found partners abroad and at home upon whom the US military depends to fight and win its wars. Missionaries brokered cooperation between the Colonial Congress and the Iroquois, forming one of the most important alliances of the Revolutionary War (Chapter 2). Adventurers and traders capitalized on their positions between societies to drag the United States into unwanted conflicts such as Samoa, in the first near-miss imperial war in the Pacific (Chapter 5). The large colonial army that the United States recruited in the Philippines was formed by soldiers who had relationships between societies that allowed them to identify potential collaborators (Chapter 7). During World War II, the agents who were able to find partners in Central Europe to fight alongside the Allies were bicultural and bilingual, using their position between societies to create advantages for US forces. The situation remains the same in Afghanistan and Iraq, where agents who are able to navigate between American forces and local rebels and militias secure America's modern allies (Chapter 8).

This book uses the power of betweenness to examine one of the more fundamental questions in international politics, "who matters?" To answer this question, I examine the role of individuals whom I describe as intermediaries. Intermediaries are people who make careers and families by crossing borders. They are people like missionaries and merchants in the eighteenth century, or translators in the contemporary world. Their influence does not arise from a central position within a society; instead, their social position between societies provides them with the power to shape the flow of information across borders. This book focuses on how these intermediaries enhanced US expansion during the eighteenth and nineteenth centuries. Intermediaries used their structural position between societies to help the United States recruit the tribes, militias, and rebels whom the United States has historically depended on to conduct its foreign policy. By selecting intermediaries and non-state allies, this book provides a systematic explanation for how one class of agents with no institutional influence shapes international politics. In doing so, it draws general lessons about the structural nature of political power while providing novel explanations of events important for the trajectory and shape of American power.

THE POWER OF BETWEENNESS AND NETWORK THEORY

Many International Relations scholars interested in security politics concentrate on the contributions of only a narrow range of agents, usually "great men." Studies of the Civil War focus on Lincoln; studies of the Second World War often focus on Roosevelt, Hitler, or Churchill; and studies of Vietnam concentrate on the American presidents – Johnson and Nixon – or their powerful staff, such as Robert McNamara or Henry Kissinger.[2] To the extent that ordinary citizens matter, it is only as a group, and even then, many studies of public opinion find the public's influence over foreign affairs is marginal.

The central problem with a focus on the "great men" is that, empirically, we know that individuals outside of nations' capitals matter quite a bit to the outcome of major world historical events, such as war, financial crises, and global trade. Historians, in particular, have repeatedly shown that individuals who do not have politically influential institutional positions frequently change world history. The consistent focus on political elites in contemporary scholarship, at the expense of individuals who live far from nations' capitals, means focusing on the agents who react to, instead of initiate, change. It leaves offstage the actor, murderer, priest, fur trader, or pawnshop owner whose daily interactions with others

---

[2] Other IR scholars find the focus on "great men" to be misguided. Changes in states' foreign policy, perhaps especially American foreign policy, should rarely be credited to individual leaders, because the structure of the international system – the balance of power or the ideas prevalent in a community – exert so much influence behind the backs of leaders. See, for example, Kenneth Waltz, *Theory of International Politics* (Boston: McGraw-Hill, 1979); Alexander Wendt, *Social Theory of International Politics* (Cambridge: Cambridge University Press, 1999).

shape global politics. While anthropologists, sociologists, historians, and students of empires have moved past political elites to focus on the ways ordinary people transform the world, many political scientists remains mired in the study of a few people.[3]

This book develops a theory about the structural conditions under which ordinary people can change international politics through the power of betweenness. In many cases, cooperation is likely stymied because agents are unaware of or do not trust potential cooperation partners. Investors in New York may be unaware of business partners in the Philippines, a farmer in Africa may not have the contacts necessary to bring his goods to market in Europe, and governments may be unaware of newly forming rebel groups. In all of these cases, there is a hole between networks: New Yorkers' circles of friends and acquaintances, for example, do not intersect with Filipinos' circles of friends and acquaintances. Using language derived from social theory, I describe these as cases where there is a "structural hole" between communities.[4]

The existence of a structural hole – a particularly information-poor environment – provides opportunities for agents whom I term "intermediaries" to play a role in international cooperation. An intermediary, a term formally defined in Chapter 1, is an agent who gains her influence from her position between societies rather than within a society. They are traders, missionaries, adventurers, and crooks whose influence comes from their skill in seeing opportunities for cooperation across borders. Intermediaries do not have significant institutional power, but they can

---

[3] Perhaps the primary exception are feminist scholars, who show the influence that women who do not have positions of political influence, such as Korean prostitutes or diplomats' wives, may have on cooperation and conflict. Cynthia Enloe, *Bananas, Beaches and Bases* (Berkeley: University of California Press, 2000); Katharine Moon, *Sex Among Allies* (New York: Columbia University Press, 1997). Several scholars within diplomatic studies have also emphasized less likely figures, such as journalists or "citizen diplomats." This scholarship, however, does not develop a framework that assesses the conditions under which these individuals are likely to matter. Eytan Gilboa, "Media-Broker Diplomacy: When Journalists Become Mediators," *Critical Studies in Media Communication* 22, no. 2 (2005): 99–120; Paul Sharp, "Making Sense of Citizen Diplomats: The People of Duluth, Minnesota, as International Actors," *International Studies Perspectives* 2, no. 2 (2001): 131–50.

[4] Ronald Burt, *Structural Holes: The Social Structure of Competition* (Cambridge: Harvard University Press, 1992); Ronald Burt, *Brokerage and Closure: An Introduction to Social Capital* (Oxford: Oxford University Press, 2005); Stacy Goddard, "Brokering Change: Networks and Entrepreneurs in International Politics," *International Theory* 1, no. 2 (2009): 249–81.

bridge structural holes, connecting buyers and sellers in international trade, or connecting states with proxy armies in the developing world.

Intermediaries' primary causal power is to connect partners across structural holes. They identify potential cooperation partners and bring them to the attention of decision-makers. Knowing the conditions under which intermediaries may fill structural holes, however, is only one step in a theory of cooperation. Even if parties are aware of one another, cooperation does not necessarily follow, because of conflicts of interest, mistrust, and cultural conflict. These problems are likely to be especially severe in instances where intermediaries are necessary to bridge structural holes, because these cases, by definition, occur where parties infrequently interact. Therefore, the parties may be unaware of, or have stereotypical views of, others' interests, may not have reputations for trustworthiness, and may make cultural blunders that hamper cooperation.

How do intermediaries promote cooperation across structural holes and avoid conflicts of interest, mistrust, and cultural misunderstanding? Intermediaries have two assets. First, by definition, intermediaries have a monopoly on information crossing borders. If intermediaries are the sole trusted means of transmitting information between communities, then they have the ability to selectively provide information or manipulate the information passed between societies. Second, intermediaries may have the ability to empathize with diverse communities. Building on socio-logical work about the nature of social skill, I argue that intermediaries between societies are better able to frame cooperation for parties because they can empathize with the interests, beliefs, and prejudices of poten-tial cooperation partners.[5] Individuals who live their lives between soci-eties can usually understand the perspective of both societies; traders, missionaries, and government agents stationed abroad make their livings appealing to people with diverse worldviews. This book outlines how they frame cooperative schemes and build trust between parties to secure international cooperation.

INTERMEDIARIES IN US FOREIGN POLICY

Intermediaries have used their power of betweenness to shape some of the most important events in the history of American foreign policy. I concentrate on how they have helped broker relationships with allies

---

[5] See, for example, Neil Fligstein, "Social Skill and the Theory of Fields," *Sociological Theory* 19, no. 2 (2001): 105–25.

across the globe, from 1776 until modern times. Since 1776, the United States has relied heavily on non-state allies – political groups, who are not states, that collectively decide to provide military assistance during a conflict – in nearly every overseas and North American conflict.

These alliances with non-state allies are fundamental to explaining how the United States rose, from its colonial origins to superpower status. Without these allies, history would have turned out differently. During the Revolutionary War, for example, the United States depended on its Native American allies, such as the Oneidas, to close major routes by which the British might invade and to collect intelligence from areas where Continentals could not easily travel.[6] During the frontier wars against Native Americans, the United States frequently depended heavily on Native Americans to fight, such as the lower Creeks in the Creek Civil War and the First Seminole War, Potawatomis in the Black Hawk War, and many Apache in the forty years of warfare in Arizona. During the Civil War, both the North and the South engaged in intense political competition to woo Native Americans, promising money, weapons, and land for alliances.[7]

Non-state allies have also participated in almost every overseas conflict. Before 1899, almost all US fighting abroad was done by non-state allies of the United States. In the First Barbary War, the United States recruited Ahmed Karamanli and helped him raise an army of local Arab Calvary. Karamanli's forces saw most of the action on the ground during the war.[8] During the Spanish–American War, the United States allied with local rebel forces – the Cuban and Filipino rebels – who did almost all the fighting on land that wore away Spanish forces.[9] After 1900, as

---

[6] Joseph Glatthaar and James Martin, *Forgotten Allies: The Oneida Indians and the American Revolution* (New York: Hill and Wang, 2007); David Levinson, "An Explanation for the Oneida-Colonist Alliance in the American Revolution," *Ethnohistory* 23, no. 3 (1976): 265–89; Jack Campisi and Laurence M. Hauptman, *The Oneida Indian Experience: Two Perspectives* (Syracuse: Syracuse University Press, 1988).

[7] Two useful overviews of Native American participation in the Civil war are Annie Heloise Abel, *The American Indian as Participant in the Civil War* (Cleveland: Arthur Clark Company, 1919); Laurence Hauptman, *Between Two Fires: American Indians in the Civil War* (New York: Free Press, 1995).

[8] M. L. S. Kitzen, *Tripoli and the United States at War: A History of American Relations with the Barbary States, 1785–1805* (Jefferson City: McFarland, 1993); Joseph Wheelan, *Jefferson's War: America's First War on Terror, 1801–1805* (New York: Carroll & Graf Publishers, 2003); Joshua London, *Victory in Tripoli: How America's War with the Barbary Pirates Established the U.S. Navy and Built a Nation* (Hoboken: Wiley, 2005).

[9] Leon Wolff, *Little Brown Brother: America's Forgotten Bid for Empire Which Cost 250,000 Lives* (New York: Longman, 1970); Louis A. Perez, *The War of 1898: The United States and Cuba in History and Historiography* (Chapel Hill: University of North

the United States became more active in global politics, the relevance of these allies increased. During World War II, the United States recruited at least fifteen non-state allies, from Albanian and Yugoslav partisans in Europe to Karen, Kachin, and Naga fighters in the highlands between India and Burma. And today, many scholars credit contemporary US non-state allies for toppling the Taliban in Afghanistan and reducing violence in Iraq.

The power of betweenness has shaped these alliances. In situations with no elite ties across borders, intermediaries are crucial bridges between societies. Missionaries, traders, and ordinary soldiers often have experience working at the intersections of societies, where they develop a crucial set of social skills that enable intersocietal cooperation. First, intermediaries may manipulate parties by creating the appearance of a harmony of interests. When intermediaries recruited Filipinos during the Spanish–American War, local US officials, who were ordered not to provide post-war promises of independence, chose to make those promises anyway, claiming that the United States had no ambition to rule the Philippines after the Spanish existed. Pratt and Wildman, the US agents who brokered cooperation, were wrong. In making this case for cooperation, they explained the interests of the US government in such a way that there appeared to be a harmony of long-term interests (see Chapter 6).

Second, intermediaries may stake their personal reputations on a deal, providing reassurances that post-war deals will be kept. Many Apache, for example, joined with the United States in hunting down other Apache between the 1870s and 1890s, proving instrumental in what may have been the costliest war in North America. The Apache, however, did not trust most local Indian Agents' promises of post-war land, because these agents had a reputation for dishonesty on the frontier. To win Apache support, General George Crook hired locals from the community who had a reputation for honesty and support of Apache causes to lead the Apache, and he built a reputation for dealing fairly and honestly with Native Americans. These personal reputations reassured the Apache that post-war promises would be fulfilled if they cooperated against others, such as Geronimo.[10]

Carolina Press, 1998); Louis A. Pérez, *Cuba between Empires, 1878–1902* (Pittsburgh: University of Pittsburgh Press, 1983).

[10] Eric Grynaviski, "Brokering Cooperation: Intermediaries and US Cooperation with Non-State Allies, 1776–1945," *European Journal of International Relations* 21, no. 3 (2014): 691–717.

Third, intermediaries may manipulate identity politics, crafting a shared sense of a common identity between cooperation partners. Cooperation may be more likely when parties hold a shared sense of identity, because the parties will better identify with one another. For example, Tomás Estrada Palma, the leader of the Partido Revolucionario Cubana (PRC), which was based in New York, used his position as the primary contact between the United States and Cuban rebels to actively solicit US recognition for the Cuban army and US intervention during the Spanish–American War. Estrada Palma's propaganda machine massaged identity issues, deftly portraying the Cuban revolution as akin to the American Revolution, with Estrada Palma cast as the Cuban Benjamin Franklin in the American Paris.[11] In doing so, he framed Cuban aspirations as in keeping with American values and traditions, making intervention more likely.

Through these mechanisms – identifying partners for cooperation, building trust, explaining (and misrepresenting) parties' interests, and managing cultural politics – intermediaries can shape cooperation between societies. Their sources of power stem from betweenness rather than institutional influence.

WHY IT MATTERS

The central chapters of this book examine the detailed history of American alliances with non-state allies, from the colonialists' alliance with the Oneidas during the American Revolution to Special Forces' interactions with local populations in Afghanistan today. These chapters are detailed examinations intended to clearly demonstrate that intermediaries matter, the source of their influence is their place between societies, and therefore a focus on institutional power creates misleading accounts of important events in international politics. To accomplish this aim requires a detailed litigating of historical evidence.

Before asking the reader to undertake these chapters, it is worth reminding the reader that the book has high stakes. Most of these stakes are more fully explored in the conclusion, where the empirical evidence can be mustered to explain just how important identifying new sources of political power is for understanding American foreign policy. In this section, I want to preview three debates in which this book intervenes.

[11] Ibid.

Networks and Agency in World Politics

The primary contribution of this book is to provide new avenues toward agency in world politics. To do so, it relies on social networks and relational sociology. One significant contribution of social network ideas in sociology has been to reach counterintuitive conclusions about sources of social influence. Work on weak ties and structural holes, for example, shows that strong ties to centers of power are liabilities in certain social situations. Yet, when IR scholars approach these topics, they do not use these ideas to discover agency in new sites of governance or new agents. Chapter 1 argues that rather than expanding the range of effective agents in world politics, network-based theories focus on the politically powerful, showing new sources of influence for empires or political leaders such as Bismarck or Kissinger. This book provides a network-based theory of influence in global politics that brings figures at the margins to the center in world politics, showing how their structural position allows them to significantly influence world events.

To make the case that intermediaries matter, I need to shift the discussion in three ways. First, this book provides a different description of the international system, moving from a state-centric image of the structure of international politics to a people-centered image. Traditional depictions of the structure of international politics emphasize states as the key agents within international structures.[12] More recently, IR scholars have included powerful international or non-governmental organizations, as well as looking to the effects of domestic politics or regime type on state preferences. Even network-based theories of international politics often emphasize states, not people, as agents.[13] The central element of all these theories is that their building blocks are corporate actors, whether states, international organizations, or some other body acting collectively. Structural theories assume corporate actors are the foundation of international structures, but studies emphasizing individuals' decision-making do not provide a structural role for individuals within world politics. Studies of foreign policy decision-making, for example, emphasize the influence of individuals' decisions over important outcomes in world

---

[12] Waltz, *Theory of International Politics*; Wendt, *Social Theory of International Politics*.
[13] Emilie M. Hafner-Burton, Miles Kahler, and Alexander H. Montgomery, "Network Analysis for International Relations," *International Organization* 63, no. 3 (2009): 559–92; Patrick Thaddeus Jackson and Daniel H. Nexon, "Relations Before States: Substance, Process and the Study of World Politics," *European Journal of International Relations* 5, no. 3 (1999): 291–332.

politics; but these studies do not place individuals in structural relations to others in ways that encourage thinking about the interrelationships between agents.

This book begins with a view of international structures in which the agents within social networks are individual people. This is necessary for the argument that follows. I propose that much of the interesting interaction in international cooperation circulates around individuals crossing borders, not individuals who live within the comfortable borders of their own society. In particular, interstate cooperation is built on interpersonal relationships that convey information, trust, and culture between societies. Political elites are rarely the agents who meet and talk often, and few political elites fight themselves. And states certainly do not have the corporeality to be the conduits of information between societies. Instead, international politics has arteries – channels of information and trust that cross borders – composed of individuals.

These arteries, whether they are built by statesmen, diplomats, traders, or priests, are by necessity the "pipes and prisms" on which international politics, and especially international cooperation, is built.[14] By showing that intermediaries – whom I will describe as the least expected arteries of international politics – matter, this book makes the case that interpersonal networks are important to study in international politics.

If we treat the social structure of international politics as one built upon these relationships between people, who are the "pipes and prisms" of information at a global level, then our accounts of agency also need to change. Thus, the second way this book tries to change conversations about agency in international politics is to adopt the view that different social positions produce different causal powers. Political elites tend to inhabit the center of dense political networks. They have access to influence because others depend on their decisions for resources and influence. Intermediaries, in contrast, who occupy positions between societies, have causal powers owing to their "betweenness."

Betweenness in international politics provides a different road to power. Intermediaries directly constitute global society in fundamental ways. They are the interconnections between societies – the traders, missionaries, and adventurers – who create global networks of exchange. Intermediaries can manipulate societies. Since they are the bridges between societies, then they can shape the information flowing across

---

[14] Joel M. Podolny, "Networks as the Pipes and Prisms of the Market," *American Journal of Sociology* 107, no. 1 (2001): 33–60.

borders. By shaping information, intermediaries can influence important outcomes in world politics, creating empires, fostering cooperation, or encouraging war.

The book's third innovation is to think about a different geography of international politics. Most IR scholars have a narrow geographical understanding of power, concentrating it in nations' capitals or at headquarters in military camps. The focus on geographic centers of political power, this book contends, is an artifact of our theories, not the reality of global politics. This book inverts this focus. It examines politics in the border areas, where societies met, traded, and fought. The conclusion to this book examines the connections between this work and borderlands histories, showing why expanding our geographic understandings of where politics happens is so important.

Rethinking American Power

The second major contribution this book makes is to intervene in contemporary debates about how we understand American power. Whereas historians of American foreign relations study a wide range of issues that contributed to the rise of American power and examine the influence of unusual agents for conquest in the American West and overseas, International Relations scholars tend to ignore these figures to concentrate on broader themes of material power or America's relations with European powers. In doing so, IR scholars commit two errors. First, they provide a historically inaccurate account of the process by which the United States expanded and how and when it first entered the international system as a major player. Second, IR scholars miss important contemporary variations in social structure that affect current events.

Most International Relations scholars spend little time discussing American adventurism overseas in the nineteenth century or the conquest of the west. Within journals dedicated to the study of foreign policy, much of the space is devoted to the Cold War, particularly issues of decision-making during the Cuban Missile Crisis or in Vietnam. As a result, foreign policy scholars (and IR scholars more generally) rarely discuss the war of 1812, the American Civil War, or the Spanish–American War, for example.[15]

---

[15] The inattention, at least in journals that largely deal with foreign policy themes, is noticeable. Three journals likely to include these subjects, because they often publish work seeking to understand US foreign policy, *Foreign Policy Analysis, International Security,* and *Security Studies,* exemplify this problem. Take the concept of "manifest destiny." Of

Why is so little attention paid to the rise of American power? One possible reason is that the United States in the nineteenth century was simply uninteresting and had few crises worthy of attention. If this is the reason for our current inattention, then as a discipline we are simply wrong. The United States concentrated on the western hemisphere in the nineteenth century, especially the American West, because it presented the most compelling security threats and the largest incentives for intervention and occupation. The United States pursued these interests regardless of great power involvement. The most seemingly innocuous cases – settling Ohio, the Louisiana Purchase, Samoa – frequently threatened to pull in European powers; and conflict with other American republics or Native Americans presented a much larger realistic threat to American commerce and expansion than did faraway European states.

The more likely reason why we do not focus on US exploits during the nineteenth century is that such a focus would undo many of our theories about the rise of American power. American material power was important for the country's rise, but the actual process by which the United States expanded saw the federal government rarely using its military forces to effectively subdue local or foreign populations. Chapter 3 shows that the war with Tripoli was largely won by foreign allies; Chapter 5 shows that forces fighting within Samoa were more important than American troops for explaining the US acquisition of the islands; and Chapter 6 shows that the US military did much less than the Philippine rebels to remove the Spanish from the Philippines. In this sense, the United States was not unique. The British Empire, unable to control its vast number of subjects, had to rely on local allies in India to subdue local populations.[16] Similarly, to win competitions against the Hapsburgs in the seventeenth-century

two papers in *Foreign Policy Analysis* that include the term, only one pays more than slight attention to the subject, and that is only to make sense of Anglo-US cooperation. In *International Security*, the last reference to manifest destiny, beyond a reference to a book title, was published about twenty years ago, and there were no references before that. John Gerard Ruggie, "The Past as Prologue? Interests, Identity, and American Foreign Policy," *International Security* 21, no. 4 (1997): 89–125. Other journals fare slightly better. *International Studies Quarterly*, if one is willing to go back 50 years, has three papers that reference manifest destiny (one references Japan's). *Security Studies* has shown slightly more interest, referencing manifest destiny a few times and providing forums on 1890s foreign policy issues. See especially Scott A. Silverstone, "Federal Democratic Peace: Domestic Institutions and International Conflict in the Early American Republic," *Security Studies* 13, no. 3 (2004): 48–102. Few papers in any of these journals emphasize key nineteenth-century international conflicts involving the United States, such as the Spanish–American War, the War of 1812, or the American Civil War.

[16] Paul MacDonald, *Networks of Domination* (New York: Oxford University Press, 2014).

Atlantic, the Dutch turned to allies in South America, going so far as to ship them across the ocean to help augment their fighting power in Africa.[17] In short, our theories of material power, designed to explain events like the great wars in Europe, may not make sense of the ways states struggled for mastery throughout much of human history, especially the United States.

One reason why IR scholars might struggle with these cases is that the allies were never states. These allies had different forms of political organization, different methods of diplomacy, and different interests. As such, state-centric images of the period do little to make sense of these alliances. The more important problem, however, is that these isolated groups were far removed from life in the United States. The preferences of presidents or secretaries of state, simply put, could not affect cooperation, because such actors had little to no information about their cooperation partners. Political elites often did not know who their allies were, they rarely met them, they did not understand them, and they had little idea about how to bargain with them. This book grounds the politics of the eighteenth and nineteenth centuries as frontier politics. Politics occurred at the places where societies met, traded, and had intercourse (often in both senses of the word). By focusing our theoretical lens on the figures who navigated the daily politics of interaction between societies, we are able to grapple with the politics of imperialism, expansion, and commerce that were part and parcel of the rise of the United States.

In the conclusion to the book, I point to three important issues that follow from emphasizing intermediaries and the allies they secure. Without taking into account the power of betweenness, IR scholars cannot understand *how* expansion happened. The crucial relationship between America and its collaborators is essential to explaining US success, both in North America and abroad. Non-state allies did much of the fighting, and sometimes even more of the winning, that secured America's objectives in war. Without focusing on betweenness, we also cannot understand *the interests* that drove expansion. Often, the people agitating for alliances abroad do so for seemingly unimportant interests – to save souls or protect a small farm. These relatively small interests, however, set into motion a process that leads to war, alliance, and expansion. Betweenness provides a theory to make sense of how small interests drive big policy change. A theory of betweenness is also important for determining

---

[17] Wim Klooster, *The Dutch Moment: War, Trade, and Settlement in the Seventeenth-Century Atlantic World* (Ithaca: Cornell University Press, 2016).

where the United States expanded. The final chapter points out that an enduring historical puzzle is why the United States went to Guam and the Philippines in 1898, yet, the real puzzle is *why only* Guam and the Philippines. Other islands, controlled by the Spanish, should have been plucked by the United States as part of the peace settlement. An emphasis on social connections, rather than strategic importance or commercial motives, is necessary to unravel these puzzles.

In other words, to understand America's rise requires looking over the shoulders of the architects of the alliances that drove US policy. These figures were adventurers, traders, and missionaries; they were not presidents or prime ministers. By appreciating how these intermediaries capture betweenness to shape policy, we can begin to take seriously events that are rarely described in IR scholarship.

Evidence and Archival Research

The third debate that this book intervenes in relates to history and historiography in international politics. Normally, political scientists interested in American foreign policy limit their attention to historical materials that emphasize the perspective of political elites. They typically focus on the sites where prime ministers or other influential figures meet and live, and they examine presidential papers, notes of cabinet or ministry meetings, records of international negotiations, or interviews with political elites. For theories that assume that political elites' preferences and beliefs drive international politics, there is a risk of confirmation bias in beginning one's work focusing on these areas of the archives, because these records are memorials to the powerful.

The purpose of this book is to question this conventional wisdom, so I take a different approach to the archival record. When examining a case of cooperation, my goal was to undo this bias by beginning with the record of what happened at the site of interaction. I want to discover what happened in those niches between societies, where messages were passed, promises were made, and intercourse happened. To do so requires a different approach to the archival record than most political scientists traditionally use.

This book, the reader will discover, uses *a lot* of primary source evidence. It does so because most traditional secondary sources are told from the perspective of what happened in the United States. I need to start from scratch. To figure out what happened at the intersections of societies, I started working with the archival record to identify the perspectives of subjects between societies. Practically, this means focusing on records preserved by ship captains, traders, missionaries, slaves, and others. I undertook exhaustive searches of records in American and British archives, focusing on daily accounts provided by naval logs, diaries, company records, and similar documents. I also talked to people in the American genealogical, American Civil War, and American Indian communities to collect privately held materials and memories. I consulted dozens of collections of private papers across the United States to piece together these histories, only some of which made it into this final book. I also read the daily, weekly, and monthly reports from overseas agents, such as commercial agents and US consuls. Only after appreciating how a war or intervention unfolded as seen by the agents who witnessed it directly did I turn to presidential papers and similar elite-level documents.

This methodological innovation – of course, long used by historians and others – is an important contribution of the book for an IR audience. Seeing the politics of alliance-making from the eyes of people between societies leads one to see the historical processes of cooperation and conflict differently. Agents at the margins wrangled over what information to pass along to agents who lived in far-off cities. They initiated and supported wars and alliances, creating *fait accomplis* that political elites could only later approve. They distorted and manipulated agents in centers of political power to get what they wanted, and what they wanted were interests (pigs and Papists) far removed from the national interest (security and commerce). One learns that the decisions taken in centers of political power often do not matter, and when they do matter, they are reactions to situations already put in play by some of the most important alliances in American political history. For IR scholars to focus only on elites' records creates problems in history and historiography that may be unrecoverable. It records an elite-bias deeply into our historical understandings of world politics and the theoretical lexicon developed to explain that history.

These issues are better explored in the conclusion. Armed with empirical examples from the book, I show the importance of historical perspective and better archival methods for IR scholarship.

PLAN OF THE BOOK

To develop this argument, Chapter 1 outlines the major theoretical claims of this book. Specifically, Chapter 1 develops a network-based account of the origins of agency for intermediaries in the international system, focusing on how agents between societies obtain influence through a monopoly on information that travels across borders. It also introduces non-state allies, showing how the rest of the book tests the theory of intermediaries' influence against existing accounts of alliance formation.

Then, the book turns to seven chapters that describe how intermediaries used the power of betweenness to shape the trajectory of America's rise. Chapters 2 and 3 focus on Early American foreign policy. Chapter 2 describes how a missionary used the power of betweenness to broker an alliance between the Continental Congress and the Oneidas in upstate New York during the American Revolution. Chapter 3 describes the same process in the First Barbary War, where a former slave and an adventurer worked together to form an alliance with local forces that won the war for the United States. Chapter 4 focuses on the Civil War era. It describes four alliances with American Indians formed during the American Civil War by the North and South. This chapter takes advantage of variations in social structure in different geographic regions to show the relationship between the power of betweenness and the structure of social relations.

Betweenness mattered for American foreign policy in the imperial Pacific. Chapter 5 provides an original account as to how an adventurer, a merchant, and a missionary managed to broker alliances between Samoans and the United States that led to a costly intervention. Chapters 6 and 7 focus on the Philippines, showing how low-level government agents pulled the United States into alliances with collaborators during the Spanish–American and Philippine–American Wars.

Betweenness continues to matter as the United States has achieved great power status. Chapter 8 extends the general framework of the book and examines how intermediaries are necessary for explaining post-war cooperation with non-state allies, including during World War II and the war in Afghanistan. In doing so, it addresses the concern that a globalized world is less likely than the nineteenth century to feature structural holes.

The conclusion of the book further explores the theoretical implications of a focus on intermediaries and non-state allies, describing the theoretical and empirical implications of recentering the study of international security on the margins of societies rather than in nations' capitals. That is, the chapter examines the tension between the borderlands and the centers of political power. In doing so, it connects these debates with more broader concerns about agency, structure, and power.

I

Power from the Margins

Political science has recently seen a resurgence of interest in international diplomacy. Much of the attention has gone to the "great men" of international politics. For example, studies related to the Vietnam War, the Cuban Missile Crisis, the Korean War, and the Cold War often emphasize presidents or high-level cabinet appointees when analyzing the origins of conflict.[1] Students of international cooperation usually focus on the same figures. Recent studies of arms control and security cooperation, for example, often emphasize the roles of presidents and cabinet-level appointees.[2] These political elites, many argue, are the "primary decision-makers" with respect to national security politics; therefore, focusing on their beliefs, preferences, personal characteristics, personalities, and so on does much to explain international politics.[3] Political scientists, of course,

[1] A few, of many, examples include Graham Allison and Philip Zelikow, *Essence of Decision: Explaining the Cuban Missile Crisis* (New York: Longman, 1999); Y. F. Khong, *Analogies at War: Korea, Munich, Dien Bien Phu, and the Vietnam Decisions of 1965* (Princeton University Press, 1992); Elizabeth Saunders, "Transformative Choices: Leaders and the Origins of Intervention Strategy," *International Security* 34, no. 2 (2009): 119–61.

[2] Eric Grynaviski, *Constructive Illusions: Misperceiving the Origins of International Cooperation* (Ithaca: Cornell University Press, 2014); Brian C. Rathbun, *Diplomacy's Value: Creating Security in 1920s Europe and the Contemporary Middle East* (Ithaca: Cornell University Press, 2014).

[3] "Primary decision maker" is in Keren Yarhi-Milo, *Knowing the Adversary: Leaders, Intelligence, and Assessment of Intentions in International Relations* (Princeton: Princeton University Press, 2014), 13. See, for example, Daniel Byman and Kenneth Pollack, "Let Us Now Praise Great Men: Bringing the Statesman Back In," *International Security* 25, no. 4 (2001): 107–46; Martha Finnemore, *The Purpose of Intervention: Changing Beliefs About the Use of Force* (Ithaca: Cornell University Press, 2003), chap. 2; Emilie M. Hafner-Burton et al., "Decision Maker Preferences for International Legal Cooperation," *International*

realize that these political elites operate under constraints. More ordinary agents, such as citizens and voters, can exert influence on political elites; however, these ordinary agents matter only when acting collectively. Public opinion and electoral results matter, but a single voter does not. A norm entrepreneur with access to organizational resources – such as wealth, prestige, and institutional influence – matters, but an individual without institutional connections does not.[4] Social movements matter, but any specific individual within a movement likely does not (unless the person has a special institutionalized role).[5]

The conventional wisdom in political science, in short, is that actors with institutional influence matter the most. These figures are central to our political and international institutions. The rest of humanity only matters, if at all, if they collectively mobilize. The argument of this book seeks to turn the conventional wisdom on its head. I show that power also lies in being *between* centers of power. This power of betweenness can sometimes matter more in shaping world history than the power that emerges from traditional centers of power. Specifically, decisions by individuals whom I call intermediaries – that is, actors with political power owing to their position between societies, such as missionaries, traders, and low-level government employees – often dramatically affect international politics.

Alliances, trade deals, and war turn on their decisions. Intermediaries' position between societies means that information often traffics through them. They can manipulate that information to create war or ensure peace. This book emphasizes how their power of betweenness shapes

---

Organization 68, no. 4 (2014): 845–76; Jack Snyder, *Myths of Empire: Domestic Politics and International Ambition* (Ithaca: Cornell University Press, 1991).

[4] See, for example, Matthew Evangelista, *Unarmed Forces: The Transnational Movement to End the Cold War* (Ithaca: Cornell University Press, 2002); Martha Finnemore, *National Interests in International Society* (Ithaca: Cornell University Press, 1996); Martha Finnemore and Kathryn Sikkink, "International Norm Dynamics and Political Change," *International Organization* 52, no. 4 (1998): 887–917.

[5] Evangelista, *Unarmed Forces*; Margaret Keck and Kathryn Sikkink, *Activists Beyond Borders* (Ithaca: Cornell University Press, 1998); Thomas Risse-Kappen and Kathryn Sikkink, "The Socialization of International Human Rights Norms into Domestic Practices," in *The Power of Human Rights: International Norms and Domestic Change*, ed. Thomas Risse, Stephen Ropp, and Kathryn Sikkink (Cambridge: Cambridge University Press, 1999), 1–38; Maria Stephan and Erica Chenoweth, "Why Civil Resistance Works," *International Security* 33, no. 1 (2008): 7–44. Collective mobilization, in some work in sociology, is the key to agents on the margins having power. See, for example, Jennifer Jihye Chun, *Organizing at the Margins: The Symbolic Politics of Labor in South Korea and the United States* (Ithaca: Cornell University Press, 2009).

cooperation, not war. This chapter outlines a theory that explains the conditions under which intermediaries become crucial for any explanation of cooperation between a state and non-state allies. The specific cases of international cooperation studied in this book are instances in which the United States formed alliances with non-state groups, from 1776 until 1945. In the chapters that follow, I trace how political elites are constrained by, and intermediaries are empowered by, the social structure of international politics. By this I mean that the way personal relationships flow across borders places a specific group of agents, who lack institutional authority, into positions where they are the primary decision-makers shaping international politics in some of the most important and most interesting instances of US security cooperation. By helping the United States find the collaborators upon which American power traditionally depends, they also help explain the rise of American power.

A NETWORK-BASED ACCOUNT OF INTERMEDIARIES' INFLUENCE

In the 1960s, Stanley Milgram conducted a small world experiment. A small world is a social system in which "even when two people do *not* have a friend in common, they are separated by only a short chain of intermediaries."[6] Milgram tested this proposition by sending letters to people in cities in the Midwest, such as Omaha and Wichita, asking them to forward the letters to someone who might know a target individual in Boston. Milgram found that most individuals were connected by no more than "six degrees" of separation, meaning that it took six iterations for a letter to be sent before finding the target person. This finding is consistent with the idea that the United States is a small world, where millions of people are closely linked to one another, whether they realize it or not.[7]

How small is the world of international politics? Most images of the international system depict it as a small system, likely much smaller than the way sociologists like Milgram describe the population of the United States. Some IR scholars think about the international social structure as

---

[6] Duncan Watts, *Small Worlds: The Dynamics of Networks between Order and Randomness* (Princeton: Princeton University Press, 1999), 4.

[7] On small worlds, see Zeev Maoz, *Networks of Nations: The Evolution, Structure, and Impact of International Networks, 1816–2001* (Cambridge: Cambridge University Press, 2011), 10–11. More generally, see Stanley Milgram, "The Small-World Problem," *Psychology Today* 2, no. 1 (1967): 61–7; Duncan Watts, *Six Degrees: The Science of a Connected Age* (New York: Norton, 2003).

the interconnections between states. If we treat states as the units of analysis, then the social structure of the international system is likely a small world, because all states in the modern era know one another directly.[8] If this is the case, there are no degrees of separation between them. They are a family rather than a society, the smallest of worlds. A second image of international diplomacy, featured in traditional diplomatic studies, treats political elites or diplomats as a small set of interconnected agents. One of the interesting features of this approach to the study of diplomacy – the limiting of diplomacy to a small group of political and institutional elites – is that it emphasizes the club-like nature of international diplomacy, characterized by the comparatively small group of individuals working on negotiations.[9] Similar to how research focusing on states as the units of socialization depict a small world, diplomatic studies traditionally represent the international system as connected through powerful political elites who meet in bilateral meetings, discuss matters in international fora, or exchange communications directly to manage international problems. The diplomatic world may be bigger than the world of states, but every high-ranking diplomat is likely connected to every other diplomat through only a few degrees of separation.

This book takes a different approach to the structure of the international system. It posits that the social system relevant to international cooperation is much more varied than the world of states or political elites. To secure one's borders, develop investment or trade partnerships, or advance political change abroad, states often work with groups with

---

[8] Many contemporary network-based descriptions of international politics point to this view, although only implicitly. See Emilie M. Hafner-Burton, Miles Kahler, and Alexander H. Montgomery, "Network Analysis for International Relations," *International Organization* 63, no. 3 (2009): 559–92; Emilie M. Hafner-Burton and Alexander H. Montgomery, "Power Positions International Organizations, Social Networks, and Conflict," *Journal of Conflict Resolution* 50, no. 1 (2006): 3–27; Maoz, *Networks of Nations*.

[9] Examples of work that emphasize the "club-like" nature of diplomacy produced by organizations include Emanuel Adler and Michael Barnett, "A Framework for the Study of Security Communities," in *Security Communities*, ed. Emmanuel Adler and Michael Barnett (Cambridge: Cambridge University Press, 1998); Jeffrey Checkel, "International Institutions and Socialization in Europe: Introduction and Framework," *International Organization* 59, no. 4 (2005): 801–26; David H. Bearce and Stacy Bondanella, "Intergovernmental Organizations, Socialization, and Member-State Interest Convergence," *International Organization* 61, no. 4 (2007): 703–33; Jeffrey Lewis, "The Janus Face of Brussels: Socialization and Everyday Decision Making in the European Union," *International Organization* 59, no. 4 (2005): 937–71; Jennifer Mitzen, *Power in Concert: The Nineteenth-Century Origins of Global Governance* (Chicago: University Of Chicago Press, 2013).

whom they have little experience. Whereas diplomats may know other diplomats, they are less likely to know of overseas firms that could be potential economic partners, they may know little about political groups in strategically insignificant parts of the world, and they may have next to no relationship with religious radicals operating in shadowy caves. Therefore, this book treats social structure as the configuration of personal ties between individuals across and within borders.

If one treats personal ties between individuals as the structure of international politics, then the system is likely a "larger world" than that depicted by most IR scholars. Agents are not so closely interconnected. The primary reason is that government agents are not likely to have close, personal ties with the diverse kinds of non-state agents with whom they need to interact. In the language of network theory, we might describe the international system as composed of clusters of individuals. By clusters, I mean there are routinized ties between individuals within an organization, such as a government, a rebel army, or a corporation, that allow those individuals to engage in common enterprises. Sometimes, these clusters will feel a sense of common purpose, such as in an organization with a name and a mission, but other times individuals are simply drawn together because of routinized interactions, such as in a market.[10]

Much of the time, there is significant interaction within clusters but very little interaction between clusters. Sociological theorists posit the idea of "structural holes" between clusters of individuals or organizations, which form when few or no individuals have ties across clusters.[11] For example, two individuals on opposite sides of a continent may never know one another. When there is a hole in the social structure – when there is a failure of agents to connect – the integration of the social structure depends on chains of intermediaries. Theories related to structural holes suggest that in order for individuals, companies, or political communities to cooperate, there must be some "bridge" between them. By bridge, I mean one or more people must have ties with both communities and can thus connect the clusters, enabling cooperation. Two companies may not realize the value of cooperating, for example, if there is no

[10] The former is described as "yoking" in Patrick Thaddeus Jackson and Daniel H. Nexon, "Relations Before States: Substance, Process and the Study of World Politics," *European Journal of International Relations* 5, no. 3 (1999): 291–332.

[11] Burt defines a structural hole in these terms: "A structural hole exists between two people or groups when either party is unaware of the value available if they were to coordinate on some point." Ronald Burt, *Brokerage and Closure: An Introduction to Social Capital* (Oxford: Oxford University Press, 2005), 25.

individual able to "see" the structural hole and realize the gains that may accrue from working together.[12] Individuals in these bridging positions are often described as brokers.

One central empirical claim this book makes is that the social structure of international politics is often characterized by structural holes. This may seem odd to IR scholars. Usually, our structural images of international politics emphasize the integration of international society in the modern era. Scholarship on diffusion of norms, practices, and technology emphasizes how the globe is becoming a single, integrated world society. Work on international cultures describes a growing, singular, international social system. Theories emphasizing trade and interaction depict the globe growing closer together in increasing levels of integration and interdependence.

These facts about the modern globe do not undermine the intuition that the whole of global social structure depends on a few links that connect societies together. If social structure is the configuration of personal ties between agents, then we will quickly discover variation in how well clusters are linked together. Sociologists have found this to be the case in much more dense social environments, such as schools and companies. Some students do not directly know one another; and opportunities for cooperation between companies are missed when few personal relationships tie those companies together. These general findings are discussed in depth in Chapter 8. I want to concentrate here on the general intuition in international politics.

The most obvious examples of structural holes are instances of "first contact," where previously isolated peoples are connected to the global community for the first time. In these cases, there is no bridge between isolated communities. To find opportunities for cooperation between these distant societies requires an agent to make contact, brokering relations between them. More often, the nature of contemporary politics does not lend itself to developing close, personal relationships between individuals working in different communities, at different levels of governance, and with different political aims.[13] Chapter 8 reviews several ways that structural holes may form: new hubs of political activity may develop with little connection to other centers (e.g., a new rebel group with no

[12] Ronald S. Burt and Don Ronchi, "Teaching Executives to See Social Capital: Results from a Field Experiment," *Social Science Research* 36, no. 3 (2007): 1156–83. More generally, see Ronald Burt, *Structural Holes: The Social Structure of Competition* (Cambridge: Harvard University Press, 1992).

[13] Burt, *Structural Holes*; Burt, *Brokerage and Closure*.

relationship to future allies), ties between groups may be disrupted (e.g., a war severs existing ties by killing well-connected leaders), or a state enters a new region of the world where it has few connections.

The closing of structural holes requires brokers to establish bridges between communities; brokers are trustworthy people who have personal connections they can use to connect clusters and secure cooperation. These figures, I argue, take advantage of structural holes to exercise power and influence in international politics. This means the world remains "small," in the language of the small worlds problem. Agents remain connected to one another when structural holes are bridged. But, the bridges are more important than IR scholars usually recognize.

If structural holes are common in international politics, their presence may constrain powerful agents within clusters but empower agents who operate between clusters. Agents with significant institutional influence, who are powerful within clusters, may be unable to generate cooperation due to their inability to identify or build trust with political elites in other clusters. Conversely, the central argument of this book is that strategically placed individuals who close structural holes likely possess power in excess of our expectations over outcomes in international politics, by virtue of having a near-monopoly on information trafficking across structural holes. In short, by focusing on the structural position of agents working between societies, we can begin to understand how seemingly ordinary agents exercise outsized influence in international politics.

The Example of Samoa

Many IR scholars are not accustomed to thinking about social structure as based on ties between individuals. This idea is crucial to the argument of this book. It is this definition of social structure that gives rise to the importance of betweenness. To illustrate, think about the relationship between two countries, the United States and Samoa. Anna Collars, in a book on religious networks in the Roman world, flippantly asks about the connections between the King of Samoa and a peasant in China. She hypothesizes that there are only a few degrees of separation between them.[14] The Chinese peasant is beyond the scope of this book, but the connections between the King of Samoa and an ordinary American citizen are at the heart of it (see Chapter 5).

---

[14] Anna Collar, *Religious Networks in the Roman Empire: The Spread of New Ideas* (Cambridge: Cambridge University Press, 2013), 14.

How was the King of Samoa connected to a resident of Maine in 1887? The King of Samoa, of course, had close relationships with a large number of political actors in Samoa (one cluster); the resident of Maine, likewise, had a large number of connections to actors in Maine (another cluster). Between them, however, there was little contact because of a structural hole. There were few American and no Samoan ships traveling between the societies. In situations such as this, only a few individuals – consular officers and a few sailors – can bridge the communities. In this specific instance, the shortest path between the King of Samoa and a resident of Maine would likely be as follows: the King of Samoa knew the American Consul, Harald Marsh Sewall, and Sewall's father was a Maine shipbuilder and significant employer in the state. Assuming that Maine was a small world separated by only a few degrees of separation, the King of Samoa was likely related to every Maine resident quite closely.[15] Yet, this small world was only made possible by Harald Marsh Sewall, the primary link between the United States and Samoa; without Sewall, the paths linking Maine's residents to Samoa would be quite long and indirect (probably trafficking through Germany).

Samoa illustrates how a planet becomes a small world because of a single individual who provides a bridge across borders. The sum of global social structure might be described in this way, highlighting patterns of relationships between individuals across which information, money, and power flows.

Three Kinds of Influential Agents

The power of betweenness described in this book comes from the importance of brokerage across structural holes. Agents without institutional authority can shape decisions by taking advantage of bridging positions between societies. To lay out how, I focus on the causal powers of intermediaries. These are agents who bridge structural holes through the use of their weak ties. This section describes intermediaries, emphasizing their betweenness.

I use the concept of centrality in social network theory to provide a convenient way to distinguish between two accounts of network structures that constrain and enable agents. The logic of centrality is that an actor central to one or more networks has access to more information,

---

[15] This assumption is safe because Maine's population was small, and Arthur Sewall was a large employer who knew political figures such as Senator Vandenberg, creating a situation in which Sewall was likely closely linked to much of Maine's population. The details of this case are explored in depth in Chapter 5.

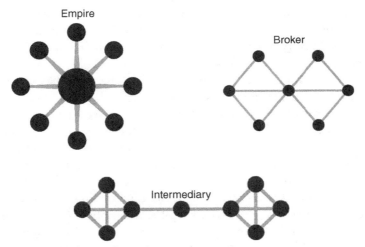

FIGURE I.I Centrality and social networks

resources, and influence than do actors who lack social connections. Yet, different agents may be central in different ways. Specifically, political elites and traditional diplomats likely have influence due to their centrality within a cluster; and intermediaries likely have influence due to their centrality between clusters.

The first type of centrality, usually captured by measures of degree centrality, suggests that people are more central to a network when they are well connected within a cluster: people gain influence, prestige, or social capital as the number and strength of their social connections increase in comparison to other agents.[16] Nexon and Wright, for example, describe one important source of power for empires and hegemons: "actors with more connections have more information about the preferences and orientations of others, than those with fewer connections," and Hafner-Burton and Montgomery describe how increasing agents' social connections increases their prestige.[17] The diagram of the empire in Figure I.I shows a state with a high degree of centrality because it is connected to many states on the periphery that do not have connections to each other.

---

[16] David Knoke, *Political Networks: The Structural Perspective* (Cambridge: Cambridge University Press, 1990), chap. I.

[17] Daniel H. Nexon and Thomas Wright, "What's at Stake in the American Empire Debate," *The American Political Science Review* 101, no. 2 (2007): 260; Hafner-Burton and Montgomery, "Power Positions International Organizations, Social Networks, and Conflict."

Another type of centrality – usually captured by measures of between-ness – highlights an agent's strategic placement. The broker in Figure 1.1 represents ideal-typical betweenness centrality. If an agent is placed between parts of a network such that the overall coherence of the net-work depends on that agent's existence, then the agent has substantial influence, even if the quantity of connections is low. Building on well-established sociological claims, Stacie Goddard argues that when net-works are fragmented by structural holes, agents who can bridge different parts can reshape international politics, because their position between influential players provides strategic flexibility, a higher potential to develop innovative ideas, and a greater likelihood of seeing their ideas diffuse.[18] Goddard concentrates on traditional diplomats, showing that agents who have strong ties to political elites in other states can broker cooperation. Henry Kissinger, for example, controlled communications between the White House and the Kremlin through his backchannel talks with the Soviet ambassador. He had elements of power that arose from his position "between" societies.[19]

These two logics of centrality point to the study of traditional polit-ical elites. Presidents, for example, are influential because they occupy a place within organizations that provides them with access to many others within a network: they are literally the center of power within the state. For instance, presidents have access to information coming from the national security bureaucracy, information from legislative and media contacts, and access to party resources that ordinary citizens do not have, making them "central" and worthy of study.[20] Other kinds of political elites who exert influence on international politics – from chief diplomats like Otto von Bismarck to chief terrorists like Osama Bin Laden – may be described as influential because they are hubs of network activity.[21]

Similarly, studies that highlight betweenness also focus on political elites. Goddard, for example, draws on some of the most powerful indi-viduals in world politics to demonstrate betweenness: Napoleon III and

---

[18] Burt, *Structural Holes*; Burt, *Brokerage and Closure*; Stacy Goddard, "Brokering Change: Networks and Entrepreneurs in International Politics," *International Theory* 1, no. 2 (2009): 249–81. See also Charli Carpenter, *"Lost" Causes: Agenda Vetting in Global Issue Networks and the Shaping of Human Security* (Ithaca: Cornell University Press, 2014).

[19] Grynaviski, *Constructive Illusions*.

[20] See, for example, Jon Western, *Selling Intervention and War: The Presidency, the Media, and the American Public* (Baltimore: John Hopkins University Press, 2005).

[21] See, for example, Marc Sageman, *Understanding Terror Networks* (Philadelphia: University of Pennsylvania Press, 2004), 141.

Bismarck.[22] In the same way, theorists describe empires, which are often the most elite states in a system, as powerful because of their betweenness. If empires are rimless hub and spoke systems, then they are powerful, in part, because they are in a structural position between the peripheral states, and goods and services from one peripheral community need to traffic through the empire to reach other communities. The language of network theory, in short, is often used within IR scholarship to describe why the powerful are powerful, highlighting added resources that may be available to actors in central positions. At present, this work reaches few counterintuitive conclusions about who matters in international politics.

A better test of the power of betweenness concentrates on individuals who gain their power *only* because of their position between societies. These individuals are common in political history. Adventurers, missionaries, and traders are three famous classes of agents who trade on their position between societies to make economic and political gains. They use their ability to navigate between societies to create opportunities for war or cooperation, depending on whether it advances their interests. These agents' power arises from their betweenness, not from strong, institutional positions of power.

I describe individuals whose power arises solely from their betweenness as intermediaries. I define an intermediary as an agent who bridges a structural hole through the use of her weak ties. The difference between an intermediary and a broker is that an intermediary must have only weak ties to one or both centers of decision-making power. Henry Kissinger, for example, was a broker to the Soviet Union. He had strong ties to Nixon and to Brezhnev. He knew them well. Kissinger was not an intermediary because of these strong ties. A missionary is more likely to be an intermediary. A missionary might have strong ties to the community in which he works, but weak, indirect ties to the government at home. He may correspond with government officials infrequently or have a passing acquaintance with people of influence. The missionary therefore does not have access to an advantageous institutional position.

In technical language, I define an intermediary as an agent who bridges a structural hole through weak ties. By weak ties in this context, I mean that the intermediary does not regularly and frequently interact with centers of power in both of those communities, and the centers of power do not have affection for or politically depend on the intermediary. Note that to qualify as an intermediary, one can have strong ties to

---

[22] Goddard, "Brokering Change."

one community and weak ties to another. This is important. Missionaries have strong ties in places where they live and work, but weak ties back home. The weak ties, this book claims, are sufficient to provide influence. The definition of weak ties I use here is similar to well-established definitions within sociology, although with an important difference. David Krackhardt lists three characteristics of a strong tie: frequent interaction, affection, and interaction over a period of time. Weak ties, conversely, are instances in which one or more of these three criteria are not met.[23] In the context of international cooperation, people strongly tied to others frequently interact over long periods of time. But, the role of affection is different. Krackhardt is trying to capture how affection helps one gain information; people gain information through acquaintances rather than friends, and friendship is characterized by affection. In the context of this book, I expand the definition of strong tie to also include political interdependence. In other words, two close friends who care for one another are strongly tied together; so too are two agents who have significant and frequent interactions and know that they depend on one another to exert political influence.[24]

In theory, any person, no matter how ordinary, can bridge structural holes so long as they have weak ties that bridge disconnects between communities. In the cases I describe later, this function is played, for example, by trade consuls with little political influence, ordinary soldiers, missionaries, ship captains, former slaves, adventurers, and plantation owners. What this unlikely cast of characters has in common is that any political power they have to shape cooperation comes from their betweenness. Their structural position, not their innate political resources owing to strong ties to governments, is the sole source of their influence.

How Common Is the Power of Betweenness?

Theories of network structure and society, developed in sociology, point to the possibility that intermediaries are prevalent in international society. When a system, like the international system, contains many structural holes, agents with weak ties are more likely to span those holes. This makes betweenness a common form of power in international politics.

---

[23] David Krackhardt, "The Strength of Strong Ties: The Importance of Philos in Organizations," in *Networks and Organizations: Structure, Form, and Action* (Cambridge: Harvard Business School Press, 1992), 216–39.

[24] The key idea is that they realize they are interdependent; a decision-maker who does not realize that the intermediary is shaping information across a structural hole does not have strong ties to the intermediary.

Some well-known properties of social networks describe why agents with weak ties are more likely to bridge structural holes than agents with strong ties. Mark Granovetter's pioneering work on the strength of weak ties found that individuals are more likely to obtain jobs through their acquaintances than through close friends.[25] One reason, important for the argument of this chapter, is that acquaintances are less likely than close friends to provide redundant information. Because close friends are usually tied together in a cluster, the informational benefits from any individual friend are marginal, because everyone in the circle likely has similar information. They know the same people. Acquaintances, by contrast, are more likely to have access to non-redundant information about firms that are hiring, because their sources of information are less likely to overlap.[26]

The principle that strong ties do not provide bridges to close structural holes is even more likely for politicians. For example, consider someone running for election. The candidate's closest advisers and friends usually have been with the candidate for a long time. This long-term, strong relationship is what earns them a friendship or a spot in the inner circle of advisers. These friends and advisers, owing to their long history of interaction, may know the same people as one another. In more formal terms, if Agents A and B are connected via strong ties, then agent A is not a bridge for B to those whom A is strongly tied to, because B likely has contact with the same agents. To reach new people, therefore, requires the candidate to use her weak ties. She trades on relationships with more distant acquaintances to find more support or more contributions. The intermediaries in this case have access to non-redundant information, making a person with weak ties more effective in creating connections.

This book makes the empirical case that this relationship is true in international politics. Throughout American political history, the United States has relied on collaborators across the world to enhance its military power. In almost every case, individuals with strong ties to the US government have not secured cooperation. Instead, agents with only weak ties to their own government, such as traders, low-level government employees, and prisoners, have helped the United States cooperate with non-state

[25] Mark Granovetter, "The Strength of Weak Ties," *American Journal of Sociology* 78, no. 6 (1973): 1360–80; Mark Granovetter, "The Strength of Weak Ties: A Network Theory Revisited," *Sociological Theory* 1 (1983): 201–33. See also Valery Yakubovich, "Weak Ties, Information, and Influence: How Workers Find Jobs in a Local Russian Labor Market," *American Sociological Review* 70, no. 3 (2005): 408–21.

[26] Granovetter, "The Strength of Weak Ties," 209.

militia groups abroad by providing access to novel strategies and connecting elites to new agents. In particular, by bridging holes across diverse
populations, these intermediaries are well-equipped to think about and
spread innovative ideas that may be conducive to cooperation.[27]

The empirical finding that strong ties are often not useful for making
connections abroad in international politics is intuitive. To gain positions
of institutional authority, individuals need to spend their time developing
and maintaining strong ties within their government or political party;
therefore, they spend less time in social positions that would encourage
the development of weak ties across communities. In other words, pos-
sessing institutional influence likely comes at the expense of developing
weak and informal ties across borders. To select one concrete example,
consider again the case of Samoa. Important nineteenth-century policymakers in Washington rarely traveled to Samoa. Why? One likely reason
is that they would not be important policymakers if they spent significant
time in Samoa: time abroad would come at the expense of time spent
developing political connections in Washington. Therefore, the people
found in brokerage positions are more often intermediaries, not political
elites.

The crucial point is that if structural holes are commonly bridged in
international politics, then there are strong reasons to believe intermediaries are doing the bridging. The power of betweenness may be a common currency of power. The search for connections abroad affect war,
imperial expansion, and international cooperation.

Intermediaries and Principle–Agent Theory

To clarify the definition of an intermediary, it is worthwhile to explore
the differences between intermediaries and agents within the principle–
agent relationship. Economists and political scientists have developed
principle–agent models to help understand cases in which a principle
delegates authority to some agent to perform a task. The public, for
example, delegates the task of foreign policy to the president, and the
Congress delegates the implementation of laws to bureaucracies.[28] For

---

[27] Markus Baer, "The Strength-of-Weak-Ties Perspective on Creativity: A Comprehensive
Examination and Extension," *Journal of Applied Psychology* 95, no. 3 (2010): 592–
601; Everett Rogers, *Diffusion of Innovations* (New York: Free Press, 2003); Brian Uzzi
and Jarrett Spiro, "Collaboration and Creativity: The Small World Problem," *American
Journal of Sociology* 111, no. 2 (2005): 462–3.

[28] George W. Downs and David M. Rocke, "Conflict, Agency, and Gambling for
Resurrection: The Principal-Agent Problem Goes to War," *American Journal of Political
Science* 38, no. 2 (1994): 362–80; Mathew D. McCubbins and Thomas Schwartz,

our purposes, figures I treat as intermediaries might also be treated as agents. US consuls abroad, for example, are agents of the US government; and soldiers in the military have tasks delegated to them by their commanders. Moreover, intermediaries and agents share one important advantage: control over information. In principle–agent theory, monitoring agents is costly for principles, because principles cannot easily gain access to agents' information. If monitoring agents is costly, then agents are empowered to pursue their interests without oversight. In the same way, intermediaries have information advantages owing to their position between societies, which are costly for political elites to eliminate. Why introduce the term "intermediaries" into the crowded lexicon of IR scholarship?

Intermediaries are distinct from agents in a principle–agent relationship for three reasons. First, many intermediaries do not consider themselves delegates of a principle. They are often brokers or third-parties, not agents of a specific party. In Chapters 2 and 5, for example, I show how missionaries helped broker cooperation overseas. These missionaries were not employed by the government when they were recruiting, and there was no policy of delegation to them. Rather, of their own initiative, they brought plans for cooperation to the US government. In this sense, they are brokers, not agents. Second, intermediaries' causal powers arise specifically from their betweenness, whereas agents' causal powers come from delegation. People count as agents whenever some task is delegated to them. Their causal powers arise from the act of delegation, which provides them a set of tasks over which they have authority. Not all agents are intermediaries. An accountant is delegated with the task of counting my money, because it is a job I do not care to spend the time doing. The accountant is not between me and my money in any meaningful sense. Her causal powers come from my act of delegation, not her social position. Intermediaries, by definition, need to do more. They need to serve as the bridges between clusters of individuals. The causal powers of an intermediary arise from this betweenness.[29] Third,

---

"Congressional Oversight Overlooked: Police Patrols versus Fire Alarms," *American Journal of Political Science* 28, no. 1 (1984): 165–79.

[29] Furthermore, the close connection in many cases between agents and intermediaries is that intermediaries want to become agents. By bringing parties together to secure some deal, intermediaries expect to be rewarded. In many cases in this book, one potential reward is a position as a government agent or an elevated position within the bureaucracy. The activity intermediaries use to obtain the position of agent, however, is different in kind from what they do once the position is obtained. For example, intermediaries might broker cooperation to get parties to reach a deal, and then expect to be rewarded

by definition, intermediaries cannot be strongly tied to centers of political power in the same way as many agents. Agents often have strong ties to their principles; the Secretary of the Interior, for example, may have strong ties to congressional committees who pass legislation. There is strong, recognized interdependence between the delegator and delegate in many principle–agent relationships. Intermediaries, by definition, cannot possess these strong ties.

In sum, intermediaries are a special set of agents whose causal power derives from their social position, not from an act of delegation. This social position – their betweenness – makes theories highlighting the causal powers of intermediaries different from the issues at the heart of conventional principal-agent theory.

BETWEENNESS AND COOPERATION

If intermediaries' social position is between two communities, how can they use that position to affect international politics? Diplomatic historians have noted how intermediaries, like those described in this book, can foment war. Intermediaries can use their weak ties to collect information about war, sometimes misrepresenting the evidence they collect. Ahmed Chalabi, described in the introduction, contributed to the Iraq War by falsifying information for the Bush administration; so too did "Curveball," the Iraqi who defected to Germany and passed on false information about chemical weapons. These are but two examples of individuals who engineer war, using claims of betweenness to gain influence.

The harder case is that intermediaries are able to help sustain international cooperation. To create war is comparatively easy. It requires asserting dire threats. To create cooperation can be much harder. Cooperation requires that partners trust each other, avoid ideological disagreement, and believe that cooperation is in their best interest. This section explains why intermediaries' betweenness provides opportunities to promote cooperation. Betweenness provides social skills that intermediaries can use to sell cooperation across borders.

---

by being tasked with monitoring the execution of the agreement. This argument will make sense of the deals conducted by the military in the field, discussed throughout the book, such as Matthew Batson and the Philippine Scouts (Chapter 4) and Frank North and the Pawnee Scouts (Chapter 6).

On the Origins of Social Skill

How can an intermediary help secure cooperation? To make sense of this concept, I turn to the idea of social skill. The concept of social skill builds on classical social theorists' insight that individuals vary in their ability to induce others to cooperate. Neil Fligstein and Doug McAdam define social skill as "the ability to induce cooperation by appealing to and helping to create shared meanings and collective identities. Skilled social actors empathetically relate to the situations of other people and, in doing so, are able to provide those people with reasons to cooperate."[30] Empathy, in particular, is important to social skill. To induce collective action, disparate groups need to cooperate; and to encourage cooperation under conditions where groups frequently interact requires providing a common meaning or purpose for group activities. Fligstein and McAdam are especially interested in the ability of social movements to defeat incumbent groups. Socially skilled agents in incumbent and challenger groups use their skill to maintain collective action in their competition with one another and to preserve group solidarity against their rivals.[31]

An approach to studying empathy that highlights social skill is different in kind from recent work in IR on the relationship of empathy and interstate cooperation. IR scholars are usually interested in empathy between potential cooperation partners, asking questions such as whether contact between enemies or common institutions can breed empathy, which might promote cooperation, or whether some political elites might have psychological predispositions against empathy.[32] On balance, studies find that although empathy may be important for international cooperation, it may not be common. As Jonathan Mercer explains, "taking the other's perspective requires extended knowledge of the other. Perspective taking between strangers is likely to be little more than ethnocentric projection."[33]

---

[30] Neil Fligstein and Doug McAdam, *A Theory of Fields* (New York: Oxford University Press, 2012), 46. See also Neil Fligstein, "Social Skill and the Theory of Fields," *Sociological Theory* 19, no. 2 (2001): 105–25.

[31] Fligstein and McAdam, *A Theory of Fields*.

[32] Neta C. Crawford, "Institutionalizing Passion in World Politics: Fear and Empathy," *International Theory* 6, no. 3 (2014): 535–57; Marcus Holmes, "The Force of Face-to-Face Diplomacy: Mirror Neurons and the Problem of Intentions," *International Organization* 67, no. 4 (2013): 829–61; Rathbun, *Diplomacy's Value*.

[33] Jonathan Mercer, "Anarchy and Identity," *International Organization* 49, no. 2 (1995): 249. On cognitive biases and barriers to empathy, see Janice Gross Stein,

Theories of the role of empathy in social skill are different in kind from those in the IR literature, because discussions of social skill highlight third parties. IR scholarship emphasizes empathy in bilateral relations, for example, asking whether the United States and the Soviet Union are capable of seeing the world through the other's eyes. Social skill is triadic. When groups cannot empathize with each other – for example, because they lack the political knowledge necessary to appeal to each other's interests – cooperation may still occur if a third party, who can empathize with potential cooperation partners, can frame cooperative ventures in appealing ways for both groups. Specifically, an intermediary can explain to both parties that cooperation is in their interests. To do so, the third party needs experience working across borders (the parties are not "strangers" to the intermediary, in Mercer's phrase) and the expertise to frame cooperation as meeting both parties' interests and ideological or identity-based needs.

This chapter posits that intermediaries, because of their position between societies, are likely to have higher levels of social skill than political elites. To develop this argument requires paying attention to a feature of Fligstein and McAdam's argument they only briefly discuss: the variation in social skill levels among individuals. Why are some people more skilled at promoting cooperation than others?[34]

Social skill among individuals might vary in two ways. On the one hand, individuals may vary in their ability to empathize with others in general. Some people, for example, are narcissists, and therefore unable to ever empathize with others. I suspect that the variance Fligstein and McAdam highlight is something of this kind. A second approach to variation in individuals' social skills, not pursued by Fligstein and McAdam, is relational.[35] A person may have a heightened ability to empathize in general, but not have the intellectual resources necessary to empathize with a particular other. President William Clinton, for example, was famous for his ability to empathize with American voters; however, Clinton may be less likely to empathize with Muslims in Iraq than would a person

---

"Building Politics into Psychology: The Misperception of Threat," *Political Psychology* 9, no. 2 (1988): 245–71.

[34] Fligstein and McAdam note the existence of variation, but they do not explain why or how individuals vary in their social skill. Fligstein and McAdam, *A Theory of Fields*.

[35] On relational sociology in general, see Mustafa Emirbayer, "Manifesto for a Relational Sociology," *American Journal of Sociology* 103, no. 2 (1997): 281–317; Nick Crossley, *Towards Relational Sociology* (New York: Routledge, 2010). In IR in particular, see the early statement in Jackson and Nexon, "Relations Before States."

with less general empathy but more experience overseas.[36] By contrast, an individual may have a special ability to empathize with a particular group – because of a long acquaintance with the group – but score low in general empathy. The person with low general ability but high specific ability possesses social skills that are more likely to mobilize cooperation.

Emphasizing a relational account of social skill is more appropriate than a general account when asking why individuals vary in their ability to relate to others. Within the context of Fligstein and McAdam's work, a relational view of social skill is not important, because they consider social skill within fields rather than within networks. Specifically, they are interested in how collective action is promoted within a field, and they define a field as "those groups who *routinely* take each other into account in their actions."[37] If agents within a field routinely interact, they likely will not vary in their level of social skill, because the most likely source of variation – experience with others – is constant.

One aim of network theory, in contrast to field analysis, is to analyze variations in how agents are interconnected. Network theory therefore does not begin with the starting point that all agents are interrelated by routine interaction. This has two important consequences. First, if social skill requires experience with others, then a relational view can highlight past experience (represented by network position) as an explanatory factor. Second, shifting to a network position from field analysis can highlight ways that agents on the margins become necessary for cooperation. When one concentrates attention on agents who routinely interact, one

---

[36] The relational concept of social skill draws for inspiration on the same classical sources as the general conception. Mead, in particular, held that individuals' ability to empathize with one another can vary depending on having common experiences, such as a shared education, language, and culture, that provide opportunities for individuals to come to understand others' perspectives (by adopting the perspective of the general other). Within fields, this may make sense: agents who routinely take one another into account within a field will likely understand the general perspective of others, and those perspectives are not too dissimilar from one another. Therefore, if there is variation in individuals' ability to empathize with one another, it is likely due to non-social differences, because social influences would not vary between individuals. See George Herbert Mead, *Mind, Self, and Society: From the Standpoint of a Social Behaviorist* (Chicago: University of Chicago Press, 1934). In the context of international cooperation, however, the situation is different. In this case, we cannot assume a shared education, language, or culture that individuals will have access to when brokering cooperation across borders. In this case, where intermediaries are attempting to frame cooperation for strikingly dissimilar parties, the intermediary needs a more specific kind of experience to know how to frame cooperation so that it seems advantageous and meaningful for the specific parties who are to cooperate. See Grynaviski, *Constructive Illusions*, 158–60.

[37] Fligstein and McAdam, *A Theory of Fields*, 168.

focuses on the extraordinarily powerful actors within the field. Marginal agents, as Fligstein and McAdam acknowledge, receive less attention. As they put it, "the downside is there might be players on the edges of fields who are pivotal to what happens within fields."[38] If individuals develop social skill in more than one field precisely because they are marginal – the argument of this book – then concentrating on social skills within networks instead of within fields is important.[39]

How do marginal agents develop social skill? Within an international context, the specific kind of social skill we are interested in is how to appeal to people from different nations or cultures. Borderlands scholarship describes these individuals as "cultural brokers": they are people who live between societies. The premise of this impressive body of scholarship is that there are individuals in borderlands contexts who have extensive experience brokering deals across borders. These people – often because of a history of interactions – are bicultural; they know how to conduct business, they understand local politics, and they can appeal to different groups' sensibilities.[40]

Building on this insight, I argue that past experiences being between societies can make an agent socially skillful as well as marginal within either society. Intermediaries' personal experiences working in communities may provide them with an understanding of agents' interests and

[38] Ibid.

[39] This argument should not be read as a criticism of their account of strategic action fields in general. My explicit claim is that focusing on fields leads an analyst to exclude elements of social position that may be useful in understanding variation in social skill. One might endorse this argument and still use field analysis to understand intermediaries' roles; for example, by considering competition between intermediaries to recruit the Cherokee for the Confederacy as a field, and then using the concept of strategic action fields to analyze competition. While I do not explicitly use this approach, it is consistent with the argument of the book.

[40] For a few works emphasizing this view from different perspectives and in different disciplines, see Margaret Szasz, ed., *Between Indian and White Worlds: The Cultural Broker* (Norman: University of Oklahoma Press, 1994); Nancy L. Hagedorn, "'A Friend to Go Between Them': The Interpreter as Cultural Broker during Anglo-Iroquois Councils, 1740–70," *Ethnohistory* 35, no. 1 (1988): 60–80; Nancy L. Hagedorn, "Brokers of Understanding: Interpreters as Agents of Cultural Exchange in Colonial New York," *New York History* 76, no. 4 (1995): 379–408; Daniel K. Richter, "Cultural Brokers and Intercultural Politics: New York–Iroquois Relations, 1664–1701," *Journal of American History* 75, no. 1 (1988): 40–67; Melford S. Weiss, "Marginality, Cultural Brokerage, and School Aides: A Success Story in Education," *Anthropology & Education Quarterly* 25, no. 3 (1994): 336–46; Fintan O'Toole, *White Savage: William Johnson and the Invention of America* (New York: Farrar, Straus and Giroux, 2005); John Hall, *Uncommon Defense: Indian Allies in the Black Hawk War* (Cambridge: Harvard University Press, 2009).

political culture. Missionaries working with American Indians, for example, may be marginal players at home, as they have few connections to their government, but their experiences make them the agents most likely to understand potential confluences of interests between Indian nations and governments. Intermediaries also often have occupations or family backgrounds that require them to practice making these kinds of appeals. Some intermediaries in this book, for example, came from bicultural families and were therefore well-equipped to understand the politics of the communities from which their parents originated. Others were traders or missionaries, whose professions required them to practice making appeals to others' interests. These kinds of experiences are likely conducive to the growth of social skills that allow actors to understand communities' perspectives and provide experiences with deal-making.

The example of Frank North's experiences with the Pawnee underscores the importance of social skill for cooperation. Frank North helped recruit the Pawnee to fight against other Native Americans in the US Civil War and in several conflicts in the post-Civil War years. The Pawnee were reluctant to cooperate with the United States because of patterns of American abuse, and American officers in the area were reluctant to cooperate with the Pawnee Scouts because of prejudice. North was a clerk at a Pawnee trading post, so he had extensive experience working with the Pawnee; he learned the language and developed ties with Pawnee traders. North would later use his experience with the Pawnee to frame cooperation, appealing to American prejudices to show that Native Americans were useful in irregular warfare, and appealing to Native American interests in land as a reason for cooperation.[41] North's niche between communities – he had weak ties to the Pawnee and to the US military – allowed him to broker cooperation, because he understood and could appeal to both parties' interests.

The level of social skill that intermediaries have in relation to others depends on their niche between societies. To frame cooperation, intermediaries need to see it as a strategy to help agents realize gains, understand parties' interests, understand parties' political culture, and also be

---

[41] George Bird Grinnell, *Two Great Scouts and Their Pawnee Battalion* (Lincoln: University of Nebraska Press, 1973); Frank Joshua North, *The Life and Experiences of Major Frank North, Originator and Commander of … "North's Pawnee Scouts" …: A Complete Record of the Battles and Engagements Participated in by This Famous Organization. Together with a History of the Pawnee Indians–Their Customs, Habits, Dances, Games and Religion*, 1924; Mark van de Logt, *War Party in Blue: Pawnee Scouts in the U.S. Army* (Norman: University of Oklahoma Press, 2010).

trusted. I argue that intermediaries' network positions – their weak ties across structural holes – provide these elements of social skill necessary to promote cooperation.

TRANSLATING SKILL INTO COOPERATION

How do intermediaries capture the power of betweenness and use their social skill to induce cooperation? IR scholars often posit examples of barriers to cooperation. This section outlines four of these barriers, showing how intermediaries can take advantage of their betweenness to secure cooperation.

Identifying Parties

The first mechanism by which intermediaries promote cooperation is through identifying potential cooperation partners. Theories of cooperation usually emphasize interstate cooperation.[42] Which states exist is common knowledge to all other states (it is a small world). If all international cooperation is interstate cooperation, then identifying partners for cooperation would be reasonably easy because the information environment is rich.[43] Many cases of international cooperation, however, occur under conditions of exceptionally low information. When firms need new overseas partners, or intelligence services want cooperation partners abroad, parties may not be aware of one another or may not actively consider cooperation as a strategy because of an unfamiliarity with others. In these situations, intermediaries are important. Recall that the logic of structural holes suggests that two parties do not have contact

---

[42] Kenneth Waltz, *Theory of International Politics* (Boston: McGraw-Hill, 1979); Charles Glaser, *Rational Theory of International Politics: The Logic of Competition and Cooperation* (Princeton: Princeton University Press, 2011); Alexander Wendt, *Social Theory of International Politics* (Cambridge: Cambridge University Press, 1999); Robert Keohane, *After Hegemony: Cooperation and Discord in the World Political Economy* (Princeton: Princeton University Press, 1984).

[43] Especially in discussions of cooperation between neighbors, such as in North America or Europe, or within multilateral institutions such as NATO. See, for example, Adler and Barnett, "A Framework for the Study of Security Communities"; Lloyd Gruber, *Ruling the World: Power Politics and the Rise of Supranational Institutions* (Princeton: Princeton University Press, 2000); G. John Ikenberry, *After Victory: Institutions, Strategic Restraint, and the Rebuilding of Order after Major Wars* (Princeton: Princeton University Press, 2001); Andrew Moravcsik, *The Choice for Europe: Social Purpose and State Power from Messina to Maastricht* (Ithaca: Cornell University Press, 1998).

with one another unless there is a broker through which information flows. Building on this logic, intermediaries are necessary for cooperation if they are the (primary) means through which agents learn of others' existence.

Intermediaries are useful for securing cooperation by identifying partners for two reasons. First, intermediaries, by definition, are able to connect parties that would otherwise remain disconnected, providing opportunities for cooperation. One example from a well-developed body of literature relates to international investment, where substantial evidence shows that international Diasporas can convert their knowledge of potential foreign investment partners into opportunities for overseas capital to obtain significant returns. Without the assistance of diasporas, social relationships might not form between capital and firms that enables the parties to identify mutually beneficial investment opportunities.[44] The same logic extends to cooperation with non-state allies. Without a bridge to identify partners for cooperation, cooperation cannot occur.

Second, intermediaries' structural position may provide them with the capability to see opportunities for cooperation that agents with more institutional influence cannot see. Scholars at the intersection of social psychology, social network theory, and organizations have discovered that individuals are not always able to understand their own network position, because people often do not have an accurate impression of the networks in which they find themselves.[45] If individuals do not have an accurate understanding of their social networks, then they are unable to "see" structural holes and as a result cannot secure cooperation.[46] Individuals without positions of institutional influence, because they are less powerful, are much more likely to sense the opportunities that network structure provides. Experiments have found that agents who do not have power, or are primed to think they lack power, are likely to be especially attuned to the structure of the social networks they find themselves within. Moreover, individuals in top spots in organizational hierarchies are less likely to understand network structure than those occupying lower structural positions. One reason that low-power actors may be highly attuned to network structure is because their dependence

[44] David Leblang, "Familiarity Breeds Investment: Diaspora Networks and International Investment," *American Political Science Review* 104, no. 3 (2010): 584–600.

[45] For an overview of this research, see Raina A. Brands, "Cognitive Social Structures in Social Network Research: A Review," *Journal of Organizational Behavior* 34, no. S1 (2013): S82–103.

[46] Burt and Ronchi, "Teaching Executives to See Social Capital."

on others makes distal ties more important.[47] Low-powered individuals, in other words, are better able to identify opportunities for cooperation because their position leads them to seek out information on to capitalize on their network ties. In the context of international politics, this means intermediaries working on the edges of societies, who may be highly dependent on their ties to centers of power, are focused on understanding how they can translate weak ties into influence and therefore are more likely to see structural holes.

Explaining Interests

A second way an intermediary's social skills may enhance the prospects for cooperation is by presenting parties' interests to each other in a way that can make cooperation more likely. Often, parties will not cooperate if there are irreconcilable conflicts of interest.[48] For example, many Native Americans refused to cooperate with the Continental Congress during the American Revolution because they perceived (correctly) that settlers' appetites for land claims posed a threat (Chapter 2); for some time, the Philippine junta in Manila refused to cooperate with the United States during the Spanish–American War because they (correctly) feared the US would colonize the Philippines after Spain left (see Chapter 6); and the United States feared cooperating with the Macabebe in the Philippine–American War because US officers (wrongly) believed Macabebe guns would be turned on American soldiers (see Chapter 7). If interests are irreconcilable, cooperation is impossible.

Intermediaries have two features that allow them to promote cooperation in the face of apparent conflicts of interest. The first feature is their monopoly on information crossing a structural hole. Recall that intermediaries are agents' primary vehicle for gaining the information on which cooperation decisions are based (by definition). This provides opportunities for intermediaries to manipulate information and make it

---

[47] T. Casciaro, "Seeing Things Clearly: Social Structure, Personality, and Accuracy in Social Network Perception," *Social Networks* 20, no. 4 (1998): 331–51; Brent Simpson and Casey Borch, "Does Power Affect Perception in Social Networks? Two Arguments and an Experimental Test," *Social Psychology Quarterly* 68, no. 3 (2005): 278–87; Brent Simpson, Barry Markovsky, and Mike Steketee, "Power and the Perception of Social Networks," *Social Networks* 33 (2011): 166–71.

[48] The cases discussed in this book are particularly difficult because the costs of defection from cooperation were high (e.g., forced removal in the cases of Native Americans) and defection could occur swiftly. On these issues, see Charles Lipson, "International Cooperation in Economic and Security Affairs," *World Politics* 37, no. 1 (1984): 1–23.

appear as if parties have a harmony of interests when there really is a conflict. This strategy was pursued in each of the overseas cases I examine, where intermediaries claimed a perfect harmony between America's and its allies' post-war visions.

The second feature of intermediaries is that they often have extensive experience working across structural holes, which gives them the political knowledge necessary to make these appeals. Intermediaries need to know how to appeal to groups' or individuals' interests in ways that make cooperation more likely. To understand the interests of different groups requires extensive experience with those groups, experience that individuals who find themselves in the position of intermediary usually have. Owing to their position between communities, intermediaries may develop a set of basic social skills that aid in cooperation, such as bilingualism and biculturalism. For example, many of the intermediaries who bridge structural holes in this book are bilingual, and some are the children of bicultural parents. Other intermediaries' occupations, such as consuls, traders, and missionaries, led them to develop not only weak ties across borders but also a broad multiculturalism that allowed them to frame parties' interests. In addition, intermediaries may develop a knack for securing cooperation; or in more contemporary language, intercommunity cooperation is a practice they are familiar with.[49] To be socially skillful, individuals need to control the way they present themselves to divergent groups (self-monitoring), understand how weak ties can lead to successful bargains, and have experience creating or dealing with cultural frames that organize cooperation. These may be learned elements of social skill; having experience brokering deals in other contexts – from being a diplomat, trader, soldier, or political prisoner – is more likely to create the relevant experience than being stationed in Washington or another capital. In summary, intermediaries are likely socially skilled because only the socially skilled are likely to find themselves bridging structural holes.

Building Trust

A third way intermediaries' social skills may be useful for generating cooperation is by building trust between communities. IR scholars often

---

[49] Emmanuel Adler and Vincent Pouliot, "International Practices," *International Theory* 3, no. 1 (2011): 1–36.

argue that states do not have enough information about others' intentions or future plans, which makes cooperation difficult.[50] In low-information environments, actors have little past history on which to evaluate the trustworthiness of specific agents across structural holes. When the costs of contracting with an untrustworthy partner are especially high, mistrust can undermine the prospects for cooperation. Theories of trust in international politics usually focus exclusively on the two parties who are to cooperate. For the United States and the Soviet Union to cooperate over arms control, for example, trust is necessary to ensure that neither party believes the other will make gains by defecting from the agreements. But a dyadic theory of trust does not fully help us understand cooperation over structural holes. In these situations, a government and a political group abroad may have little interaction with one another, but both may have a history of interaction with a broker who puts them in touch with one another. In this case, the problem of trust is slightly different: the cooperation partners may be more concerned with the trustworthiness of the intermediary, on whom they depend for estimates of the other's interests and future preferences.

One resource intermediaries have access to that is often lacking in interstate negotiations is trust formed through personal ties. Sociological theory increasingly highlights the importance of personal ties in formal and informal networks to the creation of trust.[51] Individuals often use members of their social network to evaluate the credibility of partners for cooperation. For example, I often trust my friend's evaluation of the reliability of his friend. Using personal connections to evaluate others' trustworthiness reduces the costs of gaining information and enables third-parties to proxy for the reliability of partners.[52] Intermediaries, in certain circumstances, may work hard to craft a reputation for being

---

[50] See, for example, Andrew Kydd, *Trust and Mistrust in International Relations* (Princeton: Princeton University Press, 2005).

[51] James Coleman, "Social Capital in the Creation of Human Capital," *American Journal of Sociology* 94 (1988): S95–120; Mark Granovetter, "Economic Action and Social Structure: The Problem of Embeddedness," *American Journal of Sociology* 91, no. 3 (1985): 481–510; Mark Granovetter, "The Impact of Social Structure on Economic Outcomes," *Journal of Economic Perspectives* 19, no. 1 (2005): 33–50; Robert Putnam, *Bowling Alone: The Collapse and Revival of American Community* (New York: Simon & Schuster, 2000); Brian Uzzi, "The Sources and Consequences of Embeddedness for the Economic Performance of Organizations: The Network Effect," *American Sociological Review* 61, no. 4 (1996): 674–98.

[52] Granovetter, "Economic Action and Social Structure."

honest brokers of information or successful deal-makers.[53] If successful, groups may decide to trust their cooperation partner on the word of such an intermediary, with whom they have had repeated satisfactory dealings. An intermediary can also help ameliorate credible commitment problems by promising to use her influence to ensure all sides keep their commitments or by claiming to have "inside information" that a party intends to keep its commitment.

One useful example, not discussed in this book, is the recruitment of the Apache by the US military during the Apache Wars. Some Apache bands decided to ally with the United States in the hunt for Geronimo, largely to secure their land against further encroachments. The problem was mistrust. The US agents with whom the Apache were familiar tended to have unsavory reputations: they defrauded or abused the Apache at every turn. These agents reduced Apache confidence in American promises, rather than providing the reassurances necessary to secure cooperation. General George Crook, who would eventually recruit them, worked diligently to secure a reputation for honesty, taking extraordinary steps to ensure their fair treatment by courts and government agents. The presence of a trusted intermediary, in turn, reassured the Apache about American post-war aims.[54] This case is particularly noteworthy because Crook could reassure the Apache even though no evidence supported his claim that post-war Apache land rights would be respected; in the end, the Apache who allied with the military were sent along with Geronimo to reservations outside of Apacheria.

Managing Cultural Friction

The final way intermediaries use their social skill to promote cooperation is through managing cultural friction. Ideational differences can frequently undermine cooperation, often due to ideological differences. When political elites believe there are significant ideological distances between themselves and others, they often find others more threatening,

---

[53] Paul Milgrom, Douglass North, and Barry Weingast, "The Role of Institutions in the Revival of Trade: The Law Merchant, Private Judges, and the Champagne Fairs," *Economics & Politics* 2, no. 1 (1990): 1–23.

[54] Eric Grynaviski, "Brokering Cooperation: Intermediaries and US Cooperation with Non-State Allies, 1776–1945," *European Journal of International Relations* 21, no. 3 (2014): 691–717.

which likely impedes cooperation.[55] Ideological differences between the United States and the Soviet Union, for example, contributed to tension and made cooperation more difficult. Another reason is more quotidian. Often, when communities engage in ongoing processes of cooperation, intercultural differences – really cultural blunders – emerge that threaten to undermine the process. Examples from the record of international negotiations include many instances in which agents accidently insult one another because they did not understand the other's language and culture.[56]

The following chapters show how clear these kinds of ideational threats to cooperation have been in the context of American foreign policy. US diplomatic history, some argue, is driven by political elites who have little experience with foreign nations and hold overtly hostile views about parties abroad.[57] This has manifested in many barriers for cooperation. In North America, for example, political elites were often reluctant to recruit Native Americans, such as the Pawnee discussed earlier, because they discounted their battlefield contributions as unimportant due to the color of their skin. In this case, even after the terms of cooperation were agreed to, the Smithsonian ordered that the heads of fallen Pawnee allies be returned to the Smithsonian for analysis. In Cuba, too, during the Spanish–American War, US military officers, who lacked experience with battle-hardened Cuban rebels, often discounted the potential Cuban contributions due their skin color, placing them in non-combat roles.[58]

Intermediaries' heightened social skills may make them well-equipped to reduce cultural conflicts that can undermine cooperation in three ways. First, social psychologists have found a general psychological tendency for in-groups to demonize out-groups.[59] This may reduce the

[55] Mark Haas, *The Ideological Origins of Great Power Politics, 1789–1989* (Ithaca: Cornell University Press, 2005). Common ideologies do not always produce cooperation. See Stephen Walt, *The Origins of Alliances* (Ithaca: Cornell University Press, 1987).

[56] Raymond Cohen, "International Communication: An Intercultural Approach," *Cooperation and Conflict* 22, no. 2 (1987): 63–80; Raymond Cohen, *Negotiating Across Cultures* (Washington, DC: United States Institute of Peace Press, 1991); Ole Elgström, "National Culture and International Negotiations," *Cooperation and Conflict* 29, no. 3 (1994): 289–301.

[57] See, for example, Michael H. Hunt, *Ideology and U.S. Foreign Policy* (New Haven: Yale University Press, 2009).

[58] Louis A. Pérez, *Army Politics in Cuba, 1898–1958* (Pittsburgh: University of Pittsburgh Press, 1976); Louis A. Pérez, "Supervision of a Protectorate: The United States and the Cuban Army, 1898–1908," *The Hispanic American Historical Review* 52, no. 2 (1972): 250–71.

[59] N. Miller and Marilyn Brewer, eds., *Groups in Contact: The Psychology of Desegregation* (New York: Academic Press, 1984).

chances for international cooperation, because policymakers may perceive potential cooperators as undesirable partners.[60] Intermediaries may be less likely than political elites to demonize out-groups. People who work at the margins of multiple societies tend to have a specific package of social attributes – experience working with out-groups and high self-monitoring – that makes interacting with people from different cultures easier.[61] Second, intermediaries can take advantage of their social skill and structural position to reduce cultural friction by crafting communications between parties to avoid offending others' cultural sensibilities. Successful diplomats, for example, frequently change the language of requests from their home government to ensure they do not offend foreign partners.[62] Furthermore, intermediaries may take a more active role by reframing cooperation to make it ideologically appealing.[63] When intermediaries sought to promote cooperation with the Cuban rebels during the Spanish–American War, for example, they needed to develop a common cultural frame to entice American operations on the island. They used American cultural tropes to enhance support for the intervention, for example, by comparing their own leaders to the Founding Fathers or describing their revolution as akin to the American Revolution.[64]

The argument of this chapter – and the empirical portions of the book that follow – is that intermediaries have access to these mechanisms to promote cooperation. The betweenness of intermediaries provides them with information and skills unavailable to political elites, granting them the power to shape important outcomes in international politics.

[60] Mercer, "Anarchy and Identity."

[61] David F. Caldwell and Charles A. O'Reilly, "Boundary Spanning and Individual Performance: The Impact of Self-Monitoring," *Journal of Applied Psychology* 67, no. 1 (1982): 124–27; Francis J. Flynn, Jennifer A. Chatman, and Sandra E. Spataro, "Getting to Know You: The Influence of Personality on Impressions and Performance of Demographically Different People in Organizations," *Administrative Science Quarterly* 46, no. 3 (2001): 414–42; Zuzana Sasovova, Ajay Mehra, Stephen P. Borgatti, and Michaéla C. Schippers, "Network Churn: The Effects of Self-Monitoring Personality on Brokerage Dynamics," *Administrative Science Quarterly* 55, no. 4 (2010): 639–70.

[62] Francisco Gomes de Matos, "Applying the Pedagogy of Positiveness to Diplomatic Communication," in *Language and Diplomacy*, ed. Jovan Kurbalija and Hannah Slavik (Malta: Diplo Foundation, 2001), 281–7.

[63] Jarol Manheim, "Strategic Public Diplomacy: Managing Kuwait's Image During the Gulf Conflict," in *Taken by Storm: The Media, Public Opinion, and U.S. Foreign Policy in the Gulf War*, ed. W. Lance Bennett and David L. Paletz (Chicago: University of Chicago Press, 1994), 131–48.

[64] Grynaviski, "Brokering Cooperation." Examples such as this are familiar to borderlands historians, who emphasize biculturalism in navigating through thorny identity-based issues in borderlands contexts. This is discussed more extensively in the conclusion.

COOPERATION WITH NON-STATE ALLIES

To show how intermediaries take advantage of their betweenness to pro-mote cooperation, I concentrate on the US experience with non-state allies, from 1776 until today. As the United States grew, it depended on allies at home and abroad to do much of its fighting. I refer to these groups as non-state allies.

I define a non-state ally as *a non-state political, religious, or ethnic group that coordinates military operations with a state for political purposes*, often by providing military, logistical, or material support, or actively providing intelligence by scouting, guiding, or undertaking other intelligence missions.

This definition is intentionally broad, relaxing what many IR scholars traditionally describe as a key feature of alliances: statehood. Often, IR scholars stipulate that one cannot have an alliance with a non-state actor because alliances, by definition, are compacts between sovereign states.[65] I rely on a broader definition that includes political agreements with non-state groups. To count as a non-state ally, a deal does not need to be an explicit, written agreement between sovereigns. Instead, two or more groups must decide to coordinate their military operations in order to advance their political interests. Examples of coordinated military operations are diverse, including instances where the non-state ally joins the US military en masse or serves as a guide or scout for American troops, as well as cases where the United States arms its non-state ally or uses warships to defend the non-state ally from enemy forces. Throughout this book, the terms "alliances" and "allies" are frequently used by key individuals described in the case studies, as well as by historians, to make sense of the political nature of these deals.

I also include American Indian nations through the Civil War under this definition of non-state allies. This may seem inaccurate as many American Indian communities were and are sovereign communities. Given the emphasis on American Indian studies within this book, this is an important point. Even if these nations were sovereign, they had not achieved the kind of modern statehood that American International Relations scholars usually think about when differentiating between state and non-state actors. In many ways, they were independent entities, but so too were Cuban and Philippine rebels fighting against Spain. I consider

---

[65] See, for example, James D. Morrow, "Alliances: Why Write Them Down?," *Annual Review of Political Science* 3, no. 1 (2000): 63.

Native Americans to have a family resemblance to other non-state allies, usually overseas, that the United States has relied on, and therefore count them as instances of the broader concept.[66]

Despite its breadth, this definition intentionally excludes three kinds of cases. First, a single individual cannot ally with the United States, even if she enlists for political reasons. Furthermore, groups exclusively motivated by money (mercenaries) do not count, because there are no political stakes motivating their decision-making. For a group to count as a non-state ally, there must be active cooperation. Instances where a non-state actor and a state fight against a common enemy without coordinating their operations do not count, such as when the Apache raided Mexico during the same period the United States was at war with Mexico (1848).[67] One further restriction is that I primarily concentrate on instances of cooperation between 1776 and 1945. I limit myself to cases before 1945 for evidentiary reasons. Most of the research in this book is archival, and many post-war cases are still classified, especially given the role of the Central Intelligence Agency in recruiting non-state allies during the Cold War. A final chapter briefly reviews these cases up to the War on Terror, but I give them less attention because the evidence is much more tenuous. Another advantage to examining a long period of time is that potential alternative explanations vary during these periods (e.g., the size of the US diplomatic machinery, its relative power, political elites' beliefs, and so on), as the United States moved from its weak, post-colonial status to a superpower.

To systematically investigate patterns of alliances with these groups, I attempted to collect a full dataset of known cases of cooperation. I drew up a list of major and minor American military interventions, and then read the most comprehensive accounts of the military operations available. For some, such as Native Americans in the Civil War, there are comprehensive, multi-volume accounts that list participants, making this operation possible.[68] For others, even the most comprehensive accounts do not mention or describe many non-state allies. For these latter cases, I turned to other sources, including archival evidence found

---

[66] Gary Goertz, *Social Science Concepts: A User's Guide* (Princeton: Princeton University Press, 2006).

[67] Edwin Russell Sweeney, *Mangas Coloradas, Chief of the Chiricahua Apaches* (Norman: University of Oklahoma Press, 1998), chap. 7.

[68] Annie Heloise Abel, *The American Indian as Participant in the Civil War* (Cleveland: Arthur Clark Company, 1919); Laurence Hauptman, *Between Two Fires: American Indians in the Civil War* (New York: Free Press, 1995).

in the National Archives, to find a more complete list. Even this list is incomplete, as new cases await discovery and analysis by political scientists and historians.

Table 1.1 provides a list of American non-state allies. The list is not exhaustive; it does not even cover the majority of cases described in the first part of the book, yet it represents the diversity of conflicts in which non-state allies participated from 1776 to 1945.

Most of the cases listed in Table 1.1 are instances of security cooperation with Native Americans. Their inclusion in this book is vital. Wars against Native Americans were the most common kind of conflict involving the United States. These were costly affairs, sometimes involving extraregional powers (e.g., the War of 1812), and were a primary American security concern. Yet, IR scholars, especially students of American foreign policy, treat Native Americans only briefly, if at all. When they do mention Native Americans, their focus is usually on US attitudes toward them, emphasizing, for example, manifest destiny, imperialism, or problems of difference in the discipline, without looking at Native Americans' attitudes toward the United States.[69] As a result, comparatively little attention has been paid to Native Americans as active agents whose decisions shaped American foreign policy. This is curious, in part, because historians have long noted the substantive implications of Indian decision-making for American foreign policy. As Brian Delay explains, "It is now a basic tenet of North America's colonial narrative that Indians could decisively shape the course of inter-imperial relations."[70]

From this broad collection of cases, I first selected conflicts rather than allies, including the American Revolution, the Barbary Wars, the American Civil War, Samoa, the Apache Wars, the Spanish–American War, and the Second World War. The logic behind selecting cases across such a long period is to chronicle how American foreign policy has been shaped over time by its non-state allies. By using this wide variety of cases, I can make an overwhelming case that US security policy often

---

[69] See, for example, Beate Jahn, *The Cultural Construction of International Relations: The Invention of the State of Nature* (New York: Palgrave Macmillan, 2000), chap. 4; Naeem Inayatullah and David L. Blaney, *International Relations and the Problem of Difference* (Routledge, 2003); John Mearsheimer, *The Tragedy of Great Power Politics* (New York: W. W. Norton & Company, 2001), chap. 7.

[70] Brian DeLay, "Independent Indians and the US–Mexican War," *American Historical Review* 112, no. 1 (2007): 39. See also Jeremy Adelman and Stephen Aron, "From Borderlands to Borders: Empires, Nation-States, and the Peoples in between in North American History," *The American Historical Review* 104, no. 3 (1999): 814–41.

TABLE 1.1 *US non-state allies, 1776–1945*

Overseas	Native Americans Pre-Civil War	Native Americans Civil War	Native Americans Post-Civil War
First Barbary War Ahmed Karamanli	*Revolutionary War* Delaware Maliseet Mi'kmaq Oneida Passamaquoddy Penobscot Stockbridge	*Civil War (Union)* Chippewa Creek Delaware Huron Iroquois Ojibwa Odawa Pamunkey Potawami	*Walapai War* Mojave
Spanish–American War Cuban Army Filipino Army	*Creek Civil War* Choctaw Creeks (Lower)	*Civil War (Confederacy)* Catawba Cherokee Choctaw Creek Seminole	*Cheyenne Campaigns* Pawnee
Second Samoan Civil War Tanumafili's Forces	*War of 1812* Choctaw Iroquois Osages Pawnee Sioux		*Apache Wars* Papago Pimas Walapai West Mountain Yavapai
World War II Chin (Shin) Filipino Resistance Free Thai Movement French Resistance Italian Partisans Kachin Karen Kinabalu Guerillas Korean Liberation Army Naga Partisans (Albania) Partisans (Italy) Partisans (Yugoslavia) Vietminh	*First Seminole War* Creeks (Lower)		*Snakes War* Pauite Utamilla Warm Springs
	Black Hawk War Dakotas Ho Chunks Menominees Meskwakis Potawatomis		*Great Sioux War* Crow Pawnee Shoshone
			Nez Perce War Bannock Crow

depends heavily on cooperation with these groups. Within these cases, I often need to select which groups to emphasize. For example, during the Spanish–American War, the United States had non-state allies in Cuba and the Philippines. When facing a decision about which case to select within a conflict, I discuss selection within the chapter.

TESTING THE ARGUMENT

The key causal claim in this book is that the presence of a structural hole (the independent variable) provides opportunities and resources for intermediaries to enhance the prospects for cooperation (the dependent variable) by identifying parties for cooperation, explaining parties' interests to each other, building trust, and mitigating cultural conflict (the causal mechanisms).

The Choice of Qualitative Methods

The most straightforward approach to testing this kind of causal claim is to rely on tools of Social Network Analysis, which are usually quantitative. Often, this means creating a dataset of network ties. IR scholars working with these tools have already performed these kinds of analyses at the state level, for example, by collecting data on who trades with whom, which states join the same international organizations, or which states exchange diplomatic missions.[71] These quantitative studies are usually interested in state-level official relationships, rather than the informal personal relationships addressed in this book.

One cannot, however, use quantitative methods to study the interpersonal and informal relationships with respect to non-state allies over time. The most likely strategy would be to collect all correspondence related to a case in an archive, coding an edge as an instance where one agent writes a letter to another agent. This kind of strategy, however, would produce misleading results, missing most ties between communities. Most correspondence related to the cases investigated in this book has been lost to time, many interactions were verbal rather than written, many conversations were secret with little record, and some of the non-state allies described in this book were illiterate. A large part of this book is documenting whether a specific tie existed, usually by closely reading

---

[71] See, for example, Hafner-Burton and Montgomery, "Power Positions International Organizations, Social Networks, and Conflict"; Maoz, *Networks of Nations*.

the contents of letters and looking for clues about personal connections between agents. Therefore, a database that simply counts correspondence would ignore the meat of diplomacy, which is often personal, face-to-face, and irregular. Such an approach would also overestimate some strong and direct ties. President Grant, for example, wrote to Samoan chiefs in Apia, Samoa, in the 1870s. This direct correspondence, though, does not imply a direct tie between Grant and Samoa. Rather, the letter was requested by an intermediary – Albert Steinberger – who likely helped craft the letter in order to obtain more authority in the islands (see Chapter 5). Evaluating authorship, meaning, and sense is crucial in the cases that follow, and there is no quantitative approach that would not distort or oversimplify the historical record.

Within the universe of cases of non-state allies, the only plausible strategy is a qualitative approach, which provides a richer and more accurate account of cross-border social relationships. Testing network-based arguments using qualitative techniques is increasingly common, perhaps most especially in political science.[72] I use two strategies in particular, outlined in the following sections. The first strategy is to identify observable implications of the causal processes explained earlier in the chapter, and then to test whether these observable implications are present. The second strategy is to use a variety of comparative case techniques.

Observing Intermediaries' Influence

The first strategy I use to evaluate the effect of structural holes on intermediaries' influence is process tracing. Specifically, I divide the theory into a number of empirical propositions and then deduce observable

---

[72] Carpenter, *"Lost" Causes*; Mette Eilstrup-Sangiovanni, "Varieties of Cooperation: Government Networks in International Security," in *Networked Politics: Agency, Power, and Governance*, ed. Miles Kahler (Ithaca: Cornell University Press, 2009), 194–227; Stacie E. Goddard, "Brokering Peace: Networks, Legitimacy, and the Northern Ireland Peace Process," *International Studies Quarterly* 56, no. 3 (2012): 501–15; Daniel H. Nexon, *The Struggle for Power in Early Modern Europe: Religious Conflict, Dynastic Empires, and International Change* (Princeton: Princeton University Press, 2009); Janice Gross Stein, "The Politics and Power of Networks: The Accountability of Humanitarian Organizations," in *Networked Politics: Agency, Power, and Governance*, ed. Miles Kahler (Ithaca: Cornell University Press, 2009), 151–70. In other disciplines, see Collar, *Religious Networks in the Roman Empire*; Sue Heath, Alison Fuller, and Brenda Johnston, "Chasing Shadows: Defining Network Boundaries in Qualitative Social Network Analysis," *Qualitative Research* 9, no. 5 (2009): 645–61; Sarah L. Jack, "The Role, Use and Activation of Strong and Weak Network Ties: A Qualitative Analysis," *Journal of Management Studies* 42, no. 6 (2005): 1233–59.

implications for each proposition. I evaluate each case in detail, using process tracing to identify whether the observable implications are present within the case. The empirical chapters trace how the effect of structural holes (Proposition 1) in combination with intermediaries' interests and skills (Propositions 2 and 3) helped the intermediary promote cooperation (Proposition 4). This approach, which maximizes the number of empirical predictions from a theory, generates high levels of certainty about the veracity of the conclusions drawn.[73]

Table 1.2 highlights the four propositions, and the observable implications of each proposition, that I search for in the empirical chapters that follow.

The central claim of this book is that the existence of structural holes provides opportunities for intermediaries to exercise power. Therefore, within a case, I first must identify whether a structural hole exists (proposition one). By structural hole, I mean specifically that *there were few or no interpersonal ties between alliance partners in the period before cooperation began.* Table 1.2 provides a list of four observable implications. When one or more of these observable implications are present, there is likely to be a structural hole. Specifically, the archival record may show that the parties are surprised the other exists, the parties may have no means to communicate, the existing bridges may be untrustworthy, or policymakers may lament that they know so little about the politics of a region. Most cases display at least three, and sometimes four, of these attributes. The presence of any of these observable implications would suggest the lack of direct, strong ties between political elites that could bridge structural holes.

The second proposition is that *intermediaries have an incentive to promote cooperation.* Strictly speaking, the presence of incentives is not necessary for my causal argument, which posits that the presence of structural holes produces opportunities and resources for intermediaries. Yet, understanding intermediaries' incentives is important for two reasons. The causal argument is a condition of possibility argument. Structural holes make it possible for intermediaries to exercise influence,

---

73 See Derek Beach and Rasmus Brun Pedersen, *Process-Tracing Methods: Foundations and Guidelines* (Ann Arbor: University of Michigan Press, 2013); Andrew Bennett, "Process Tracing and Causal Inference," in *Rethinking Social Inquiry: Diverse Tools, Shared Standards,* 2nd ed. (Lanham: Rowman & Littlefield, 2010), 207–20; David Collier, "Understanding Process Tracing," *PS: Political Science & Politics* 44, no. 4 (2011): 823–30; Alexander George and Andrew Bennett, *Case Studies and Theory Development in the Social Sciences* (Cambridge: MIT Press, 2005).

TABLE 1.2 *Observable implications*

Proposition 1: Structural hole	*Observable implication 1*: Awareness The future parties to cooperation are unaware of each other's existence
	Observable implication 2: Communications Infrastructure The future parties to cooperation have no reliable method for communicating with one another
	Observable implication 3: Negative Affect Existing ties between communities carry an (almost) entirely negative affect, often prompted by untrustworthy individuals, cultural or racial prejudice, or a past history of violence
	Observable implication 4: Reflexivity The future parties to cooperation lament their lack of knowledge of the others' affairs
Proposition 2: Intermediaries' incentives	*Observable implication 5*: Self-interest Bridging the structural hole realizes, or is perceived to realize, personal rewards, such as financial or career benefits
	Observable implication 6: Group Interests Bridging the structural hole realizes, or is perceived to realize, the parties' interests with whom an intermediary identifies
	Observable implication 7: Esteem Benefits Intermediaries are drawn to bridge structural holes due to the esteem benefits they anticipate
Proposition 3: Social skill	*Observable implication 8*: Language Skills Intermediaries can speak the languages of the parties
	Observable implication 9: Biculturalism Intermediaries have experience working or living within both communities
	Observable implication 10: Brokerage Experience Intermediaries have experience developing deals between communities, for example, through trade or as low-level diplomats (trade consuls)
Proposition 4: Cooperation mechanisms	*Observable implication 11*: Identification Mechanism The historical record shows that the intermediary was the primary agent for identifying cooperation partners. Without the intermediary, there is evidence that the parties would remain unaware of one another
	Observable implication 12: Interests Mechanism The intermediary "explains" the parties to each other in a way conducive to cooperation, often by portraying the parties as having a harmony of interests

(*continued*)

TABLE 1.2 (*cont.*)

Observable implication 13: Building Trust
The intermediary builds trust between the parties, often
by staking her personal reputation on the reliability
of a cooperation partner or framing information in a
way that reassures one or more parties about others'
intentions

Observable implication 14: Mitigating Cultural Conflict
The intermediary helps the parties avoid identity-based
conflicts that might undo cooperation

---

but they do not make it certain that intermediaries will choose to do so.
Intermediaries, in theory and in fact, can choose not to use their influence to bridge structural holes, especially when they have incentives to
not promote, or even to hinder, cooperation. To translate these conditions of possibility into direct political behavior requires the intermediary to have incentives to exert influence. Furthermore, the presence of
incentives is important for evaluating much of the specific case material assessed here. In select cases, such as the Philippines and Samoa, it
remains a historical controversy to assert that missionaries or consular agents acted as intermediaries and promoted cooperation. Assessing
incentives in these cases is important: it shows agents had good reasons
to support cooperation and lends confidence to the argument that they
did in fact do so.

Three observable implications related to intermediaries' incentives
may be present in the archival record, corresponding to three kinds of
incentives intermediaries may have to promote cooperation. First, there
may be evidence that intermediaries believe cooperation will pay, for
example, by advancing a career or a means of financial gain. Second,
the archival record may provide evidence that intermediaries sincerely
believe that cooperation is in the interest of one or more parties with
whom they identify. In other words, an intermediary might identify with
the well-being of one or more communities and thus has an interest in
improving that party's well-being. Finally, the archival record might provide evidence that intermediaries enjoy the esteem benefits (the attention)
drawn from promoting cooperation. Evaluating incentives may appear
difficult in the abstract, but the archival evidence is strikingly clear in
almost every case.

A third component of my argument is that *intermediaries are socially
skilled agents, able to promote cooperation by understanding parties'*

worldviews. There is no direct way to test this argument because empathy is difficult to observe in the historical record. I believe, however, that three indirect implications are observable: intermediaries have linguistic skills, are bicultural (i.e., have practice working in the relevant political cultures), and have experience with cross-cultural brokerage. The first two observable implications are proxies; I assume that bilingualism and biculturalism may provide a way to understand others' identities and interests. Brokerage experience may be more direct. If people have a track record of promoting cooperation, they likely have a higher ability to empathize with others.

The final proposition is that *intermediaries are necessary for cooperation because without the intermediary, parties for cooperation may not be identified, parties would assume their interests conflict, there would be insufficient trust, and/or there would be no cultural frame to enable cooperation.* These four mechanisms by which intermediaries may enhance cooperation each have several observable implications, although I collect them into four categories listed in Table 1.2. For example, I argue that in the presence of structural holes, intermediaries are necessary for the identification of cooperation partners, which means the historical record shows (a) no other agents were familiar or in contact with both parties, and (b) the intermediary actively put the parties in contact with one another.

Testing Strategies

Process tracing, outlined in the previous section, often provides firm evidence for the role of the intermediary. In some cases, however, I set the process tracing evidence against alternative explanations. Two alternative explanations, in particular, that are treated throughout the case material may cut against my argument.

Alternative Explanation (Political Influence): Politically Well-Connected Agents Played the Role of Intermediary, Promoting Cooperation through Strong Ties between Communities. The political influence explanation suggests that particularly well-connected agents brokered cooperation by using their strong ties. This cuts against the argument that intermediaries – agents who by definition have weak ties – were causally important in the process. One variation of the political influence hypothesis is that intermediaries were ordered to secure cooperation. If intermediaries were under orders to promote cooperation, especially from Washington, it is unlikely they were causally important for cooperation. The existence of top-down orders would imply the absence of a structural hole, because it would mean politically influential agents knew about and trusted potential cooperation partners. Moreover, it would suggest that cooperation could have occurred without the help of an intermediary, because Washington could simply select another person had the intermediary not existed.

Alternative Explanation (Structural Determinism): Cooperation with Non-State Allies Would Have Occurred Due to a Harmony of Interests, Regardless of the Intermediary's Contribution. This explanation, familiar to security scholars, posits that interests drive alliance behavior regardless of agents' roles.[74] If interests drive cooperation without being conditioned by intermediaries' role in framing cooperation, then intermediaries are causally unimportant.

I use several comparative case study techniques to enhance the evidence for the role of intermediaries and to undermine the alternative explanations. In several chapters, I analyze within-case variation, disaggregating a case into the periods before and after cooperation. In doing so, I can compare periods of non-cooperation and cooperation, showing that the intermediary's presence played a role in producing different outcomes. There are two benefits to analyzing within-case variation. If factors that alternative explanations point to, such as political influence or structural factors, are constant before and after cooperation begins, then they are unlikely to explain the turn toward cooperation.[75] By screening out some of these factors, I have more confidence in the special roles played by intermediaries. Moreover, analyzing within-case variation provides evidence for counterfactual analysis, which I use in several of these cases.[76]

Several cases also afford opportunities for between-case comparisons. In Chapter 1, I examine the case of the Oneidas and their alliance with the colonists. The Oneida are one of five major groups of Iroquois who lived in the Great Lakes region; the other four chose to remain neutral or ally with the British. By comparing Oneida and Mohawk decision-making, I can

---

[74] See, for example, Walt, *The Origins of Alliances*; Waltz, *Theory of International Politics*.

[75] Analyzing within-case variation by treating it as an interrupted time series is extraordinarily useful for discounting alternative explanations, even if interrupted time series designs cannot provide direct evidence for a claim. See Grynaviski, *Constructive Illusions*, 45–46.

[76] James Fearon, "Counterfactuals and Hypothesis Testing in Political Science," *World Politics* 43, no. 2 (1991): 169–195; Eric Grynaviski, "Contrasts, Counterfactuals, and Causes," *European Journal of International Relations* 19, no. 4 (2013): 823–46.

isolate specific causal factors related to intermediaries and screen out structural factors such as geography, ideology, and power that should affect both groups in the same way. Furthermore, I examine cases where the United States chose to cooperate with one ally instead of another. In Chapter 8, for example, I evaluate why the United States chose to support Hoxjde's partisans in Albania and Tito's in Yugoslavia. In both cases, the decision to support one non-state ally meant not cooperating with other rival partisan groups within the state. Once again, structure may push the United States to form alliances, but structural explanations are not sufficiently precise to determine with whom the United States will ally.[77]

THE EVIDENCE

To collect evidence related to the roles intermediaries play requires working with primary source materials. In most of the cases addressed in this book, existing secondary sources treat non-state allies as an aside and do not concentrate on their contribution or the manner in which cooperation came about.[78] In some cases, the secondary literature barely mentions non-state allies. Therefore, I turned to primary source documents to identify who cooperated with the United States and how those alliances formed. The archival work contained in this book is extensive enough that a few words on how I approached the archival record are necessary.

IR scholars usually focus on the diplomatic record produced by high-ranking officials, especially meetings between heads of state or documents produced by government agencies or committees. The archival research in this book is qualitatively different, because the scope of agents is much broader. Therefore, the kinds of evidence are much more varied, including, for example, Army enlistment papers, ships' logs, consular records, court martial records, personal papers, private family papers, and county records. I concentrate, whenever possible, on the documents of individuals who were candidate brokers, whether these documents appeared in personal papers or government archives. I also spoke with members of a number of Native American groups, listening to their oral traditions related to the Civil War in particular. In one case, I worked with the online American genealogical community to obtain a

---

[77] On "most-similar" designs, see George and Bennett, *Case Studies and Theory Development in the Social Sciences*, 80–1.
[78] The notable exception is the First Barbary War, discussed in the next section, as well as the role of Samuel Kirkland in the Revolutionary War.

Civil War-era diary. In addition, I paid special attention to contemporaneous accounts, including newspapers, memoirs, and relevant congressional testimony.

One contribution of this book is to show that IR scholars' selective
attention to the historical record, focusing on the papers of a small number of policymakers, biases their interpretations. Often, IR scholars (and
some diplomatic historians), interested in the preferences and perceptions
of political elites, begin and end their evidentiary searches in presidential papers and political memoirs. Unsurprisingly, the evidence they find
in the papers or memoirs of political elites underscores the influence of
those elites.[79] Most political memoirs, for example, read as exercises in
narcissism.

I focus on agents closer to the action. Examining how cooperation
unfolded on the ground shifts the interpretive emphasis away from
what decision-makers believed to why they believed it. Specifically, it
moves the spotlight toward the agents who shaped the information
moving across societies, and away from decision-makers who often
reacted to intermediaries' efforts. By looking past the papers of political
elites, I hope this book will underscore the importance of expanding
the sources consulted, as well as provide a bridge to the more nuanced,
contemporary diplomatic history that emphasizes a more diverse range
of agents and more attention to broader sets of sources in the archival
record.

One limitation this work faced was the sparseness of documents produced by US non-state allies. In all cases, I rely exclusively on archives
located in the United States and the United Kingdom. In contemporary
diplomatic history, one standard for work is the extent to which international events are given "international histories," meaning that the
perspectives of participants other than the United States are represented
through evidence produced by those communities.[80] This book sometimes falls short of that standard, and this may introduce one important bias into the evidence. Often, a western intermediary worked with

---

[79] In some cases, political elites intentionally obfuscate the roles of private actors in
presidential records. See, for example, Max Holland, "Private Sources of U.S. Foreign
Policy: William Pawley and the 1954 Coup d'État in Guatemala," *Journal of Cold War
Studies* 7, no. 4 (2005): 70–1.

[80] On international history, see Caroline Kennedy-Pipe, "International History and
International Relations Theory: A Dialogue beyond the Cold War," *International Affairs*
76, no. 4 (2000): 741–54; Odd Arne Westad, "The New International History of the
Cold War: Three (Possible) Paradigms," *Diplomatic History* 24, no. 4 (2000): 551–65.

a counterpart abroad, and it is difficult to identify the level of agency exercised by the non-western intermediary without examining direct evidence.[81] One wonders whether agents from North Africa, the Philippines, or Samoa, for example, shaped intermediaries' perceptions of events in the same way the intermediaries I focus on shaped their preferences.[82] While I recognize this problem, there is no way to avoid the resulting bias from concentrating on western intermediaries. I attempted to find evidence related to non-western intermediaries, but they typically did not leave an archival record, at least that I can identify. An international history of these conflicts is therefore beyond the scope of this book. The cost is a biased interpretation that may slightly overemphasize western intermediaries, but it comes with the benefit of being able to show how western intermediaries mattered.

CONCLUSION

The central argument developed in this book is that attention to great powers and "great men" may do more to confuse our understanding of the history of American foreign policy than to illuminate it. Rather than beginning with the assumption that these agents are the most important in international politics, this book begins work from the ground up, by first asking, "Whose contributions were essential for the achievement of American war aims?" In most of the cases canvassed in this book, the work of non-state allies was essential for military success and, in cases where these allies were not essential, they contributed to the war effort in ways that reduced the costs of military operations and enhanced the legitimacy of overseas military operations. I then ask, "Who secured the cooperation of these non-state allies?" In every case, political elites were constrained by their structural position, unable to see opportunities for cooperation. Even after opportunities for cooperation were identified, political elites did not have the social skill to secure cooperation, due to issues related to trust and political culture. Instead, intermediaries – agents with weak ties

---

[81] On how this might bias the interpretation of events, in a North American context, see Michael A. McDonnell, "Maintaining a Balance of Power: Michilimackinac, the Anishinaabe Odawas, and the Anglo-Indian War of 1763," *Early American Studies: An Interdisciplinary Journal* 13, no. 1 (2015): 42–3.

[82] If these agents mattered, of course, it would confirm the argument of this book, because these agents, acting as intermediaries, would work through intermediaries to broker cooperation. Yet, who mattered would expand to include many more agents from overseas.

across structural holes – had structural positions that enabled the kinds of social skill necessary to secure cooperation. The chapters that follow track the development of American foreign policy, from the country's founding until today, showing how a focus on intermediaries provides a better understanding of the development and trajectory of the rise of American power.

2

Rebels or Savages

Most military histories of the American Revolution focus on white forces. Schoolchildren in the United States learn about the Continental Army, the Battle of Yorktown, the crossing of the Delaware, and survival at Valley Forge. They also learn about irregular forces, such as the Minutemen at the Battles of Lexington and Concord. Less attention has been paid, in the popular imagination, to the contributions of the colonists' non-white allies, especially Native Americans. Across the thirteen colonies, American Indians formed alliances with the belligerents. Many Cherokees cooperated with the British, attacking the Carolinas, Georgia, and Virginia; so too did the Ohio Indians – Delawares, Shawnees, and others – who fought in the west. Conversely, the colonists formed alliances with the Oneidas and Tuscaroras, the Stockbridge Indians, and many other American Indians in the northeast. Historians interested in the Revolutionary War have focused on these important alliances, showing that they were materially important for the war.[1]

I focus on cooperation between the colonists and the Oneidas and the Tuscaroras, one of the most studied cases of cooperation during

---

[1] For an overview of some of these cases, see Colin Calloway, *The American Revolution in Indian Country: Crisis and Diversity in Native American Communities* (Cambridge: Cambridge University Press, 1995); Colin Calloway, "Sentinels of the Revolution: Bedel's New Hampshire Rangers and the Abenaki Indians on the Upper Connecticut," *Historical New Hampshire* 4 (1990): 271–95; Barbara Graymont, *The Iroquois in the American Revolution* (Syracuse: Syracuse University Press, 1972); James Leamon, *Revolution Downeast: The War for American Independence in Maine* (Amherst: University of Massachusetts Press, 1995); James H. O'Donnell, *Southern Indians in the American Revolution* (Knoxville: University of Tennessee Press, 1973).

the Revolutionary War. Beginning in 1775, these nations declared a pro-American neutrality, aiding the colonists through the collection of intelligence and helping them engage in diplomacy with other American Indians. In 1777, they formed an alliance, fighting alongside Patriot forces.[2] Their contribution was important. The strategic problem confronting the Continental Congress with respect to the northern frontier was the long border with British-controlled Canada. British troops were based across the border, and if the border was left undefended, the British would obtain an important strategic advantage. Compounding the difficulty, many Iroquois nations joined the British, adding manpower and intelligence gathering capabilities to the already overwhelming British advantage. The threat from pro-British Iroquois was sufficiently strong to require an extensive dedication of resources. In 1779, Washington ordered the Sullivan Expedition into Iroquoia to burn down the villages and fortifications of Iroquoia loyal to the Crown. Over 3,000 soldiers – a sizable commitment for the Continental Army – dedicated their summer to campaigning against Iroquois warriors instead of British soldiers.[3]

Oneida and Tuscarora were two of six nations of Iroquois who composed the Iroquois Confederacy in 1776. In this chapter, I refer to them collectively as the Oneidas.[4] They were the only two nations who sided with the Patriots. Their decision led them to exit the confederacy, left them prey to raids from Indians and attacks from the British, and forced them to leave their lands for protection elsewhere. These non-state allies were important for the defense of New York during the war, and they gained an impressive reputation on the battlefield. The Oniedas fought at the battles of Oriskany and Saratoga in 1777 and Barren Hill in 1778. They raided and were raided by other, pro-British Iroquois. They spied in Canada and upstate New York, providing vital information about British military plans. They conducted raids to disrupt British food supplies. They even brought supplies to Valley Forge to help feed the Continental Army.[5]

[2] David Levinson, "An Explanation for the Oneida-Colonist Alliance in the American Revolution," *Ethnohistory* 23, no. 3 (1976): 271–2.

[3] Max M. Mintz, *The Seeds of Empire – The American Revolutionary Conquest of the Iroquois* (New York: New York University Press, 1999); Glenn Williams, *Year of the Hangman: George Washington's Campaign Against the Iroquois* (Westholme: Yardley, 2005).

[4] When referring to Oneidas, I am following a common convention of referring to Oneida and Tuscarora decision making. The Tuscarora were a separate nation living in and around Oneida lands but tended to follow the lead of Oneida decision makers. Only when describing the Tuscarora specifically do I refer to them separately.

[5] Joseph Glatthaar and James Martin, *Forgotten Allies: The Oneida Indians and the American Revolution* (New York: Hill and Wang, 2007); Graymont, *The Iroquois in the*

Unfortunately for the Oniedas, cooperation did not yield significant dividends. In the short term, the war devastated the Oniedas. Fighting in the Mohawk Valley was vicious, and the Oneida were prime targets. Their villages were burned, they lost their long-standing alliances within Iroquoia, and many died from fighting or hunger. In the long term, the fighting did nothing to help the Oneidas secure their post-war position in the United States. In the years after the American victory, the Oneidas' and Tuscaroras' settler allies encroached on their land; in fact, they lost their land more quickly than other Iroquois who fought against the United States.[6]

Cooperation between Oneidas and the Continental Army is a puzzle for International Relations scholars, who emphasize strategic or broad cultural factors at the expense of a politics of agency. The Oneidas made no strategic gains from cooperation. As one scholar bluntly explains: "What benefits did the Oneida reap from their allegiance to the victorious Americans? Unfortunately, the answer to this question is *absolutely none*."[7] They were left largely homeless, their crops and villages were destroyed, and the United States quickly displaced them.

Geographic factors commonly cited by IR scholars also do not explain the difference in alliance decisions by the Oneidas and other Iroquois.[8] Stephen Walt's balance of threat theory describes how states should balance against geographically near threats.[9] These geographic arguments cannot explain Oneida decision making. The 1771 map (Figure 2.1) shows the geographic position of the Iroquois nations: the Mohawks, who were the most loyal British allies, lived east of the Oneida, and the other British-allied nations lived to the west. The Oneida nation's geographic position was not special in the senses described by IR scholars.

American Revolution; David J. Norton, *Rebellious Younger Brother: Oneida Leadership and Diplomacy, 1750–1800* (DeKalb, IL: Northern Illinois University Press, 2009), 90–110.

[6] Graymont, *The Iroquois in the American Revolution*, 292–6. More generally, see Laurence M. Hauptman, *Conspiracy of Interests: Iroquois Dispossession and the Rise of New York State* (Syracuse: Syracuse University Press, 1999).

[7] Levinson, "An Explanation for the Oneida–Colonist Alliance in the American Revolution," 276.

[8] In making this statement, I am specifically referring to theories in International Relations about geographic factors that emphasize proximity to threats. I do not intend this as a broader statement to discount the importance of broader, cultural influences that have a geographic element, such as kinship ties across borders or changing patterns of trade and settlement among the Iroquois (and the Oneidas in particular).

[9] Stephen Walt, *The Origins of Alliances* (Ithaca: Cornell University Press, 1987).

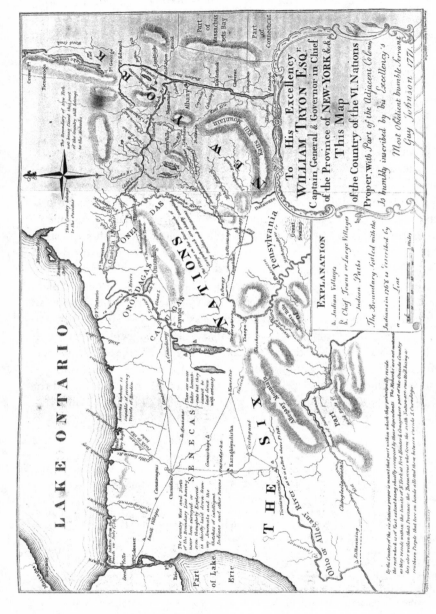

FIGURE 2.1 Map of Iroquois by Guy Johnson, 1771. Courtesy of the American Antiquarian Society

Familiar arguments about ideology and culture also do not explain Oneida decision-making. International Relations scholars often argue that common cultures produce alliances. In the case of the Oneidas, however, culture and ideology present more puzzles than solutions. The Oneidas shared a rich common life with the other Iroquois nations. They had shared in the Iroquois Confederacy for centuries, shared language and cultural practices, and had similar religious beliefs until shortly before the war. The ideological explanation for alliances predicts that the Oneidas would work together with the other Iroquois nations; instead, they allied with the Patriots, with whom they shared none of these cultural factors. Therefore, ideological or religious differences cannot explain divergent alliance decisions.

Why did the Oneidas cooperate with the Americans while other Iroquois cooperated with the British? This chapter argues that cooperation between the Oneidas and the Continental Army was brokered by Samuel Kirkland, a missionary. Traditionally, Iroquois relations with the settlers were brokered by British agents, especially the Johnson family who lived in the region. During the Revolutionary War, most Iroquois looked to Johnson to interpret what the war meant to them, and partly as a result, they allied with the British. The Oniedas, by contrast, turned to Kirkland, who had lived with them for about a decade. Kirkland had worked hard during those years to build trust with the Oneidas, preaching an anti-Anglican faith (New Presbyterianism) and explaining the growing revolutionary sentiment in a way that appealed to the Oneida. This brokerage explains why the Oneidas and Tuscaroras allied with the Continental Army, whereas Senecas, Cayugas, Onondagas, and Mohawks allied with the British.

The conclusions reached in this chapter are not novel. Cooperation between the colonists and the Oneidas is a well-studied case, and many historians reach the same conclusion about Kirkland's role: the conventional wisdom is that there was a structural hole, bridged by socially skilled intermediaries. The titles and subtitles of major biographical and historical works of figures in the era – *The White Savage* or *Man of Two Worlds* – convey the importance of brokerage. Yet, historians and scholars working within American Indian Studies do not place their findings within the context of social network theories or the politics of alliance formation as understood by International Relations scholars. While their findings are suggestive of theory, they do not outline the causal mechanisms through which intermediaries promote cooperation. Therefore, I turn to the historical record, not to revise central claims, but to find details overlooked by historians that are central to testing the claims in Chapter 1.

Before beginning this chapter, I want to reiterate a point made in Chapter 1 about referring to Indian nations as non-state allies. By non-state ally, I do not mean a community that has fully lost its sovereignty. In fact, Indian nations' ability to choose who to align with is what makes them interesting for this book. Instead, when discussing American Indian nations, I mean that their political communities did not have many of the trappings of European states that IR scholars usually associate with statehood. There are interesting parallels, for example, between the Oneidas, discussed in this chapter, or the Lumbee, described in Chapter 4, to rebels fighting for independence against Spain in the Philippines and Cuba, described in Chapter 6. In both instances, war is in part motivated by a defense of sovereignty against more traditional European powers who want to deny that sovereignty. The term non-state ally is imperfect, but captures the sense of communities struggling for statehood that is characteristic of the American Indian experience from the founding until today.

COOPERATION WITH THE ONEIDAS

This chapter makes two arguments. First, a structural hole existed between revolutionary political elites and their future American Indian allies in modern-day New York. Second, closing this structural hole required an intermediary – an agent with weak ties between communities – who could secure cooperation. Building on existing American Indian Studies scholarship, I argue that intermediaries were essential for securing important alliances during the Revolutionary War. Specifically, Samuel Kirkland – a Presbyterian missionary to the Oneidas – brokered cooperation by suggesting a policy of alliance, building a reputation for trustworthiness, explaining American interests to the Oneida in a way conducive to securing cooperation, and managing identity-based threats to cooperation.

Structural Holes and the Emergence of Samuel Kirkland

The social relationship between the Oneidas and the colonists during the Revolutionary War was complex and dynamic. Before the war, British agents tended to dominate negotiations with the Iroquois. The most important figure was Sir William Johnson. By the time of the

Revolutionary War, Johnson had lived in the region for decades. He immigrated to North America, bought land among the Mohawks, and learned their language and customs – he also took a Mohawk mistress. Over time, he used his connections to the Mohawks to enhance his fortunes, as a trader and a landowner. Trading on his position between London and the Mohawks, he was appointed the agent to the Iroquois during King George's War, a position he held until he died shortly before the American Revolution. In the language of Chapter 1, British agents – especially Johnson – were intermediaries between Crown and Indians. They controlled the flow of information between societies, and they profited from this monopoly on information, trade, and control over military and diplomatic relations. Moreover, these official British figures were bicultural. Johnson had lived among Mohawks for years; one recent biographer referred to him as the *White Savage* to explain how he was viewed by himself and his contemporaries.[10]

In the years before the Revolutionary War, the politics around Iroquoia began to change. The first change in social structure was the emergence of a new center of political power. When the colonists became rebels and established political bodies, such as the Continental Congress, and military forces, such as the Continental Army, it generated new political authorities that had little connection to Iroquoia. In social network terms, it created a new "hub" of political activity that was not connected to the old pathways by which diplomacy between Iroquoia and London traditionally took place. The emergence of new hubs of power may require new agents to broker relations.

The formation of rebel centers of power therefore created a structural hole. A structural hole is a case where two sets of political authorities do not have trusted relationships through which information flows. In this case, the pathways by which Iroquois negotiated with the British – especially through the Johnson family – did not provide a reliable bridge to centers of revolutionary political power, because Johnson was tightly allied with the British.

The second change was the entry of new agents, uncontrolled by British political authorities, into Iroquoia. The most important new figure was Samuel Kirkland, a missionary from the Presbyterian Church. Kirkland attempted to create his first mission among the Seneca in

---

[10] Fintan O'Toole, *White Savage: William Johnson and the Invention of America* (New York: Farrar, Straus and Giroux, 2005). This is described in more detail later in the chapter.

the early 1760s. It quickly failed as the Seneca distrusted Kirkland.[11] Kirkland next settled among Oniedas, and this second attempt at a mission was enormously successful. I will explain his success later, at this point, I am only describing the changing social structure. The critical point is that Kirkland was independent of Johnson's influence. He came from the College of New Jersey where ideas contrary to British interests had spread, he was opposed to Johnson's Anglican faith, and he had connections to patrons who supported the rebellion against the British.[12] Unlike Johnson, Kirkland had the ability to connect the Oneidas to the colonists who opposed British rule.

Chapter 1 identified several observable implications of a structural hole. If the parties are unaware of one another, communication is costly, and if there is mistrust, cooperation will likely not occur. In every other case in this book where there is a structural hole, there is a period before cooperation begins – usually quite a long period – where one can find measurable evidence of these features of social structure. This case is strikingly different. The moment a structural hole might open because of the creation of a new center of power – the moment the revolutionaries decided to fight the British – it was almost immediately closed by Kirkland. His already established position among the Oneidas provided immediate brokerage opportunities.

Therefore, to show that Kirkland closed a structural hole requires a counterfactual exercise. Would a structural hole have existed without Kirkland occupying a brokerage position? I believe there are three reasons it is likely a structural hole would have formed. First, there is reflexive evidence that British agents realized Kirkland's role.[13] In 1775, Guy Johnson, William's nephew and successor, ordered Kirkland to remain at Johnson's home to prevent him from spreading his ideas among the Oneidas.[14] The British reflexively understood that severing social ties by imprisoning Kirkland provided an advantage. Second, the pathway through which the structural hole closed, empirically, was directly through

---

[11] Alan Taylor, *The Divided Ground: Indians, Settlers and the Northern Borderland of the American Revolution* (New York: Random House, 2006), 52–4.

[12] Samuel Kirkland Lothrop, *Life of Samuel Kirkland, Missionary to the Indians* (Boston: Charles C. Little and James Brown, 1847); Graymont, *The Iroquois in the American Revolution*, 34.

[13] Letter from Guy Johnson to Samuel Kirkland, February 14, 1775. Samuel Kirkland Collection, Hamilton College Library Digital Collections. Kirkland denied that he was meddling with politics. See A Speech of the Oneida Chiefs to Guy Johnson, February 23, 1775. Samuel Kirkland Collection, Hamilton College Library Digital Collections.

[14] Graymont, *The Iroquois in the American Revolution*, 62–3.

Kirkland. He traveled to the Second Continental Congress in Philadelphia in 1775, asking for the creation of official lines of communication with the Iroquois.[15] No other agent acted so quickly and so decisively.[16] Third, Kirkland was a trusted agent. The Oneida did not trust other agents – the Tryon County Committee of Safety, for example – because of a long history of land depredations.[17] Conversely, the white residents mistrusted

---

[15] Glatthaar and Martin, *Forgotten Allies*, 90.

[16] Levinson cites two additional go-betweens for the Onieda and the Continental Congress. The first was Aaron Crosby who was a missionary to Onohaghkwage. Like Kirkland, the British accused Crosby of political interference. Proceedings of Colonel Guy Johnson with the Oneidas and Oughquageys, 1775. John Romeyn Brodhead, *Documents Relative to the Colonial History of the State of New York*, vol. 3 (Albany: Weed, Parsons and Company, 1857), 549–55. Yet, there is strong evidence against Crosby having a dominant role. When Crosby arrived, Kirkland was given the task of assisting him. Letter from Andrew Elliot to Samuel Kirkland, April 9, 1772. Samuel Kirkland Collection, Hamilton College Library Digital Collections. Kirkland found that Crosby had difficulty working with the Oneidas because he did not speak their language. Letter from Samuel Kirkland to Andrew Elliot, November 19, 1771. Samuel Kirkland Collection, Hamilton College Library Digital Collections. Although Kirkland reported that Crosby's language skilled improved by 1773, even as late as 1774, Crosby relied on Kirkland for support in translating documents into "Indian." Letter from Samuel Kirkland to Andrew Elliot, March 28, 1773; Letter from Crosby to Kirkland, January 29, 1774. Samuel Kirkland Collection, Hamilton College Library Digital Collections. These language problems were significant, leading Crosby to "weep in secret" and write to Kirkland, asking him to come and help. Letter from Samuel Kirkland to Jerusha Kirkland, March 24, 1773. Samuel Kirkland Collection, Hamilton College Library Digital Collections. The conclusion one might draw is that Crosby was less effective in appealing to the Oneidas in the years before the Oneidas joined the Patriots, in part, because he lacked social skill (biculturalism and bilingualism). The second pathway Levinson cites is the Committee of Public Safety for Tryon County. Levinson notes that the Committee of Public Safety had contacts with the Oneidas as early as 1775, showing that the Oneidas had more than one route to discuss political matters with rebels. The problem with Levinson's assertion that the Oneidas might have had a bridge to Philadelphia through the Committee is dating. By 1775 (as I show later), the Oneidas already have sympathies with the colonists. Contact with the Committee of Public Safety appears to come after the Oneidas had decided on a strategy of informal cooperation (pro-colonial neutrality) and not before. Moreover, the speeches listed in the *Minute Book* of the Committee do not lend much support for this view. Samuel Ludlow Frey, *The Minute Book of the Committee of Safety of Tryon County* (New York: Dodd, Mead and Company, 1905), 32–3. Another possible bridge was James Dean, a missionary and translator who worked closely with Kirkland. His biculturalism and bilingualism, however, would confirm the central arguments of this book. See Karim M. Tiro, "James Dean in Iroquoia," *New York History* 80, no. 4 (1999): 391–422.

[17] Even if they were trusted agents, the County political leaders would have been an ineffective bridge. While the *Minute Book* of the Committee lists one meeting with the Oneidas, by the time of the war, the Committee had effectively shut down. At the Battle of Oriskany (1777), many Committee members were killed or captured by the British. See Frey, *The Minute Book of the Committee of Safety of Tryon County*, 32–3, 146.

the Oneidas. The fiancé of the commander of Fort Schuyler, the fort near the Oneidas, explained, "I hope you [will] not put much trust on Our Indians they are a Sett of people not to be trusted on."[18] Her husband shared this sentiment. He believed the Oneidas were bloodthirsty, and feared they would turn on the settlers and kill them. This provides evidence that negative affect may have continued to create a structural hole had Kirkland not worked to close it. While indirect, I believe the best evidence is that if Kirkland had not set up a mission prior to the revolution, cooperation would not have occurred: a structural hole would have prevented the diffusion of information. Only Kirkland's role as intermediary linked hubs of Oneida and revolutionary political activity.

The structural hole that Kirkland closed did not last long. Once Kirkland drew the Oneidas into the Patriots orbit, they quickly developed social ties to leaders in the Continental army. Oneida warriors met with George Washington at Valley Forge, met with and scouted for the Marquis de Lafayette, and were drawn into meetings with local political elites in Tryon County and elsewhere in New York.[19] The social structure, in short, changed after the Oneidas began to cooperate with the Continental Army, because cooperation produces social connections. Yet, such later connections do not undermine Kirkland's influence in the period before cooperation began, especially 1773 through 1775.

Brokering Cooperation

Samuel Kirkland used his status as an intermediary to broker cooperation. In this section, I show how Kirkland built trust between the Patriots and the Oneidas, and how he used this trust to create the political and cultural preconditions for cooperation. Before doing so, I first want to establish that Samuel Kirkland was a model intermediary. Chapter 1 described two features of intermediaries. First, intermediaries connect two centers of political power across a structural hole. Kirkland served this role for many Oneidas and the Patriots. Second, intermediaries have weak ties to one or both centers. Kirkland, while enjoying strong ties to political elites within Iroquoia, had weak ties to Continental political elites.

---

[18] Letter from Catherine Van Schaick to Peter Gansevoort. In David A. Ranzan and Matthew J. Hollis, eds., *Hero of Fort Schuyler: Selected Revolutionary War Correspondence of Brigadier General Peter Gansevoort, Jr.* (Jefferson, NC: McFarland, 2014), 68.

[19] Norton, *Rebellious Younger Brother*, 91–9.

To appreciate how weak Kirkland's ties were to Patriot centers of power requires a bit of biographical background. Kirkland was born in 1741, the son of a minister. Little is known about his family's political connections, although they do not appear to have amounted to much. After attending common schools, he enrolled at Eleazer Wheelock's school in Lebanon, Connecticut.[20] During his time there, he likely learned Mohawk and other Indian languages.[21] After graduating, he attended the College of New Jersey, leaving halfway through his senior year to begin a mission among the Senecas (which failed). After leaving the Seneca, Kirkland created a successful mission among the Oneidas. This mission, which was successful as explained later, created strong ties to the Oneida.

Kirkland, however, had only weak ties to centers of colonial political power. These weak ties were created first at Wheelock's school and then as a missionary. Through Wheelock, Kirkland gained the attention of prominent religious and political figures. Yet, Kirkland knew none of these figures well, worked at best indirectly for them among the Iroquois, never had a position of institutional influence until after helping the Patriots recruit the Oneida, and appears not to have had an intimate relationship with any political elite. His weak ties, however, provided him with a position *between* the Oneidas and the Continental Congress that closed the structural hole between the Oniedas and the Patriots.

Social Skill

Kirkland exemplified the ways in which intermediaries can broker cooperation. Early in Kirkland's missionary work, he came to appreciate the importance of social skill. One observable implication of social skill is bilingualism.[22] Kirkland preached in English and in Iroquoian languages. He recognized the importance of doing so, and he encouraged others to learn the language.[23] He was also bicultural. By living with the Oneidas for more than a decade, Kirkland intimately understood their political culture. Kirkland reflexively understood the importance of social skill. In his writings to other missionaries, he encouraged them to follow his

---

[20] Lothrop, *Life of Samuel Kirkland, Missionary to the Indians.*
[21] Eleazar Wheelock, *A Brief Narrative of the Indian Charity-School In Lebanon in Connecticut, New England* (London: J. and W. Oliver, 1767).
[22] Letter from Samuel Dunlop to LBCB, July 2, 1773. Samuel Kirkland Collection, Hamilton College Library Digital Collections.
[23] Letter from Samuel Kirkland to Aaron Crosby, January 19, 1773. Samuel Kirkland Collection, Hamilton College Library Digital Collections.

example, stressing the importance of bilingualism, trust-building, and biculturalism for missionary work.

The consensus of many historians is that Kirkland's social skill was necessary for cooperation between the colonists and Oneidas.[24] One study by an ethnohistorian summarizes the influence arising from his social skill: "Without doubt, the most important precipitating cause of the Oneida-Colonist alliance was the influence of Samuel Kirkland. At the time of the Revolution, Kirkland had been with the Oneida for about ten years and was quite influential in the Oneida nation. He was the religious leader, supervised the educational activities, set societal rules (it was he who abolished the consumption of alcoholic beverages), counseled the sachems and warriors, settled arguments, supplied the poor with food, clothing, and shelter, and, when required, served as an interpreter."[25] These comments are noteworthy because the author is among the few who are critical of the claim that Kirkland's influence played the sole role in influencing the Oneidas. While describing other potential necessary conditions for cooperation, such as strained Oneida–Iroquois relations, even the most skeptical account gives Kirkland the lion's share of the credit for the alliance.

Building Trust

How did Kirkland use his social skill to promote cooperation? One primary mechanism was trust-building. Kirkland learned early that building trust with the Oneidas was essential for his career as a missionary. Often, whites who lived near the Iroquois did not practice what they preached, literally. This inspired mistrust: whites appeared hypocritical and they did not keep their word. Kirkland sought to maintain a reputation for trustworthiness. He did not drink, he did not buy Indian lands, and he engaged in charity. In doing so, he believed he could convert more Oneidas to Christianity. When compared to his rival in the area – the British Agent, Sir William Johnson – this mattered. Kirkland vowed never to take any Indian lands. Johnson, in contrast, had become rich from

---

[24] Glatthaar and Martin, *Forgotten Allies*; Graymont, *The Iroquois in the American Revolution*, 55–66; Mintz, *The Seeds of Empire*, 10–11. Earlier accounts place even more emphasis on Kirkland. See Lothrop, *Life of Samuel Kirkland*, 237–40; Francis Whiting Halsey, *The Old New York Frontier: Its Wars with Indians and Tories; Its Missionary Schools, Pioneers and Land Titles, 1614–1800, by Francis Whiting Halsey* (New York: C. Scribner's Sons, 1902), 155.

[25] Levinson, "An Explanation for the Oneida–Colonist Alliance in the American Revolution," 284.

seizing Indian lands. During times of poverty, Johnson could not deliver important, promised trade goods. Kirkland used his meager stores to buy food and supplies during times of crisis. Johnson promised to curtail settlers' demands for land, but he was unable to do so. This shattered the Oneidas' trust in Johnson and enhanced their trust in Kirkland.[26]

In the lead up to the war, small issues became tests of trustworthiness. Joseph Glatthaar and James Kirby Martin, who wrote a recent book on the Oneidas in the American Revolution, describe several of these incidents. One notable issue was the importance of a blacksmith. As the Oneidas transitioned under Kirkland's leadership to adopt modern farming, they needed a blacksmith to make and repair tools. At the time, the only blacksmith was at Sir William Johnson's home, forcing the Oneidas to travel a hundred miles. Johnson refused to provide a local blacksmith. To do so would reduce the Oneidas' dependence on him. The Oneidas were not convinced. Probably on Kirkland's advice, they petitioned the Royal Governor of New York directly. Glatthaar and Martin explain that Johnson's rejection of the blacksmith conveyed "the misleading impression that both he and the British government did not care about their needs. As for Kirkland, because he had served as an advocate for the Oneidas, he gained yet more stature as the person committed to their well-being."[27] This pattern would repeat itself as Kirkland advocated for a church for the Oneidas and other issues, and Johnson would reject these requests for fear of undermining his own influence as a broker to the Oneidas.

By the time of the American Revolution, this mistrust had affected alliance politics. Exposure to white settlers – their fraudulent land deals and unfair treaties – had left many embittered. At a 1776 meeting among the Iroquois, a Cayuga sachem explained, "White people, particularly the *Americans,* are in nature treacherous and deceitful," and if they win the war, they will "turn and fall on the *Indians.*"[28] Most Iroquois did not trust the Patriots, but the Oneidas did because of Kirkland. In their meetings, the issue of trust did not undermine cooperation as it did in meetings in other Iroquois nations. The Oneidas evaluated the Patriots differently because Kirkland staked his high-quality reputation for trustworthiness on the patriots protecting the Oneidas after the war.

---

[26] Glatthaar and Martin, *Forgotten Allies*, 73.
[27] Ibid., 71.
[28] Ibid., 107.

Shaping Interests and Cultural Frames

Kirkland had a monopoly on information, which provided him an opportunity to shape Oneida perceptions of their interests. He was also a news source for many Iroquois during the period when they were making decisions about Oneida policy. His news helped the Oneidas and Tuscaroras determine where their interests lay in the war, particularly during the critical period of 1774 through 1777. By 1775, the Oneidas had decided to help the rebel cause. Although officially neutral, they provided intelligence and scouting reports.[29] By 1777, as fighting began in and around Iroquoia, neutrality proved untenable and the Oneida formally allied with the rebels. Although 1777 marked the beginning of official cooperation, Oneidas' understanding of their interests appeared to crystallize in 1775.

During this critical period, Kirkland appears to have been the sole (or at least primary) source of political news. His correspondence shows that in November 1774, he began to receive detailed political information about the First Continental Congress.[30] At the same time, he was meeting with Oneida and other Iroquois sachems.[31] Kirkland told British agents that he was not meddling with politics, but he admitted to rebel agents that he was translating the proceedings in Philadelphia for the Oneidas[32] Later that summer, he traveled to the Second Continental Congress. While there, Kirkland highlighted the importance of the Oneidas and asked Congress for funds and assurances to get the Oneidas to cooperate.[33] Philip Schuyler, the commander of the fort being built in the region, also used Kirkland to communicate with the Oneidas and asked for his opinion about other agents whom he might send to them.[34]

---

[29] Oneida Declaration of Neutrality, June 1775. Samuel Kirkland Collection, Hamilton College Library Digital Collections.

[30] Letter from Stephen West to Samuel Kirkland, November 2, 1774; Letter from Stephen West to Samuel Kirkland, November 4, 1774; and Letter from Timothy Edwards to Samuel Kirkland, November 12, 1774. Samuel Kirkland Collection, Hamilton College Library Digital Collections.

[31] Letter from Samuel Kirkland to Jerusha Kirkland, November 22, 1774. Samuel Kirkland Collection, Hamilton College Library Digital Collections.

[32] Letter from Samuel Kirkland to Andrew Elliott, March 28, 1774. yhm-arc 0000.190, Item 54b. Samuel Kirkland Papers, Hamilton College Library.

[33] Entry for July 13, 1775. *Journals of the Continental Congress, 1774–1789*, vol. 2 (Washington, DC: Government Printing Office, 1905), 177–84.

[34] Letter from Philip Schuyler to Samuel Kirkland, January 5, 1776; Letter from Kirkland to Schuyler, March 11, 1776. Samuel Kirkland Collection, Hamilton College Library Digital Collections.

The majority of historians have concluded that Kirkland used this monopoly on information to shape Oneida perceptions of their interests in cooperation. There is little direct evidence in the historical record, although the absence of evidence may confirm Kirkland's role. Kirkland explicitly refused to write about any political activity before 1776, because he worried his communications would be intercepted by British agents and used by Johnson to arrest him or force him to leave Oneida lands.[35] Historians have interpreted the record, however, to show that Kirkland likely fused two mechanisms through which control over information can promote cooperation: explaining interests and creating cultural frames.

Kirkland's time as a missionary made him adept at combining western political and religious ideas with Iroquois culture. To win converts to Christianity, he needed to find a way to fit or graft Christian ideals onto Iroquoian aspirations. First, sharing was an important norm within Iroquoian culture. Kirkland drew connections between sharing and the Christian conception of charity. Second, the Iroquois used feasts as rituals for thanksgiving as well as requickening. Kirkland drew connections between these traditional rituals and Christian feasts after worship as well as communion. Furthermore, Kirkland had settled in areas where the Oneida warrior class had political clout. Kirkland used military and martial imagery in Christianity ("soldiers of Christ") to connect to Iroquoian martial themes.[36] These are only three examples; as he preached, he likely drew many more comparisons between Oneidas' traditional beliefs and the Christianity he preached.

Kirkland helped the Second Continental Congress craft its diplomatic language in the same way. When Kirkland traveled to the Second Continental Congress in July 1775, he only hoped the Iroquois would remain neutral. After briefing decision-makers in Philadelphia, Kirkland helped the Congress draft a speech to the Iroquois. The speech frames the dispute in ways that Kirkland thought would appeal to the Iroquois,

---

[35] Letter from Samuel Kirkland to Andrew Elliott, March 28, 1774. yhm-arc 0000.190, Item 54b. Samuel Kirkland Papers, Hamilton College Library. Kirkland's journals rarely mention political activity until after 1776, although the crucial period between February 1775, when he was accused of meddling by Guy Johnson, and the fall of 1776 is missing. There are, however, hints, such as conversations in October and November 1774 regarding "civil affairs," especially concerning correcting "wrong intelligence!!" that Kirkland believed had confused the Iroquois. See the entries between October 12 and November 16, 1774. Walter Pilkington, ed., *The Journals of Samuel Kirkland* (Clinton, New York: Hamilton College, 1980), 96–7.

[36] Glatthaar and Martin, *Forgotten Allies*, 60–1.

using terms familiar to Iroquois diplomacy, highlighting their shared living place in North America, and describing the conflict as an internal issue between father and son that did not require Iroquois intervention.[37] In addition, Kirkland advised local political leaders on how to navigate the complicated world of Iroquois diplomacy. In 1777, when many Onondagas died of a disease outbreak, Kirkland encouraged General Schuyler to begin condolence ceremonies before the British could so, in order to win Onondaga support for the patriots.[38]

In the same way that Kirkland drew connections between the Oneidas' religious views and Christianity, he also drew connections between the revolution's political goals and the Oneidas' political concepts. Kirkland drew close connections, in particular, between the ideas of freedom in the revolutionary rhetoric and Iroquois customs. The Iroquois, as a whole, did not recognize British sovereignty over their nations; they considered themselves a "free people." These republican ideals, of course, were exactly the aim of the revolution. If all the Iroquois had an affinity for republican ideals of freedom, why did only the Oneidas favor the rebellion? Glatthaar and Martin argue that Kirkland played an important role: "Like the Oneidas, other Iroquois nations held basic ideas about freedom in common with the rebels. What they lacked was regular exposure to patriot commentary."[39] Kirkland would translate parts of the minutes of the Continental Congress for the Oneidas, and he explained the rebellion against the British from the rebels' perspective.[40]

In summary, Kirkland provided three necessary ingredients for an alliance. First, he created the necessary social connections between the Oneidas and the Patriots, without which no alliance would be possible. Second, he provided a trusted means of communication, and he used the trust the Oneidas had in him to make the Patriots' promises appear more reliable than those of Johnson and the British. Third, he crafted an impression of shared interests and a common worldview at stake in cooperation. Moreover, no other figure during the period was capable of doing so much to further cooperation because no other figure was as well inserted between societies.

---

[37] Entry for July 13, 1775. *Journals of the Continental Congress, 1774–1789*, vol. 2 (Washington, DC: Government Printing Office, 1905), 177–84.

[38] Norton, *Rebellious Younger Brother*, 91.

[39] Glatthaar and Martin, *Forgotten Allies*, 106.

[40] Karim M. Tiro, *The People of the Standing Stone: The Oneida Nation from the Revolution Through the Era of Removal* (Amherst: University of Massachusetts Press, 2011), 43–4.

COMPETITION BETWEEN INTERMEDIARIES

One advantage of studying the Oneida in the American Revolution is that it provides a lens into competition between intermediaries. In most of the cases assessed in this book, two states did not compete for the same allies. In the American Revolution, the British and the Americans recognized the importance of the Oneidas, and they competed to win them as allies. In addition, while the Oneidas allied with the Americans, the Mohawks and other Iroquois allied with the British, and these different decisions provide a unique lens through which to evaluate the influence of social structure on alliance politics. In this section, I show that the Mohawks had a different social relationship with the British than did the Oneidas. I argue that this difference in social structure helps explain the Oneida's different alliance choices.

The difference in Oneida and Mohawk decision-making cannot be explained by differences in their strategic geographic position. As explained in the introduction to this chapter, the Mohawks were located further east (closer to Albany) than the Oneidas, but other Iroquois who allied with the British were located further west (farther from Albany). The Oneidas' geographic position, therefore, was not special. The Oneidas were also more powerful than some nations in the Confederacy, but weaker than others. Therefore, relative power cannot explain Oneida decision-making. Furthermore, the Oneidas and the other Iroquois shared a similar political culture. Some historians have noted that the Oneidas made further strides than other Iroquois in adopting European cultural and farming practices, but this difference cannot explain variation in alliance behavior, because Mohawk political leaders, such as Joseph Brant, had adopted the same European mores. These westernized Mohawks allied with the British. Therefore, westernization cannot explain the choice of alliance politics. Moreover, different economic positions cannot explain differences in alliance commitments. All the Iroquois nations were dependent on European trade goods, and all the Iroquois nations traded in the same kinds of commodities. Why then did the Oneidas and Tuscaroras (and only them) decide to ally with the colonies against the British?

To understand this variation requires understanding the relationship between the Mohawks and the British. As noted earlier, before the American Revolution, the primary bridge between Iroquoia and British centers of political power was the Johnson family. By the end of the previous century, the Mohawks had recognized the opportunities available in being situated so close to settlers. Hendrick, a Mohawk, played a central role in this process. In the early eighteenth century, Hendrick realized that he and the Mohawks might profit by inserting themselves between Britain and other Indian nations. In an attempt to make himself an intermediary, Hendrick adopted western dress and became Christian. The British, however, were not prepared to accept Hendrick. "Successful go-betweens," Fintain O'Toole, a biographer of William Johnson explains, "need partners. They need to deal with people like themselves, people who are useful to their side precisely because they have become a little like the other. Hendrick needed, from the British empire, someone who would imagine him and his fellow-Indians, not as savage bogeymen, but merely human beings with different notions. As an Indian who had become partly European, he required a European who could become partly Indian."[41] William Johnson, who settled in the Mohawk Valley in 1738, provided that bridge to the British world.

William Johnson, born in Ireland, quickly established himself as a bridge between the Mohawks and the British. Once Johnson settled in the Mohawk Valley, he established himself as a trader and inserted himself between the Mohawks and traders in Albany. In fact, he was so effective that traders in Albany attacked him more than once.[42] Johnson's rise to prominence occurred during King George's War (1744–1748), and the Mohawks sought to use the conflict to acquire more influence. As "keepers of the eastern door" in the Iroquois Confederacy, they controlled contact between settlers who lived to the east and Indians who lived to the west. Capitalizing on this position, they profited at treaty negotiations in Albany, Boston, and Montreal between 1744 and 1745, though they continued to favor a policy of neutrality. After William Johnson intervened in 1746, they changed their policy. By the following year, Johnson led the Mohawks to war. His growing biculturalism is underscored by contemporaneous records. At a conference in 1747, Johnson showed up at the head of a Mohawk party, dressed as a war chief. According to his biographer, Johnson "came dressed in blanket, loincloth, leggings and moccasins, his face painted with vermilion and verdigris, his hair drawn back and decorated with ribbons."[43]

The shift in Mohawk policy, from neutral to British allies in King George's War, was the result of Johnson's influence. He used his status

---

[41] O'Toole, *White Savage*, 15.
[42] Ibid., 43.
[43] Ibid., 76.

among the Mohawks to achieve a higher position within New York society. The Mohawks told Governor Clinton in 1747 that "[f]or these twelve months past and better, we have minded nor listened to nobody else."[44] The best evidence indicates Johnson had a deep level of social skill. By 1746, Johnson was clearly bilingual and bicultural. He understood Mohawk cultural and political practices, and he used this knowledge to secure their cooperation and his authority among them.[45]

By the American Revolution, Johnson had created strong ties to the Mohawks. He had developed a relationship (essentially an unofficial marriage) with Molly Brant, an important Turtle Clan matron, which enhanced his ties to the Mohawks. This relationship also brought him closer to Joseph Brant, an influential Mohawk leader who would lead many British Iroquois forces during the Revolutionary War. Johnson also become a direct agent of the British government, providing him with strong ties in London and New York.[46] In short, Johnson capitalized on his structural position between the Mohawks and the British Empire to create strong ties to London.

Shortly before the Revolutionary War began, William Johnson died. His nephew, Guy Johnson, replaced him as the British agent. Guy Johnson and Joseph Brant worked to create a pro-British Iroquois alliance. In so doing, the Johnson family's political connections flowed outward into western Iroqouia. The Senecas – the "keepers of the western door" – were furthest from the settlers. When the British met with the Senecas to convince them to ally with the empire, Brant attended the conference. Details of the 1777 meeting that led the Senecas to join the Mohawks are sketchy (at best), but Brant appears to have had a significant role. First, as an Iroquois, Brant participated in the decision-making process. This may have been important. At the meeting, the British agents

---

[44] In ibid., 77.

[45] Ibid., 81.

[46] Many American Indian scholars might object to treating William Johnson rather than Joseph or Molly Brant as the key intermediaries. The Brant family, like Johnson, was socially skilled. They also helped provide Johnson with contacts among the Mohawks that gave Johnson significantly more influence than he may otherwise have had. I agree with these assessments. However, I concentrate on William Johnson because he had developed a strong relationship with many Mohawks that effectively closed the structural hole by the late 1740s at the latest. In this sense, Hendrick is a more likely candidate for helping Johnson close the structural hole given his role early in Johnson's career. In making this claim, I am referring to the social structure. I agree, as explained later, that Brant's social position is important for explaining Mohawk policy and do not mean to diminish it.

were "outsiders," which meant they could make a case for an alliance but could not participate in the meetings where decisions were made. Brant could participate in these meetings, likely using his "insider position" to secure cooperation. When Cornplanter – an important Seneca – spoke in favor of neutrality, Brant could use his social position within Iroquoia (as a fellow member of Wolf Clan) to marginalize him.[47]

How did Brant recruit the Mohawks successfully and Kirkland the Oneidas? Historians give two theories that are consistent with the argument of this book, but which the historical record cannot successfully adjudicate between. The first theory gives more agency to the Oneidas and Mohawks than this chapter has done so far. The close connections between the Mohawks and the British, in this account, meant the Mohawks had a privileged status within the Iroquois Confederacy. By monopolizing diplomatic ties to Johnson, the Mohawks gained political influence and economic rewards. In this view, the Oneidas' political goal was to remove the Mohawks – especially Brant – from his role as intermediary to the British settlers. Therefore, the Oneidas capitalized on Kirkland – their weak tie to the Continental Congress – to gain influence with the new political power growing in North America. In doing so, the Oneidas hoped to displace the Mohawks as the intermediary nation between whites and the Confederacy.[48]

A second interpretation gives more agency to Kirkland. In this view, Kirkland understood the Oneidas' mistrust of the British and saw Johnson's failure to promote Oneida interests. Kirkland used this dissatisfaction to establish his own position as a broker between the Oneida and the Patriots. To do so, Kirkland sought to distribute goods to prevent the need for Oneidas to travel to the Johnson family's home.[49] Kirkland intentionally denied Johnson his monopoly on the Iroquois, inserting himself as an intermediary. In addition, he worked to establish further mistrust; for example, he prompted the Oneida to make requests, such as for a blacksmith, that he knew Johnson would deny (as described earlier). Kirkland then used the political connections he created, as explained earlier in the chapter, to develop trust and cooperation between the Oneidas and the Patriots.

---

[47] The most comprehensive treatment of this event and the historiographic controversies surrounding it is in Thomas Abler, ed., *Chainbreaker: The Revolutionary War Memoirs of Governor Blacksnake as Told to Benjamin Williams* (Lincoln: University of Nebraska Press, 1989), 58–80.

[48] Taylor, *The Divided Ground*, 84–5.

[49] Tiro, *The People of the Standing Stone*, 43.

Regardless of each party's level of agency, two inferences can be drawn from the competition between Johnson and Kirkland. First, agents on the ground in the 1770s understood the dramatic stakes of brokerage. There was a heavy political competition to occupy the niche between societies, and life and death hung on the outcome. Second, Johnson failed to bring the Oneidas onto the British side, in part, because he lost his monopoly on information between whites and Iroquois. Access to Kirkland opened a broader range of diplomatic possibilities for the Iroquois, which likely would not have existed if Kirkland could not bridge the structural hole between Iroquoia and Philadelphia.

CONCLUSION

In sum, from its earliest days, the United States depended on unusual, bicultural figures to recruit and sustain alliances with non-state allies to fight its wars. The findings of this chapter are not localized to the case of the Oneida. Figures between white and Indian society loom large in military histories of North American warfare, from wars before the American Revolution through the closing of the west. Kirkland is a particularly notable example. His weak ties to Oneida society allowed him to form a bridge upon which information and trust could flow. His understanding of Oneida culture and politics allowed him to frame cooperation as in the Oneida's interests. And, he helped manipulate information to make the parties trust one another enough to support joint operations.

Understanding cases such as the Oneidas is crucial for understanding American diplomatic history and how the United States emerged as a great power. North America saw frequent and intense war involving Native Americans, from well before the American Revolution until the beginning of the twentieth century. From the wars in Virginia and Massachusetts in the early days of the colonies to the Wounded Knee Massacre (1890), first the settlers and later the United States was fighting in intense, constant warfare in North America. These wars were not side affairs. They were some of the most central challenges facing the United States at its birth. Alliances with Native Americans were common. The first major alliance was likely in the Pequot War (1634–1638), where English colonists formed an alliance with Narragansetts and Mohegans to fight the Pequots. The British and French recruited allies during King William's War (1699–1697), the French recruited in King George's War (1744–1748), and they both recruited again during the French and Indian War (1754–1763). During and after the American Revolution, this pattern continued. In every major war against Native Americans – including the Seminole Wars, the Creek Wars, the Apache Wars, the wars on the Plains, as well as many others – the settlers or the United States formed alliances.

If I scholars take brokerage seriously, it will have a number of concrete advantages. One advantage is it helps IR scholars understanding the findings of new international histories of North America. For many historians, many of the central concepts in this book – especially brokerage and social skill – find an easy home in these cases. Politics on the frontier were intercultural: individuals or even whole communities who could play the role of middlemen profited. To tell the story of the politics around American survival and expansion, therefore, requires focusing on the intermediaries who brokered deals across borders and secured land, weapons, and support. Scholars who study the period concentrate on a multilevel politics of brokerage. Colonists and Indians understood that brokerage positions could pay, and depending on the level of analysis one adopts, brokerage can be represented in different ways as individuals, nations, and larger political groups attempted to fill these roles.[50]

Without understanding the politics of brokerage, IR scholars cannot navigate much of American political history. The Iroquois are only one case among many. The politics of brokerage *was* international politics in the eighteenth century. To understand military success or failure, how the United States expanded, commercial success along the frontier, or any myriad of other important outcomes, we need to understand how cooperation formed and what the main issues were that threatened cooperation. Moreover, the key figures on the frontier were not necessarily the colonial elites. The ways these elites – colonial governors, important landed interests, British and French political agents and others – understood politics were dramatically affected by the opportunities and threats presented to them by intermediaries who worked and lived along the frontier. Understanding intermediaries' interests and how they profited from

[50] See Nancy L. Hagedorn, "'A Friend to Go Between Them': The Interpreter as Cultural Broker during Anglo-Iroquois Councils, 1740–70," *Ethnohistory* 35, no. 1 (1988): 60–80; Nancy L. Hagedorn, "Brokers of Understanding: Interpreters as Agents of Cultural Exchange in Colonial New York," *New York History* 76, no. 4 (1995): 379–408; Daniel K. Richter, "Cultural Brokers and Intercultural Politics: New York–Iroquois Relations, 1664–1701," *Journal of American History* 75, no. 1 (1988): 40–67; Timothy Shannon, *Iroquois Diplomacy on the Early American Frontier* (New York: Viking, 2008). For a broader overview, see Margaret Szasz, ed., *Between Indian and White Worlds: The Cultural Broker* (Norman: University of Oklahoma Press, 1994).

brokering cooperation is therefore essential to the story of American foreign policy in its first centuries.

The years of the American Revolution were early in American political history. By the end of the nineteenth century, North America had changed. Settlers had moved west, trains and telegraphs crossed much of the country, and the sheer size of the American population should close structural holes. The chapter on the American Civil War shows that these changes did indeed close some structural holes between whites and Native Americans. Cherokees, for example, had close contacts with politicians in Washington. Yet, many American Indian groups along and even behind the frontier continued to have little contact with the US government. The following chapters examines these variations in social structure to understand the role of structural holes in enabling agency.

3

Pirates and Hookahs

In the 1780s, the United States sought to negotiate treaties with the states on the Barbary Coast. Ships from the Barbary States frequently seized European ships, turning their crews into slaves until their governments made "tributes" to have them freed. The United States authorized its representatives in Europe – John Adams, Thomas Jefferson, and Benjamin Franklin – to conclude an agreement to prevent the capture of American sailors. With this purpose in mind, on February 16, 1786, John Adams dropped his card off at the Tripolitian representative in London. Adams was invited in and, to his delight, was able to talk to the Ambassador "by a little Italian and French with some Langua Franca." Then, as Abagail Adams told her son John Quincy, the servants brought in two hookahs – "long Pipes, one for Pappa and the other of Monsieur la Turke, with two cups of Coffe. Pappa took both and resting the bowl of the Pipe upon the floore, while the stem was in his mouth smoaked away, taking a sip of Coffe and a Whif at his Pipe" until a secretary yelled out "Monsieur vous êtes un veritable Turk."[1] John Adams was so excited by the meetings, which he thought portended a quick agreement, that he sent word to Jefferson, then living in Paris, to come to London.

When Jefferson arrived, their hopes were dashed. The Ambassador demanded more than the United States would pay. And when Adams and Jefferson "took the liberty to make some inquiries concerning the Grounds of their pretentions to make war upon Nations who had done them no injury," the response was "it was founded on the laws of their

---

[1] For Abagail Adams' account, see Abagail Adams to JQM, February 16, 1786. *AFC*, Vol. 7, 40–1.

Prophet, that it is written in their Koran, that all nations who should not have acknowledge their authority were sinners, that it was their right and duty to make war upon them where they could be found, and to make slaves of all they could take as Prisoners, and that every Musselman who should be slain in battle was sure to go to Paradise."[2]

The Barbary Coast would become an important issue for the United States in the following years. Since the 1780s, Jefferson had decided that paying ransom to the Barbary States ran counter to American policy. When he entered office, he sought to fight, rather than continue to pay tributes. The war would last four years, was the first overseas conflict involving the US military, and was an important motivation for development of the US Navy.

Most American military operations were naval. Even before Tripoli declared war, a squadron had been dispatched to the Mediterranean, whose primary object was to deter the Barbary States from taking Americans ships.[3] After the war began, this small squadron was tasked with the blockade of Tripoli. The naval war did not go well. The small American squadron needed to not only blockade Tripoli, but also blockade Tripoli's ships in Gibraltar and protect convoys moving across the Mediterranean, and it frequently had to leave or change stations to take on water and supplies. As a result, the blockade of Tripoli's harbor was so porous that Tripolitian corsairs could run the blockade and then sneak back to port. In one incident in 1802, three corsairs slipped the blockade, capturing the *Franklin*, and then reentered Tripoli's harbor with its prize. American and Swedish ships watched in broad daylight.[4] The US commodore in charge of the squadron in 1803 had his commission revoked for incompetence. Later that year, the United States lost the *Philadelphia* to Tripoli when it struck ground near the harbor. The US fleet, while gallantly minimizing its losses by burning its own ship, had now given Tripoli the *Philadelphia's* 307 sailors as hostages. The following year was no better: US naval engagements with Tripoli, despite escalating significantly, were at best indecisive and at worst enhanced Yusuf's domestic position by rallying opinion against the United States.[5]

[2] American Commissioners to John Jay, March 28, 1786. *PTJ*, Vol. 9, 358.
[3] Smith to Tuxtun, April 21, 1801. *NDBW*, Vol. 1, 428–9.
[4] Joshua London, *Victory in Tripoli: How America's War with the Barbary Pirates Established the U.S. Navy and Built a Nation* (Hoboken: John Wiley & Sons, 2005), 110–11.
[5] Accounts of the effectiveness of American naval operations differ. The most bullish recent account, which is more interested in the heroism of American forces rather than providing an accurate assessment of military operations, is Joseph Wheelan, *Jefferson's*

The outcome of the war, therefore, rested heavily on land operations. In the middle of the war, Ahmed Karamanli, Yusuf's brother, led an army across modern-day Libya from Egypt. Ahmed's army – a non-state ally of the United States – seized Derna (then Derne), the second most important city in the region, and threatened Tripoli itself.[6] These land-based operations, which resulted in the capture of Derna and threat-ened to install a new leader in Tripoli, led Yusuf to reduce his demands and agree to a peace treaty with the Jefferson administration.[7] In short, Ahmed's efforts were crucial for ending the war after American forces failed.

This chapter asks about the origins of cooperation between the United States and Ahmed Karamanli. Why did the United States and Karamanli engage in cooperation on the Barbary Coast? The chapter shows that Ahmed's decision to cooperate with the United States is in many respects puzzling. I show that Ahmed did not trust the United States and that most American officials opposed cooperating with Ahmed. Moreover, Ahmed had good reasons to distrust the United States: in the end, it would renege

War: America's First War on Terror, 1801–1805 (New York: Carroll & Graf Publishers, 2003). This account more closely follows Frank Lambert, *The Barbary Wars: American Independence in the Atlantic World* (New York: Hill and Wang, 2005), 123–55; London, *Victory in Tripoli*; A. B. C. Whipple, *To the Shores of Tripoli: The Birth of the U.S. Navy wand Marines* (Annapolis: Naval Institute Press, 1991). On alternative factors reinforcing the blockade's failure, see Kola Folayan, "Tripoli and the War with the U.S.A., 1801–5," *The Journal of African History* 13, no. 2 (1972): 261–70.

[6] I refer to them as Ahmed and Yusuf because they are brothers who share the same last name.

[7] Some of the historical literature disagrees about the central role of Derna. Some his-torians, for example, credit a story that Yusuf read American newspapers, discovering that there was a Mediterranean Fund to fund the war, or the continued presence of the Navy. Lambert, *The Barbary Wars*, 153–5. These partisan accounts owe their origin to Republicans support and Federalists opposition to the fund and not to knowledge of what Yusuf read. Robert J. Allison, *The Crescent Obscured: The United States and the Muslim World, 1776–1815* (Chicago: University of Chicago Press, 1995), 32. The bal-ance of the evidence, instead, points to the capture of Derna as the central factor that influenced Tripoli to end the war. Tobias Lear – the American representative who met with Yusuf – credited the land-based operations led by William Eaton and Ahmed Karamanli. Lear to Eaton, June 6, 1805. *NDBW*, Vol. 6, 92. Moreover, the peace treaty between the United States and Tripoli reads like a straightforward exchange, where Yusuf returned the American prisoners (for a reduced price) and promised peace, and the United States, in a secret article, agreed to "immediately" hand over Ahmed and his family. One can infer from the terms of the treaty that capturing Ahmed was therefore an importance incentive for Yusuf. "Treaty of Peace and Amity between the United States and Tripoli." *NDBW*, Vol. 6, 81–2. Furthermore, the timing of the decision points to a central role for Derna. Only in May, a few weeks after Derna's capture, did Yusuf show a willingness to seriously negotiate, pointing to the battle's role. Farfara to Lear, May 30, 1805. *NDBW*, Vol. 6, 65.

on every term of cooperation that Ahmed believed was promised. How did the two parties build sufficient trust to make cooperation feasible?

Two key intermediaries played an outsized role in the First Barbary War. The first intermediary was James Leander Cathcart, who is a paradigmatic example of an intermediary. Cathcart had been captured more than a decade earlier in the United States' first encounter with the Barbary Coast, living for eleven years as a slave in Algiers. During that time, he became acquainted with Barbary politics, learning about the language, culture, and political system. When he returned to the United States after securing his freedom, he was turned around and sent to Tripoli to act as the American Consul. Cathcart's familiarity with Barbary politics provided him with the skill necessary to realize that cooperation with Ahmad may be in American interests. Cathcart was ill-equipped, however, to see this plan reach fruition. William Eaton, then the Consul to Tunis, whom one biographer called the American Lawrence of Arabia, picked up on Cathcart's plan, tracking down and initiating a process of cooperation with Ahmad.[8] These figures, who owed their influence to their place between societies, would exercise decisive influence.

STRUCTURAL HOLES

The specific instance of cooperation of interest in this chapter is Ahmed Karamanli and American decision-makers in Philadelphia or Washington (the capital moved during the period). American relationships with rebels in the Barbary States are an instance of a structural hole. Recall that by structural hole, I mean there are no direct personal relationships linking decision-makers in the communities who are cooperating. If a structural hole was present, then we would see few or no relationships across the Atlantic linking Washington to Ahmed.

The Jefferson administration had no knowledge that Ahmed Karamanli – its future ally – existed. As one historian put it bluntly: "scarcely anyone mentioned Hamet [Ahmed] as a plausible alternative to his brother."[9] Why? To gain information about Ahmed would require diplomats abroad to forward his name to Jefferson. A close reading of the diplomatic correspondence, however, includes only one mention of Ahmed before Cathcart proposed cooperation. This mention was in an abbreviated history of the

---

[8] Samuel Edwards, *Barbary General: The Life of William H. Eaton* (Englewood Cliffs: Prentice Hall, 1968), 268.
[9] Wheelan, *Jefferson's War*, 234.

regime, written in French, and forwarded with little comment to the State Department by Cathcart. Instances in which political elites do not know about others mark the clearest instance of a structural hole – there are no interpersonal relationships to transmit information.

If communication were efficient and cost-free, then perhaps the Jefferson administration could have directly engaged Ahmed when discussing cooperation, making an intermediary unnecessary. The historical record shows, however, that communication was costly and inefficient. One anecdote underscores the difficulty of communicating in the age of the sail. After Tripoli declared war, the US consuls on the Barbary Coast took extraordinary steps to get a message to Washington. William Eaton chartered a foreign ship at his own expense, sending it in ballast directly to the United States with the news.[10] Even with this extraordinary effort, the communication did not arrive until August 13, four months later. If communication from Tunis to the United States was slow, communication from the United States to the Barbary Coast was almost non-existent. Not only were ships slow, but political crisis in the State Department, yellow fever in the capital, and the move from Philadelphia to Washington all delayed correspondence.[11] In July 1801, James Leander Cathcart complained to the State Department that "I have had but one letter from the department of State" since his arrival in 1799, and he was "uninform'd of the intentions of the govt." The US Consul in Algiers wrote in obvious frustration that "the Government of The U. States pays no attention to our Communications it is 10 Months That I have not had any letter from the department of State. War Sir will Shortly be the result of detention and Neglect."[12] Even if the parties were aware of one another, technology and inattention meant would reinforce the structural hole between the Barbary Coast and the United States.

The existence of a structural hole may seem odd to scholars who have followed debates about Jefferson's foreign policy. Several historians have emphasized Jefferson's experience managing closely related problems on

---

[10] Eaton to James Madison, April 10, 1801. *PJM: SS*, Vol. 1, 78–82.

[11] On the confusion during the move, when all of the papers were packed, see Madison to O'Brien, May 27, 1800. *Diplomatic Instructions of the Department of State, 1801–1906*. M28, R5. RG 59. Madison to O'Brien, July 29, 1800. *Diplomatic Instructions of the Department of State, 1801–1906*. M28, R5. RG 59.

[12] Cathcart to James Madison, July 2, 1801. *PJM: SS*, Vol. 1, 372; O'Brien CD, May 12, 1801. *PJM: SS*, Vol. 1, 167. In fact, communications likely grew worse as many American ships began to make for port as soon as they heard news that Tripoli had declared war, limiting opportunities to send mail. William Willis to Madison, April 22, 1801. *PJM: SS*, Vol. 1, 111.

the Barbary Coast. Between 1784 and 1795, there was extensive deal making with Morocco and Algeria to free American ships. Jefferson was a Commissioner in some of these earlier negotiations.[13] If Jefferson's personal experiences during these negotiations meant he had ties to Ahmed Karamanli, then there was no structural hole. Did Jefferson develop personal relationships with figures who would help the process of cooperation more than a decade later?

Despite opportunities for Jefferson to learn about Barbary politics, he learned very little because of how the negotiations proceeded. In May 1784, Congress empowered its representatives in Europe – Benjamin Franklin, John Adams, and Thomas Jefferson – to negotiate with the Barbary States.[14] The nature of these negotiations prevented Jefferson, in particular, from learning much about them. The instructions that empowered the commissioners to negotiate did not include any funds. The Commissioners explained to Congress that without funds, there could be no negotiations.[15] Moreover, the Commissioners did not have much knowledge of Barbary politics. Adams, Franklin, and Jefferson, in the effort to learn more about the Barbary States, attempted to get information from their counterparts in Europe. They were able to acquire information on the strength of Barbary naval forces, but even finding out how much other Europeans paid was time consuming and difficult. Jefferson remarked, "Either shame or jealousy makes them wish to keep it secret."[16] Moreover, the Commissioners decided they were not empowered to go to the Barbary Coast themselves, preventing direct personal contact.[17]

[13] Entry September 17, 1776. United States Continental Congress, *Secret Journals of the Acts and Proceedings of Congress*, vol. 2 (Boston: Thomas B. Wait., 1820), 10. On these negotiations, see Ray Irwin, *The Diplomatic Relations of the United States with the Barbary Powers, 1776–1816* (Chapel Hill: University of North Carolina Press, 1931), 20–105; Wheelan, *Jefferson's War*, 32–54.

[14] Thompson with Instruction and Commissions, May 16, 1784. *PTJ*, Vol. 7, 261. The likely reason they were empowered to treat with Barbary States was news from Europe that Algiers was planning to begin capturing American ships. See John Adams to Robert Livingston, July 12, 1783. *PJA*, Vol. 15, 105.

[15] John Adams to Gerry, September 9, 1784. *PJA*, Vol. 16, 318; American Commissioners to the President of Congress, November 11, 1784. *PTJ*, Vol. 7, 494.

[16] Jefferson to Monroe, February 6, 1785. *PTJ*, Vol. 7, 639.

[17] March 19 and March 20, 1785. *Diary of John Adams*, Vol 3, 173–5. Adams wrote to Congress that he believed the Commissioners in Europe may be able to make it work if Congress authorized the use of the French Consuls to carry on the negotiations, arranging the terms by correspondence with the Commissioners in Europe. Adams likely held this view because of his desire to conserve funds. A letter written on the same day, from the American Peace Commissioners as a whole, favored sending an American minister

These negotiations left Jefferson dissatisfied. For Jefferson the statesman, negotiating with the Barbary States ran contrary to American interests. Jefferson favored force over diplomacy.[18] For Jefferson the intellectual, his encounter with the Barbary States likely left him dissatisfied with his understanding of politics in the region. Jefferson scholars conclude that around this time he reengaged with the study of Arabic and purchased several books on Ottoman politics. It is a reasonable inference that Jefferson knew that he did not understand Barbary affairs.[19] Unfortunately, the books Jefferson purchased were likely little help in understanding the concrete nature of politics in Tripoli in the early nineteenth century.[20] They certainly did not contain references to the intricacies of Tripolitian politics such that Jefferson could make well-informed decisions about alliances.

In these kinds of situations, where political elites are unaware of one another and there are no reliable means for direct interaction, structural holes appear that require brokerage. The limited interactions between political elites in the United States and the Barbary powers left opportunities for a few individuals with unusual pedigrees – especially Cathcart and Eaton – to play outsized roles in generating cooperation.

to Morocco. See John Adams to President of Congress, September 10, 1783. *PJA*, Vol. 15, 273; American Peace Commissioners to the President of Congress. September 10, 1783. *PJA*, Vol. 15, 286. The received the same advice from Holland. See Dumas to John Adams, February 25, 1785. *PJA*, Vol. 16, 532–3.

[18] For one early statement, see Jefferson to Monroe, February 6, 1785. *PTJ*, Vol. 7, 639; John Lowell to Thomas Jefferson, December 18, 1784. *PTJ*, Vol. 7, 577–8. On Adams' contrary view, see John Adams to Gerry, December 12, 1784. *PJA*, Vol. 16, 452–3; John Adams to Jay, December 15, 1784. *PJA*, Vol. 16, 466–8.

[19] See Kevin J. Hayes, "How Thomas Jefferson Read the Qur'ān," *Early American Literature* 39, no. 2 (2004): 247–61; Denise A. Spellberg, *Thomas Jefferson's Qur'an: Islam and the Founders* (New York: Alfred Knopf, 2013), 124–57.

[20] The books listed by Hayes focused on the Ottoman Empire, including one that was over a century old and another focusing on Egypt, although also including short descriptions of other regions in the Ottoman Empire. Neither includes chapters on any of the Barbary States. Sir Paul Rycaut, *The History of the Present State of the Ottoman Empire: Containing the Maxims of the Turkish Polity, the Most Material Points of the Mahometan Religion, Their Sects and Heresies, Their Convents and Religious Votaries. Their Military Discipline, with an Exact Computation of Their Forces Both by Sea and Land …* (London: C. Brome, 1686); Sauveur Lusignan, *A History of the Revolt of Ali Bey, Against the Ottoman Porte: Including an Account of the Form of Government of Egypt; Together with a Description of Grand Cairo and of Several Celebrated Places in Egypt, Palestine, and Syria: To Which Are Added, A Short Account of the Present State of the Christians Who Are Subjects to the Turkish Government, and the Journal of a Gentleman Who Travelled from Aleppo to Bassora* (London: J. Phillips, 1783).

LEARNING ABOUT BARBARY POLITICS

The central question this book asks is who has influence in deciding schemes for cooperation. The conventional wisdom in International Relations scholarship tends to posit that political elites matter. Unlike the other cases described in this book, the clear answer given by every historian who has studied the Barbary wars is that the war effort advocated by elites – naval adventures – was a remarkable failure. Instead, a seemingly odd case of cooperation, whose idea originated in the mind of a former slave turned US consul in Tripoli, and an unusual adventurer led to cooperation. Their position between societies was a necessary ingredient for their success.

Whose Idea?

The Jefferson administration's strategy to win the war against Tripoli focused on naval power. Since the 1780s, Jefferson was convinced that Barbary naval forces were weak. Policymakers concluded that a show of force in the Mediterranean would quickly cajole Tripoli into changing its position.[21] Most of the American diplomatic staff reached the same conclusion. For example, the US Consul at Genoa wrote, "I trust a Squadron will ere this be in the Straights to shew those Barbarians what the Americans are & can do."[22] Because the Jefferson plan did not anticipate ground forces, it included no provisions for, or appreciation of, potential regional allies.

Unsurprisingly, the origins of the idea to cooperate with Ahmed Karamanli did not come from someone in the Congress or White House, but from someone who had extensive experience with Barbary politics: James Leander Cathcart.[23] Cathcart, who was the US Consul to Tripoli at the start of the war, had an unusual background for a diplomat. He had been captured onboard his ship in 1785, and enslaved along with four other crewmen and his captain for about eleven years. While in captivity, he rose through the ranks of slaves, eventually rising to be the

---

[21] Their belief that force would produce results was likely confirmed by the views of Americans in Europe, who wrote frequently about the need for a naval force.

[22] Humphreys, CD 276, May 8, 1801. *PJM: SS*, Vol. 1, 147. See also Humphreys, CD 55, July 18, 1796. *NDBW*, Vol. 1, 167–8; Barnes to Jefferson, March 19, 1801. *PTJ*, Volume 33, 364; Humphreys, CD, April 14, 1801. *PJM: SS*, Vol. 1, 92–3.

[23] Eaton to Smith, August 19, 1802. In Charles Prentiss, *The Life of the Late Gen. William Eaton* (Brookfield: E. Merriam & Co., 1813), 225.

Pasha's Christian Secretary. Cathcart was freed to go to Philadelphia and represent Algiers's position in treaty negotiations. Cathcart was so unimportant that the United States refused to pay "any part of the expense of this journey," in other words, refusing to even pay for Cathcart's passage home from captivity. Cathcart paid his own way.[24]

During his time in Algiers, Cathcart learned about the society, culture, and politics on the Barbary Coast, making him socially skilled. As a slave in Algiers, he met with Americans sent to negotiate his release, met with and knew the Pasha and his advisers, logged vessels in and out of port and spoke with their captains and other states' consuls, learned the language, came to understand the religion, and became acquainted with the methods by which Ottoman leaders gained and clung to power. The development of these linguistic skills, biculturalism, and experience with cross-cultural brokerage are consistent with the theory advanced in Chapter 1. Cathcart survived in the world of Algiers by navigating its political culture, and he was attentive to the international negotiations over his fate. In the language of this book, Cathcart was developing the kind of specific social skill that would later help him induce cooperation: he understood parties' interests, as evidenced by his linguistic skills, biculturalism, and time spent in Algiers.[25] There were likely few Americans, if any, who possessed a better understanding of Barbary politics.

Before Cathcart left for the United States, he decided that he wanted to return to Algiers as Consul. The US Consul to Algiers, did not give him a stellar recommendation: "He has neither the talent nor the dignity of character necessary for the purpose."[26] Yet, few people probably applied for the position of consul to a Barbary State. The job meant leaving rich opportunities in the New World to be ignored by one's own government in Africa and abused by one's host, without much hope for political or commercial rewards. Cathcart was quickly appointed in 1797, and he returned to Tripoli in 1798.[27]

Cathcart was not authorized to create an alliance. His instructions permitted him to negotiate with the Barbary leaders to secure new treaties, report on stores of weapons and troop positions, and take careful

[24] Barlow, CD 6, May 4, 1796. *NDBW*, Vol. 1, 154.
[25] James Leander Cathcart. *Journals, 1792* and *Negotiations at Algiers*. Reel 1. Cathcart Papers.
[26] Barlow, CD 6, May 4, 1796. *NDBW*, Vol. 1, 155.
[27] Secretary of State to Barlow, December 3, 1796. *NDBW*, Vol. 1, 182–3.

notes of their commerce.[28] They did not anticipate plotting the overthrow of the government. Cathcart's mission to Tripoli was a disaster. When he arrived, relations were already so tense that he was not allowed off the ship. Promised deliveries from the United States then failed to appear. Shortly thereafter, Yusuf Karamanli chopped down an American flag pole, declaring war against the United States.

Stuck on his ship, Cathcart developed the plan for an alliance with rebels that would later win the war. In July 1801, he wrote to the Secretary of State that the naval war could not realize American objectives in the region. Even if America won a favorable treaty through the naval war, it would not produce the desired outcome in the long-term, because "even allowing that we conclude a peace upon our own terms, the first time our frigates are off their guard or employed upon other service, his cruisers will capture Americans in retaliation for having imposed upon him terms which he may consider humiliating." Therefore, the only solution was regime change, because "so long as Joseph the Bashaw lives our commerce will not be secure." By "dethroning the present Bashaw & affecting a revolution in favor of his Brother Hamet, who is at Tunis, & thereby insure the United States the gratitude of him and his successors." He recommended that William Eaton, then the Consul to Tunis, be given the task of engineering cooperation with Ahmed.[29]

Without the authority to do so, Cathcart directed Eaton to begin negotiations with Ahmed, who was then in Tunis, to overthrow Yusuf. It was on Cathcart's advice, not instructions from the United States, that Eaton would recruit and form plans with Ahmed.[30]

The fact that a plan for cooperation with rebels should come from the region and not from the seaboard of the United States should be no surprise. But, it does exemplify two themes in this book. The first theme is that the origins of the plan came from an agent socially skilled with reference to the Barbary Powers. In addition to Cathcart's skills cited earlier – bilingualism, biculturalism, and experience brokering cooperation – he also had a near monopoly on information moving between Tripoli and the United States. This provided him with a unique position, making it possible to craft a menu of options that would make cooperation appear obvious. The second theme is that the decisions leading to

---

[28] Pickering to Cathcart, December 20, 1798. *Diplomatic & Consular Instructions*. M28, R5. RG 59.
[29] Cathcart to Madison, July 2, 1801. *Despatches from Tripoli*. M466, R2. RG 59. NARA.
[30] Cathcart to Eaton, June 29, 1801. *NDBW*, Vol. 1, 493–5.

and surrounding the war were not made in the nation's capital. Cathcart
was cavalier with his authority. He asked Eaton, for example, to negotiate with Ahmed a month before he even notified the State Department
that a plan was afoot to depose Yusuf. This decision initiated a process of
cooperation that would later fundamentally change the war. The Jefferson
administration did not even know about Ahmed's existence until much
later, after months of scheming and plotting.

EATON'S MISSION

Onboard the ship that took Cathcart to Tripoli was William Eaton, sent
to Tunis as Consul. William Eaton would seize on Cathcart's advice
to recruit Ahmed, engineering the first attempt at an overseas regime
change in American history. Eaton, as I will show in this section, was a
model intermediary who used his position between societies to marshal
cooperation.

Who Was William Eaton?

William Eaton's background shows he is a poster child for the strength of
weak ties hypothesis. Recall that in Granovetter's formulation, individuals are often successful when they have a large number of acquaintants
through whom they can access enhanced information. Eaton pursued this
strategy with enormous success.

Eaton came from a family of modest means. He joined the Continental
Army during the Revolutionary War and later attended Dartmouth. He
briefly worked for the Vermont Legislature and then joined the military. In the military, he first briefly went to Philadelphia, where he "saw
to it that men in positions of power became aware of him." He does
not appear to have done this by forming close ties to anyone in particular in Philadelphia, but instead "he spent most of his time in the
War Department, making the acquaintance of Secretary Knox and his
civilian and military subordinates," as well as meeting some members
of Congress.[31] Eaton's ability to develop acquaintances with a broad
spectrum of individuals was later enhanced because of his war record.
He commanded a fort against an Indian attack that earned him credit
in Philadelphia, and he went on a famous scouting mission, where he

---

[31] Edwards, *Barbary General: The Life of William H. Eaton*, 34.

learned the language of and dressed like the Miami people, bringing back intelligence of their war plans. These accomplishments made Eaton one of the first heroes of the campaigns in the wars in the Old Northwest. In 1795, he returned to Philadelphia briefly, and his war record provided him with more opportunities to meet political elites.[32]

There are two differing views in the biographical and historical literature about Eaton's ties to Philadelphia. One view holds that Eaton gained the appointment through strong ties with the Adams administration, especially the Secretary of State, Timothy Pickering, whom he described to his wife as his "respected, loved, honored *friend*."[33] To support the view that Eaton had strong ties, one would point to a few key moments in the historical record. Eaton named a mud fort after Secretary Pickering, which may have earned him some notice, but since 1795 he had been under shadow of suspicion and had been court martialed by the army. He was suspended and confined to Fort Pickering. He considered leaving the army, but before he did, he returned to Philadelphia during the summer of 1797. For some reason, left obscure in this historical record, he was sent to make arrest and seize the papers of an agent involved in the Blount Conspiracy, an international conspiracy to aid the British in the southwest. Afterward, he was appointed Consul to Tunis, leaving for his post in the winter of 1798.[34] If Eaton was Pickering's close friend, and used this friendship to secure the mission in support of the Blount investigation and later the job of consul, then he would have strong ties to the Adams administration. This would undermine the argument of this book because Eaton would count as a political elite and not an intermediary.

The best historical evidence shows, however, that Eaton had only weak ties to the Jefferson administration. First, there is slim to no evidence of a close friendship between Pickering and Eaton. Eaton did not often correspond with and likely rarely visited him.[35] More

---

[32] Ibid., 39–45.

[33] William Eaton to Eliza Eaton, August 15, 1800. In Prentiss, *The Life of the Late Gen. William Eaton*, 179.

[34] Edwards, *Barbary General*; Prentiss, *The Life of the Late Gen. William Eaton*.

[35] If they were friends, it was not because of face-to-face meetings. Eaton's only opportunity to meet Pickering appears to have been in the summer of 1797 and there is simply no evidence pointing to their meeting or developing affective ties. Moreover, during the latter half of the summer, there is clear evidence that they did not talk. Pickering refused to correspond directly with Eaton from July until September, during the period that Eaton was being selected as Consul, because of complications involving Blount's impeachment from Congress. Even then, Pickering wrote that the only reason for his correspondence with

importantly, even if Eaton had strong ties to Pickering, they likely would not have transferred to the Adams administration in general or the Jefferson administration. Pickering and Adams distrusted each other since shortly after Adams's election, and by the summer of 1799, they despised each other.[36] Pickering, therefore, had left the State Department a few years before Eaton began forwarding plans for cooperation with Ahmed. Even if Eaton had ties to important figures in the Adams administration, he had no ties to Jefferson. Pickering's relations with the Jefferson administration were so cool that Pickering sought to have New England leave the country![37] This is a crucial point to underscore. Given Pickering's change in status between Eaton's appointment and the beginning of the war – to an opponent of the government – even if strong ties helped Eaton gain his position, they would not have provided him influence.[38]

Eaton likely had weak ties to the presidency at the moment when cooperation began. This situation, however, creates a puzzle. If Eaton had weak ties, why was he selected? One possible reason is that Eaton's pursuit of weak ties – his ability to make himself known – provided him with an advantage in gaining the post. Another possible reason is that he had studied Arabic and Ottoman politics, making him more qualified than many. Perhaps it was also a political reward for his part in Blount's investigation. Most importantly, there probably was no real competition. Working as the American Consul to Tunis offered little prospect for career advancement or commercial opportunity, and it promised a significant amount of misery.

Eaton was to ensure he was on his guard against a Mr. Ripley, who had some part in the plot. Pickering to Eaton, September 19, 1979. Pickering Papers, Reel 7. There is also no correspondence from Pickering to Eaton in the first half of the year, leading me to believe they were not close friends then. Therefore, if they were friends, it was a fast blossoming friendship beginning sometime in early summer and lasting until early July. During this period, the evidence for a friendship simply does not exist. From a close examination of the correspondence between Pickering and Eaton during Eaton's years as Consul, there is little mark of friendship, let alone warmth. Therefore, I conclude that Eaton had weak ties to Pickering.

36 Gerard H. Clarfield, *Timothy Pickering and the American Republic* (Pittsburgh: University of Pittsburgh Press, 1980), 198–9. See also Gerard H. Clarfield, *Timothy Pickering and American Diplomacy, 1795–1800* (Columbia: University of Missouri Press, 1969).

37 Clarfield, *Timothy Pickering and the American Republic*, 211–28.

38 When he arrived and discovered these limitations, he promised his wife he would return in less than two years. William Eaton to Eliza Eaton, April 6, 1799. In Prentiss, *The Life of the Late Gen. William Eaton*, 153.

Eaton's Incentives and Social Skill

Eaton's selection was fortuitous for cooperation. He was a socially skilled agent. He had experience promoting cross-cultural brokerage, from when he fought in the wars against Native Americans. Perhaps most important, by the time Eaton recruited Ahmed Karamanli, he had lived in Tunis for several years, making him bicultural and fluent in Arabic. Moreover, even before the war began, Eaton favored the use of force over negotiation. A few months after arriving in Tunis, Eaton wrote to the Secretary of State about the humiliation of the United States at the hands of the Barbary powers: "*nothing but terror will check the insolence of these demands on our generosity!*"[39] Shortly after the Bey of Tripoli declared war against the United States, Eaton wrote to the Secretary of State that "[w]hile we are in difficulty with Tripoli it seems to me good policy to be on good terms with Tunis," where Eaton was posted. But, if the United States had grown tired of the "sink of Jewish perfidy," then it should provide Eaton "a transport with *One thousand marines*, between twenty and thirty eight years of age, native Americans, and properly officered, under convoy of a 44 gun frigate."[40] Eaton pledged that he would surprise Tunis and destroy the Bey's arsenal. The Jefferson administration, probably smartly, ignored Eaton's advice to fight two wars at once.

The presence of a socially skilled agent who favored the use of force (and therefore would consider military cooperation) was essential to US cooperation with Ahmed. Without Eaton, there was literally no one else who could engineer the scheme for cooperation. The story of Eaton's recruitment of Ahmed, and how they together marched to Derna, has been retold in many histories of the First Barbary War. In the following section, I provide a brief history to show how Eaton used his position as an intermediary to make political elites on both sides of the Atlantic believe that cooperation was in their interests, to build trust, and to manage cultural friction.

The First Coup

When Cathcart wrote to Eaton, suggesting he recruit Ahmed, Eaton quickly began the process of cajoling Ahmed into fighting against his brother. Eaton's correspondence first mentions Ahmed in a letter written

[39] Eaton, CD 22, June 24, 1800. *NDBW*, Vol. 1, 358.
[40] Eaton, CD 35, April 10, 1801. *PJM: SS*, Vol. 1, 78–82.

on September 5, 1801, in which he describes a project in concert with the "rightful Bashaw of Tripoli." Eaton explains that his plan is to attack from land with Ahmed, and the navy should bombard from the sea. Eaton, of course, had no authority to unilaterally make American military policy.

From the start, Eaton's plan was unlikely. The first problem was mistrust. For the scheme to work, Ahmed needed to know that the United States would provide material support. Ahmed's distrust was sensible. Eaton himself had been given no assurance that the United States would favor cooperation, and his letters to the Secretary of State are full of pleas for such reassurances.[41] Without any authority to do so, Eaton counseled Ahmed that support was coming. The second problem was Ahmed's interests. In late 1801 or early 1802, Yusuf agreed to allow Ahmed to return home, promising that he could rule the important city of Derna. Eaton, on sick leave in Leghorn, vowed to return to Tunis to "defeat this project."[42] When Eaton returned to Tunis in March, Ahmed was on the verge of returning to his brother. Eaton made two arguments to convince Ahmed that cooperation with the United States was in his interests. Eaton's first argument, which was likely a straightforward lie or unwarranted guess, was that Yusuf would "cut his throat." Therefore, cooperating with the United States was Ahmed's only option for survival. Moreover, Eaton offered the carrot and stick of American policy. He denied Ahmed passage on an American ship, saying "instead of my influence to assist his passage to the Kingdom of Tripoli I should give it to have him and his retinue carried prisoners of war to the United States; but if he would adhere to his former arrangements I did not doubt but that before the expiration of four months he might be offered to his people by an American Squadron."[43]

Sometime around the winter of 1802/1803, Ahmed returned to Derna as requested by his brother. But instead of supporting Yusuf's rule, Ahmed revolted. Ahmed anticipated US naval support for his rebellion, probably because of Eaton's promises.[44] Eaton, of course, had no authority to

[41] Eaton to Madison, September 5, 1801. In Prentiss, *The Life of the Late Gen. William Eaton*, 209. Eaton to Madison, December 13, 1801. In ibid., 213.

[42] Eaton to Madison, February 12, 1802. In Prentiss, *The Life of the Late Gen. William Eaton*, 213.

[43] Eaton to Madison, March 18, 1802. Eaton, CD 22, June 24, 1800. *NDBW*, Vol. 2, 90–1.

[44] Hamet to Jefferson, January 20, 180; Journal of James Leander Cathcart, February 27, 1803; and Affidavit of Seid Ahmet Gurgi, February 20, 1803. *NSDW: Vol. 2*, 347, 350, and 363.

order the navy to intervene. Without the promised US assistance, Ahmed quickly lost. He retreated and eventually traveled to Egypt.[45]

This first attempt at cooperation created two problems. On the one hand, the refusal of American assistance to Ahmed created problems of mistrust: Ahmed would want more visible signals that the United States would support his efforts before undertaking another uprising against Yusuf. On the other hand, the failed uprising convinced some influential Americans that cooperation with Ahmed was not helpful. As Tobias Lear explained to Madison, "He is now in Egypt, driven by his brother from Darne, where it is presumed he might have made a stand, had he been a man of any force or influence; which, from the best accounts I can collect, he is not."[46] To move the parties to cooperate, Eaton needed to convince the United States that Ahmed was useful, and convince Ahmed that the United States was trustworthy.

The Second Attempt at Cooperation

Eaton and Cathcart realized that if Ahmed was to be successful, he needed more support from the Navy. Getting this support was difficult. The US Navy knew that Eaton had no authority to mount a land invasion of Tripoli, and the Navy refused to take orders from William Eaton.[47] Eaton and Cathcart fumed at the refusal. Cathcart, in particular, pointed out that the Naval Officers blocking cooperation had no understanding of Barbary politics, and he insisted that in the future, trade consuls be authorized to overthrow governments.[48]

To sell cooperation, Eaton needed to travel home. He spent much of 1803 and early 1804 in the United States, trying to convince policymakers to support cooperation. His central argument was that cooperation with Ahmed would significantly advance American interests. We do not have a record of any of his meetings with the Cabinet or Jefferson; however, the arguments he made in a letter to the Speaker of the House likely reflect his arguments to the administration. The first argument he made was that cooperation with Ahmed was crucial for influencing Yusuf: "I am convinced that our captives cannot otherwise be released." As evidence, he cited the 1802 uprising, claiming that his "arrangements with the rival

---

[45] Nissen to Cathcart, July 15, 1803. *NSDW*, Vol. 2, 486.
[46] Lear to Madison, November 3, 1804. *NDBW*, Vol. 5, 116.
[47] See the correspondence in Prentiss, *The Life of the Late Gen. William Eaton*, 222–7.
[48] Cathcart to Madison, August 25, 1802. *NDBW*, Vol. 2, 253.

Bashaw did more to harass the enemy in 1802 than the entire operations of our squadron." He also ruled out the other options. Naval action, he rightly argued, had been ineffective in ending the war, and negotiating with Yusuf was an insult to the flag: "as an individual, I would rather yield my person to the danger of war in almost any shape, than my pride to the humiliation of *treating* with a wretched pirate for the random of men who are the rightful heirs of freedom."[49] These arguments may have resonated with the Jefferson administration, which was seeking an end to a costly war.[50]

Despite Eaton's attempt to win support for his plan, the Administration did not endorse it. Jefferson likely did not take a position on cooperation. While at sea back to Africa, Eaton explained to a friend: "The President becomes reserved. The Secretary of war *believes we had better pay tribute*. He said this to me in his own office. Gallatin, like a cowardly Jew, shrinks behind the counter. Mr. Madison *leaves every thing to the Secretary of the navy department*."[51] Yet, Jefferson authorized commanders in the field to pursue cooperation if they believed it would be successful. The instructions for Captain Samuel Barron from the Secretary of the Navy explain this clearly: "With respect the Ex-Bashaw of Tripoli, we have no objection to you availing yourself of his co-operation with you against Tripoli – if you shall upon a full view of the subject after your arrival upon the Station, consider his co-operation expedient. The subject is committed entirely to your discretion."[52] The Cabinet likely found cooperation to be unnecessary. Writing to Tobias Lear, Madison explained that "[o]f the co-operation of the Elder brother of the Bashaw of Tripoli we are still willing to avail ourselves, if the Commodore should Judge that it may be useful," yet, "less reliance is to be placed on his aid, as the force under the orders of the Commodore is deemed sufficient for any exercise of coercion which the obstinacy of the Bashaw may demand."[53] In other words, no one was enthused by Eaton's plan because everyone thought the war would be won at sea. But, Eaton was authorized, if the situation called for it and the commanders in the field approved, to cooperate.[54]

---

[49] Eaton to Col. Dwight, 1804 (Undated). Prentiss, *The Life of the Late Gen. William Eaton*, 267.
[50] Extracts of letter, Undated. Ibid., 245–46.
[51] Eaton to Col. Dwight, 1804 (Undated). Ibid., 266–67.
[52] Smith to Barron, June 6, 1804. *NDBW*, Vol. 4, 152–3.
[53] Madison to Lear, June 6, 1804. *PJM: SS*, Vol. 7, 288.
[54] When Eaton arrived in the Mediterranean, he needed to continue selling the plan because of Commodore Baron's reluctance. He used these same arguments. See Eaton to Baron,

Selling cooperation to Washington may have been easier than selling it to Ahmed. Recall that in late 1802, Ahmed had risen up against his brother, expecting American support. The support predicted by Cathcart and Eaton did not arrive. In 1804, Ahmed thus needed more assurances of the US intention to support resistance. Eaton himself understood the problem. Jefferson had authorized cooperation (if Barron approved), but he had not done so publicly, and he provided Eaton with no written assurances to give Ahmed. As Eaton explained, "I carry with me no evidence whatever, from our government, of the sincerity of their intentions towards the friendly Bashaw." Because there was no direct evidence from Jefferson, Eaton planned to stake his personal reputation: "I have no alternative but to place my breast in this breach of confidence and good faith. This I am resolved to do, and, by exposing my temporal salvation, convince the ally and the world of a consistency and fidelity in my country which, I myself am convinced, does not exist with our administration any further than considerations purely individual render it convenient."[55] In other words, Eaton decided that because Jefferson would not provide written assurances of US support, or even supplies to signal forthcoming support, Eaton would himself fight alongside Ahmed to send a signal of Jefferson's intentions that Jefferson neither desired nor expected.

Eaton's plan, however, would prove overly simplistic. When returning to the Mediterranean, he discovered that Ahmed had moved to Egypt and become embroiled in its internal rebellions. Eaton adventure with Ahmed in Africa is an amazing story, extensively chronicled in existing accounts of Eaton's life.[56] In this chapter, I briefly describe only three of the problems faced on their trip because they exemplify how Eaton used his structural niche between societies to secure cooperation.

August 21, 1804; and Eaton to Barron, September 8, 1804. Enclosed in Eaton to Smith, September 18, 1804. *NDBW*, Vol. 5, 36–8. One aspect that I do not discuss here is that Eaton also played the role of intermediary between political elites in the United States and naval commanders in the Mediterranean. Throughout the ordeal, Eaton represented himself as having more direct authorization than in fact he had, to secure the approval and assistance of the Navy. For example, he wrote to Barron that he had the express authorization of the Secretary of the Navy to place himself in charge of all land operations, which almost certainly was untrue. See Eaton to Baron, February 14, 1805. *NDBW*, Vol. 5, 353–4. His allies appear to have understood the challenges posed by his lack of authority. See, for example, Hull to Eaton, December 24, 1804. *NDBW*, Vol. 5, 215.

55 Eaton to Col. Dwight, 1804 (Undated). In Prentiss, *The Life of the Late Gen. William Eaton*, 266–7. See also Eaton to Smith, September 18, 1804. *NDBW*, Vol. 5, 34.

56 Edwards, *Barbary General: The Life of William H. Eaton*; London, *Victory in Tripoli*; Prentiss, *The Life of the Late Gen. William Eaton*; Wheelan, *Jefferson's War*.

The first moment important for cooperation was the meeting between Eaton and Ahmed, which took place sometime in early February 1805.[57] At this meeting, Ahmed and Eaton agreed to a Convention (a treaty) that articulated sets of compatible interests. Ahmed would cooperate with Eaton only if the United States would restore him to power; if he was not restored, there was no reason to go on the expedition. The Second Article of the Convention made this promise: "The government of the United States shall use their utmost exertions ... to reestablish the said Hamet Bashaw in the possession of his sovereignty of Tripoli."[58] The problem, however, was that the United States had no intention of pledging itself to place Ahmed on the throne. Samuel Barron, under whose authority Eaton was working, was clear: "I wish you to understand that no guarantee or engagements to the exiled prince, whose cause, I repeat it, we are only favoring as the instrument to an attainment and not in itself as an object, must be held to stand in the way of our acquiescence to any honorable and advantageous terms of accommodation which the present Bashaw may be induced to propose."[59] In short, no one provided Eaton with the authority to describe the interests of the United States as identical to Ahmed's interests.[60] Although he refused to endorse Eaton's promises, Barron appears to recognize that despite being unauthorized, they were necessary for enlisting Ahmed's help. Ahmed, however, was unaware that Eaton lacked this authority, because Eaton was the primary link between decision-makers in Washington and himself. Eaton's structural position between societies, in other words, enabled him to misrepresent American intentions and policy, creating the appearance of a harmony of interests.

The second issue related to supplies. To recruit an army required money, and to move thousands of soldiers, along with their camp (their family), across the desert in 1805 was an enormously expensive undertaking. The issue of supplies was important; if Ahmed moved and the promised supplies did not arrive, then the mission would fail. As Ahmed himself put it,

---

[57] Eaton to Hull, February 2, 1805. In Prentiss, *The Life of the Late Gen. William Eaton*, 294.

[58] "Convention." In Eaton to Smith, February 13, 1805. In ibid., 297–8.

[59] Barron to Eaton, March 22, 1805. *NDBW*, Vol. 5, 439. See also Barron to Smith, April 6, 1805. *NDBW*, Vol. 5, 485–6.

[60] Eaton appears to acknowledge the irregularity of an American agent negotiating a treaty. See his discussion of how it can "do no mischief" in Eaton to Barron, April 29, 1805. Prentiss, *The Life of the Late Gen. William Eaton*, 345.

"Friend, you must have courage; do not think about money because the occasion demands heavy expenditure. It is a matter of making war, and war calls for money and men."[61] On the trek, this lack of supplies led to a mutiny among the Arab troops on April 10.[62]

The Convention signed by Eaton and Ahmed provided reassurances that supplies would be forthcoming. This was beyond Eaton's authority to promise: he was authorized to spend only $20,000. The Convention promised that the funds would be repaid to the United States from the tribute from Denmark, Sweden, and the Batvian Republic to Tripoli.[63] By negotiating a treaty in which Ahmed promised to repay the difference later, Eaton could claim he was in effect spending no more than $20,000, although he was borrowing much more.[64] Once again, Eaton was aware that he had no authority to borrow money on behalf of the United States. Eaton's plan was to reassure Ahmed of US intentions by providing (borrowing) the resources for the expedition, likely representing these funds (at home and in Egypt) as implicitly approved by the US government.[65] To establish Ahmed's trust with the United States, Eaton promised supplies and sold himself into debt, staking his personal credit (literally) on American intentions.[66]

A third issue relates to the problems of establishing a cultural frame to make cooperation between Christians and Arabs possible. Eaton found that relations between Christians and Arabs at the time were framed through mistrust and conflict. Eaton explained, "We find it almost impossible to inspire these wild bigots with confidence in us, or to persuade them that, being Christians, we can be otherwise than enemies to Musselmen."[67] This problem would present itself in a variety of ways. For example, when supplies were short, the Arabs were concerned that the

---

[61] Ahmed Karamanli to Eaton, about January 15, 1805. *NDBW*, Vol. 5, 279.

[62] Eaton's Journal, April 10, 1805. Prentiss, *The Life of the Late Gen. William Eaton*, 325–6.

[63] Eaton may have haggled for the addition of tribute. The terms Ahmed proposed earlier included only a promise of perpetual peace, repayment of American assistance, and the prizes from capturing Derna. See Bufuttil to Barron, November 1, 1804. *NDBW*, Vol. 5, 110.

[64] Eaton to Smith, February 13, 1805; and Eaton to Barron, February 14, 1805. *NDBW*, Vol. 5, 350–4.

[65] Eaton anticipated that the supplies would not be forthcoming. See Eaton to Dwight, September 20, 1804. *NDBW*, Vol. 5, 42–3.

[66] Eaton to Barron, April 29, 1805. Prentiss, *The Life of the Late Gen. William Eaton*, 340–6.

[67] In Louis Wright and Julia MacLeod, *The First Americans in North Africa: William Eaton's Struggle For a Vigorous Policy Against the Barbary Pirates, 1799–1805* (Princeton: Princeton University Press, 1945), 169.

Christians, acting collectively, would kill them; the Arabs and Christians thus camped at different sites and often traveled at different times. Chapter 1 identified these kinds of cultural disagreements as threats to cooperation.[68]

On several occasions, Eaton attempted to present common cultural frames to make sense of their joint enterprise. However, Eaton did not appreciate his allies' culture. He wrote about their strange customs and referred to the troops he would command as having "no sense of patriotism, truth or honor" – Eaton was indeed a creature of his times. Yet, Eaton recognized their religiosity and displayed tolerance toward their culture because he worried that difference might threaten cooperation. For example, he attended a marriage that he found distasteful.[69] He also attempted to explain why Americans in particular were trustworthy, even though most Christians would refuse to cooperate with most Muslims. He explained that American religious pluralism meant he would not refuse to engage or cooperate with others regardless of their religious views. He also painted an odd view of his religion, in which there were separate heavens for Americans, "Papists," and Muslims, but they could visit one another.[70] In doing so, he was providing an interpretation of religious differences that allowed for cooperation instead of confrontation to appear natural.

Each of these ways that Eaton encouraged cooperation is an example of the power of betweenness. Since the United States and Ahmed could not directly communicate, Ahmed's impressions of the United States formed on the basis of what Eaton said and did. Eaton used this monopoly on information to push Ahmed to cooperate.

Eaton's march was successful. He captured Derna, forcing Yusuf Karamanli to settle with the United States. In the resulting peace treaty negotiations, the United States abandoned its support for Ahmed Karamanli. This should have been no surprise, despite Eaton's pretense that it was. The United States would not, in accordance with a Convention signed by an agent, continue to fight to install one brother on the throne over another. Cooperating with Ahmed was essential for winning the battle, but abandoning him was essential for winning the peace.

---

[68] The cases involving Native Americans will focus on these exact kinds of issues at camps and how they can derail cooperation.

[69] Eaton's Journal, April 5, 1805. Prentiss, *The Life of the Late Gen. William Eaton*, 318–20.

[70] Eaton's Journal, March 30, 1805. Prentiss, *The Life of the Late Gen. William Eaton*, 312–14.

CONCLUSION

The consensus among most historians who study the Barbary Wars bears out the role of betweenness in genera ting political power. Agents without institutional influence can become important when they are able to manipulate information across a structural hole. Specifically, James Leander Cathcart, a former slave, identified Ahmed Karamanli as a potential cooperation partner; and William Eaton, a consul with few strong ties to centers of political power in the United States, was able to exploit the situation. They lobbied, cajoled, and manipulated the US government and Ahmed, creating an alliance. Most historians recognize that Eaton and Cathcart's, influence derived their their unique social position and that they used their position between societies to find partners for war.

The sharp difference between this case and the others in this book is time. The Barbary Wars were the earliest American involvement overseas; the other overseas cases took place in the age of steam, after ships became faster and telegraph lines, radios, and telephones sped communication. The United States also developed a more professional diplomatic corps, built global intelligence apparatuses, and became more tightly tied to an economically interdependent world. The Barbary Wars thus serve as a "most-likely" case for the influence of an intermediary. The rest of this book shows that Eaton is not an anomaly. Consistently, wars are won due to the recruitment of non-state allies, like Ahmed Karamanli and his army, through the influence of the weak and their ability to manipulate information across structural holes.

4

Red, Blue, or Gray

Between 1862 and 1865, American Indians across the continent wrestled with their position "between two fires," in Laurence Hauptman's phrase. Should they fight? And if so, should they wear blue or gray?

Almost every aspect of the American Civil War was shaped by alliances the Union and the Confederacy made with American Indians. At least 20,000 Native Americans joined the armed forces in the North and the South. Companies of Indians fought in some of the most important battles of the war: the Wilderness, the Battle of the Crater, Pea Ridge, and dozens more. Individual Native Americans also acted as guides, served as spies, and piloted ships. While the total number of American Indians in the war was never very high, constituting at most 1 percent of the war's total manpower, some theatres were dominated by concerns about whom they would ally with and how many men they could bring to bear. The Kansas Home Guard, for example, was composed of 3,000 Native Americans who fought for the Union, and there were plans to recruit several thousand more by the end of the war; it faced off against forces raised by the Confederacy in the Cherokee Nation.[1] Within theatre, they were the dominant fighting forces. At the same time, tribes in the west continued to fight against the Union and Confederacy, with significant uprisings in Minnesota (the Dakota War or Sioux Uprising, 1863–1865), conflicts with the Navajos and Apaches in Arizona and New Mexico and the Cheyennes, Arapahos, Kiowas, and Comanches in Kansas and

---

[1] For general overviews, see Annie Heloise Abel, *The American Indian as Participant in the Civil War* (Cleveland: Arthur Clark Company, 1919); Laurence Hauptman, *Between Two Fires: American Indians in the Civil War* (New York: Free Press, 1995).

Colorado, and unrest in the Pacific Northwest (the Snake War, 1864–1869).[2] These wars, often suspected of being triggered by Confederate agents, brought attention from the Union, drawing down manpower needed to defeat the Confederacy.[3]

By placing competition between North and South over the recruitment of Indian allies at the center of the politics of the Civil War, the conflict acquires an international dimension.[4] In a legal sense, American Indian decision-making in regard to US allies constituted international politics, because many Indian nations were legally sovereign states.[5] In a political sense, the Civil War opened up space for independent alliance decision-making that had been closed for many Indians since the War of 1812. After the War of 1812 ended, most American Indians did not have a potential alliance partner besides the United States.[6] During the American

[2] On the Dakota War, see Gary C. Anderson, *Through Dakota Eyes: Narrative Accounts Of The Minnesota Indian War Of 1862*, ed. Alan Woolworth (St. Paul: Minnesota Historical Society Press, 1988); Scott W. Berg, *38 Nooses: Lincoln, Little Crow, and the Beginning of the Frontier's End* (New York: Vintage, 2012); Kenneth Carley, *The Dakota War of 1862: Minnesota's Other Civil War* (St. Paul: Minnesota Historical Society Press, 1976). On the Snake War, see Scott McArthur, *The Enemy Never Came: The Civil War in the Pacific Northwest* (Caldwell: Caxton Press, 2012); Gregory Michno, *Deadliest Indian War in the West: The Snake Conflict, 1863–1868* (Caldwell: Caxton Press, 2007).

[3] Francis Paul Prucha, *The Great Father: The United States Government and the American Indians* (Lincoln: University of Nebraska Press, 1984), 437 and 440.

[4] To date, International Relations scholars have focused on British decision-making, that is, the dog that didn't bark rather than the dog that did. This is an odd omission, not justified by the historical record. A review of Lincoln's correspondence, held at the Library of Congress, shows more documents related to Indian Affairs during the Civil War than those related specifically to the British. A focus on the British thus ignores Lincoln's dramatic concern with Sioux-related issues and strips Lincoln from his historical connections to the frontier. If one were to come to the historical record without eyes blinkered by IR scholarship, one would likely focus on alliance politics with Native Americans, rather than the less politically and strategically salient issues overseas.

[5] Three early nineteenth-century Supreme Court decisions, known collectively as the Marshall Trilogy, found that Indian nations were "foreign states." The practical consequence of these decisions was to deny states any role in negotiating and signing treaties with Indian Nations; because they were like any other sovereign state (in some senses), only Congress was empowered by the Constitution to negotiate and sign treaties with them. Frank Pommersheim, *Broken Landscape : Indians, Indian Tribes, and the Constitution* (New York: Oxford University Press, 2009), 87–124.

[6] American Indians could and did make alliances with one another; however, the last major attempt to create an alliance system to balance against the United States was Tecumseh's, which ended with his death in 1813. Instead, intra-American Indian conflicts often involved one party making alliances with the United States, such as in the Black Hawk War (1832), the Yakima War (1855–1858), and the Rogue River Wars (1855–1856). A fuller investigation of the history of intermediaries' influence over American foreign policy would include examples from the Indian Wars, although see Thomas Dunlay, *Wolves for the Blue Soldiers: Indian Scouts and Auxiliaries with the United States*

Civil War, by contrast, the emergence of the South as a major power led
to more flexible alliance choices and the space for decision-making grew.
Especially in the West, everyone realized the importance of American
Indians' decisions for the balance of power, and both the Union and the
Confederacy paid close attention.[7]

The American Civil War provides a useful arena in which to test
whether the presence of structural holes creates opportunities for agents
who have little institutional influence to play an outsized role in shaping cooperation. The ways that structural holes were produced varied
dramatically in different regions in the 1860s. Table 4.1 summarizes
these differences. The Odawa, Ojibwe, and Potawatomi who enlisted
in Company K of the First Michigan Sharpshooters spoke little English,
lived on reservations, and had sparse contact with whites in the southern part of the state. The Pawnee Scouts were similar to Company K,
with the notable exception that they were further west and lived in communities even more sparsely populated by white settlers. The Lumbee
who volunteered to guide Sherman's Army through the swamps near the
border of North and South Carolina in 1865 were comparatively well-
integrated into local politics: they spoke English and lived on parcels of
land just like their white neighbors. Yet, the war produced a structural
hole between these potential northern allies, and they had only fleeting
contact with armies moving near their homes. There was no structural
hole between white and Cherokee society, which provides the ability to
vary an important scope condition to determine its effects on the influence of intermediaries. If variations in social structure help explain the
politics of agency in each of these settings, then it lends credibility to the
view that the argument of Chapter 1 likely explains cases across a wide
terrain in international politics.

To select cases, I first divided cooperation into two forms. Some
American Indian political communities cooperated in ad hoc, informal

---

Army, 1860–90 (Lincoln: University of Nebraska Press, 1982); John Hall, *Uncommon
Defense: Indian Allies in the Black Hawk War* (Cambridge: Harvard University Press,
2009); Daniel K. Richter, "Cultural Brokers and Intercultural Politics: New York-Iroquois
Relations, 1664–1701," *Journal of American History* 75, no. 1 (1988): 40–67.

[7] If these nations were legally sovereign, why refer to them as non-state allies? As explained
in Chapter 1, this term is inexact because of changes over time to US constitutional law
and international law. American Indians' sovereignty is often the subject of legal and political debate. To remind the reader, I mean the term "state" in the European usage common to International Relations scholarship. This implies more than legal sovereignty; it
also implies the other trappings of a modern state. The choice of the term non-state allies
does not imply any larger point about the sovereignty of American Indian Nations.

TABLE 4.1 *Causes of structural holes in Civil War cases*

Ally	Cause of structural hole	Modern state
Company K	Linguistic, cultural, institutional	Michigan
Pawnee Scouts	Linguistic, cultural, institutional, geographic	Nebraska
Lumbee	Geographic, transitory actors	North Carolina
Cherokee	No structural hole present	Oklahoma

arrangements. Throughout the war, Native Americans cooperated with the Union Army during operations in the South, acting as river pilots, guides, and intelligence agents.[8] Often, these arrangements were temporary because cooperation began and ended when the army passed through the territory. I focus on the Lumbee as an example of informal cooperation, because the other cases I investigated provided an insufficient evidentiary basis to draw any conclusions. Much more common was the enlistment of American Indians in the Union and Confederate armies. In selecting which groups to focus on, I maximized geographical diversity, including instances of cooperation near the frontier (the Pawnees) as well as cooperation in heavily settled areas (the Lumbees). Furthermore, I selected cases where the choice sets were different. Native American historians often describe resistance or accommodation as two political strategies that tribes might use to protect themselves against white settlement. I selected cases where cooperation is best described as an act of resistance (the Lumbee cooperating with the Union Army was an act of resisting the Confederacy), an act of accommodation (the Odawa, Ojibwe, and Potawatomi), and instances in which cooperation was a strategy to win support in claims against other Native Americans, not directly related to the Civil War (the Pawnee). I also selected the Cherokees because they made one of the largest contributions to the war effort and are a case where I can relax the scope condition that a structural hole is present.

Before describing these cases, I first want to describe my approach to studying Indian participation in the Civil War and how it differs from most historians. The history of American Indians in the Civil War is fascinating; so much so that historians, novelists, and filmmakers have produced compelling work about their role. Almost all of this work is narrative, showing how important Native Americans were to the war and

---

[8] Several of these cases are described in Hauptman, *Between Two Fires: American Indians in the Civil War.*

the effects of the war on their communities. I cannot use the same narrative approach. Most military histories concentrate on the contributions of American Indians to the war after they enlist or form alliances. The important question at the heart of this book – why did they fight? – has received much less attention. One reason for the inattention to recruitment is the quality of the historical evidence. The historical record, in the form of unit histories or recollections of other soldiers, is long on American Indians' contributions to specific battles or how they behaved in camp, but short on the politics of why they joined. I do not, therefore, narrate the recruitment because doing so requires a significant amount of historical imagination that is inappropriate in this book. Rather than providing a narrative account of the origins of American Indian participation in the war, I make careful inferences from a fractured historical record, spending more time dealing with historiographical questions and rendering judgments about the quality of evidence to compare my explanation with alternative explanations.

THE CHEROKEES

The largest contribution of soldiers by Native Americans to either North or South came from the Five Civilized Tribes who lived in and near Indian Territory. I focus on the Cherokees. By the end of the war, thousands of Cherokees served in the army in both the North and the South. More than 3,000 Native Americans enlisted in the Home Guard, who served in and around Fort Gibson in Oklahoma.[9] They were matched against thousands of Confederate Indians, led by Stand Watie, the only Native American Brigadier General in the Civil War. The Confederate Cherokees were perhaps the longest-serving Confederate soldiers. They fought at the Battle of Wilson's Creek (August 1861), one of the first major battles of the war, and Stand Watie was the last Confederate general to surrender (June 1865).[10] Their most pronounced presence was in the area around Cherokee Nation, where they often constituted the most effective fighting force in the theatre. Beyond its importance to the war, the alliance also

[9] For enlistment numbers, see the Regimental Descriptive Books. 1st Indian Home Guard, 2nd Indian Home Guard, 3rd Indian Home Guard. Book Records of Volunteer Union Organizations. RG 94, NARA.

[10] Clarissa W. Confer, *The Cherokee Nation in the Civil War* (Norman: University of Oklahoma Press, 2007), 158; William Garrett Piston and Richard W. Hatcher III, *Wilson's Creek: The Second Battle of the Civil War and the Men Who Fought It* (Chapel Hill: University of North Carolina Press, 2000), 160.

had long-lasting effects on the Cherokee Nation. Battles and raids were fought in and around Indian Territory. In the end, between 33 percent and 50 percent of the Cherokee died during those four years, and for many parts of Cherokee Nation there was "almost total destruction"; everything was destroyed, including farms, homes, and churches.[11]

The history of Cherokee participation in the Civil War is drastically different from that of other Native Americans. There was no significant structural disconnect between the Cherokee and white political elites. Therefore, I can use Cherokee participation in the Civil War to explore whether intermediaries matter when structural holes are not present. I show that when political elites know one another well, intermediaries become less important.

Absence of Structural Holes

The Cherokee relationship with the Confederacy and the Union was special in comparison to the others described in this chapter, because there was no structural hole between societies. To a large measure, this is due to Cherokee political history. Unlike the other American Indians described in this chapter, many Cherokee (especially the wealthy in Cherokee Nation) had largely assimilated by the Civil War.

To understand their social connections requires understanding the social relationships between two groups of Cherokees in the nineteenth century. On the one hand, a minority of the Cherokee, often (and sometimes quite inaccurately) called "half-bloods," had largely assimilated to American society.[12] They often had a biracial family history, were wealthy, spoke English, farmed the land, and many owned slaves. To defend their property and garner social relationships with white society, they more or less strived to "imitate the plantation society of the white South."[13] This group, associated with the Ridge Party, tended to favor cooperation with Federal authorities during the era of removal and had sympathies for the South during the war. On the other hand, a majority of Cherokees, described (also often inaccurately) as "full bloods," were generally not wealthy and did not own slaves. Many within this faction, associated with the Ross Party during the Civil War, strove to maintain a

---

[11] Confer, *The Cherokee Nation in the Civil War*, 144–5.

[12] The terms "half-blood" and "full-blood" were commonly used, though often inaccurate.

[13] Theda Perdue, *Slavery and the Evolution of Cherokee Society, 1540–1866* (Knoxville: University of Tennessee Press, 1979), 58.

distinctive Indian identity, supported abolition, and opposed removal-era land concessions.

Both parties had social relationships that linked the Cherokee Nation to centers of political power. First, neither group had barriers to communication with political elites. The Ridge Party's leaders, which gravitated toward the Confederacy, were Cherokees who were likely to speak English and Cherokee, were raised in western-style schools, had children attending elite colleges, and had biracial heritages.[14] That the Ridge Party, who supported assimilation, had contacts with white political elites is no surprise. Perhaps more surprising is the existence of strong ties between those often called "full bloods" and white political elites. The leader of the latter group, John Ross, developed political connections between the majority of Cherokees and the government. John Ross had the same background as Cherokee in the Ridge Party. Ross had a Scottish father and Cherokee mother. As a child he learned English, in addition to Cherokee, and his tutor was from Inverness. His bilingual, biracial, and bicultural background helped him economically in the years before the war: he created a trading post, secured Federal contracts, and in 1812 joined Andrew Jackson's army working with Cherokee soldiers.[15] By the time of the Civil War, Ross had become wealthy and owned many slaves.[16] No significant linguistic or cultural barriers precluded either faction from reaching out to political elites in the white world.

Representatives of both parties had long histories of corresponding with and lobbying American political elites. Stand Watie, who led the Ridge Party during the Civil War, and John Ross both traveled to Washington on several occasions to meet and sign treaties. Ross had over forty years of experience navigating Washington politics; Watie had less experience (he was much younger), but gained political connections when he and his brother helped sign the treaties that culminated in the loss of the Cherokees' lands and the Trail of Tears.[17]

These ties continued into the years right before the Civil War. Ross had direct political ties to Washington. In the decades before the Civil War, Ross spent an enormous amount of time in Washington City, lobbying

---

[14] See for example James W. Parins, *John Rollin Ridge: His Life and Works* (Lincoln: University of Nebraska Press, 1991).

[15] Stanley Hoig, *The Cherokees and Their Chiefs: In the Wake of Empire* (Fayetteville: University of Arkansas Press, 1998), 125–8.

[16] Ibid., 207–8.

[17] Daniel Blake Smith, *American Betrayal: Cherokee Patriots and the Trail of TEars* (New York: Henry Holt, 2011), 177.

for Cherokees' rights in the age after removal. His most recent visit to Washington City had occurred in the year before the alliance with the Confederacy formed, and he had stayed for at least four months. During the visit, he spoke with the Secretary of the Interior and the Commissioner of Indian Affairs, attended services at a local church, and stayed in the Willard Hotel.[18] While there, he lobbied Congress and kept a close eye on national politics, such as the heated controversy surrounding the 1860 election.[19] One might go on about how well Cherokee political elites were integrated into American politics. They had lost many important legal and political battles, but they appeared to have formed strong connections across societies.

Intermediaries' Roles

If there was no structural hole between Cherokee society and Washington or Richmond, then I expect intermediaries to have played less of a role in cooperation. To show that the empirical record bears this out, I examine three moments when important alliance decisions were made in the early years of the Civil War. When describing each, I show that the four mechanisms by which intermediaries can promote cooperation were not necessary given the extended political interactions between Cherokees and whites, and specifically the interactions between Watie, Ross, and white leaders.

The first overtures toward cooperation came from the Confederate government. In the spring of 1861, months before the Battle of Bull Run, the Confederacy and the Watie faction began to make overtures toward one another. Jefferson Davis appointed Albert Pike, a former lawyer to the Indians in the region, as a commissioner to win their support for treaties.[20] Some historians credit Pike with playing the role of intermediary, closing the structural hole between Richmond and Cherokee Nation. Regular contact between Cherokees and other Confederate government agents undermines this view. In addition to Pike, other Confederate elites traveled to the region to seek the Indians' cooperation, including Brigadier General Benjamin McCulloch who commanded Confederate forces in the

---

[18] John Ross to Sarah Stapler, March 25, 1860. *Papers of Chief John Ross*, Vol. 2, 436–7. John Ross to William Ross, about June 1860. *Papers of Chief John Ross*, Vol. 2, 447–9.

[19] John Ross to Mary Ross, May 1, 1860. *Papers of Chief John Ross*, Vol. 2, 441–3.

[20] Walter Lee Brown, *A Life of Albert Pike* (Fayetteville: University of Arkansas Press, 1997); Robert Lipscomb Duncan, *Reluctant General: The Life and Times of Albert Pike* (New York: E. P. Dutton, 1961).

area. The Confederate Secretary of War was not only interested in generating support among the Cherokee. Confederate plans were much bigger, and they armed Choctaw, Chickasaw, and other Native American units.[21]

In the first few months, Ross chose a policy of neutrality. He argued that the Cherokees had signed treaties with the United States, and he was not inclined to break those treaties.[22] Why did Ross choose to remain neutral? Ross's main concern during the Civil War era was to preserve Cherokee unity. The divisions between the Watie and Ross factions risked splitting the Cherokee Nation apart. The last period of deep division, in the decade following the Trail of Tears, saw incredible violence as the Ridge and the Ross parties struggled over the responsibility for removal. Any decision to aid either side in the Civil War risked a renewal of violence, because loyalties within the Cherokee Nation were split between North and South.[23]

Unable to get Ross to form an alliance, the Confederacy sought a different strategy to form an alliance. Confederate officials were aware of divisions within the Cherokee Nation.[24] Realizing that Ross was less likely to cooperate with Confederate officials, influential figures within Arkansas who knew Watie wrote directly to him, asking him to raise a force himself. They argued that enlisting Cherokees as Confederates would serve his interests, because a Union victory would lead to the abolition of slavery.[25] Watie quickly raised a force. The primary advantage for Watie's party was that forming an early alliance with the Confederacy could shift the balance of power within the Cherokee Nation, arming Watie's forces while Ross's party clung to a tenuous neutrality.[26]

As the summer of 1861 progressed, Ross began to change his mind. By the fall, he called for a conference of Cherokees to formalize an alliance with the South. Two factors led Ross to conclude that he needed to form an alliance with the Confederacy. The primary concern was the status of Ross's faction within the Cherokee Nation. Watie's alliance with the

[21] Walker to Cooper, May 13, 1861. Edward Everett Dale and Gaston Litton, *Cherokee Cavaliers: Forty Years of Cherokee History as Told in the Correspondence of the Ridge–Watie–Boudinot Family* (Norman: University of Oklahoma Press, 1939), 104–5.

[22] John Ross, Proclamation, May 17, 1861. In *Papers of Chief John Ross, Vol. 2*, 469–70; Ross to Bean et al., May 18, 1851. In *Papers of Chief John Ross, Vol. 2*, 470–1.

[23] Confer, *The Cherokee Nation in the Civil War*, 46–8; Hoig, *The Cherokees and Their Chiefs*, 219–20.

[24] Perdue, *Slavery and the Evolution of Cherokee Society, 1540–1866*, 130–1.

[25] Wilson and Washbourne to Watie, May 18, 1861. Dale and Litton, *Cherokee Cavaliers*, 106–7.

[26] Confer, *The Cherokee Nation in the Civil War*, 54–5.

Confederacy led to dissension, because it was at odds with the Cherokees' official policy of neutrality; in addition, Watie now had armed soldiers who were able to call on the Confederacy as allies. By forming an alliance with the Confederacy and raising his own regiment, Ross could preserve Cherokee unity and reduce Watie's relative strength. The new units were to be commanded by John Drew, Ross's relative.[27] Another issue Ross raised was the fear of encirclement. In his address to the Cherokees in August, Ross concluded that the Cherokees in Indian Territory had been surrounded by the Confederacy and its Native American allies.[28] Especially in the period after the Confederate victory at Bull Run, an alliance appeared strategically necessary.

The history that follows, which is so important for Cherokee political history, is beyond the scope of this book. The crucial question this book asks is about the relationship of social structure to international cooperation. The argument in Chapter 1 is that the presence of structural holes increases opportunities for intermediaries to play a role in securing cooperation. A close analysis of the case of the Cherokees bears out that the inverse is also true: the absence of a structural hole means intermediaries are unnecessary for cooperation to occur. First, no one was needed to identify partners for cooperation. The Cherokees and the Confederacy were aware of one another and thought about alliances in the very first days of the war. Second, no one needed to explain the parties' interests to one another. Ross and Watie understood the politics of the Civil War extraordinarily well; they were also well informed about what was happening on the battlefield and in the Indian Territory. Similarly, the Confederacy knew about politics in the Cherokee Nation. As explained earlier, the Confederacy knew and corresponded frequently with Cherokee leaders and understood internal political quarrels. Moreover, there is little evidence that any intermediary played any role in building trust or mitigating cultural conflict. In short, Ross and Watie, along with their friends and families, were sufficiently plugged into the culture and politics of white society that they had no need of intermediaries to carry or make sense of messages.

---

[27] On unity, see for example John Ross, Annual Message, October 9, 1861. *Papers of Chief John Ross*, Vol. 2, 492–5. On concerns over Watie's strength, see ibid., 57.

[28] John Ross, Address to Cherokees, August 21, 1861. In *Papers of Chief John Ross*, Vol. 2, 479–81; Gary Moulton, *John Ross: Cherokee Chief* (Athens: University of Georgia Press, 1978), 171–2.

Why Were the Cherokees Different?

A critic of the argument that intermediaries matter might point to the Cherokees. If the Cherokees were important to the war effort, and Cherokees had strong social ties to political elites in Richmond, then why believe that structural holes are generally important in world politics?

The Cherokees, however, in fact underscore the central claim that brokerage and social structure are important to theories of cooperation and conflict. The Civil War, though, is the wrong time period in which to examine US–Cherokee relations to understand a structural hole's effects. Before the Civil War, structural holes were central to the politics of Cherokee removal and leadership struggles. Many historians suggest that the early nineteenth century saw a significant structural hole between Cherokee and white society; most Cherokee could not speak English, and most whites distrusted Cherokees because of racial prejudice. In the decades before the war, this structural hole created a competition over who would broker white–Cherokee relations. The Ridge Party – who profited from signing a treaty with the Federal Government – is an example. It claimed to speak on behalf of the Cherokees, using its leaders' biracialism, biculturalism, and bilingualism to make the claim that they represented the "civilized" elements of Cherokee society. The Ross Party contested the Ridge Party's role as brokers. Arguing against the treaties of dispossession, the Ross Party claimed to be better representatives – better intermediaries – between Cherokees and white society. John Ross was selected as leader of the Cherokee Nation because, in part, his status as a biracial, bilingual person provided opportunities for him to compete with the Ridge party. This competition was premised on the importance of finding a bridge to white society, and the stakes were high because whoever played the bridging role would have an outsized impact on removal.[29] By the time of the Civil War, this argument was still ongoing. The question was not whether a structural hole would be closed, but rather who would represent Cherokee society? Would cooperation form across Watie's ties to the Confederacy? Or across Ross's ties to the Union?

The Cherokee therefore show an important variation in social structures not explored in Chapter 1. Variations in social structure affect level of agency. By 1861, the structural hole was closed between white and Cherokee society. There were direct political connections between

---

[29] Confer, *The Cherokee Nation in the Civil War*; Hoig, *The Cherokees and Their Chiefs*; Moulton, *John Ross: Cherokee Chief*.

Cherokee political elites, and Richmond. This meant that intermediaries – people whose sole influence arises from their position between societies – were displaced by political elites. The alliance between the Confederacy and the Cherokee, however, underscores the power of brokerage. The ability to represent societies provides valuable forms of political power for which people fight and die.

COMPANY K

One form that cooperation took during the Civil War was the enlistment of American Indians into regiments composed primarily of white soldiers. Unlike the recruits in Kansas or Oklahoma, where American Indians were predominately surrounding by other Indian soldiers with whom they shared much in common, Indian soldiers who served alongside white units would likely have faced social isolation and prejudice. I focus on Company K of the 1st Michigan Sharpshooters. One cannot make a case that Company K, by itself, turned any battles in the east. A single company, or even a single regiment, was too small. When Company K fought in the Battle of the Wilderness (1864), for example, they were fewer than 100 men in a force that exceeded 100,000.[30] Unlike the other units discussed in this chapter, Company K was used like most other companies in the Civil War; in their case, thrown into grueling battles in Virginia. They saw the most fighting during Grant's Overland Campaign, where they fought at Wilderness, North Anna, and Spotsylvania, and then later at Petersburg.[31] Colonel Deland, who was the regimental commander, wrote of them after Petersburg, that "[i]n every action in the campaign the Indians have stood bravely up to the work and won the admiration of all." They also shared the same fate as the white companies; Deland reports they "lost 16 killed, 25 wounded and 17 missing in action."[32] Some of those missing in action were captured and sent to Andersonville, an infamous prison camp in Georgia. One can only imagine how their

[30] Gordon C. Rhea, *The Battle of the Wilderness May 5–6, 1864* (Baton Rouge: Louisiana State University Press, 2004).

[31] Field and Staff Muster Roll, 1st Michigan Sharpshooters, April 30 to August 31, 1864. Compiled Records Showing Service of Military Units in Volunteer Union Organizations, Michigan. M594, R85, RG 94, NARA. On the regiment in general, see Raymond J. Herek, *These Men Have Seen Hard Service: The First Michigan Sharpshooters in the Civil War* (Detroit: Wayne State University Press, 1998).

[32] Deland to Robertson, August 5, 1864. Regimental Letter, Order and Courts-Martial Book, 1st Michigan Sharpshooters, Vol. 3. RG 94, NARA.

skin color affected their fate in the prison camp, compared to their white peers.

Why did Native Americans in Northern Michigan choose to cooperate with the US Army in 1863?[33] Their enlistment is puzzling. Native Americans' history in Northern Michigan would not have inspired confidence in the Union. They had reached two agreements in the previous decades with the Federal government – the 1836 Treaty of Washington and the 1855 Treaty of Detroit – which promised concessions to the Anishinaabek that were never delivered.[34] In the years immediately preceding the Civil War, their land was again under threat as settlers were moving into and claiming land reserved for Anishinaabek; moreover, annuities were unpaid, the blacksmith provided by the federal government was incompetent, and the schools were underfunded.[35] If the Anishinaabek were under threat for dispossession of their land from the Union, why did they enlist in such large numbers? Understanding their participation requires, in part, understanding the importance of socially skilled intermediaries who brokered cooperation across the structural hole that divided Native American society from white society.

Structural Hole

Native Americans in Northern Michigan had few social connections to lawmakers and military officials in the region; the result was a structural hole that provided intermediaries with opportunities to broker cooperation.

One likely cause of the structural hole was linguistic differences. Many Anishinaabek could not speak English and had limited contact with white settlers. Institutional and demographic patterns were even more important. Institutionally, the federal system to administer Indian Affairs put in place an Indian Agent, who was entrusted as liaison between the Native Americans and the Federal Government. During this period, Indian

---

[33] Anishinaabek is the collective term for the Odawa, Ojibwe, and Potawatomi
[34] Matthew Fletcher, *The Eagle Returns: The Legal History of the Grand Traverse Band of Ottawa and Chippewa Indians* (East Lansing: Michigan State University Press, 2012); James M. McClurken, *Our People, Our Journey: The Little River Band of Ottawa Indians* (East Lansing: Michigan State University Press, 2009).
[35] Collective Letter to Lincoln, June 21, 1859. Letters Received, Office of Indian Affairs, 1824–1880, Mackinac Agency, 1828–1880, M235, R406, RG 75. NARA; Burns et al. to Secretary of State, March 16, 1860. Letters Received, Office of Indian Affairs, 1824–1880, Mackinac Agency, 1828–1880, M235 R406, RG 75. NARA.

Agents were often supposed to prevent direct contact between Indians and Washington; in the Mackinac Agency that administered Northern Michigan, this meant the Indian Agent, Dewitt C. Leach, was supposed to prevent Native Americans from visiting the White House.[36] This policy had the effect of funneling official communication through one specific agent – Leach – providing him with a brokerage position.

If the Indian Agent limited contact with Washington, then one would expect the Indian Agent to span the structural hole. If Leach played this bridging role, then it might undermine the argument advanced in Chapter 1 if he had strong ties to Washington. Leach was more powerful than many agents. He was a former Republican Congressman and may have had strong ties to Washington and party ties to Lincoln.[37]

Leach, however, did not broker cooperation with the US Army. The correspondence from Leach's Mackinac Agency shows no interest by Leach in recruiting soldiers for the war. Instead of enlisting Native American support, he spent more time working on other aspects of Federal Indian policy, such as the concentration of reservations.[38] One likely reason why Leach did not play this role was his views of Native Americans. Recall that one observable implication of structural holes is an intense dislike for other parties. If one does not trust another group, then it is difficult to form direct ties to secure cooperation. Leach held strongly negative views about those whom he was supposed to help.[39] Perhaps for this reason, Leach never lifted a finger to help the army's recruitment efforts.

Michigan lawmakers shared Leach's views: prejudice prevented them from considering the Ojibwas, Odawas, and Potawatomis as a potential source of recruits. In the early years of the war, the state legislature refused to allow Native Americans to join because, as the editors of

---

[36] Fitch to Greenwood, March 29, 1860. Letters Received, Office of Indian Affairs, 1824–1880, Mackinac Agency, 1828–1880, M235, R406, RG 75, NARA. Official delegations sometimes had different experiences and were encouraged to go to Washington. See Herman J. Viola, *Diplomats in Buckskin: A History of Indian Delegations in Washington City* (Bluffton, SC: Rivilo Books, 1995).

[37] Daniel Stafford Mevis, *Pioneer Recollections: Semi-Historic Side Lights on the Early Days of Lansing* (Lansing, MI: Robert Smith Printing Company, 1911), 120.

[38] Leach to Dole, October 17, 1863. No. 230. In United States Office of Indian Affairs. *Annual Report of the Commissioner of Indian Affairs, 1863* (Washington, DC: GPO, 1864), 374–80; Leach to Dole, October 7, 1864, No. 247. In United States Office of Indian Affairs. *Annual Report of the Commissioner of Indian Affairs, 1864* (Washington, DC: GPO, 1865), 444–7.

[39] Leach to Dole, October 7, 1864, No. 247. In United States Office of Indian Affairs. *Annual Report of the Commissioner of Indian Affairs, 1864* (Washington, DC: GPO, 1865), 444–7.

the Detroit *Free Press* wrote, "every man knows the system of warfare adopted by these demi-savages, and the civilized people of the northern states will hardly consent this year [1861] to become responsible for the performances of such allies."[40] As the Civil War wore on and the state needed to fill draft quotas, Michigan lifted its restrictions against Indian participation. The structural hole produced by lawmakers' and Leach's racism lingered; to recruit American Indians required some agents who knew them and could appeal to them.

Intermediaries' Roles

The structural hole between Native Americans in the north and centers of political power elsewhere created powerful opportunities to shape communication between societies. Before asking how socially skilled agents secured cooperation, we first must identify who these agents were. The intermediaries I focus on are the recruiters, especially Edwin Andress and Garrett Graveraet.[41]

Edwin Andress, who would become the Captain of Company K, was a socially skilled intermediary.[42] Andress's experience among the American Indians in Northern Michigan emerged from his experience as a trader in the region. His nephew recalls that his experience working at the store and

---

[40] In Raymond J. Herek, *These Men Have Seen Hard Service: The First Michigan Sharpshooters in the Civil War* (Detroit: Wayne State University Press, 1998), 25.

[41] Michelle Cassidy, by contrast, points to native religious and political leaders as possible cultural brokers, especially Peter Greensky, who had two sons in Company K, and Mwekewenah, who joined with some of his followers. Cassidy's account is consistent with the argument of this book. Both figures were bicultural and bilingual. Moreover, at least Mwekewenah may have recruited others from Northwestern Michigan, framing cooperation as a strategy that could help preserve land. I do not pursue this account, although its central findings fit with the argument in Chapter 1. Cassidy's account is limited to Native Americans who came from near Grand Traverse Bay and Little Traverse Bay, and therefore does not help us understand why the majority of the recruits, who came from Isabella, Saginaw, and Pentwater further south, enlisted. In addition, Cassidy's account, to some extent, is subsumed by my own because she agrees that the recruiters convinced the figures she emphasizes – Mwekewenah and the Greensky brothers – to enlist. If Cassidy is right about the influence of the recruiters, especially Graveraet whom I also emphasize, then our accounts are complementary. Michelle Cassidy, "'The More Noise They Make': Odawa and Ojibwe Encounters with American Missionaries in Northern Michigan, 1837–1871," *Michigan Historical Review* 38, no. 2 (2012): 30. Cassidy is referring explicitly to Mwekewenah, although Graveraet also recruited the Greensky brothers. See Compiled Military Service Records. Benjamin and Jacob Greensky. Co. K, 1st MI SS. RG 94, NARA.

[42] Descriptive Book, 1st Michigan Sharpshooters, Vol. 2. Book Records of Volunteer Union Organizations, RG 94, NARA.

trading with local American Indians improved his social skill: "German, French and Indian. He is reported to have talked these three different languages one after the other with his customers. He traded for furs with the Indians and added to his vocabulary of the Indian language by making a written note of every new word. It was said he had a vocabulary larger than some of the Indians themselves." In the language of Chapter 1, his experience living at the intersections of societies made him a socially skilled intermediary. He was bilingual, had experience with cross-cultural brokerage, and likely was bicultural.[43] Although Andress had a significant amount of social skill, he did not have any institutional power. He was a trader at the frontier of American settlement; unsurprisingly, there is no record of his having any political influence or close connections to political leaders in the rest of the state. Andress did have some ties to Native Americans, owing to a career trading with them, although there is no record that he knew any who were influential. In fact, family lore describes him as an interesting figure: after the war he served on a whaler before stealing a rowboat to leave the ship in the West Indies. He earned money for the return voyage by playing violin while a friend danced, as well as selling soap.[44] Andress had no strong ties to centers of political power, to say the least.

With the First Sharpshooters forming, Andress was sent to recruit among the Native Americans in the region. The way he recruited shows that strong ties did not feature in the enlistment process. He enlisted recruits from three towns, but he secured the most recruits at a July 4 festival at a reservation in Oceana County. According to county records, Andress gave a speech, followed by Pay-baw-me, which was translated by Louis Genereau.[45] Using local intermediaries appears to have been successful: more than 20 recruits signed up that day, and more joined shortly thereafter.[46] This form of recruitment – popping up and giving

---

43 J. Mace Andress, "A Bit of Spice: Pages from an Intimate Autobiography" n.d., in author's possession, being donated to Lower Traverse Bay Bands of Odawa Indians. The author is grateful to Chuck Lott for providing him with this and his correspondence with Andress' descendants, which confirms Andress' knowledge of local languages. See also Compiled Military Service Records. Edwin Andress. Co. K, 1st MI SS. RG 94, NARA; and Edwin Andress, Civil War Pension Records. 311.699, 201,283. RG 94. NARA.

44 Ibid., 4.

45 Genereau was also recruited on the same date by Andress. Compiled Military Service Records. Louis Genereau. Co. K, 1st MI SS. RG 94, NARA; and Edwin Andress, Civil War Pension Records. 311.699, 201,283. RG 94. NARA.

46 Louis M. Hartwick and William H. Tuller, *Oceana County Pioneers and Business Men of to-Day: History, Biography, Statistics and Humorous Incidents* (Pentwater News Steam Print, 1890), 45–6; Hauptman, *Between Two Fires*, 133–4.

speeches – requires one to appeal to enlistees; it does not require strong ties to them. I return to this point shortly.

Garrett Graveraet was an even better recruiter than Andress. Graveraet was a school teacher in Little Traverse Bay; his father was white and his mother was an Anishinaabe, making him culturally and linguistically fluent in both worlds. According to Laurence Hauptman, Graveraet perfectly embodied this role: "he was the perfect candidate, the cultural mediator" because "[a]s a Franco-Indian with one foot in each world, he understood both the indigenous peoples of Michigan and the non-Indians."[47] Graveraet likely had strong ties within the Native American community, but there is no record of his having any political influence in the south (and certainly not Washington); he therefore counts as an intermediary. The soldiers Graveraet recruited came from areas near his home, in Bear River, LaCroix, Little Traverse, and Northport, showing the importance of social connections for securing cooperation.[48]

Intermediaries' position between societies and their social skills were essential to brokering cooperation. The regimental leadership understood that sending white officers with no experience with American Indians would fail. This became clearest after Petersburg, when almost all the

---

[47] Hauptman, *Between Two Fires*, 129–30. See also Herek, *These Men Have Seen Hard Service*, 35–6.

[48] Descriptive Book, 1st Michigan Sharpshooters, Vol. 2. Book Records of Volunteer Union Organizations, RG 94, NARA. William Driggs, whom army records also list as a top recruiter, appears at first anomalous. He was the son of a Congressman and there is no evidence that he had any experience with Native Americans before the war. If Driggs played a fundamental role, then it may count as evidence that agents with significant institutional influence (his father) played an important role in promoting cooperation. A closer examination, however, shows there is likely more to the story. Deland had assigned William A. McClellan (about whom we know little) to Driggs to aid him in his recruitment; McClellan, who was likely not a political elite and most probably was bilingual and bicultural, appears to have done the lion share of the recruiting work. Special Order 30, June 22, 1863. Regimental Letter, Order and Courts-Martial Book, 1st Michigan Sharpshooters, Vol. 3. RG 94, NARA. First, a careful comparison of the Descriptive Muster Rolls and the original enlistment papers show that Driggs was less successful; the enlistment paperwork often credits William McClellan and not Driggs. Moreover, the only mass recruiting event that Driggs attended was on May 18 in Isabella, although almost all of the recruits were credited to William McClellan (about whom we know little). In general, Driggs' recruiting numbers were slow, and he primarily enlisted one person at a time, mostly located near his home in East Saginaw. See, for example, Compiled Military Service Records. Louis Bennett. Co. K, 1st MI SS. RG 94, NARA; and Edwin Andress, Civil War Pension Records. 311.699, 201,283, RG 94. NARA. The original enlistment paper is most likely right, in part because the Descriptive Muster Roll shows Driggs recruiting all across Michigan on the same day or on consecutive days.

officers who were bilingual had died or left the service: Andress was hurt and Graveraet died from wounds at Spotsylvania. Colonel Deland thought that filling these positions was "essential." The problem was that they needed an intermediary, or someone "who can speak indian and who has influence among them." Although Deland ordered white officers home from the regiment to recruit, he did not believe they would be successful, due to their inability to appeal to the Native Americans in Michigan, and likely also because of the structural hole between settlers in the south of the state and Native Americans in the north.[49] In short, Deland understood the problems produced by network structure and the importance of social skill for closing the hole. He also understood the fundamental role played by Andress and Graveraet in forming the initial network.

The Politics of Cooperation

Intermediaries' social skills were recognized to be important, but how did these skills translate into cooperation? The closest analysis of the limited evidence points to two of the four mechanisms – identifying parties and explaining interests – outlined in Chapter 1. This evidence, however, is limited because there are no full accounts of what intermediaries said when recruiting. First, there is strong circumstantial evidence that socially skilled recruiters played a crucial role in identifying who was willing to fight. Garrett Graveraet and William Driggs, for example, recruited in their hometowns, consistent with the idea that they may have known candidates who were willing to enlist. Moreover, Deland's statements cited earlier, where he wrote that he needed to find people who were bilingual and knew the Anishinaabe language, imply that without an intermediary, recruiting was difficult because opportunities for cooperation would be missed.

The most important role for intermediaries, however, was likely that they could appeal to the interests of the Anishinaabek. Historians who study Company K have reached different conclusions about why they fought. Eric Hemenway cites cultural norms that valorize fighting; Raymond Herek believes that Native Americans may have taken the fact that they were paid the same as white soldiers as a signal of political equality, encouraging their participation; and Hauptman and Cassidy

---

[49] Deland to Robertson, August 5, 1864. Regimental Letter, Order and Courts-Martial Book, 1st Michigan Sharpshooters, Vol. 3, RG 94, NARA.

suggest that Native Americans fought to demonstrate that their land rights should be respected.[50] Yet, everyone agrees that land may have been a decisive factor due to the threats posed to Anishinaabek during the Civil War years, especially with the reopening of treaty negotiations and the imminence of the threats they faced.

If land was a major motivating factor, then we can reach two conclusions. First, the logic of enlistment may have, in part, been to demonstrate loyalty to the Union to win leverage in future treaty negotiations. This is the conclusion that Laurence Hauptman and Michelle Cassidy reach, with the former writing, "The Ottawa and Ojibwa enlisted in the Civil War in part in hopes of gaining the trust and leverage for a new Treaty arrangement."[51] This is consistent with the only surviving snippet from a speech to Company K by Nock-ke-chick-faw-me. He began by talking about the costs of losing: "If the South conquers you will be *slaves, dogs*. There will be no protection for us; we shall be driven from our homes, our lands and the graves of our friends."[52] But, the majority of the speech talks about the importance of fighting well, not drinking, and

---

[50] Author's interview with Eric Hemenway; author's correspondence with Raymond Herek, June 17 and June 18, 2015; and Cassidy, "'The More Noise They Make'"; Hauptman, *Between Two Fires*. Another potential reason is that they enlisted for the money. Indians in Michigan were often poor, and the bounty (about $100) may have enticed them. The evidence in support of the bounty argument, however, is not overly compelling. First, the amount was likely insufficient. The economic explanation for enlistment usually highlights the incredibly large bounties that might be paid for enlisting; the bounty paid to men from Niles, Michigan who enlisted was about $1000 (between the contributions from the town, the county, and private citizens). The bounties paid to American Indians, in comparison, were quite small. On the difference in bounty payments, contrast Peter Bratt, "A Great Revolution in Feeling: The American Civil War in Niles and Grand Rapids, Michigan," *Michigan Historical Review* 31, no. 2 (2005): 58; Herek, *These Men Have Seen Hard Service*. Perhaps more importantly, funds were raised for many bounty men to support the families of soldiers; for Indians, there is no evidence that these locally raised funds (beyond pensions) were available. The economic cost for a family of losing an income would have likely outweighed the gains from enlistment. Second, the level of combat motivation exhibited by Company K is inconsistent with the economic explanation. James McPherson's analysis of the reasons for enlistment in the Civil War suggests that "bounty men" – those whose initial motivation was economic – developed a reputation for shirking combat; the logic is that if one joins for money rather than ideological convictions, then one is less likely to fight. Company K, on all accounts, had a high combat motivation in contrast to the picture McPherson paints of bounty men, suggesting that the initial motivation for enlistment may not have been financial. See James McPherson, *For Cause and Comrades: Why Men Fought in the Civil War* (Oxford: Oxford University Press, 1997), 5–13.

[51] Hauptman, *Between Two Fires: American Indians in the Civil War*, 133.

[52] In Herek, *These Men Have Seen Hard Service*, 59.

not deserting in order to influence whites' opinions of Native Americans, perhaps implying that this was an important moment to win over popular sympathy.[53]

If fighting was a strategy to gain leverage for future land deals, who decided upon this strategy? Did the Ojibwe, Odawa, and Potawatomi decide themselves to use the war as an opportunity to win support for their land rights? Or, did intermediaries frame this as an appropriate strategy?

Intermediaries most likely framed cooperation as a strategy likely to advance Indian interests. If the Anishinaabek made the decision to enlist, and intermediaries were unimportant, one would expect to see a different recruiting pattern than took place. If Native Americans independently reached that decision, then recruitment should have moved faster and been uniform. Large groups might even have volunteered, and perhaps have traveled to the army camp to enlist. Instead, recruitment records show that the opposite was the norm. Recruiters had to travel to reservations, prodding and poking men to enlist. These observations about recruiting patterns are underscored by the wider politics in the region. Intermediaries frequently engaged in misrepresentation of deals. The Mackinac Agency, which had jurisdiction over Native American affairs in the region, received many complaints about deliberate misrepresentation of parties' interests or policy positions with respect to treaty negotiations and annuity payments.[54] There are hints in the record that Andress may have misrepresented the situation and made promises for bounty and pay for services in excess of what was permitted.[55] The abuse of power by intermediaries between Native Americans and the Federal government is a critical part of the story of dispossession, including during the Lincoln

---

[53] There is also some evidence that cultural issues threatened to derail. Due to language barriers and racism in the army, Company K did not interact with other soldiers, and when they did, cultural differences led them to resist elements of the soldier's life. A soldier in Company K remarked that "they had to be handled with soft gloves," and interactions by the officers worked through a bicultural intermediary as a result. Ibid., 36–7.

[54] See, for example, Enclosures to Fitch to Mise, May 22, 1858. Letters Received, Office of Indian Affairs, 1824–1880, Mackinac Agency, 1828–1880, M235, R406, RG 75, NARA. Sometimes, there are also thanks given to Individuals who they believe represented them well. See Grand River Ottawas and Chippewas, November 23, 1858. Letters Received by the Office of Indian Affairs, 1824–1880, Mackinac Agency, 1828–1880, M235, R406, RG 75, NARA.

[55] Special Order 34, June 23, 1863. Regimental Letter, Order and Courts-Martial Book, 1st Michigan Sharpshooters, Vol. 3. RG 94, NARA.

Administration, when problems with Indian Agents became particularly sinister.[56]

The recruitment of the Anishinaabek by Andress and Graveraet demonstrates the power of betweenness. Deland, the regimental commander, felt constrained by the network structure that produced structural holes between white and Anishinaabe society. It prevented him from brokering cooperation without intermediaries to do the recruitment. Moreover, Andress and Graveraet, two institutionally unimportant agents, played a more decisive role in recruitment than did Leach, the Indian Agent, or Driggs, whose father had influence in both communities. Their social skills that allowed Andress and Graveraet to bridge the structural hole enabled them to influence cooperation in unexpected ways.

PAWNEE SCOUTS

One interesting feature of the Civil War is that the war in the east created a power vacuum in the American west as Federal soldiers were taken away from frontier posts to fight against the Confederacy in other theatres. Especially in the Great Plains, Indians hostile to the United States quickly noticed the absence of US regulars, and they began to raid more settlers and harass more trails. Unable to move significant military assets west, the United States increasingly relied on friendly Native Americans to enhance their strength, especially in the Plains.

The Cheyenne and Sioux were two of the most significant enemies the United States faced on the northern Plains. During the Civil War and the years preceding it, a long-simmering conflict escalated as white settlers, Mormons, and prospectors headed to California increased traffic over lands held by these Plains Indians. The wars that followed led to intense confrontations. The Sand Creek Massacre (1864), for example, saw a Colorado Militia kill unarmed Indians, mostly women and children. In part as a result of the massacre, conflict across the region drastically escalated, leading to wars and expeditions against the Plains Indians for more than a decade. The Battle of Little Big Horn (1876), perhaps the most famous event in these wars, showcases the intensity of the conflict: General Custer intentionally targeted Indian women and children (planning to use them as hostages) and the resulting battle saw hundreds of casualties. The level of conflict at this time

---

[56] David Nichols, *Lincoln and the Indians: Civil War Policy and Politics* (Columbia: University of Missouri Press, 1978).

in modern-day Colorado, Minnesota, Nebraska, and nearby areas was so significant that it frequently took Lincoln's attention, and sometimes Federal troops, away from the American Civil War to respond to settlers' concerns about their safety on the frontier.[57]

The dearth of Federal troops available to respond to problems on the frontier provided important opportunities for non-state allies – American Indians who would cooperate with the United States instead of fighting against it – to play an important role in campaigns in the west. The alliance between the United States and the Pawnee is one of the longest-lasting of these alliances, and it was substantively important. In the 1865 Powder River Expedition, the first company of Pawnee proved effective soldiers and scouts on an ineffective expedition. The most significant battle on the expedition was on the Tongue River, where somewhere between 35 and 63 enemy American Indians were killed; the Pawnee found those campgrounds. In addition, the Pawnee also killed 23 enemies when operating independently of the main body of troops. In short, despite being a small part of a larger command, the Pawnee outperformed the rest of the regular soldiers combined.[58] From these beginnings sprang the formation of more Pawnee units. In 1867, two companies of scouts were defending the Union Pacific Railroad. Three companies of Pawnee Scouts took to the field again in 1869 during the Republican River Expedition, where they literally led the charge at the Battle of Summit Springs. In 1873, the scouts were raised again to fight against the Sioux at the Red Cloud Agency, where they daringly snuck into the Sioux camp to drive off their horses, limiting Sioux mobility in the decisive battle of the campaign.[59]

How was cooperation between the United States Army and the Pawnee brokered? The conventional wisdom is that cooperation formed because the Pawnees and the settlers shared common enemies on the Plains, and the agent who brokered cooperation was General Curtis, who had substantial institutional authority. I demonstrate, however, that a detailed examination of the historical record shows the influence of Frank North, a clerk at the Pawnee Agency with no institutional influence but

[57] Berg, *38 Nooses*; Bruce Hampton, *Children of Grace: The Nez Perce War of 1877* (Lincoln: University of Nebraska Press, 1994); Hugh J. Reilly, *Bound to Have Blood: Frontier Newspapers and the Plains Indian Wars* (Lincoln: University of Nebraska Press, 2011).

[58] Connor to Barnes, Report of the Powder River Expedition, October 4, 1865. In David Wagner, *Patrick Connor's War: The 1865 Powder River Indian Expedition* (Norman: University of Oklahoma Press, 2010), 269–75.

[59] See Dunlay, *Wolves*, 155–63; Mark van de Logt, *War Party in Blue: Pawnee Scouts in the U.S. Army* (Norman: University of Oklahoma Press, 2010).

significant social skill. Frank North, who would later take the Pawnee on tour in Wild West Shows, helped identify the Pawnee as potential cooperation partners, recruited the Pawnees, and framed cooperation for the US Army in a way that made cooperation possible.

Structural Hole

The Pawnees who would work with the army lived in Nebraska Territory, on the Pawnee Reservation along the Loup River. Of the cases of Native Americans during the Civil War era, the Pawnee provide an instance of the greatest cultural and geographic distance between centers of power in Washington and recruits living on the Reservation, creating a structural hole.

Few interpersonal ties united Pawnees to the white world. Before moving to their reservation in 1857, the Pawnee had only limited contact with whites. No religious network bound these societies together, as was sometimes seen with other Native American and white communities. A mission to the Pawnees was established in 1834, but it was never very successful and the mission station was closed by 1846.[60] In addition, Pawnees and settlers could not speak to one another because there was no common language. The correspondence of the missionaries who lived among the Pawnee show the Pawnees' limited knowledge of English, and the even smaller number of white settlers (including the missionaries) who spoke Pawnee: one was more likely to find someone fluent in Pawnee and French than Pawnee and English.[61] No whites lived on Pawnee lands at the reservation. The reservation was founded on land formerly farmed by Mormons, but the Mormons were evicted and moved to Utah before the Pawnees arrived. Two schools were built, but attendance was low and there is no evidence these schools bridged the linguistic or cultural divide between white and Pawnee society. The Indian Agents appointed to the Pawnee were often not trusted, probably with good reason.[62]

The surrounding communities provided the Pawnees only a few social ties to the military. The first town near their land, Columbus, Nebraska

[60] John Dunbar, Journal, 1835. Richard Jensen, ed., *The Pawnee Mission Letters, 1834–1851* (Lincoln: University of Nebraska Press, 2010), 47; Dunbar to Green, June 30, 1846. Ibid., 541–5.

[61] See for example Ramney to Greene, October 2, 1846. Jensen, *The Pawnee Mission Letters, 1834–1851*, 556–8.

[62] David Wishart, *An Unspeakable Sadness : The Dispossession of the Nebraska Indians* (Lincoln: University of Nebraska Press, 1994), 174–85.

was founded in 1856 by settlers from Columbus, Ohio. The population that first year was 13 men; the entire county had only 35 settlers. Platte County's population steadily increased, but not until years after the Pawnees began to cooperate; the population reached almost 2,000 people in 1870.[63] This thin connection, between those who lived in and around Columbus and worked to navigate between the Pawnees and the new town, became the social connection between the army and the reservation. Two of these settlers from Ohio, the North brothers, became the intermediaries who helped the Pawnee join the army in the 1860s and beyond.

The North Brothers

The most significant recruitment of Pawnee Scouts occurred in 1864 and 1865.[64] How was the alliance formed and what role did intermediaries

---

[63] Nicholas Aieta, "Frontier Settlement and Community Development in Richardson, Burt, and Platte Counties, Nebraska, 1854–1870" (Dissertation, University of Nebraska, 2007), 85–6.

[64] Historians debate two earlier episodes. First, some historians cite recruitment in the year before the one I concentrate on here. See Eugene Ware, *The Indian War of 1864: Being a Fragment of the Early History of Kansas, Nebraska, Colorado, and Wyoming* (Topeka, KS: Crane and Company, 1911). Following contemporary scholarship, I believe this recruitment did not occur and thus do not focus on it here. See Thomas Dunlay, *Wolves for the Blue Soldiers: Indian Scouts and Auxiliaries with the United States Army, 1860–90* (Lincoln: University of Nebraska Press, 1982), 264; Mark van de Logt, *War Party in Blue: Pawnee Scouts in the U.S. Army* (Norman: University of Oklahoma Press, 2010), 50.

The second instance is when Pawnees cooperated with the United States military was in 1857, during the Cheyennes Expedition of 1857. On June 4, 1857, Colonel Edwin Vose Sumner recruited five Pawnee scouts, led by Ta-ra-da-ha-wa, called "Speck-in-the-Eye" by the white troops, at Fort Kearny in Nebraska Territory. Robert Peck, a Private in the First Calvary, wrote the only surviving account of the expedition that highlights the scouts. He explains that Sumner believed the Pawnees would prove useful, in part because of their "hereditary enmity for the Cheyennes." Percival Lowe, *Five Years a Dragoon ('49 to '54)* (Kansas City, MO: Franklin Hudson, 1906), 247–48. One might believe this episode is theoretically important because it credits Sumner, who had strong ties to military and political elites, with recruitment. If Sumner, an agent with strong ties to Washington, brokered cooperation with the Pawnees in 1857, then it is unlikely that an intermediary – an agent with weak ties across a structural hole – is crucial for cooperation.

I do not focus on it for three reasons. First, the Pawnee commitment was tiny (five Pawnees), and there does not appear to have been a political decision to cooperate. Second, the empirical record is too short to evaluate. The only account crediting Sumner with the idea comes from Peck, who wrote a short account forty years later. Robert Morris Peck, "Recollections of Early Times in Kansas Territory, from the Standpoint of a Regular Calvalryman," *Transactions of the Kansas State Historical Society, 1903–1904* 8 (1904): 494. Peck was not with Sumner during the recruitment episode, and his account

play in its formation? I argue that one particularly obscure person, Frank North, brokered cooperation between the Pawnees and the US military.

The origins of cooperation are related to the problems the US military faced in 1864, as violence intensified between settlers and the Arapaho, Cheyenne, Lakota, and Sioux in the region. The Platte River valley, in particular, was the site of much violence. The Sioux continued to raid settlers and travelers as well as Pawnee settlements. In August 1864, Major General Samuel Curtis led a campaign against the Sioux. He stopped at the Pawnee Indian Agency, where 70 or more Pawnees volunteered to act as scouts and guides for the army. Another two or three hundred Pawnees offered to join Curtis, but the Indian Agent, Benjamin Lushbaugh, refused because it would leave the Pawnee remaining behind undefended against more Sioux raids.[65]

Why did the Pawnee volunteer? Two explanations for US–Pawnee cooperation run counter to the argument of this book. The first argument is that cooperation was determined by structural factors. Specifically, the Pawnee and the Sioux held a deep enmity toward one another; cooperation with the United States, therefore, was a natural response by the Pawnee to Sioux attacks. Thomas Dunlay explains: "Outnumbered and losing population, the Pawnees were on the defensive; they still adroitly made off with other people's horses, but only to lose them to the Sioux. Their relations with the white were uneasy, marked by accusations of thievery and war scares, but they could not afford another enemy."[66] To

is also inaccurate with respect to other important details of Sumner's attitudes toward the Pawnee, making his account wholly unreliable. See van de Logt, *War Party*, 43–8. Third, even if the case is deviant because Sumner did the recruiting himself, it may be the exception that proves the rule. Sumner was age sixty in 1857, and would become the oldest field general during the Civil War. His first service on the frontier was in 1832, during the Black Hawk War, and he remained on the frontier for much of the period between 1832 and 1857. William Wallace Long, "A Biography of Major General Edwin Vose Sumner, U.S.A., 1797–1863" (Dissertation, University of New Mexico, 1971). During the Black Hawk War, Sumner probably relied on Indians as scouts and guides when he was a junior officer with little institutional influence, or at least was aware that others were relying on Native Americans. Hall, *Uncommon Defense* ; Louis Pelzer, *Marches of the Dragoons in the Mississippi Valley* (Iowa City: State Historical Society of Iowa, 1917). If Sumner had gained extensive experience working with Native Americans during the decades preceding 1857, then he likely had experience with cross-cultural brokerage and perhaps also some level of biculturalism, which developed in the period preceding his obtainment of positions of institutional influence. In other words, when Sumner was not politically important, serving as a junior officer on the frontier, he learned to "see" structural holes, providing a crucial source of social skill later in life.

[65] Lushbaugh, Pawnee Agency, September 30, 1864. *ARCIA*, 382–3.
[66] Dunlay, *Wolves*, 148.

make matters worse, 1864 was a particularly difficult year in the Pawnee Agency. A drought followed by pests had completely destroyed the Pawnee crop, and the Sioux attacked the Pawnees during their annual hunt, preventing them from obtaining meat.[67] Disease had also led to a sharp drop in the number of Pawnees, making defense more difficult. Cooperation with the US military might provide defense and much needed supplies. Dunlay's explanation is similar to structural explanations highlighted by realists: the Pawnee and the military needed one another, and they drew closer because of a common threat. Mark van de Logt makes this precise argument: "Scout service allowed the Pawnees, equipped with weapons supplied by the U.S. government, to exact revenge on their Sioux and Cheyenne enemies – and to be paid for it. The Pawnees were not 'duped' into fighting against people of their own race by the American government, as has sometimes been charged. They welcomed the invitation to join the United States in a military alliance against common foes."[68]

The emphasis on structural factors may explain Pawnee decision-making, but American decision-making remains puzzling. Whereas the Pawnee may have had only one option to survive, American political and military elites tended to oppose alliances with the Pawnee. As the Indian Agent who succeeded Lushbaugh explained, "Many whites who were unacquainted with the tribe, and some evil-disposed persons who had had trouble with members of the tribe, charged the Pawnees with being in League with the Sioux and other hostile Indians, who had been for some time previous committing so many depredations and atrocities on the plains."[69] Due to these anti-Pawnee views, many in the west were afraid of the Pawnee, sparking the "Pawnee War" in 1859.[70] The war, really an expedition, saw no deaths, but the fact that an expedition was raised to attack the Pawnee shows that cooperation was not inevitable. If individuals who saw the Pawnees as a menace had framed cooperation for the US military, rather than intermediaries who favored cooperation, then cooperation would likely not have occurred. Moreover, even if they realized they had a common enemy, an alliance was not inevitable. American military elites tended to discount the potential Pawnee contribution throughout the early period of cooperation, claiming the Pawnees were more trouble than they were worth. If one discounts a potential

[67] Lushbaugh, Pawnee Agency, September 30, 1864. *ARCIA*, 382–3.
[68] van de Logt, *War Party*, 241.
[69] Taylor, Pawnee Indian Agency, September 15, 1865. ARCIA, 1865, 420.
[70] A description of the terror of nearby settlers of the Pawnee during the late 1850s is in Reuben Hazen, *History of the Pawnee Indians* (Fremont Tribune, 1893), 39–49.

ally's contribution, one is unlikely to seek cooperation. To understand why an alliance formed thus requires understanding who convinced US decision-makers that cooperation with the Pawnee would serve US interests, and how they made their case.

To secure cooperation between the United States and the Pawnee required someone to frame cooperation for American decision-makers. This brings us to the second question: whose idea was it to cooperate with the Pawnee? The conventional wisdom is that the idea originated with General Samuel Curtis. If Curtis developed the plan to recruit the Pawnee, then it would cut against the central argument of this book, because Curtis had significant institutional authority. Curtis had earlier served in Congress as a Republican, led the Army of the Southwest before the Battle of Pea Ridge (1862), and was assigned to stamp out fighting in Minnesota and Dakota Territory. If the idea of cooperation began with Curtis or was precipitated by his orders, then it makes the influence of intermediaries minimal at best.

It is very unlikely, however, that Curtis had the sudden inspiration to cooperate with the Pawnee without help from intermediaries. The origins of the account crediting Curtis with the decision relate to a report by Benjamin Lushbaugh, the Indian Agent. In his 1864 report on the Pawnee Indian Agency, Lushbaugh worried that Curtis would take too many Pawnee away from the Agency, leaving the rest of the Pawnee undefended. He recommended that if Curtis wanted to recruit more Pawnee, he would need to leave a company of cavalry to replace them.[71] Historians wrongly take Lushbaugh's report as evidence that cooperation with the Pawnee was Curtis's idea. In writing the report, he is explaining why he did not agree to Curtis's request to enlist Pawnees from the reservation. Lushbaugh's report provides no broader evidence that the inspiration for cooperation came from Curtis rather than another source.

In contrast to the focus on political and military elites, this chapter advances the argument that an intermediary – specifically Frank North – likely suggested the idea to Curtis. Frank North is an ideal-typical intermediary. North's father moved to Iowa and then Nebraska in 1855; Frank followed in 1856 when he was about 16 years old. Frank had little institutional influence. He settled in Columbus, then a new town, and started a farm; his older brother James ran a ferry across the Loup River. In 1860, when Frank was 20, he took a job as a clerk at the Genoa Indian Reservation, where he learned the Pawnee language and customs. His

[71] Lushbaugh, Pawnee Agency, September 30, 1864. *ARCIA*, 382–3.

younger brother Luther, who would later also serve in the scouts, briefly joined the military.[72] On North's family's account, "It was at the suggestion of Frank North that General Curtis, when he was sent to Nebraska to suppress insurrection by the Sioux and Cheyenne Indians, employ Pawnee Indians as scouts."[73]

Frank North position between communities helped make him socially skilled. When working at the Pawnee Agency, he became fluent in Pawnee and would become the key source for academic work on the Pawnee language. He was also bicultural. As described later, Frank and Luther adopted Pawnee customs and habits with ease when they fought alongside them. In addition, as a clerk on the reservation as well as living within the community, Frank North likely learned how to cut deals between whites and the Pawnee in order to survive and prosper.[74] The depth of Frank North's social skill is related in more detail in the next section of this chapter.

Frank North was likely the source of inspiration for cooperation. In 1864, the trader at the Pawnee Agency sent Frank to accompany Federal troops to Fort Kearny. During the trip, General Curtis "took a fancy" to Frank, learning about his close relationship to the Pawnee. During this trip, a weak tie formed between North and Curtis. This is not as far-fetched as it may sound. Travel across the plains by horse was slow – horses usually walked at about three miles an hour. The more than 100-mile trip would have provided them a good opportunity to become acquainted. During the trip, Curtis and North discussed raising a force of Pawnees. North returned to the Pawnee Agency and recruited another white man – McFadden, who was bilingual and had some military experience – to help.[75] By all accounts, the actual work of identifying and recruiting the Pawnee was left to North. After they left for Fort Kearney, the Pawnee, led by McFadden and North, were deployed as vedettes to screen the army's advance.[76]

A couple of days after reaching Fort Kearney, Curtis left the main body of troops and traveled with Frank North, two Pawnees, and a company

---

[72] Luther North, Company K, Second Nebraska Cavalry, Compiled Military Service Record, RG 94, NARA.

[73] Untitled Historical Sketch of Family. Box 1, Folder 1, Series 4, RG 232 (Luther Hedden North Papers), Nebraska State Historical Society.

[74] George Bird Grinnell, *Two Great Scouts and Their Pawnee Battalion* (Lincoln: University of Nebraska Press, 1973), 18.

[75] Grinnell, *Two Great Scouts and Their Pawnee Battalion*, 71.

[76] Curtis, Orders, September 2, 1864. *United States War Department. The War of the Rebellion: a Compilation of the Official Records of the Union and Confederate Armies*. Serial 85, Ch. 53, 36,

of cavalry to Fort Riley, Kansas. This trip was much longer, as it required them to cross more than 200 miles of prairie. During this trip, Curtis and North discussed the prospects of raising a company of Pawnees.[77] It was probably during these conversations on the trip to Fort Riley, if the North family's history is accurate, that North raised the idea of forming a company. North returned to Columbus with permission to raise a company of scouts. In late 1864 and early 1865, he enlisted 91 men to form the first company of Pawnee Scouts, to be led by North.[78]

North was essential to identifying and recruiting the Pawnee as cooperation partners. Curtis had no experience working with the Pawnee, did not know the language, and probably did not have the idea before two long marches with North. North, who was socially skilled – he was bicultural and bilingual – could shape Curtis's understanding of the contribution the Pawnee might make to the army. In short, the weak tie that formed between Curtis and North was the tie across which information flowed to build cooperation between the United States and the Pawnee. Moreover, if an agent other than North had represented the Pawnee Agency, especially one of the "evil-disposed" agents who thought the Pawnee were enemies who hung around Columbus, cooperation would likely not have occurred. Such an agent would likely have presented the Pawnee as a threat rather than a potential ally.

Framing Cooperation

While the conventional wisdom does not give Frank North the credit for the recruitment of the Pawnee Scouts, it does highlight his importance for ensuring an effective alliance was not disrupted by racism and mistrust. Technically, this is beyond the purview of this book; I am interested in where cooperation comes from rather than why it persists. But, a brief discussion is warranted because it shows how and why social skill is necessary to manage intercultural cooperation.

From the beginning, the Pawnee faced two important challenges in cooperating with American forces. The first challenge was racism amongst the US military and society at large. Many soldiers who would serve with the Pawnee found them "barbaric, offensive, and annoying."[79]

---

[77] Luther North. "The Pawnee Battalion." January 21, 1922. Folder 1, Box 1, Series 2, RG 232 (Luther Hedden North Papers), Nebraska State Historical Society.

[78] Descriptive Book, Pawnee Indian Scouts (Nebraska). Vol. 1. Book Records of Volunteer Union Organizations. RG 94, NARA.

[79] van de Logt, *War Party*, 55.

The extent of this racism is evidenced by the orders given by the leader of the first expedition with a Pawnee Company in 1865: "You will not receive overtures of peace or submission from Indians, but will attack and kill every male Indian over twelve years of age."[80] These sentiments reflect government policies beyond the US Army. At the Mulberry Creek Massacre in 1869, nine former Pawnee Scouts were killed by Federal troops. When the identity of the Pawnee was discovered, the five survivors were allowed to bury the dead and return home. After the survivors left, an officer acting on orders from the Surgeon General's office, dug up the graves and removed their heads. After boiling the flesh off their heads, he sent the skulls back to the Army Medical Museum; the skulls later found their way to the Smithsonian. It is worth noting that despite a long campaign to have the remains returned, the Smithsonian did not agree to let the Pawnee bury the remains until 1995.[81]

A related but more specific threat to cooperation was the difference between Pawnee and American (really European) norms related to warfare. The Pawnee culture had norms of warfare that were explicitly barred by the US military. For example, for the Pawnee, torture, scalping, horse stealing, and other kinds of Plains Indians norms were socially meaningful. These practices were taboo for many regular officers. Conversely, the norms of the US Army, in particular those related to drilling and marching, were perceived as necessary elements of military life by army officers, but made little to no sense for the Pawnee.

Given these stark challenges, Frank North had a hard time securing continued cooperation. North, however, had enough social skill that he could appeal to the Pawnee while identifying threats to cooperation. According to Mark Van de Logt, who has written the most comprehensive account of the scouts, rather than trying to "change" the Pawnee, he and his brother Luther adopted their customs, effectively becoming leaders of a Pawnee war party attached to the army. When the first Pawnee arrived at Fort Kearny in 1865, for example, the commander required the Pawnee to be drilled in the army's manual. After more than a week of trying, North interceded and ended the exercise. The Pawnee language had no words to describe the maneuvers they were to undertake, and the Pawnees likely could not understand the utility of the exercises.[82]

---

[80] Ibid., 64.

[81] James Riding In, "Six Pawnee Crania: Historical and Contemporary Issues Associated with the Massacre and Decapitation of Pawnee Indians in 1869," *American Indian Culture and Research Journal* 16, no. 2 (1992): 101–19.

[82] van de Logt, *War Party*, 59.

Perhaps learning from this experience, North did not require the Pawnees to adopt western norms for warfare, and he continually interceded to ensure they could practice their own traditions. He let them fight without uniforms, allowed them to focus on first driving off horse herds rather than engaging combatants, sang at their celebrations (including scalp dances), distributed spoils and engaged in Pawnee gift exchange, sang their death song, allowed them to carry their medicine bundles, and he let them say their prayers and wear their face paint.[83] North sometimes wrapped a red scarf around his head and put on war paint before leading the Pawnee into the field. The Pawnee named him Pani Leshar, which means Pawnee Chief.[84]

In sum, the structural hole between the Pawnee and the military provided opportunities for Frank North to promote cooperation. He used his position between Pawnee and white society, and his social skill, to ward off threats to cooperation. His continued intervention ensured that Pawnee customs and traditions were respected, preventing cultural conflict from ruining cooperation.

LUMBEE GUIDES

The most difficult aspects of cooperation to study during the Civil War are the informal and transitory episodes of cooperation between American Indians and the Northern and Southern armies. As the armies moved through the South, American Indians approached them to act as guides and scouts. In most of these cases, there are few records left behind to make any judgments about who these people were and why they helped. In this chapter, I focus on the Lumbee who cooperated with Sherman's Army in 1865, where a historical record fortunately exists.

In 1864, William Tecumseh Sherman, commanding a Union army, completed his (in)famous March to the Sea. In the winter, he and Ulysses S. Grant decided that Sherman would continue to demoralize the South by marching through the Carolinas. In January, Sherman traveled north, inaugurating the Carolinas Campaign. After crossing into North Carolina in March, the spring rains began to fall. Sherman's troops found the roads were impassable and the Lumbee River and its surrounding

[83] Ibid., 244–5.
[84] Ibid., 66.

swamps were treacherous to cross.[85] Sherman wanted to make haste, to prevent the Confederate commander, Joe Johnston, from concentrating forces.[86] To speed his army through such awful conditions, Sherman relied on Lumbees to help guide his forces through the area and find places to forage for supplies.

To understand cooperation between the Lumbee and Sherman's army requires a bit of background. In 1864, many Lumbee lived in and around Scuffletown, North Carolina (modern-day Pembroke). Their relationship with the Confederacy, especially the local Confederate Home Guard, had become increasingly strained. Historically, the Lumbee had been considered a free people of color, able to vote and serve in the military (e.g., in the War of 1812). Since the 1820s, however, North Carolina law began to restrict the rights of people of color, removing their right to vote and restricting gun ownership and ability to serve in the militia. The Lumbee also increasingly became the target of predatory land claims. Local whites would tie a mule up on Lumbee property or put a hog in a Lumbee smokehouse, and then bring over the local sheriff. The Lumbee would be forced to sell part of his property to avoid jail time. The restriction on Lumbee rights became acute in 1861, when many were conscripted to work at Fort Fischer alongside freed blacks and slaves. Not only were the work conditions abysmal, many Lumbee interpreted this as eliminating their status as free persons, and they began to hide (or "lie out") in the swamps in and around Robeson County to avoid predatory white behavior.[87]

In late 1864 and early 1865, tensions between the Confederate Home Guard and the Lumbee Indians escalated. Around December 1864, James Barnes came by the farm of Allan Lowery, claiming that Allan's sons had stolen a hog (in the tradition of "tied-mule" stories, this may have been a way to force Allan to sell his land). Allan's son, Henry Berry

---

[85] John Barrett, *Sherman's March Through the Carolinas* (Chapel Hill: University of North Carolina Press, 1956), 123–5; William T. Sherman, *Memoirs of General W.T. Sherman* (New York: Jenkins and McCowan, 1890), 293–94.

[86] Sherman to Terry, March 12, 1865. In Brooks Simpson and Jean Berlin, eds., *Sherman's Civil War: Selected Correspondence of William T. Sherman, 1860–1865* (Chapel Hill: University of North Carolina Press, 1999), 826.

[87] Karen Blu, *The Lumbee Problem: The Making of an American Indian People* (Cambridge: Cambridge University Press, 1980), 45–65; Malinda Maynor Lowery, *Lumbee Indians in the Jim Crow South: Race, Identity, and the Making of a Nation* (Chapel Hill: University of North Carolina Press, 2010), 14–15; Gerald M. Sider, *Lumbee Indian Histories: Race, Ethnicity, and the Indian Identity in the Souther United States* (Cambridge: Cambridge University Press, 1993), 158–61.

Lowery, along with a group of friends and relatives, tracked down and shot Barnes. The Lowery band (named after Henry Berry) then killed a particularly cruel Confederate conscription agent, known to force Lumbee men to work at Fort Fisher and for assaulting Lumbee women. The Lowery band also began to raid the plantations of rich, slave-owning whites and distributed the gains to the poor in Robeson County. To stop the raids, the Confederate Home Guard went to the Lowery farm, less than a week before Sherman arrived, and shot Henry Berry's father Allan and his brother William. After Sherman left, a local "war" broke out. The most interesting aspects of the story of Henry Berry's resistance to the Confederate Home Guard, and later the Klu Klux Klan – including his escapes from jail, how he became a Lumbee Robin Hood figure, and what his legacy has meant for Lumbee attitudes toward social justice – unfortunately occurred after the specific episode of cooperation of interest, and thus are only tangentially related to cooperation with Sherman's army, so I must leave them aside.[88]

Structural Hole

Against this background, we can focus on the politics of cooperation between the Lumbee Indians and Sherman's army. The specific episode of cooperation that I am interested in is the provision of guides and scouts by the Lumbee to Sherman's army in 1865. There was a clear structural hole between the Lumbee and the Union army, although for different reasons than those described elsewhere in this book. Unlike other American Indians described in this chapter, no linguistic or cultural barriers separated the army and the Indians. The only language the Lumbee spoke was English, and they were intimately familiar with white culture. Moreover, the Lumbee were integrated in many ways into the community in North Carolina. They were not confined to a reservation on the frontier, but lived in a region with many whites, at the intersection of major railroad lines on which they traveled.[89] From the Lumbee perspective, the problem was not too little contact with Southern society but too much.

---

[88] In general, see Anonymous Manuscript, p. 1. Folder 5, Wishart Family Papers, circa 1830–1999, Southern Historical Collection, The Wilson Library, University of North Carolina at Chapel Hill; William McKee Evans, *To Die Game: The Story of the Lowry Band, Indian Guerrillas of Reconstruction* (Baton Rouge: Louisiana State University Press, 1971).

[89] Blu, *The Lumbee Problem*, 39–45.

The Lumbee had no social relationships with the Union army because they were behind enemy lines; not because of linguistic or cultural problems. The circumstances of Sherman's advance likely prevented close social contacts. First, Sherman's army was a northern army and likely had few social connections in the south, especially to persons of color in North Carolina. Moreover, the army did not stay in the region for long, and it had not marched through the area before. Moving north from Savannah, it did not linger longer than necessary in the region where the Lumbee lived.[90] The only delay was caused by rain. No direct social connections were present that would have made the Union aware of the Lumbee, and there were certainly no strong ties between the Officer Corps and Lumbee political leaders in and around Scuffletown.

Escaped Prisoners and the Politics of Cooperation

Why did the Lumbee Indians guide Sherman's army through the swamps surrounding Robeson County? One potential explanation for cooperation is that a harmony of interests drove cooperation. Given the precarious position of the Lumbee in North Carolina, they naturally sympathized with the Union.[91] If the balance of power drove alliance behavior – if local threats from the Home Guard were sufficient to force the Lumbee to ally with Sherman – then intermediaries played little role.

Structure alone, however, is insufficient to explain cooperation. Although Lumbees sympathized with the Union, they were likely wary of cooperation. The costs of collaboration were excessively high. It was likely common knowledge that Sherman's army was not planning on staying. As a result, collaborators had no protection. Hector Oxendine, who helped guide the army, was shot for collaboration, proving that these costs were not hypothetical.[92] Cooperation was not necessarily in the Lumbees' self-interest. Moreover, if the Lumbee Indians had heard anything about the army, it was likely about the devastation left in the wake of Sherman's advance. Sherman's army did not just take food and

---

[90] The army crossed the Peedee, south of the Lumber River, on March 6, and was in Fayetteville by March 12. Therefore, the army would have been traveling through the general region for six days at most, but likely only three days in the area near the Lumbee. On Sherman's account of their progress, see Sherman, *Memoirs of General W.T. Sherman*, 292–95.

[91] Author interview with Alex Baker, Public Relations Manager with the Lumbee Tribe concerning their oral tradition, May 31, 2011.

[92] Author interview. Malinda Maynor Lowery, July 1, 2015.

supplies from white property-owners, but also from the poor who lived in the region, including slaves and freedman alike.[93]

If cooperating with Sherman required prodding, then whose idea was cooperation? Escaped Union prisoners of war helped Lumbees decide to cooperate. Contemporary accounts describe escaped Union prisoners who were in the swamps with the Lowery band. Where did they come from? In 1864, as Sherman's army approached Georgia, the Confederates hurried to move its prisoners out of the infamous Andersonville Prison to camps around the south. One of these camps was the Florence Stockade in South Carolina. The prisoners probably escaped when the prison first opened in September 1864, making their way across the border into North Carolina. They settled in the swamps near Scuffletown, where the Lowery band was lying out.[94]

These escaped Union prisoners only had weak ties to centers of political power. The prisoners had, at best, weak ties to Sherman's army; they were likely not high-ranking officers and probably had never been with Sherman. They also had weak ties to the Lumbees who guided Sherman. While they may have had strong ties to Henry Berry – living in the swamps and fighting together may have produced strong, affective ties – by oral tradition, Henry Berry and his band did not help Sherman directly. Instead, relations of the band helped. Hector Oxendine, the only person we can identify positively as a guide, had two cousins in the Lowry band. Through his cousins, Hector Oxendine would have known the prisoners, although likely not as well as Henry Berry and others who were in hiding with them.[95]

These escaped prisoners likely shaped Lumbee views. The conventional wisdom among those who hunted the Lowery band was that the Union prisoners helped shape Lumbee attitudes toward the Union, providing the Lumbee with an interest in Union success. In an anonymous manuscript on the origins of the Lowry band, the author describes the Lumbee as supporters of the Confederacy until the Union prisoners arrived: "The

---

[93] Jacqueline Glass Campbell, *When Sherman Marched North from the Sea: Resistance on the Confederate Home Front* (Chapel Hill: University of North Carolina Press, 2003).

[94] Mary Lowry Deposition, May 28, 1867; Thompson Deposition, May 27, 1865. Letters Received, Second Military District, 1867–1868, Box 9, RG 393, NARA. See more generally Lorien Foote, *The Yankee Plague: Escaped Union Prisoners and the Collapse of the Confederacy*, Escaped Union Prisoners and the Collapse of the Confederacy (Chapel Hill: University of North Carolina Press, 2016).

[95] On the oral tradition not linking the Lowery band directly to guiding Sherman, author interview. Malinda Maynor Lowery, July 1, 2015.

escaped prisoners, by talking and reading to them used their best efforts to turn their friendship towards the General (U S) government. They were successful in ingratiating themselves with the Scuffletonians."[96] The timing of Lowery resistance adds credibility to this view. The Lowery band became increasingly violent beginning in December 1864; the Union prisoners, if they escaped from the Florence Stockade, could not have arrived until early October at the earliest, placing them in Robeson just weeks before the Lowery Band began to actively resist the Homeguard.[97] The timing is perfectly consistent with an emphasis on their role: shortly after the prisoners arrive, Henry Berry and his men begin raiding white plantations, and a few months later their families are guiding Sherman through the swamps.

There is strong evidence that the escaped prisoners used their position between the Lumbee and Sherman's army to secure cooperation. The prisoners, first, may have framed cooperation as if it was in the Lumbees' interests. If the anonymous manuscript is accurate, then the prisoners likely explained that the Union's advance would help defeat the Confederacy in the larger war, and with it, the local Confederate power base that abused Lumbees.[98] Moreover, the prisoners may have been the

---

[96] Anonymous manuscript, p. 1. Folder 5, Wishart Family Papers, circa 1830–1999, Southern Historical Collection, The Wilson Library, University of North Carolina at Chapel Hill. The account in the manuscript should be read with caution. On the author's account, the Lumbee had supported the Confederacy, trying to enlist in the army, but were unable to do so. Feeling dejected, the Union prisoners capitalized on their feelings to win their support. The warm Lumbee feelings for the Home Guard are inaccurate. It does not follow, however, that the author is wrong about the prisoners' influence. The escaped prisoners may have been instrumental in turning a strategy of quiet resistance into one of open collaboration with the North.

[97] I surmise the period of late September to early October as the earliest, because the first prisoners did not enter the Florence Stockade until September 15. Assuming that the prisoners were part of this attempt or those that occurred on the following three days, they would have needed to travel more than 50 miles over several significant rivers while evading capture. This would place them in the swamps near Scuffletown in October. On the opening of Florence, see Paul G. Avery and Patrick H. Garrow, "Life and Death at the Florence Stockade, American Civil War, Prisoner of War Camp, South Carolina," in *Prisoners of War: Archaeology, Memory, and Heritage of 19th- and 20th-Century Mass Internment*, ed. Harold Mytum and Gilly Carr (New York: Springer, 2013), 41–58. On how slow traveling was after escape, see Luther Dickey, *History of the 103d Regiment, Pennsylvania Veteran Volunteer Infantry, 1861–1865* (Chicago: L.S. Dickey, 1910), 110–11.

[98] Anonymous Manuscript, p. 1. Folder 5, Wishart Family Papers, circa 1830–1999, Southern Historical Collection, The Wilson Library, University of North Carolina at Chapel Hill. Another plausible reason, not treated in the literature or the oral tradition, is that the Lumbee who acted as guides volunteered to guide Sherman's men to white plantations to steer them away from Lumbee property, a strategy that may have been

agents who put the Lumbee into direct contact with the Sherman's forces. Lorien Foote's history of escaped Union prisoners explains that a primary goal was to establish contact with Sherman's army.[99] When Sherman approached Scuffletown, the escaped union prisoners likely approached the army in order to escape the South. This would provide an opportunity for the Lumbee to become guides for Sherman's men. For a guide to approach and work with Sherman's army, they likely had a person familiar with the military to help them make it safely through Sherman's pickets and to vouch for their reliability. This process of closing a structural hole by identifying partners for cooperation and putting them into contact with one another is essential to cooperation.

In sum, the limits of the historical record, and the recollections in the Lumbee oral tradition, are insufficiently precise to know *how* the prisoners framed cooperation. But, the historical record shows that a Lumbee uprising and cooperation with the Union occurred at the same time that a set of intermediaries moved into the neighboring swamps, and the conventional wisdom among some is that these intermediaries played a role, although it is unclear exactly how. The politics of local cooperation in Robeson County in 1865 is therefore consistent with the argument of Chapter 1. Agents with weak ties across a structural hole likely helped engineer informal cooperation, helping Sherman's advance.

CONCLUSION

During the American Civil War, a significant source of manpower came from Native American communities, stretching from the far north to the Deep South, and from the frontier to well-settled eastern communities. Historians have long sought to understand and document Native Americans' role in the war. Yet, this book is one of the first to take seriously their participation in the war in order to understand larger lessons for international politics.

One reason why IR scholars may not have studied Native Americans is the inability of existing theories to take intermediaries seriously. Over the past few decades, American Indian scholars have placed the "culture broker" at the center of their work. These figures, who navigate between societies, often drastically affect politics, especially on the frontier. White

---

suggested to them by the prisoners. This strategy would make sense if the Lumbee had heard of the effects of Sherman's army on communities in Georgia.
[99] Foote, *Yankee Plague*, chap. 6.

and Indian societies respond to one another in ways that are mediated by the individuals who help them to make sense of one another. IR scholars can learn from these ideas. Politics on the frontier were closely tied to personal connections; to cooperate requires trust and a common cultural framework that makes cooperation meaningful. Intermediaries spent significant time cultivating this trust, such that they could bridge the structural hole between white and Indian society. In doing so, they provided the social cement that encouraged cooperation. The same patterns exhibited overseas are evident at home.

IR scholars have avoided the politics of agency partly because they limit their attention to a relatively small slice of international politics. By any reasonable method of counting, most of American military history is a history of wars against American Indians. Yet, IR scholars interested in American foreign policy spend less time assessing the Indian Wars than they do minor Cold War crises with no practical significance. As a result, the way we explain American foreign policy to students and policymakers is presentist and limited. A close look at some syllabi in undergraduate course work on American foreign policy shows zero readings that make more than casual mention of the longest, most intense period of warring in American history.

The discounting of American Indian history has practical consequences. The history of the wars against American Indians were the primary means by which the United States developed a continental empire. They also furnished the formative experiences that would affect the United States military and political elites as they began to expand overseas. The same personnel who fought against Geronimo, for example, fought in Cuba and the Philippines. Simply put, one cannot understand how the United States began to transition to an international power in the early twentieth century without understanding the political experiences of political and military elites in the preceding decades; and to understand those experiences requires making American Indian Studies – and the conceptual vocabulary of brokerage, frontiers, and borderlands – more central to our understanding of international politics.

5

Pigs and Papists

The American annexation of Samoa in 1900 was a crucial development in the history of American foreign policy. At first glance, Samoa does not seem so important. Samoa was never economically or strategically important. The islands are small and had a small population with a tiny economy. The only strategically important part of the islands – Pago Pago harbor – was undeveloped and unfunded; the United States declined to annex it in the 1880s when Germany tried to trade it for other Samoan islands. Despite these low stakes, the United States became involved in a rivalry, sometimes intense, to contain growing German influence on the islands. On at least two occasions, war rumors reached the front page of American newspapers, sparking international conferences to manage the risks of war. The final crisis was dangerous enough that Germany drew up its first plans to attack the United States. The interesting features of the Samoan tangle, then, concern why the United States got dragged into three conflicts, two involving Germany, when no one cared.

The conventional story of great power entanglements over Samoa focuses on the drama of colonial powers, brought into competition over the few remaining regions left for colonization. Paul Kennedy's *Samoan Tangle*, for example, concentrates on great power behavior at the several international conferences dedicated to Samoa as a window into understanding the origins of broader conflicts, such as the rise of Anglo-German tensions. Other diplomatic historians are interested in Samoa because it affords an excellent lens to consider American attitudes toward imperialism in the forgotten decades of the 1870s and 1880s.[1]

[1] Paul M. Kennedy, *The Samoan Tangle: A Study in Anglo-German-American Relations,*

Conversely, scholarship emphasizing Samoan perspectives, usually by anthropologists, tries to understand what western intervention meant for political, economic, and social change on the islands.[2] These studies are important. The conventional wisdom regarding US imperialism is that it emerged in the 1890s, around the Spanish–American War and the Boxer Rebellion, and quickly faded by 1914. The case of Samoa, however, shows that imperialists in the US Senate and within the State Department were aggressively and successfully pushing for American expansion three decades earlier. As John Bassett Moore, an early political scientist who was in the State Department for much of these crises, remarked, "The significance of the Samoan incident lies not in the mere division of territory, but in the disposition shown by the United States long before the acquisition of the Philippines, to go to any length in asserting a claim to take part in the determination of the fate of a group of islands, thousands of miles away, in which American commercial interests were so slight as to be scarcely appreciable."[3]

The central contention of this chapter is that focusing on the great power drama misreads the history of this dramatic episode in the development of American foreign policy. I concentrate on US alliances with Samoans. Over three decades, the United States military or political agents formed alliances with rebel groups on the islands on at least three different occasions. These alliances are puzzling, in part, because the United States frequently shifted who it was allied with, as well as the degree to which it was willing to use force to support its allies.

To understand these shifting alliances requires understanding the influence of the western agents who navigated between the United States and Samoa. These agents – an adventurer, a dishonest plantation owner, and a missionary – manipulated the United States into active support, and even war, for Samoans' interests. These intermediaries used the power derived from betweenness to drive the politics of military entanglement and later annexation.

1878–1900 (St. Lucius: Irish University Press, 1974); Sylvia Masterman, *The Origins of International Rivalry in Samoa, 1845–1884* (G. Allen & Unwin, 1934); George Herbert Ryden, *The Foreign Policy of the United States in Relation to Samoa* (New Haven: Yale University Press, 1928).

[2] J.W. Davidson, *Samoa Mo Samoa: The Emergence of the Independent State of Western Samoa* (Melbourne: Oxford University Press, 1967). One work that moves back and forth well between perspectives is R.P. Gilson, *Samoa 1830 to 1900: The Politics of a Multicultural Community* (Melbourne: Oxford University Press, 1970).

[3] John Bassett Moore, *Four Phases of American Development: Federalism-Democracy-Imperialism-Expansion* (Baltimore: Johns Hopkins Press, 1912), 190.

Focusing on Samoa is important. In the context of this book, Samoa provides a "most likely" case for a theory of intermediaries. Only a very small number of American agents were in Samoa during the three crises in the late nineteenth century. Therefore, examining the politics of US entanglement in Samoa enables one to understand how agents exploit structural holes in an almost perfect setting. In this sense, Samoa is also a helpful case because of its paired contrast with the Philippines, explored in Chapter 7. During the Philippine–American War, the site of institutional authority moved from Washington to Manila as tens of thousands of American soldiers and many political and military elites began the occupation in 1899. In terms of late nineteenth-century American foreign policy, the conflicts in Samoa and the Philippines are thus on opposite ends of the spectrum, as Samoa was such a low priority and the number of agents involved was so small.

Studying Samoa also raises an important methodological point, more thoroughly explored in book's conclusion. Even though Samoa is a most likely case for a theory of the role of intermediaries, their influence is not obvious. The conventional wisdom in fact gives intermediaries little role. Paul Kennedy, a historian who focuses on power and great power politics, explores Samoa through the lens of political elites in the great powers, telling the story of the Samoan intervention without giving a significant causal role to intermediaries. His work, as well as others, begins with the papers of high-level political elites and focuses on great power conferences.

This book pursues a different approach. I focus on what was happening between societies, beginning with missionary records and consular correspondence, for example. This bottom-up view emphasizes the historical record from the perspectives of those with lived experiences of it. It shows how mistaken histories that only emphasize the elites in great powers may be. Intermediaries –agents living between societies – framed the great powers' interests for those living in far-off cities such that wars and alliances reflected intermediaries' interests rather than national interests. To understand why alliances formed and wars broke out, one must begin by looking at those at the intersections of societies who manipulated others into doing what they would not have otherwise done. The importance of this more comprehensive perspective is described more fully in the conclusion.

The discussion of Samoa has four parts. The first part characterizes the structural hole that existed between Samoa and Washington, showing that information flowing across the Pacific was limited and provided opportunities for intermediaries to exert influence. The remaining three parts concentrate on US cooperation with Samoans during three periods: 1875, 1888–1889, and 1898–1899. In each part, I identify the location of decision-making, showing that agents capitalized on their position between societies to broker cooperation.

STRUCTURAL HOLES

In the nineteenth century, few links existed between Samoa and Washington, forming a structural hole. The first observable implication of a structural hole is a lack of awareness; during much of the nineteenth century, few American decision-makers knew much about Samoa because there were few Americans in Samoa who could intelligently report on conditions on the ground. Most foreign residents established themselves at Apia Bay, in the community known as "the Beach." The first Europeans to arrive were deserters, escaped prisoners, and survivors of shipwrecks, collectively known as beachcombers.[4] They were followed in the 1850s by the London Missionary Society, which had established a small presence in Samoa; next came the American, British, and German consuls, who were primarily tasked during the early years with helping ships find provisions. In sum, there were about fifty foreign residents. By 1880, the Beach grew, although not by much. The 1880 Municipal Census found 176 foreign male residents; the largest foreign presence, however, was from Niue, another Pacific island, and they were likely indentured laborers living on German plantations.[5] Missionaries lived and traveled throughout Samoa, especially as part of the London Missionary Society, but the numbers of westerners preaching in Samoa always remained small.[6]

What the community lacked in size, it made up for in intrigue. After a visit in 1856, the captain of the USS *Independence* described the Beach as "the most immoral and dissolute Foreigners that ever disgraced humanity, principally composed of Americans and Englishmen, several of whom had been Sidney [sic] convicts," where "anarchy, riot, debauchery which render life and property insecure."[7] Robert Louis Stevenson, author of *Treasure Island* and *The Strange Case of Dr. Jekyll and Mr. Hyde*,

---

[4] Lelani Leafaitulagi Grace Burgoyne, "Re-Defining 'The Beach': The Municipality of Apia, 1879–1900" (Dissertation, University of Auckland, 2006), 8.

[5] Ibid., 8–9.

[6] Gilson, *Samoa 1830 to 1900*, 98–9.

[7] In ibid., 180.

FIGURE 5.1 View of Main Street, Apia, Samoa, ca. 1897. Courtesy of Council for World Mission archive, SOAS Library

retired to Samoa. Describing the Beach as he found it in the 1890s (see Figure 5.1), he wrote: "Here, then, is a singular state of affairs: all the money, luxury, and business of the kingdom is centered in one place; that place excepted from the native government and administered by whites for whites; and the whites themselves holding it not in common but in hostile camps, so that it lies between them like a bone between two dogs, each growling, each clutching his own end."[8]

Even worse than western merchants were the strange and petty group of figures that occupied consular positions. The first regularly appointed American commercial agent arrived in 1853. He was almost immediately replaced the following year by a second agent who was convinced he could make his "pile" in Samoa by seizing and auctioning off US merchant ships found unfit; of course, he found as many were unfit as might line his pockets. This agent was replaced in 1856 by a third, who sequestered his predecessor's property and tried him in absentia for his conduct.

[8] Robert Louis Stevenson, *A Footnote to History: Eight Years of Trouble in Samoa* (New York: Charles Scribner's Sons, 1892).

The third agent was then dismissed and briefly imprisoned in the United States over the affair.[9] Unsurprisingly, the State Department characterized the information it received about Samoa as "scanty," providing evidence that decision-makers in Washington reflexively understood they had no direct, strong ties to the islands.[10]

A second observable implication of a structural hole is a poor communications network, making direct contact between decision-makers costly and difficult. Samoa was far removed from normal shipping routes. Few ships visited the islands, and the telegraph was far away. This remoteness had practical consequences for communications with the eastern seaboard of the United States. The first American consul was appointed in 1841 by a passing captain, but he did not receive his official commission for seven years.[11] No US navy ships visited during those years, and he often had to wait three years for dispatches to arrive from Washington.[12] The situation improved over time, but not remarkably. When Steinberger arrived in the islands in the early 1870s, described at length in the next section, the US Consul had already waited two years to receive his commission, and he was forced to travel to San Francisco to obtain it.[13] Even in an emergency, rapid communication was impossible. At the height of the 1888 crisis describe later, the US Vice Consul and a Navy Commander needed urgent instructions from Washington. To make contact as quickly as they could, they set sail on September 14, 1888, to make contact with a US mail steamer headed to Australia, meeting it the next day. The mail steamer went to Sydney, where a telegram was dispatched to San Francisco, arriving on September 29. By the time it was stamped as received in Washington, on October 1, more than two weeks had past.[14] Even then, the short telegram had little information, no context, and described only the elements of the situation that the Commander wanted to have presented to Washington.

---

[9] Gilson, *Samoa 1830 to 1900*, 233–9.

[10] Fish to Steinberger, March 29, 1873. Volume 3. Diplomatic Instructions of the Department of State, 1801–1906, Roll 154, National Archives, College Park.

[11] Gilson, *Samoa 1830 to 1900*, 151. Even then, the 1848 commission was as commercial agent, a lower grade than Consul.

[12] Ibid., 164.

[13] Foster to Fish, August 22, 1874. Despatches from US Consuls in Apia, Samoa. Roll 3, T27. RG 59, NARA II.

[14] Telegram. Blacklock to Bayard, September 4, 1898. Box 129. General Correspondence. Thomas Bayard Papers, LC. [Telegram misfiled.] Entry for September 14, 1888, *Adams' Deck Log* 5-2-1888 to 11-1-1888; Entry for September 15, 1888, *Adams' Deck Log* 5-2-1888 to 11-1-1888, RG 24, NARA.

This kind of political situation, in which groups have little official contact, is when intermediaries are likely to fill a structural hole. The only information available to political agents in Washington, London, and Berlin came from a small group of commercial representatives, companies, and ship captains, as well as an occasional reporter. These figures "explained Samoa" to their capitals and could pick and choose who their country might support in the frequent Samoan civil conflicts.

STEINBERGER IN SAMOA

The first episodes of cooperation between the United States and Samoa occurred in the mid-1870s. In 1875, British sailors intervened in Samoa to preserve the power of Malietoa Laupepa, the recently deposed king. In the field, they met the recently created Samoan militia, organized and trained by an American at the behest of President Grant's Special Agent in Samoa, Colonel Albert Steinberger. The proximate cause of hostilities was Laupepa's decision to deport Steinberger, leading to an open revolt against the king. Why did the militia revolt? And why did it ally itself with Grant's agent?

I argue that Albert Steinbeger, an agent with weak ties to political elites in Washington and Samoa, managed to broker cooperation across a structural hole. Steinberger, as a Special Agent to the islands, had an almost exclusive monopoly on information, providing him opportunities to frame cooperation for Samoans and Americans, raise a militia, and build trust.

To understand the alliance between Samoa and the United States, a bit of background is necessary. The Samoan islands are ideal to grow copra, made from cocoanuts. Between 1870 and 1872, a German firm began to make the first major land purchases in Samoa. Until then, Samoans had been reluctant to cede land; intra-Samoan conflict, however, led Samoans to trade land for guns. Soon after, US companies became interested in Samoa. William H. Webb, a shipowner from New York, sought to create a steamship line from San Francisco across the Pacific. If the line were successful, then land in Samoa, a stopping point, might gain value. Webb's agents began purchasing land in Samoa, forming the Central Polynesian Land and Commercial Company (CPLCC). The CPLCC was unscrupulous; for example, it bribed a senator to support its foreign venture.[15]

---

[15] Barry Rigby, "The Origins of American Expansion in Hawaii and Samoa, 1865–1900," *The International History Review* 10, no. 2 (1988): 229.

Webb hired a trader familiar with Samoa to scout harbor facilities. By 1875, the CPLCC claimed to own 180,000 acres of Samoan land, or about half of the islands, and told shareholders that an American-influenced government would soon become a reality.[16]

To establish US support for annexing Samoa, and thus creating the stop on the steamship line, some official US presence in Samoa was needed. Webb's agent managed to convince the White House to send Commander R.W. Meade to Samoa in 1872. When Meade arrived, he negotiated a treaty with local Samoan political leaders to make the harbor at Pago Pago an American naval station. But, much to the consternation of the CPLCC, Meade did not try to extend US influence at Apia and the Beach. Instead, he returned to Tutuila, the island where Pago Pago is located, and tried to build support for his agreement with local chiefs. For the CPLCC, this was a bitter disappointment. To bolster US support for a protectorate, Webb needed an explicit commitment, beyond harbor rights. His agent drafted a petition for local Samoan leaders, in English of course, asking for American annexation of Samoa.[17] In 1872, President Grant supported these designs on Samoa. The Meade Treaty received Grant's endorsement and was submitted to the Senate, despite being negotiated by a ship captain with no authority whatsoever to enter negotiations over annexation. The treaty was rejected.[18]

With Congress refusing to endorse the political arrangements necessary for CPLCC success, Webb recommended that Grant send Colonel Albert Steinberger to Samoa. With high-level commercial and political interests in Samoa, one might expect an agent with strong ties to Washington to be sent there to broker cooperation. And Steinberger's mission would eventually become so fantastic that many historians have posited that he must have had secret connections to the White House. For example, some say, perhaps he served with Grant during the Civil War and had dirt about the President? If these accounts of Steinberger's strong ties were true, then it would cut against the argument of this book: Steinberger, who recruited a Samoan militia, would not count as an intermediary. Steinberger more realistically, gained his position through weak ties. He was a CPLCC clerk from San Francisco and therefore an employee of

---

[16] Barry Rigby, "Private Interests and the Origins of American Involvement in Samoa, 1872–1877," *The Journal of Pacific History* 8 (1973): 76.

[17] The annexation request was also submitted through commercial rather than diplomatic channels. See John Alexander Clinton Gray, *Amerika Samoa* (New York: Ayer Publishing, 1980), 60.

[18] Ryden, *The Foreign Policy of the United States in Relation to Samoa*, 42–82.

Webb's.[19] It is difficult to tell why Webb selected Steinberger, although we can be sure it had little to do with connections to the White House than with Steinberger's willingness to go.

Steinberger was given secret instructions from the White House that set extraordinary limits on what he might do in Samoa. He was to look for "a harbor where their steam and other vessels may freely and securely frequent" and advise Samoans "against making grants of their lands to individual foreigners." Steinberger, and here his orders were clear, was not a representative of the US government, and he was "to avoid conversation, official or otherwise, with any persons respecting the relations between this and any other country."[20] Steinberger had no institutional authority to do much in the islands.

When Steinberger arrived, Samoa was entering a political crisis. One problem was the sale of land to Europeans. To gain access to resources and funds, Samoans had begun to sell land. Communal ownership, however, meant that Samoans did not often own the land they sold. Upon Steinberger's arrival, this was creating problems as Samoans had begun to realize that a land scramble of the previous few years had led them to forfeit rights that would be difficult to reclaim. And, these land sales were so irregular that it was becoming unclear who owned what.[21] Samoans therefore were looking for assistance in reclaiming their land and resisting predatory sales.

On Steinberger's first mission, he used his monopoly on information to build trust between the United States and Samoans. Steinberger's instructions to caution against land sales were popular.[22] Steinberger, however,

---

[19] Rigby, "Private Interests and the Origins of American Involvement in Samoa, 1872–1877"; Rigby, "The Origins of American Expansion in Hawaii and Samoa, 1865–1900." Webb made these requests for other administrations as well. See Letter. Samuel Barlow to Thomas Bayard, February 13, 1888. Box 120, J General Correspondence. Thomas Bayard Papers, LC. For a long time, the decision to send Steinberger perplexed historians. Several theories about his past circulated at the time: he was said to be a mining expert, rifle manufacturer, ex-army officer, office clerk, or a friend of Grant's from the 1850s who had dirt about the president. Gilson, *Samoa 1830 to 1900*, 296. For a modern discussion of several of these theories, see Stephen W. Stathis, "Albert B. Steinberger: President Grant's Man in Samoa," *Hawaiian Journal of History* 16 (1982): 86–111; Martin Torodash, "Steinberger of Samoa: Some Biographical Notes," *The Pacific Northwest Quarterly* 68, no. 2 (1977): 49–59.

[20] Fish to Steinberger, March 29, 1873. Volume 3. Diplomatic Instructions of the Department of State, 1801–1906, Roll 154, National Archives, College Park. Fish goes so far as to imply that it would be illegal for Steinberger to meddle in the affairs of other states.

[21] Gilson, *Samoa 1830 to 1900*, 280–8.

[22] For example, shortly after Steinberger's first mission, the Samoans began to stridently protest land sales, leading the Prussian fleet, in one case, to burn a Samoan village to the

went much further than cautioning against land sales. During the first mission, he explained American interests in such a way that Samoans began to favor American annexation. Steinberger told the Samoans that if Samoa became an American protectorate, then their land might be reclaimed. In doing so, he promised to support Samoa against the American and German interests. Barry Rigby, the historian who has done the most to document Steinberger's missions, argues that these promises meant he "immediately established a bond of trust with the sorely abused Samoans."[23] These promises were not authorized. Also against instructions, he began to interfere with local Samoan politics, helping, for example, to draft a new constitution. With the new constitution in hand, as well as letters asking for American protection, Steinberger returned to the United States to make his report to Grant and to Congress.[24] The idea of a Samoan protectorate appears to have intrigued Grant, but there was no political support on Capitol Hill.

Within a year, Steinberger was sent on a second mission to Samoa as Grant's Special Agent. The origins of the second mission are more interesting than the first, because it shows how intermediaries may profit financially from brokering cooperation. The crucial agent in the second mission was Orville E. Babcock, Grant's corrupt private secretary. Babcock, later famous for corruption after his indictment in the St. Louis Whiskey Ring, promised that Steinberger could "have" Samoa in exchange for silver shares.[25] The idea of trading Samoa for silver was only the first swindle. The Secretary of State and the Congress refused to pay Steinberger's salary, and, with the CPLCC on the verge of bankruptcy, Steinberger had no funds to return to the islands. To finance his trip, he turned to the German firm and signed a secret contract in which he promised to protect German interests against Samoan and American interests in exchange for money and a ship. Steinberger therefore intended to capitalize on his position between communities for financial gain.

---

ground. Coe to Davis. August 28, 1874. CD. 53. Despatches from US Consuls in Apia, Samoa. Roll 3, T27. RG 59, NARA II.
[23] Rigby, "The Origins of American Expansion in Hawaii and Samoa, 1865–1900," 229.
[24] See A.B. Steinberger, *Report Upon Samoa, or the Navigator's Islands, Made to the Secretary of State* (Washington, DC: Government Printing Office, 1874).
[25] Rigby, "Private Interests and the Origins of American Involvement in Samoa, 1872–1877," 230. The correspondence over silver continued into 1880, lending confidence to the thin trail Rigby points toward. See Steinberger to Babcock. January 4, 1980, Silver Cliff Colorado; Steinberger to Babcock. January 28, 1880, Palmer House Chicago. Folder 377, Box 6. Orville E. Babcock Papers, The Newberry Library, Chicago.

When Steinberger returned to Samoa, he needed to provide the Samoans with evidence that the United States had an interest in preserving Samoan autonomy and land. Doing so was difficult because Steinberger was explicitly barred from making any political promises or statements of US policy: the Secretary of State's instructions read that his "functions will be limited to observing and reporting upon Samoan affairs and to impressing those in authority there with the lively interest which we take in their happiness and welfare."[26] Steinberger was explicitly not authorized to do more.

If Steinberger wanted power, he thus needed some signal that he had authority in Samoa – sharing his instructions would not be helpful. To win more influence on the Beach and in Mulinuu, he used his connections with Babcock to earn passage on the USS *Tuscarora*. Babcock convinced the ship's captain to help Steinberger gain influence by playing along with any plans he had. When Steinberger arrived, the captain explained to the Beach that Steinberger had a political function in addition to the normal commercial functions permitted to consuls. After assembling the chiefs, he said Steinberger was "sent by the President of the United States to remain among you ... to assist you in organizing your government."[27] His arrival on a naval vessel, with public endorsement from its captain, signaled that he had authority. Steinberger immediately made public promises to protect Samoan and American interests, and he thus received a warm welcome from both groups.[28]

Steinberger capitalized on the opportunity to obtain political power. When he returned to Samoa, there was a constitutional crisis. In particular, the constitution drafted during his first visit had established a dual kingship to avoid conflict between two aspiring groups. While the Malietoa agreed on a single candidate, Laupepa, the Tupua had a more difficult choice between two candidates.[29] Steinberger immediately began to canvass Samoa to figure out a response; in the end, he decided to establish a single kingship with a term limit, giving Malietoa Laupepa the first term and thereby delaying the thorny decision on who among the Tupua

[26] Fish to Steinberger, December 11, 1874. Volume 3. Diplomatic Instructions of the Department of State, 1801–1906, Roll 154, RG 24. NARA II.
[27] Rigby, "The Origins of American Expansion in Hawaii and Samoa, 1865–1900," 231.
[28] Foster to Hunter. May 22, 1875. CD 17. Despatches from US Consuls in Apia, Samoa. Roll 3, T27. RG 59, NARA II.
[29] Foster to Hunter. February 8, 1975. CD 6. Despatches from US Consuls in Apia, Samoa. Roll 3. T27. RG 59, NARA II.

should hold office.[30] His more important constitutional innovation was to eliminate the king's executive and legislative powers and create an office of premier, who held ultimate power over the executive functions of the office, was the primary judge on the Supreme Court, and took part in the legislature. Steinberger himself occupied the premiership, making him in many ways an "absolute dictator."[31]

Steinberger also used this opportunity to search out Samoans to join a militia. While in Baltimore, Maryland, between the missions, Steinberger met with John Latrobe, telling him of the opportunities to profit by playing parties against one another. For Latrobe's assistance, he got a quarter of all the profits.[32] Latrobe's mission in Samoa was to organize and lead the Samoan militia, dedicated to protecting the Laupepa–Steinberger government. This militia became important, as it was formed by Steinberger's agent and not Laupepa's, and therefore would support Steinberger and not Laupepa in the event of a crisis.

The problem Steinberger faced over the next year was how to maintain a balance between the private and public interests that put him in office. It was a real pickle. He had to balance his secret deals with German firms with his official position as US Consul, as well as represent the Samoans interests in his capacity as premier. He failed. Any decision to favor European land claims against Samoans would risk his premiership; any decision to favor Samoan land claims risked undermining his support on the Beach; and any decision to favor a particular commercial interest, such as maintaining his secret agreement with the Germans, risked alienating other commercial interests. It quickly became apparent that Steinberger, working through a land court, intended to support the Samoan interests that installed him into power against all the foreign powers' commercial interests. This led his support on the Beach to

---

[30] Constitution. Enclosure 1. Foster to Hunter. February 8, 1975. CD 6. Despatches from US Consuls in Apia, Samoa. Roll 3, T27. RG 59, NARA II.

[31] For the term "dictator" or "absolute dictator," see Petition addressed to Captain Stevens by foreign residents. Encl. 6 to Mr. Foster to Mr. Hunter. January 18, 1876. CD 39 Despatches from US Consuls in Apia, Samoa. Roll 4, T27. RG 59, NARA II;. Foster to Hunter. January 5, 1876. CD. 35 Despatches from US Consuls in Apia, Samoa. Roll 4, T27. RG 59, NARA II; Williams and Foster. Apia, Samoa December 31, 1875. Encl. 6 to Foster to Campbell. September 20, 1876. CD. 30. Despatches from US Consuls in Apia, Samoa. Roll 4, T27. RG 59, NARA II.

[32] Copy of Articles of Agreement between A.B. Steinberger and John H.B. Latrobe of Baltimore, MD. Enclosure. Foster to Hunter. March 18, 1876. CD 44. Despatches from US Consuls in Apia, Samoa. Roll 4, T27. RG 59, NARA II.

collapse.[33] By the end of the year, the American Consul became suspicious and inquired about Steinberger's mission with the State Department.[34]

Soon, Captain Stevens of the HMS *Barracouta* arrived. Europeans on the Beach convinced him that Steinberger was a fraud. Stevens met with Laupepa in December. He demanded to see Steinberger's orders. When Steinberger refused, Stevens told Laupepa that Steinberger was probably operating off-script and should be removed from office. Laupepa refused. Even if Steinberger was ignoring the interests of the Beach, he continued to defend Samoan land claims.[35] Unable to make headway with Laupepa, Stevens seized Steinberger's ship and found his real instructions aboard, along with his secret contract and correspondence with the German firm.[36] With these finds in hand, which showed that Steinberger was corrupt, had no authority from Washington to lead the Samoan government or form a militia, and had lied since his return to Samoa, Stevens again talked to Laupepa. This time, he coerced the Malietoa to order Steinberger to leave the government and the islands.[37]

Steinberger's arrest was unpopular in Samoa, and it helped build trust in Samoa for the United States. As Barry Rigby explains, because the US and British consuls were unpopular owing to land sales, "Far from discrediting Steinberger in the eyes of the Samoans, the *Barracouta* incident

---

[33] Foster to Hunter. February 8, 1975, CD 6. Despatches from US Consuls in Apia, Samoa. Roll 3; Godeffroy to Steinberger. May 5, 1975. Enclosure. Foster to Hunter. March 18, 1876, CD 44. Despatches from US Consuls in Apia, Samoa. Roll 4, T27. RG 59, NARA II. These complaints were later compounded with charges that the Samoans under Steinberger had the audacity to try Americans for crimes, such as manslaughter, committed in Samoa. Foster to Department of State, September 6, 1875, CD 25. Despatches from US Consuls in Apia, Samoa. Roll 4; Foster to Hunter, October 3, 1875. Despatches from US Consuls in Apia, Samoa. Roll 4, T27. RG 59, NARA II; Foster to Hunter, January 3, 1876, CD 34. Despatches from US Consuls in Apia, Samoa. Roll 4. T27. RG 59, NARA II.

[34] Foster to Hunter. October 3, 1875, CD 30. Despatches from US Consuls in Apia, Samoa. Roll 4, T27. RG 59, NARA II.

[35] Minutes of a Meeting at Mulinuu Point. Various dates in December 1875. Enclosure 1. Foster to Hunter. January 5, 1876, CD 35. Despatches from US Consuls in Apia, Samoa. Roll 4, T27. RG 59, NARA II.

[36] These are enclosed in Foster to Hunter. March 18, 1876, CD 44. Despatches from US Consuls in Apia, Samoa. Roll 4, T27. RG 59, NARA II.

[37] Once removed, Foster, the American consul, delegated authority to Williams, the British consul, who delegated authority to Stevens, who took Steinberger aboard the *Barracouta*. This plot, leading to the British imprisonment of an American who was lawfully in Samoan office, would see all of the westerners fired for misconduct. See the enclosures in Foster to Hunter. March 18, 1876, CD 47. Despatches from US Consuls in Apia, Samoa. Roll 4, T27. RG 59, NARA II.

actually increased his credibility and that of the United States."[38] The other organs of the Samoan government revolted, deposing Malietoa Laupepa for deporting Steinberger. When Stevens insisted they reinstate Laupepa, the Samoans refused. On March 13, 1876, the British intervened, sending sailors to seize the guns in the capital. The Samoan militia, egged on by Steinberger's supporters, including Latrobe, fought to defend what they thought was America's official representative to Samoa. The ensuing fight killed somewhere between eight and ten Samoans and three British sailors.[39] Relying on the militia that Steinberger had trained, now in revolt against Laupepa, the Samoans won.

Steinberger's time in the islands is important to this book for three reasons. First, the locus of the politics of security cooperation in Samoa in the 1870s, despite involving the United States, the British Empire, and Germany, was in Samoa. Agents in the islands – Steinberger, the US. Consul, and a British ship captain – were far more important than decision-makers in Berlin, London, and Washington. It was the agents *between* Samoa and the United States who mattered; not decision makers who led either community. Moreover, Steinberger's ability to create cooperation was premised on his structural niche between powerful individuals and organizations. Steinberger was at the center of a complicated web in which he was the only person who connected many parties. Arriving in a warship gave him influence over Americans, he had earned support from the Germans by secretly pledging to line their pockets, and he gained Samoan support by promising to protect their land. Moreover, Steinberger had a complete monopoly on information. No one in Samoa knew his instructions from Washington, only the Germans knew about his secret agreement with the Godeffroy House, and Steinberger's close relations with the Samoans meant he was the person they trusted the most. Steinberger, somehow, managed to be the critical agent who could fill structural holes across the Pacific, and between the Beach and the rest of Samoa. He used this niche to create a militia that defended his interests against consular authorities on the Beach.

Second, the way Steinberger used this niche highlights at least three of the four causal mechanisms identified in Chapter 1. Steinberger identified Samoans who would cooperate with the United States by recruiting Samoans with Latrobe to join the militia. Moreover, Steinberger explained

[38] Rigby, "The Origins of American Expansion in Hawaii and Samoa, 1865–1900," 232.
[39] Gilson, *Samoa 1830 to 1900*, 324–31; Ryden, *The Foreign Policy of the United States in Relation to Samoa*, 142.

the parties' interests to one another such that they believed there was a harmony of interests. He suggested, for example, that the United States intended to protect Samoan autonomy under a protectorate and reported to Grant that Samoa was willing to accept US guidance. He also provided reassurances of US intentions by cultivating a personal reputation for preserving Samoan interests during his time as premier. His ability to perform these functions depended on his structural niche: he was especially well-equipped to broker cooperation across a structural hole because he was the only agent with ties between Apia and Washington.

Despite being only a minor case of cooperation, Steinberger's missions helped create lasting American interest in the islands, setting the stage for later competition. Ten years later, jingoists in the United States treated Steinberger's promises of protection for Samoans as precedent for US interests in the islands. Steinberger's record of supporting Samoan interests also meant that Samoans might turn to Washington for future help against aggressive German commercial interests.[40]

LEARY, MOORS, SEWALL, AND THE HURRICANE

In 1888, another war broke out in Samoa, but this one risked war between the great powers. Since Steinberger left Samoa, German and American commercial interests had grown. The Godeffroy House ("the German Firm"), in particular, had developed successful copra plantations. It also installed a friendly government, led by Tamasese, into power that favored German commercial interests. When a rebellion broke out in Samoa against the German-backed Tamasese regime, Germany began to actively intervene, deploying sailors on shore, moving warships to Samoa, and sending troops onto its beaches. In a string of battles, the rebellion routed the Germans and their allies, leading Germany to bombard their enemy on the shores.[41] On January 15, 1889, President Grover Cleveland, in a message to Congress, announced that "[a] recent collision between the forces from a German man-of-war stationed in Samoan waters and a body of natives rendered the situation so delicate and critical that the warship *Trenton,* under the immediate command of Admiral Kimberly,

---

[40] See, for example, "Statement of Harold M. Sewall, of Maine, Consul-General of the United States to Samoa." January 11, 1889. Box 2, Folder 18. George Bates Samoa Papers. Special Collections at the Morris Library, University of Delaware.

[41] In Gray, *Amerika Samoa,* 86.

FIGURE 5.2 Headlines during the crisis. Thomas F. Bayard Papers, Library of Congress. Author thanks Tina Bernsten for producing the image

was ordered to join the *Nipsic,* already at Samoa."[42] Kimberly's orders were to "extend full protection and defence to American citizens and their property" and to "[p]rotest against the subjugation of the country and the displacement of native government by German rule enforced by German arms and coercion."[43] Apia Harbor was soon crowded: the great powers had sent the USS *Trenton, Vandalia,* and *Nipsic,* HMS *Calliope,* and SMS *Adler, Olga,* and *Eber.*[44] Rumors of war soared in Germany and the United States as the US Congress held hearings and the German Admiralty asked for strategic plans for a war against the United States.[45]

Then, on March 15, the barometer dropped and the winds intensified; the next day, a hurricane swept into the harbor, wrecking the assembled ships. Only the *Calliope* survived; all six American and German ships were wrecked or beached. In the middle of the hurricane, Samoans and

[42] "Message Relative to the Samoan Question," January 15, 1889. *The Public Papers of Grover Cleveland: March 4, 1885–March 4, 1889.* Washington, DC: GPO, 1889. pp, 470–1.

[43] Cleveland to Rear-Admiral Lewis Kimberly, January 10, 1889. In *Letters of Grover Cleveland, 1850–1908,* ed. Allan Nevins (Boston: Houfflin, 1933), 196–7.

[44] Entry for March 11, 1889. *Trenton's Log Book,* 11-29-1888 to 5-30-1889. RG 24, NARA.

[45] Charles S. Campbell, *The Transformation of American Foreign Relations: 1865–1900* (New York: Harper & Row, 1965), 81; Kennedy, *The Samoan Tangle,* 80.

FIGURE 5.3 View of the USS *Vandalia* from the wreckage of the USS *Trenton*. Courtesy of Naval History and Heritage Command

sailors from all of the great powers worked together to rescue survivors.[46] As Paul Kennedy explains, "The prospect of military action in Samoa was literally blown away, and tempers further cooled with the realization that the warships lost were probably worth more than the group itself."[47]

US–German tensions were in part the result of an active alliance between the US Navy and the rebellion against the German-backed regime. Beginning in 1888, the US Navy had begun to intervene in defense of a rebellion led by Mata'afa. As the civil war in Samoa escalated, US naval vessels conducted operations to defend Mata'afa, the rebellion's leader. The central question I am interested in is why the United States had so deeply committed to aid Mata'afa?

---

[46] Gray, *Amerika Samoa*, 87–91.

[47] Kennedy, *The Samoan Tangle*, 86. Losses from the Hurricane were substantially higher than any potential gains. The *Nipsic*'s recently installed electric lights were worth more than the largest US complaint against Germany. Moors' interest on Samoa, valued at $40,000 (and probably exaggerated), was worth less than a third of the machinery aboard the *Vandalia* alone. And, the estimate to simply buy Samoa from the Germans was 330,000 pounds, or less than 1.7 million dollars. The total lost in the hurricane was three million dollars.

The case of Samoa in 1888 and 1889 is interesting because there were two parallel routes by which Americans tried to gain aid for Mata'afa. One route agents took was to use strong ties to political power to invite American intervention on his behalf. The conventional wisdom, provided by Paul Kennedy, follows this pathway. He finds that the decision to send a significant naval force to Samoa was produced by well-connected individuals who used the press and their influence in the Senate to agitate for an increased US commitment.[48] If this conventional wisdom is correct, then it cuts against the argument of this book, because these figures would have capitalized on their institutional authority in Washington, rather than their position between societies, to secure cooperation with Mata'afa's forces. The first part of this section argues that the conventional wisdom is wrong. A close analysis of the archival record shows that these individuals failed to persuade Washington to take a more active stand. Instead, the alliance formed because of weak ties. Naval intervention occurred because of a passing relationship between navy captains and merchants in Apia, where these merchants frame the politics of Samoa in ways that made naval intervention to support Mata'afa appear to be a natural outgrowth of their orders.

The next section first lays out the argument for strong ties because it forms the diplomatic context in which intermediaries operated. In doing so, it shows the insufficiency of an explanation emphasizing the interests or beliefs of political elites. Then I describe the view from Apia, showing how merchants used their position between societies to convince the US Navy to support Mata'afa.

The Political Track

Beginning in the 1880s, German commercial interests became as politically adventurous as Steinberger had been in the previous decade. In August 1887, a German-backed coup installed Tupua Tamasese into the kingship in Samoa, supported by troops trained by Eugen Brandeis, a clerk from the German firm. Brandeis became, in many ways, the German Steinberger. George Ryden, who wrote one of the first histories of the conflict, remarked that "the only difference between the two was that Brandeis remained in power longer than Steinberger.".[49] The new Brandeis–Tamasese government was enormously unpopular with Samoans, as it imposed crippling

---

[48] Kennedy, *The Samoan Tangle*, 79.
[49] Ryden, *The Foreign Policy of the United States in Relation to Samoa*, 374.

taxes and eliminated Tamasese's political rivals.[50] By 1888, much of Samoa was in rebellion, rallying around Mata'afa. Brandeis, again following Steinberger's precedent, raised a Samoan army to defend the Tamasese regime and equipped it with German guns.[51]

Recognizing that Samoan intrigues might cause problems amongst the great powers, a conference was held in Washington in 1887, led by Thomas Bayard, the US Secretary of State. Participants could not reach an agreement on Samoan affairs. The Germans recommended creating a government led by a strong Prime Minister, which Bayard thought a thin veil for German annexation. Yet, Bayard, who favored Samoan autonomy, did not have a bargaining chip he was willing or able to trade. The conference ended in deadlock in Washington, while events on the ground in Apia were moving quickly.[52]

While Bayard and the German and British ministers met in Washington, the Brandeis–Tamasese regime consolidated its power, naming Tamasese King and Brandeis his Premier.[53] Americans in Samoa soon began to complain about discriminatory treatment against US commercial interests. The primary complainant was H.J. Moors, who in the 1880s was the largest American landowner in Samoa. Moors had moved to Samoa in the 1870s and started a trading firm, possibly with money or labor from blackbirding (i.e., kidnapping indigenous peoples and transplanting them to plantations to work).[54] He achieved some notoriety among the British for a case in which Moors captured a foreign worker who ran away from his plantation with her child. The child died during the escape, and the mother was brought back "lashed to a pole like a pig, and a severe public flogging was administered by Moors."[55] Later, Moors was caught

---

[50] CD 90. March 27, 1888. Despatches from US Consuls in Apia, Samoa. Roll 16, T27. RG 59, NARA II; CD 119. Sewall to Rives. May 24, 1888. Despatches from US Consuls in Apia, Samoa. Roll 16, T27. RG 59, NARA II.

[51] Record of Current Events. Enclosure 0. CD 150. September 11, 1888. Despatches from US Consuls in Apia, Samoa. Roll 16, T27. RG 59, NARA II.

[52] Samoa Conference at Washington, Protocols. June 25, 1887–July 26, 1887. Box 1. First Samoan Conference 1887. Records of International Conferences, Commissions and Expositions, RG 43, NARA 2.

[53] CD 165, April 25, 1887, Despatches from US Consuls in Apia, Roll 15, T27. RG 59, NARA II.

[54] Mandy Treagus, "Crossing 'The Beach': Samoa, Stevenson and 'The Beach at Falesá,'" *Literature Compass* 11, no. 5 (2014): 318.

[55] See Doug Munro and Stewart Firth, "Samoan Plantations: The Gilbertese Laborers' Experience, 1867–1896," in *Plantation Workers: Resistance and Accommodation*, ed. Brij V. Lal, Doug Munro, and Edward D. Beechert (University of Hawaii Press, 1993), 111–12. See also Newell to Thompson. September 6, 1899, Malua Samoa. CWM/LMS South Seas Incoming Correspondence Box 45 1899, Folder 4.

falsifying claims for damages caused by the 1899 conflict; his claims were the only ones denied. After his Samoan intrigues, Moors would go on to purchase Nassau Island, somehow convincing a *Washington Post* reporter that he had single-handedly converted the islanders from cannibalism to pork lovers.[56]

Moors had a sympathetic ear in Apia. The US Consul in Samoa, Harold Marsh Sewall, was unusually important for the post. He was the son of Arthur Sewall of Maine, who led a shipbuilding empire and would later run for Vice President. Sewall arrived in Samoa on July 18, 1887, and was immediately convinced that the Brandeis-Tamasese government was a threat to US interests. Sewall forwarded dozens of complaints over the next few months to the Secretary of State, most of them petty and many originating in Moors' disputes with Germans. These included important issues, such as a German monopoly on copra production, as well as odd schemes, such as altering the prejudice of German beer drinkers against American light beer.[57] The implication of these complaints was clear: only annexation of Samoa would protect American interests. When complaining about the Germans enclosing a piece of Moors land, for example, Moors asked the State Department, "Could not the United States annex Samoa Tamasese and all? And so impress upon the German diplomats that they cannot play fast and loose with a country so great as ours."[58]

One complaint, over the disputed ownership of a pilot house in Apia, merits special attention, because it shows how aggressive Sewall was in framing issues for the State Department, and the latter's lack of interest.

---

[56] The full title does justice to the reporting: "An American Monarch: How H. J. Moors Became King of the Cannibal Islands... An Adventurous Youth, He Discovered an Almost Depopulated Island, Over Which He Established a Protectorate and Taught the Inhabitants to Eat Roast Pork Instead of Human Flesh – Now He Owns Two Islands, a Yacht, and a Troup of Dancers. Cannibal Enterprise that Failed. Traveling Guests of the King. Cannibals to Be Recruited. The Island Queen." December 3, 1893, *Washington Post*, 10.

[57] CD 90, Sewall to Rives, March 27, 1888. Despatches from US Consuls in Apia, Samoa. Roll 16; "The Political Situation in Samoa," April 23, 1888. Despatches from US Consuls in Apia, Samoa. Roll 16; Sewall, "German Land Claims," April 23, 1888. Despatches from US Consuls in Apia, Samoa. Roll 16. Sewall, "Complaints of American Citizens," April 30, 1888. Despatches from US Consuls in Apia, Samoa. Roll 16; CD 120, Sewall to Department of State, May 24, 1888. Despatches from US Consuls in Apia, Samoa. Roll 16; CD 124, Sewall to Rives, June 18, 1888. Despatches from US Consuls in Apia, Samoa. Roll 16, T27. RG 59, NARA II.

[58] Moors to Sewall, October 5, 1887. Enclosure 1. CD 35, October 8, 1887, Despatches from US Consuls in Apia, Roll 15, T27. RG 59, NARA II; CD 15. August 13, 1887, T27. RG 59, NARA II; and Ryden, *The Foreign Policy of the United States in Relation to Samoa*, 407.

In 1887, the German consulate and an American, Billy Coe, each claimed to own a pilot house on the shore at Apia. The German Consul reasonably suggested that Germany should occupy the house and pay Coe rent until a court of arbitration might form. Coe refused, even though it represented no net financial loss. By itself, the pilot house should not merit attention, but it shows how Sewall tried to frame issues for Washington. Sewall did not mention that Billy Coe was a political opponent of the German regime and had recently been jailed by Tamasese's forces.[59] Instead of framing the issue as a political issue specific to Billy Coe, Sewall framed the issue as a credibility issue for the United States. Writing to the State Department, Sewall suggests that force might be necessary to install Coe in his pilot house, although he did remark that "only a show of force would be necessary" to evict the German consular clerk. In an understated response, the Assistant Secretary of State wrote to Sewall that he "fails to see what ground there is for making the case" a "special and urgent matter," especially since Germany was willing to pay rent.[60]

Sewall tried to use his political influence to sway Washington. His first strategy was to influence Thomas Bayard, the Secretary of State, to resist German intrigues, raising the specter of German annexation.[61] The only solution to German monopolies in Samoa, Sewall would repeatedly argue, was to use force, either by taking the islands or protecting Samoans who chose to trade with US rather than German firms.[62] When Sewall made this argument in his correspondence from Apia, he left Bayard unconvinced. Bayard wrote to Sewall that despite "an appeal to me for prompt action to sustain native Government in Samoa and check German aggression," he would not act, because "I have not been able to decide that any violation of international law as affecting the United States or of our treaty tights with Samoa has yet been committed by Germany," and it seemed that Sewall's "suggestions would lead to a departure from our

---

[59] CD 163, Hamilton to Porter, April 25, 1887, Despatches from US Consuls in Apia, Samoa, Roll 15, T27. RG 59, NARA II; CD 166. Hamilton to Porter. May 15, 1887, Despatches from US Consuls in Apia, Samoa, Roll 15. T27. RG 59, NARA II.

[60] CD 91, February 1, 1888 (With Enclosures). Despatches from US Consuls in Apia, Samoa, Roll 16; CD 93, T27, RG 59, NARA II. February 25, 1888. Despatches from US Consuls in Apia, Samoa, Roll 16, T27. RG 59, NARA II; Rives to Sewall, February 28. 1888. Reprinted in Exec. Doc. No. 31, *Executive Documents of the Senate, 50th Congress, Second Session* (GPO: Washington, DC, 1889).

[61] CD 90, Sewall to Rives, March 27, 1888. Despatches from US Consuls in Apia, Roll 16, T27. RG 59, NARA II.

[62] See, for example, Consular CD 107. Sewall to Rives, May 24, 1888. CD 107. Despatches from US Consuls in Apia, Samoa. Roll 16, T27. RG 59, NARA II.

position as a Neutral and place this Government [the United States] as an ally of Samoa in an attitude of belligerency to Germany." Bayard further states that Sewall's recommended policy would likely require "placing in useless jeopardy the vaster interests of our own countrymen." He recommended that Sewall remember he was a consul, which meant he was not entrusted with diplomatic functions.[63] A "disappointed" Sewall wrote back, asking for naval commanders visiting Samoa to be given direction for a "show of force" that he was sure risked no conflict with Germany.[64] Bayad, though, found the idea of war over Samoa ridiculous.

After Sewall and Moors failed to influence Washington from the Beach, they traveled to the United States to testify to Congress about the situation in Samoa, and they kept up a lively correspondence with the US media.[65] During the crisis years of the late 1880s, Moors' letters were published in newspapers across the country, his petitions to the Secretary of State were answered, and his protests against German encroachments on his property rights were given attention, even in the President's annual message to Congress.[66]

In addition, Sewall, now a former consul to Samoa, began to give interviews to newspapers across the country in which he read aloud a letter from Moors about the injustice of German rule. The headline for the *Boston Daily Advertiser* noted, he was "a man who knows what he was talking about."[67] Sewall used his family's connections to a member of the Senate Foreign Relations Committee to have hearings held on Samoa in executive session.[68] Sewall testified at those hearings that the ships at or

---

[63] Bayard to Sewall, January 6, 1888. Box 119, General Correspondence. Thomas Bayard Papers, LC.

[64] Sewell to Bayard, February 4, 1888. Box 120, General Correspondence. Thomas Bayard Papers, LC.

[65] Sewall to Rives, August 16, 1888, CD 147, Despatches from US Consuls in Apia, Samoa. Roll 16, T27. RG 59, NARA II; H.J. Moors, *Some Recollections of Early Samoa* (Apia, Western Samoa: Western Samoa Historical and Cultural Trust, 1986), 60–7.

[66] For the broad sweep of Moors' engagement with the press, see "Samoan Merchants." Evening Bulletin [San Francisco]. January 26, 1886. "Troublous Times in Samoa: Foreign Residents Insulted by Germans and Natives." November 25, 1888. *New York Times*, 5. "Samoan Broils: The German Influence Causes Mischief." November 25, 1888. *Los Angeles Sunday Times.* "The Samoan Difficulty." December 22, 1888. *The Sentinel: Milwaukee.* "Samoan Strife: Full Details of Late Doings on the Islands." February 17, 1889. *Los Angeles Times.*

[67] See for example "Bad Faith in Samoa." January 23, 1889. *Boston Daily Advertiser;* "Feeble Diplomacy. How Bayard Protected Uncle Sam's Interests." December 21, 1888. *Los Angeles Times.*

[68] The exact nature of the connection is unclear but clearly firm. Harold Marsh and his father corresponded with William Frye before and after 1888, and Arthur even named

on the way to Apia were insufficient because they were intended only to protect American property. He argued that the Germans had anticipated these instructions, and knew how to continue to gain influence in Samoa without provoking a naval incident. Rather, Sewall suggested, the United States needed to provide more direct support for Samoans, rather than for the Americans living in Samoa.[69]

Paul Kennedy suggests that Sewall, an agent with strong ties to Washington, caused Washington to rethink its position on Samoa, leading to greater American engagement. Specifically, Kennedy argued that the decision to send ships to Samoa was largely a reaction to news accounts and Senate pressure.[70]

Public opinion does not explain the alliance with Mata'afa. The House Committee on Foreign Affairs made clear its position in January. Its Chairman was "not alarmed," thought the newspapers exaggerated the threat, and believed the troubles would go away by themselves. One Congressman thought the stories about Germans stabbing Americans in Apia were made up. Another said the issue had not yet been important enough for him to look into the matter. Many in the Senate agreed, stating that only if the United States lost its rights to Pago Pago should it think about escalating the conflict.[71]

The Secretary of State, Thomas Bayard, was even clearer. He was not going to respond to Samoan intrigues. He argued publicly with Sewall, whom he fired from the State Department, saying that no American was injured in Samoa (not quite true), that it was not the job of the United States to provide Samoa with a stable government, and he had no interest in placing the United States between rival commercial firms.[72] In an hour-long meeting with Sewall, Bayard was even more strident. He told Sewall that "we had no policy of annexation," he demanded that the Germans be treated "frankly and kindly," and he read a telegram in which the Germans promised neutrality, explaining that the United States

---

a ship after Frye afterward. See James Burton. "Ship "William P. Frye" builders, Arthur Sewall & Co." Prints and Photographs Division. Library of Congress.

[69] "Statement of Harold M. Sewall, of Maine, Consul-General of the United States to Samoa." January 11, 1889. Box 2, Folder 18. George Bates Samoa Papers. Special Collections at the Morris Library, University of Delaware.

[70] Kennedy, *The Samoan Tangle*, 79.

[71] "Our Flag Was Insulted." January 21, 1889. *Washington Post*, 1.

[72] "To Keep an Eye upon Us." February 1, 1889. *Washington Post*, 1. For Sewall's dismissal, see "Consul Sewall asked to resign." February 8, 1889. *Washington Post*, 2.

"would assume that the German government was perfectly friendly to the natives of Samoa, and meant to let them exercise their own choice freely in electing their rulers."[73] Bayard wrote a private letter to a friend in which he described the concern over Samoa as purely political: "It is difficult to describe the singular bitterness of feeling which seems to control the republican managers – and which has led to a systematic obstruction, misrepresentations, and aspersion of the administration in every department, and towards none so fiercely as the department of state in which I am."[74] In sum, no substantial policy change issued from Washington until after the hurricane at Apia; Sewall had done little to engineer cooperation or affect US policy.[75]

Why did Sewall's strong ties fail? One reason, suggested by the media at the time, was that Sewall had lost his monopoly on information. Sewall left Samoa in August, when events on the ground were moving fast. By the time he testified in December, his information was out of date, and Bayard, not Sewall, knew more about the crisis. As the *Washington Post* explained, "[H]e can know very little more about recent events in the Samoan islands than Senator Frye himself knows."[76] If the *Washington Post* account is right, it underscores the argument of this book: when agents lose their position between societies, their influence declines. More importantly, the action was not in Washington but in Apia, where events were thickening the Samoan tangle without Sewall's input.[77]

---

[73] Meeting Notes. Bayard and Sewall. November 14, 1888. Box 131, General Correspondence. Thomas Bayard Papers, LC.

[74] Bayard to Judge Wales. February 1, 1889. Letter Book 1888–1891, December 10–March 1. Vol. 203. Secretary of State Book 10. Thomas F. Bayard papers, LC.

[75] Samoa was not unique as a political football. Issues more relevant to the election, such as seals and fisheries disputes, were also politicized. For the Cleveland administration, these issues were more important because they concerned debates before and not after the November elections that Cleveland lost. See, for example, Letter. Deringer to Bayard, August 29, 1888. Box 129, General Correspondence. Thomas Bayard Papers; Letter. Illegible to Bayard, September 18, 1888. Box 130, General Correspondence. Thomas Bayard Papers, LC. By the election, the fisheries scandals had turned into an international scandal, sometimes called the Murchison-Sackville Affair, to which some credit Cleveland's loss in November. This occupied much of Bayard's time and may explain the slow British responses to US inquiries. For an overview, see Marc-William Palen, "Foreign Relations in the Gilded Age: A British Free-Trade Conspiracy?" *Diplomatic History* 37, no. 2 (2013): 217–47.

[76] "Samoa to be Sacrificed." January 7, 1889. *Washington Post*, 2.

[77] Blacklock to Rives. September 11, 1888. CD 147. Despatches from US Consuls in Apia, Samoa. Roll 17, T27. RG 59, NARA II.

The Unofficial Track

Robert Louis Stevenson arrived in Samoa in 1889 and immediately began drafting a history of the troubles on the islands.[78] Stevenson's history presents a strikingly different account of the conflict than that provided by diplomatic historians, in part, because he was more acquainted with Apia than with Washington. Stevenson credits two individuals as critical to US policy in Samoa: H.J.Moors and Captain Richard Leary. These agents used their position between societies to shape cooperation and war in Samoa. Taken together, Stevenson writes, "they were partizans; it lacked but a hair they should be called belligerents."[79]

This section outlines the process of US escalation in support of Mata'afa between October and November 1888. Following this record closely is important. If political decision-making in Washington explains the alliance with Mata'afa, then cooperation should begin in 1889, after Washington reacted to political events in the Senate or the media. Instead, events began months before Washington had begun to debate what to do in Samoa, and brinksmanship between the US and German navies was already well underway. After reviewing this track record of political and military events, I then ask which agents brought about the alliance, showing that Moors' position between Samoa and American naval vessels allowed him to shape American foreign policy toward the islands.

On October 6, 1888, Charles Scanlon reported that Tamasese's warriors had come to his home, threatening him at gun point. When Scanlon said he was an American, Tamasese's warriors left without hurting him. They returned later, this time threatening his pigs at gun point.[80] This "pale atrocity," as Robert Louis Stevenson characterizes it, should not have become much of an issue. The pigs, in the end, seem to have been given a reprieve. When Americans objected to the offense, Tamasese offered to compensate Scanlon for the pigs, first offering 1,000 dollars

---

[78] Stevenson, *A Footnote to History*. On its composition, see Stevenson to Sidney Colvin. November 25, 1891, 365–72. *The Letters of Robert Louis Stevenson, Vol III 1887–1891*. Edited by Sidney Colvin. New York: Greenwood, 365–72.

[79] Ibid., 185.

[80] Record of Events. CD 152. October 8, 1888. Despatches from US Consuls in Apia, Samoa. Roll 16, T27. RG 59, NARA II. Killing enemies' livestock as a kind of coercion was a common tactic used by Tamasese forces. See Record of Current Events. Enclosure 0. CD 150. September 11, 1888. Despatches from US Consuls in Apia, Samoa. Roll 16, T27. RG 59, NARA II. Blacklock suggested it was Scanlon, and not the pigs, who was threatened on October 6, with the threat to the pigs occurring earlier. See Record of Events. CD 152. October 8, 1888. Despatches from US Consuls in Apia, Samoa. Roll 16, T27. RG 59, NARA II.

per month in gold to lease his property, and then offering him a position at the German firm.[81] Scanlon took pride in refusing to accept any compensation.[82]

The threats on Scanlon's pigs marked the first instance where the US Navy began to cooperate with Mata'afa. Before the pigs "crisis," most of Mata'afa's support came from US merchants. H.J. Moors, the plantation owner who frequently and constantly complained to Washington of German threats to his property, had a strong relationship with Mata'afa. He provided advice, food, and guns for Mata'afa's rebel fighters.[83] Moors would develop a record of intrigue. In 1899, Moors would encouraged Mata'afa to rebel, although this time against the United States.[84] Two decades later, Moors again tried to incite Samoans to revolt, this time against New Zealand. As the commission assigned to investigate claims arising out of the 1899 conflict decided, he had "a constitutional tendency to take much interest in whatever events are happening about him."[85] Yet, Moors' help was strictly financial. He had no navy.

Moors' primary asset though was his position between societies. When ship captains entered Samoan waters, they usually had little information about the islands and did not understand its contemporary politics. Upon arrival, they therefore turned to their nationals living in the islands for gossip, supplies and advice. These Americans would sail out to meet the incoming American vessels, offering food, fresh water, and friendship. They also had a political role. When the *Nipsic* arrived its captain explained how these Americans – "trustworthy and responsible" people" from the Beach – met with him and helped him form his impression of the Brandeis–Tamasese regime.[86] They were the only source of news about

---

[81] Affidavit of Charles Scanlon. October 10, 1888. Enclosure 9. CD 160. November 6, 1888, Despatches from US Consuls in Apia, Samoa. Roll 16, T27. RG 59, NARA II; Record of Events. CD 152. October 8, 1888. Despatches from US Consuls in Apia, Samoa. Roll 16, T27. RG 59, NARA II.

[82] Stevenson, *A Footnote to History*, 150–1.

[83] On advice, see Gerald Horne, *The White Pacific: U.S. Imperialism and Black Slavery in the South Seas After the Civil War* (Honolulu: University of Hawaii Press, 2007), 120–2. Gray, *Amerika Samoa*, 85; Moors, *Some Recollections of Early Samoa*, 74–5. On delivery of food and espionage, see Stevenson, *A Footnote to History*, 184–5.

[84] "Claims of American Citizens, Apia, in the Samoan Islands." House of Representatives, 62 Congress, 3rd Session, Doc. No. 1257, 27–8.

[85] "Claims of American Citizens, Apia, in the Samoan Islands." House of Representatives, 62 Congress, 3rd Session, Doc. No. 1257, 27–8.

[86] Mullan to Whitney, November 25, 1888. Folder 1, Box 668. Subject File, U.S. Navy, 1775–1910, VI – International Relations and Politics, 1887–1894, Samoa. RG 45, NARA.

the islands. The navy depended on these agents who navigated between societies.

In May 1888, the USS *Adams* arrived in port, captained by Richard Leary.[87] One of the "trustworthy and responsible people" who greeted him was almost certainly H.J. Moors, the small merchant who complained so bitterly to the State Department about his treatment.[88] Moors may have had his assistant William Blacklock along, who in his position as Vice Consul was the highest-ranking American in the islands.

As Germany escalated its commitment to help the government, Moors and Blacklock exerted pressure on Leary to help Mata'afa. At first, it did not work. When Leary first arrived, he befriended German Captain Fritze of the *Adler*.[89] They ate together and socialized. Even in September, as the crew of the *Adams* was watching the German navy begin to conduct military operations to defend the Brandeis-Tamasese regime against Mata'afa, Leary did little. On September 2, the *Adams* watched two armed boats head to Mulinuu Point, unloading personnel to help build forts and guard the German-led government headquartered there.[90] Two days later, they watched the *Adler* ferry about 125 armed men for the Tamasese regime.[91] Then, the Adler threatened to open its guns on the revolutionaries' undefended wives and children unless they surrendered. The *Adams* did nothing but protest. Leary vainly wrote a

---

[87] Entry for May 31, 1888. *Adams' Deck Log* 5-2-1888 to 11-1-1888, RG 24, NARA.

[88] I infer that it was Moors from ship logs from the period. For example, in the weeks following Scanlon's pigs, Moors provided stores to the *Nipsic* on November 13, 14, 17, 19, 22, 28, and 29. See Entries for November 13, 14, 17, 19, 22, 28, and 29, 1888. *Nipsic's Log Book,* October 10, 1888 to April 9, 1889, RG 24, NARA. The *Nipsic's* log books have detailed entries about who provided stores; I infer that the *Adams* likely received them from the same source. Moors was also involved when the navy rebuilt a bridge, which was controversial for reasons that are more confusing than the pigs. See Receipt. Apia Tax-Payers to Peter Paul and John Skelton, January 31, 1889. Enclosure. Correspondence respecting Affairs in Samoa, Printed for the use of the American Commissioners in Berlin. Samoan Conference at Berlin 1889. Despatches from US Commissioners-Protocols. Box 1. Second Samoan Conference, 1889, RG 43, NARA II.

[89] They visited on a number of occasions. See Entry for May 31, 1888 *Adams' Deck Log* 5-2-1888 to 11-1-1888; Entry for July 5, 1888, *Adams' Deck Log* 5-2-1888 to 11-1-1888; Entry for July 22, 1888 *Adams' Deck Log* 5-2-1888 to 11-1-1888; Entry for August 20, 1888 *Adams' Deck Log* 5-2-1888 to 11-1-1888; Entry for August 20, 1888, *Adams' Deck Log* 5-2-1888 to 11-1-1888, RG 24, NARA.

[90] Entry for September 2, 1888, *Adams' Deck Log* 5-2-1888 to 11-1-1888; Entry for September 9, 1888, *Adams' Deck Log* 5-2-1888 to 11-1-1888; Entry for September 10, 1888 *Adams' Deck Log* 5-2-1888 to 11-1-1888. The US Vice-Counsel came on board to consult Leary the following day. Entry for September 3, 1888, *Adams' Deck Log* 5-2-1888 to 11-1-1888, RG 24, NARA.

[91] Entry for September 5, 1888, *Adams' Deck Log* 5-2-1888 to 11-1-1888, RG 24, NARA.

calm but moving letter to the captain of the *Adler,* asking for more consideration for the lives of women and children.[92] Fritze, not disputing the charge that he intended to target women and children, responded that Leary should take it up with the German Consul.[93]

Moors and Blacklock began to use their position to pressure Leary to take up Mata'afa's cause. Blacklock complained bitterly to the State Department that Leary refused to intervene unless American lives were at stake, writing, "We might as well be without a Man of War if he cannot interfere" because "her presence here does not awe anyone."[94] He wrote to Leary about an incident where some property was damaged – a few of his workers' homes were hurt and some banana trees cut down – prognosticating that "American lives will be in danger if this outrage is quietly winked at."[95] This latter point is important. Leary was authorized to intervene if American lives and property were threatened. Yet, Leary continued not to act.

By the end of September, Leary had finally become concerned enough that Germany was intensifying its commitment to the government. Perhaps as the result of Blacklock's needling, Leary sought new instructions. He tried to make contact with Washington, sailing to meet a mail steamer who could more quickly get a telegram to Washington about the impending hostilities, and asked, "Could not the United States get in ahead till things are settled Must act at once."[96] New orders from Washington would not come. Washington was embroiled in election year scandals involving British diplomats. Drawing new orders requiring British cooperation against Germany was impossible.[97] Therefore, not a word was sent to Leary.

[92] Leary to Fritz, September 6, 1888. Enclosure 4. CD 150. September 11, 1888. Despatches from US Consuls in Apia, Samoa. R16, T27. RG 59, NARA II.

[93] Fritz to Leary, September 7, 1888. Enclosure 5. CD 150. September 11, 1888. Despatches from US Consuls in Apia, Samoa. R16, T27. RG 59, NARA II.

[94] CD 150. Blacklock to Rives. September 11, 1888. Despatches from US Consuls in Apia, Samoa. R17, T27. RG 59, NARA II.

[95] Blacklock to Leary. September 11, 1888. Enclosure 9. CD 150. September 11, 1888. Despatches from US Consuls in Apia, Samoa. R16, T27. RG 59, NARA II. Leary investigated the complaint, and the culprits promised to repair the homes. See Leary to Blacklock. September 9, 1888. Enclosure 10. CD 150. September 11, 1888. Despatches from US Consuls in Apia, Samoa. R16, T27. RG 59, NARA II.

[96] Telegram. Blacklock to Bayard, September 4, 1898. Box 129, General Correspondence. Thomas Bayard Papers, LC. Entry for September 14, 1888, *Adams' Deck Log* 5-2-1888 to 11-1-1888; Entry for September 15, 1888, *Adams' Deck Log* 5-2-1888 to 11-1-1888, RG 24, NARA.

[97] Bayard did briefly search for information, although this was ineffective. The British did not respond, and the Germans promised they were indifferent. Telegram. Coleman to

When Leary returned to Samoa, the situation grew worse as a family fled to the *Adams* for protection, Tamasese forces prepared an attack on Mata'afa, and Tamasese boats began to capture supplies meant for Mata'afa's men in the harbor.[98] Germany intervention, however, was unsuccessful and Mata'afa's men kept advancing.

Then, the pigs "crisis" occurred. After Scanlon's pigs were held at gunpoint, Leary wrote to the commander of the *Adler* that he was "desirous of locating responsibility for violations of American rights" and wanted to know if they were under German protection.[99] When the *Adler's* commander responded the next day that he did not want to intervene in a political dispute, Leary repeated his question, adding that "[u]nder the shadow of the German fort at Mulinuu atrocities have been committed."[100] When he did not hear from Fritze, Leary led a party to the Scanlon house, only yards from Tamasese forces, making it seem like he was garrisoning the house. He then threatened to bombard Tamasese forces until they left Mulinuu.[101] Tamasese, who argued that this was obviously a "pretend" plot to aid Mata'afa, withdrew on October 11.[102]

The Scanlon home was a convenient pretext to get involved. It was near Mulinuu, the neutral ground and seat of government occupied recently by Tamasese and German forces. By defending Scanlon's home, Leary could make a difference while claiming only to be protecting American property.[103] Once Tamasese abandoned Mulinuu, Leary

Bayard, October 3, 1888. Box 130, General Correspondence. Thomas Bayard Papers, LC; Note. JBM (John Bassett Moore) to Bayard, October 16, 1888. Box 130, General Correspondence. Thomas Bayard Papers, LC. The Murchison Letter incident meant that Bayard's correspondence regarding British Affairs was dominated by the attempt to have British diplomats meddling in American politics censured.

[98] Entry for September 16, 1888, *Adams' Deck Log* 5-2-1888 to 11-1-1888; Entry for September 23, 1888, *Adams' Deck Log* 5-2-1888 to 11-1-1888, RG 24, NARA.

[99] Leary to Fritz. October 7, 1888. Enclosure 2. CD160. November 6, 1888. Despatches from US Consuls in Apia, Samoa. R16, T27. RG 59, NARA II.

[100] Fritz to Leary. October 8, 1888. Enclosure 3. CD 160. November 6, 1888. Despatches from US Consuls in Apia, Samoa. Roll 16. Leary to Fritz. October 8, 1888. Enclosure 4. CD 160. November 6, 1888. Despatches from US Consuls in Apia, Samoa. R16, T27. RG 59, NARA II.

[101] Stevenson, *A Footnote to History*, 140–57. On the politics of neutrality and Mulinuu Point, see Record of Events. September 4, 1888. Enclosure 1. CD 160. November 6, 1888. Despatches from US Consuls in Apia, Samoa. R16, T27. RG 59, NARA II.

[102] Tamasese to Leary. October 11, 1888. Enclosure 6. CD 160. November 6, 1888. Despatches from US Consuls in Apia, Samoa. R16, T27. RG 59, NARA II

[103] Mulinuu was fortified by Tamasese in September, with German support. Record of Current Events. Enclosure 0. CD 150. September 11, 1888. Despatches from US Consuls in Apia, Samoa. R16, T27. RG 59, NARA II.

claimed Tamasese had lost his right to rule because it was the seat of government.[104]

Blacklock and Leary were not done. Later in October, after the *Adler* accidently hit an American house while trying to preventing Mata'afa's men from raising a canon lost in the harbor, Leary argued that Fritze should not conduct military operations in Apia Harbor. To "safeguard" American interests, Blacklock persuaded Leary to garrison the US Consulate in Apia, in theory ensuring the consulate's protection, but more importantly placing American troops on the Beach.[105] Notices were placed in Apia that the marines were ready to provide aid.[106] Fritze was "astonished" at the overreaction.[107] Then, on November 11, Leary notified Tamasese that Scanlon's property was taken from the Scanlon home, and if it was not returned, "I shall be at liberty to take such action as will in future enforce a wholesome respect for the American flag and the lives and property under its protection."[108]

The Germans began to play this game, too; Americans and Germans justified their military actions through specious claims about protecting their compatriots' property. From the German perspective, if Mata'afa's forces happened to be near German property, then they were justified in shelling his positions.[109] From the US perspective, if Mata'afa happened to quarter his forces on or near American property, then Leary might intervene without violating his orders. One episode, called Leary's "Big Bluff" by Moors, highlights the dangers in this form of competition.[110] On November 14, Leary heard from Mata'afa that the *Adler* intended to bombard Mata'afa's forces. Blacklock, Leary, and the British Consul met during the night, agreeing that they would defend Mata'afa if they could

---

[104] Meeting Notes. February 4, 1889. Box 136, General Correspondence. Thomas Bayard Papers, LC

[105] Record of Events. September 4, 1888. Enclosure 1. CD 160. November 6, 1888. Despatches from US Consuls in Apia, Samoa. Roll 16. See also Leary to Fritz, October 24, 1888. Enclosure 17. CD 160. November 6, 1888. Despatches from US Consuls in Apia, Samoa. R16, T27. RG 59, NARA II

[106] Blacklock. Notice to all American Citizens. Undated. Enclosure 27. CD 160. November 6, 1888. Despatches from US Consuls in Apia, Samoa. R16, T27. RG 59, NARA II.

[107] Fritz to Leary, October 26, 1888. Enclosure 18. CD 160. November 6, 1888. Despatches from US Consuls in Apia, Samoa. R16, T27. RG 59, NARA II.

[108] Leary to Tamasese, November 11, 1888. Folder 1, Box 668. Subject File, U.S. Navy, 1775–1910, VI – International Relations and Politics, 1887–1894, Samoa. RG 45, NARA II. It is unclear what the property was, and is only described as an "article."

[109] Becker. Notice to all Samoans. October 25, 1888. Enclosure 29. CD 160. November 6, 1888. Despatches from US Consuls in Apia, Samoa. R16, NARA II.

[110] Moors, *Some Recollections of Early Samoa*, 75.

claim he was on American property.[111] When the *Adler* steamed out the following morning to bombard Mata'afa, it was followed by the *Adams*, with Moors and Blacklock on board.

There are two versions of what happened next. The most spectacular version has it that before the *Adler* could fire on Mata'afa's men, the *Adams* interposed itself between the ship and the shore and ran out its guns, training them on the German ship and also coming so close to the *Adler* that its guns could not elevate above the *Adams*. Leary sent a note to the German commander: "I have the honor to inform you that having received information that American property in the Latoga vicinity of Laulii, Lotoanuu, and Solo-Solo is liable to be invaded this day, I am here for the purpose of protecting the same."[112] The *Adams's* Logbook has a less exciting account, recording that the *Adams* and HMS *Lizard* followed the Germans to Mata'afa's headquarters and sent the note, but there is no record of the ship's guns being run out.[113] There are reasons, though, to prefer the more exciting account: the *Adams's* log for those hours confuses times and events, and Leary had an incentive to downplay his brinksmanship with the German ships in his official log. Regardless, the *Adler* eventually left, leaving Mata'afa's forces safe. Blacklock, the Vice-Consul, wrote, "By delaying the Mata'afa attack the Tamasese people can strength their strong hold and otherwise improve their position."[114] The *Adams* and the *Nipsic* continued supporting Mata'afa, likely using Moors to provide arms and coordinate naval support until the rest of the ships arrived in 1899.[115]

---

[111] Records of Events. Enclosure o. CD 166. December 3, 1888. Despatches from US Consuls in Apia, Samoa. R17, T27. RG 59, NARA II.

[112] In Henry Collins Walsh, "Captain Leary at Samoa," *Ainlee's Magazine* 3, no. 5 (June 1899): 744.

[113] Entry for November 14, 1888, *Adams' Deck Log* 11-2-1888 to 2-4-1888, RG 24, NARA.

[114] Blacklock to Rives, December 3, 1888. Apia Samoa. Enclosure No. o Record of Current Events. In House Docs, No. 1, NARA

[115] Leary to Whitney. U.S.S. Adams, Apia Samoa. December 2, 1888. House docs No 3. Meeting Notes. February 4, 1889. Box 136, General Correspondence. Thomas Bayard Papers, LC. Leary to Wallis, November 27, 1888. Folder 1, Box 668. Subject File, US Navy, 1775–1910, VI – International Relations and Politics, 1887–1894, Samoa. RG 45; Leary to Tamasese, November 27, 1888. Folder 1, Box 668. Subject File, US Navy, 1775–1910, VI – International Relations and Politics, 1887–1894, Samoa. RG 45. NARA. I draw the conclusion that Moors was used to channel guns from Entries for November 20, 1888, and January 23 and January 25, 1889. *Nipsic's Log Book*, October 10, 1888 to April 9, 1889; Mullan to Fritze, December 18, 1888. Folder 1, Box 668. Subject File, U.S. Navy, 1775–1910, VI – International Relations and Politics, 1887–1894, Samoa, RG 24, NARA. Mullan, the commander of the *Nipsic*, appears to

Embarrassingly for the State Department, Moors and Leary's scheme quickly became common knowledge. The following February, after reports reached Berlin about problems in Samoa, Bismarck had Count Arco, the German Ambassador to Washington, talk to the Secretary of State. Arco explained to Bayard that Leary and Blacklock were at the bottom of the trouble. The ambassador reported a fairly accurate portrayal of much of Leary's activities in Samoa, from the Scanlon incident through the end of November. He and the Secretary of State then argued about whether $210 was sufficient compensation for Scanlon's pigs. Bayard, promising to consult Leary, reported that he doubted "enflaming statements."[116] However, Bismarck was right. A war in Samoa had almost occurred because of Moors' influence and Scanlon's pigs.

The pattern of brinksmanship between 1888 and 1889 is important for understanding the origins of alliance making in the islands. Two clear conclusions can be drawn from the record. The first crucial point to draw from this history is how uninvolved political elites were in the decision-making. While Leary, Blacklock, and Moors were moving toward a direct alliance with Mata'afa, policymakers in Washington and Berlin were unaware of happenings in Apia and congratulating each other on reaching an understanding. Bayard thought it sufficient to simply let their subordinates know that they should consult with one another and their governments to ensure the mutual defense of property.[117] If they did consult, Bayard "saw no reason to suppose that any question could arise that we could not readily settle."[118] Bayard was unaware that those subordinates were pointing cannons at one another.

The second crucial point concerns the strength of weak ties. Personal connections and social skill provided Moors with the ability to influence Leary. Moors met Leary in the course of supplying Leary's ship. Over time, these weak ties would become stronger. At one point, Moors' friendship with Leary was intense enough that he went on a spy mission

---

have lacked talent for Leary's game, as the *Adler* was able to sneak out of Apia to bombard Mata'afa. Mullan to Fritze, December 23, 1888. Folder 1, Box 668. Subject File, U.S. Navy, 1775–1910, VI – International Relations and Politics, 1887–1894, Samoa. RG 45, NARA.

[116] Meeting Notes. February 4, 1889. Box 136, General Correspondence. Thomas Bayard Papers, LC.

[117] Letter. Bayard to Count Arco, November 21, 1888. Box 132, General Correspondence. Thomas Bayard Papers, LC.

[118] Meeting notes. Bayard and Arco. Undated. Box 132, General Correspondence. Thomas Bayard Papers, LC.

with Leary to the Tamasese camp because "Leary dared me to do so."[119]
These weak ties to a single ship captain were augmented by a substantial
amount of social skill. Moors and Blacklock had lived in the islands for
many years, they deeply understood Samoan politics and culture, and
their livelihoods depended on brokering deals between Europeans and
Samoans. Their structural niche between societies, in other words, made
them "trustworthy and responsible" people whom the navy could depend
on to explain American interests. Faced with a structural hole, decision-
makers have little recourse but to turn to agents whose weak ties are the
only sources of information.

When Blacklock and Moors incited Leary to defend the pigs, it set
in motion events to which Washington had to react. The *Adams*'s and
Nipsic's reports of action in Samoa motivated Cleveland to send additional ships. As the situation on the ground grew worse for the Brandeis–
Tamasese forces, and Germans began to be returned without their heads,
the Germans escalated the conflict. On January 5, a telegraph arrived in
Washington from Auckland. The Commander of the *Nipsic* sent word
that Germany had lost twenty sailors and thirty were wounded in a battle against Mata'afa.[120] Germany, in retaliation, was shelling villages and
placing neutrals' lives and property in danger, in particular, by inspect-
ing American ships in the harbor.[121] Unfortunately, there is no record of
the Cabinet meetings where these decisions were reached, but the USS
Trenton and the USS *Vandalia* were sent to Samoa the following week.
Admiral Kimberly was then granted institutional authority and sent to
Samoa.[122] Kimberly never had a chance to exert official influence. Only

---

[119] Moors, *Some Recollections of Early Samoa*, 72. The *Adams* also purchased supplies
from Moors. See Entry for November 20, 1888, *Adams' Deck Log* 11-2-1888 to
2-4-1888.

[120] Telegram. To Bayard. January 5, 1889. Box 134, Undated, General Correspondence.
Thomas Bayard Papers, LC.

[121] The policy of looking for Americans was reasonable. Besides the active involvement
of Moors and Leary, an American reporter named Klein had embedded himself with
Mata'afa's forces and was present when Germany took 50 casualties on a particularly
bloody day. See Meeting notes. Bayard and Arco. January 8, 1889. Box 134, General
Correspondence. Thomas Bayard Papers, LC. For Klein's account, see John C. Klein.
"Affidavit of John C. Klein." January 14, 1889. No. 1. Correspondence respecting Affairs in Samoa, Printed for the use of the American Commissioners in Berlin.
Samoan Conference at Berlin 1889. Despatches from US Commissioners-Protocols. Box
1. Second Samoan Conference, 1889, RG 43, NARA II.

[122] Proposed Telegram to Admiral Kimberly. Undated. Box 134, General Correspondence.
Thomas Bayard Papers, LC.

five days after he arrived, the hurricane defused the crisis.[123] Washington never had its say as the politics of the Beach drove events.

THE UNITED STATES GOES TO WAR

Ten years after the hurricane swept into Apia, the great powers faced the most substantial fighting in Samoa yet. In January 1899, Mata'afa, the American ally in the 1889 civil war, assumed the throne in Samoa. Now a German ally, Mata'afa created a provisional government, deposing his rival Tanumafili's American-backed government. By March, the United States was actively fighting in Samoa, this time against Mata'afa, on land and sea.

On March 14, Admiral Kautz, aboard the *Philadelphia,* opened fire on war canoes trying to occupy Mulinu'u Point. Following this, American and British warships bombarded the coast, weakening Mata'afa's forces in order for Tanumafili's forces to gain ground. They ferried hundreds of Tanumafili's followers from nearby islands and trained them. A force of Americans and British then landed on the coast, and in cooperation with Tanumafili's forces, cleared the coasts before moving inland on April 1. With tensions escalating, the HMS *Torch* arrived with news that the great powers had decided once and for all to let a joint commission decide the fate of the islands; the great powers did not want a war over Samoa.[124]

Why did the United States decide to enter the Samoan tangle again? And, when it did so, why did it ally against Mata'afa in 1899, after being allies in 1888 and 1889? The conventional wisdom posits that great power decision-making led to the alliance, because the great powers poor institutional solution to the 1889 crisis sowed the seeds of a future civil war. I argue that the conventional wisdom is wrong. The institutional solutions produced by the 1889 crisis were certainly inept, but they did not directly lead to an alliance between the US Navy and Tanumafili. Instead, British missionaries took advantage of a structural hole to choose their preferred candidate and ensure military backing by the United States.

---

[123] The *Trenton* left for Samoa from Panama in January, but it took two months to reach the islands, in part because it visited Tahiti en route. See Entries for January 13, February 22 and 23, and March 2 and 11, 1889. *Trenton's Log Book,* November 29, 1888 to May 30, 1889.

[124] Paul Kennedy, "The Royal Navy and the Samoan Civil War, 1898-1 899," *Canadian Journal of History* 5, no. 1 (1970): 57–72; Kennedy, *The Samoan Tangle,* 154–5; Moors, *Some Recollections of Early Samoa,* 149–52.

The Institutional Explanation

The conventional wisdom about the emergence of conflict in 1898 is that western-imposed political institutions were incapable of resolving conflicts between Samoans or western interests on the islands.[125] An institutional explanation is not presented as an alternative explanation in Chapter 1, yet it is an important alternative to consider here. If the institutions that the great powers imposed on Samoa contributed to the crisis in 1898 and 1899, then the seeds of alliances were formed in the capitals of the great powers, rather than on the Beach in Samoa; intermediaries, in other words, would have mattered less than I expect.

After the hurricane, the three powers met in Berlin in April 1889 to consider the problem of Samoa. The result – the conference's General Act of June 14, 1889, or the Berlin Act – reorganized the government of Samoa to avoid future great power competition. The Berlin Act's primary aim was to prevent competition between the great powers over the administration of Samoan affairs. To avoid this competition, the Act created a single judge – a "chief justice of Samoa" – who was to be appointed by Sweden if the great powers failed to agree on a nominee. The chief justice would be the king of Samoa's principal legislative adviser and was tasked with making decisions about leased land, settling disputes between the great powers and Samoa, and overseeing disputes within Apia. In addition, the Act created a President of the municipality in Samoa. All this was to be paid for by the Samoan government, requiring heavy taxes.[126]

The most controversial issue at the conference was the appointment of a king. The great powers wanted firm rules for the election of kings, because leadership controversies often led to dissension in the islands. They agreed the king should generally be selected by "the laws and customs of Samoa," and any dispute should be peacefully settled by the Chief Justice. Selection of the first king, however, needed a more specific method. Owing to the conflict with Germany in 1888, Bismarck staunchly opposed Mata'afa, who had beheaded German sailors.

---

[125] All the major works on Samoa concur in this assessment. See Gilson, *Samoa 1830 to 1900*, chap. 16; Gray, *Amerika Samoa*, 92–98; Kennedy, *The Samoan Tangle*, chap. 3; Ryden, *The Foreign Policy of the United States in Relation to Samoa*, chap. 14; Masterman, *The Origins of International Rivalry in Samoa, 1845–1884*.

[126] "General Act Providing for the Neutrality and Autonomous Government of the Samoan Islands." In *Treaties, Conventions, International Acts, Protocols and Agreements Between the United States of America and Other powers, 1776–1909*. Senate, 61st Congress, 2nd Session, Document No. 357. Washington: GPO, 1910, 1576–89.

Similarly, Tamasese, the German puppet, was not a strong candidate, because Britain and the United States opposed his candidacy. With the two most popular candidates facing opposition from each side, the great powers agreed to select Malietoa Laupepa, the Samoan who had turned against Steinberger (as described earlier in the chapter).[127]

Unfortunately, Samoans were wholly unaware of what was happening in Berlin, and they reached a different conclusion to the controversy over the kingship: they appointed Mata'afa as king (*Tupu o samoa*) and Laupepa as the vice king (*Sui Tupu o Samoa*). When word of the Berlin Conference's conclusions about the kingship reached Samoa, Laupepa claimed power and deposed Mata'afa. In the ensuing conflict in 1893, Britain and Germany sent warships to aid Laupepa, who easily prevailed over Mata'afa. Mata'afa was exiled and sent to the Marshall Islands with his most important supporters. Almost immediately, a second rebellion began, led by Tamasese's son.

If the government in Samoa was already unstable, matters soon became worse in 1898. Malietoa Laupepa – the only candidate that the great powers had agreed upon – died in August. The consuls now faced the question of whom to support. The only candidate most Samoans would support was Mata'afa, and by November, Mata'afa and his supporters expected him to become king. His challengers were Laupepa's son, Tanumafili, who was collaborating with Tamasese (the younger, being the son of Tamasese who ruled with Brandeis). To bolster their chances, Tanumafili and Tamasese colluded to "run" together on a "ticket," with Tanumafili as king and Tamasese as his vice-king. Tanumafili and Tamasese had support from the US and British agents. Despite this collusion, Mata'afa was overwhelmingly popular.

Empowered by the Berlin Act, the Chief Justice, William Lea Chambers, heard the case and ruled that Mata'afa was ineligible, making Tanumafili the unopposed candidate. After reaching this decision, Mata'afa and his supporters revolted against the court, leading to war in which the United States deployed soldiers into the islands.

---

[127] There were rumors that Laupepa had formed a secret alliance with the German government while imprisoned. See Kasson to Blaine. May 5, 1889. Samoan Conference at Berlin 1889. Despatches from US Commissioners-Protocols. Box 1. Second Samoan Conference, 1889, RG 43, NARA II; Kasson to Blaine. May 11, 1889 (no. 26). Samoan Conference at Berlin 1889. Despatches from US Commissioners-Protocols. Box 1. Second Samoan Conference, 1889, RG 43, NARA II.

The conventional wisdom is that the crisis was sparked by institutional problems created by the Berlin Act.[128] The Berlin Act had two problems. First, it relied on laws and customs that did not exist in Samoa. The First Article suggested that Laupepa's replacement should be "elected according to the laws and customs of Samoa."[129] What were these laws and customs? As the American Consul, Luther Osborn, tried to explain to Washington, "there is no <u>law</u>" regarding succession, and the Samoan custom was "for the chiefs of each group of districts to get together, and to each elect a king, and then go to war, and for the unsuccessful party to remain OUT [sic], and sulk, and refuse to recognize the government and defy the authority of the king in power."[130] While exaggerated, this is more or less accurate. The second problem was great power interests, which divided power among unpopular figures within Samoan society, none of whom wanted to cooperate with one another. Henry C. Ides, an American Chief Justice in Samoa, may have put it best: "The natives were to be governed by a King whom the majority did not obey; the Whites by a German President of the Municipality, who was also to act as adviser to a King that did not want his advice; and over all was set a Swedish Chief Justice to intervene in the disputes that were certain to ensure."[131] Paul Kennedy echoed this judgment, writing that "the underlying cause" of the resumption of fighting "lay undoubtedly with the faulty phraseology of the Berlin Act."[132] The great powers created a structure in which competing interests needed to cooperate, and they relied on laws and customs that did not exist, all of which created institutional problems.

The creation of a Chief Justice is particularly important for the events that followed. Some scholars think the Berlin Act's provisions encouraged the war in 1899 because they led to the selection of an unpopular king. The Chief Justice who heard the case, William Lea Chambers, was an American. On December 31, when he ruled in favor of Tanumafili,

[128] Variants of the institutional argument are present in Gilson, *Samoa 1830 to 1900*; Ryden, *The Foreign Policy of the United States in Relation to Samoa*; Kennedy, *The Samoan Tangle*.

[129] See Article 3, Section 6 in "General Act Providing for the Neutrality and Autonomous Government of the Samoan Islands." In *Treaties, Conventions, International Acts, Protocols and Agreements Between the United States of America and Other Powers, 1776–1909*. Senate, 61st Congress, 2nd Session, Document No. 357. Washington: GPO, 1910, 1576–89.

[130] Osborn to Moore. CD 71. November 29, 1899. Despatches from US Consuls in Apia, Samoa. R25, NARA.

[131] In Ryden, *The Foreign Policy of the United States in Relation to Samoa*, 552.

[132] Kennedy, *The Samoan Tangle*, 155.

Mata'afa's supporters swept into Apia, overwhelmed Tanumafili's forces, and forced them to flee with Chambers onto a British ship in the harbor.

The institution, however, did not explain the civil war. Chambers reasoned that the Protocols to the General Act prevented Mata'afa from becoming king because Bismarck had refused his selection in 1889.[133] If Chambers's interpretation was correct, then the institution required him to select Tanumafili, the unpopular candidate. This legal explanation, however, is not compelling. A plain text reading of the Protocols does not exclude Mata'afa. On May 22, 1889, Bismarck did remark, "The principle of the election of a King was therefore acceptable, but he [Bismarck] was bound to make one exception, in the person of Mataafa, on account of the outrages committed by his people, and under his authority, upon dead and wounded German sailors lying on the field of action." But, the Protocol goes on in the next several paragraphs to show that the other powers refused to agree to this provision.[134] Moreover, the American representatives worried that barring a candidate from office would represent an anti-democratic approach by the great powers. Therefore, instead of explicitly barring Mata'afa from seeking the kingship in 1889, they simply chose his rival, Malietoa Laupepa, to occupy the kingship. No explicit language barred Mata'afa from the throne.[135] In addition, the Protocols themselves are generally not binding, and Germany had withdrawn its objections. There was therefore no legal case to bar Mata'afa.

Chambers had earlier reached this same conclusion. In a letter to Moors written two months earlier, Chambers explained that Mata'afa has "the same right to aspire to the kingship as any other Samoan, and if the people elect him as Malietoa's successor in a rightful manner, according to the laws and customs of Samoa, why shouldn't he have the office?"[136] When Chambers announced the trial, he similarly gave no

---

[133] A few days before the case began, he wrote, "I cannot propose anything contrary or at variance with the Treaty, and must stick close to it." W.L. Chambers to Moors, November 30, 1898, Apia Samoa. In Moors, *Some Recollections of Early Samoa*, 119.

[134] In fact, the American representative was ordered not to consent to an election in which the most popular candidates could not run. See Kasson to Blaine. May 11, 1889. Samoan Conference at Berlin 1889. Despatches from US Commissioners-Protocols. Box 1. Second Samoan Conference, 1889, RG 43, NARA II.

[135] "Protocols of Conferences between Great Britain, Germany, and the United States, respecting the Affairs of Samoa. Berlin, April 29-June 14, 1889." In *British and Foreign State Papers. 1888–1889, Volume LxxxI*. London: Her Majesty's Stationary Office, 1889. 1251–2.

[136] W.L. Chambers to Moors, Apia Samoa October 5, 1898. In Moors, *Some Recollections of Early Samoa*, 116.

hint of any language disqualifying Mata'afa from seeking office.[137] Only mid-trial did Chambers change his mind. He claimed he was not aware of the Berlin Act until the British Consul presented it into evidence in the final two days of the trial. Therefore, the legal claim rests on the odd conclusion that the Chief Justice of the Treaty Powers, in the words of one journalist, had "never taken the trouble to possess or open the only book which annotates and explains the Act."[138] Even then, this could not constitute a legal case, because the German representative in Apia withdrew Bismarck's reservation, saying Germany welcomed Mata'afa's election.[139] Therefore, the claim that decision-making among the great powers – the "faulty phraseology of the Berlin Act" in Kennedy's terms – led to the crisis is unlikely at best.

Paul Kennedy, who tends to favor the institutional explanation, rightly points out that had savvier individuals occupied positions of authority, the outcome may have been different. The Chief Justice, for example, may have sided with Mata'afa, forestalling war; US and British naval commanders may have been less aggressive, interpreting their orders less liberally; and German commercial and consular agents may not have engaged in collaboration with Mata'afa at all. The great power condominium, in other words, did not eliminate the seeds of conflict, but neither did it create the kind of conflicting interests that often lead political scientists to credit political institutions as causes of conflict.

The Missionaries

To understand how the United States and Britain formed an alliance with Tanumafili – an 18-year-old student who asked only to be left in school – requires understanding why Chambers decided to issue a judgment for the less popular party, and why he demanded that the navy enforce his decision. The last section showed there was no political or legal rationale for the decision, undermining institutional explanations. This section claims that missionaries framed support for Tanumafili for Chambers,

---

[137] Supreme Court of Samoa. "To all persons." December 9, 1898. Volume 1. Box 1. Records relating to the Samoan High Commission. RG 43. NARA II.

[138] John George Leigh, "The Samoan Crisis and Its Causes," *The Fortnightly Review* 65 (May 1, 1899): 727. Chambers' claim that he never opened the Protocols is even odder than Leigh recounts: it implies that a Chief Justice had never "opened the book" that created the office of Chief Justice or given the Chief Justice rules and jurisdiction for deciding claims.

[139] Moors, *Some Recollections of Early Samoa*, 133–4.

FIGURE 5.4 Group portrait of missionaries and families, Samoa, ca. 1890–1900. Courtesy of Council for World Mission archive, SOAS Library

prompting him to sow the seeds for an alliance with the United States. Chambers did not speak the language, understand Samoan traditions, or know its politics. when facing on the most consequential decisions in the kingdom's history, he turned to the London Missionary Society for guidance. The missionaries (Figure 5.4) used this opportunity to secure install Tanumafili in power, provoking an alliance with the United States.

Chambers represents, in a microcosm, a case where a structural hole may be produced in intimate surroundings. Chambers was from Georgia; he spent most of his professional life as a banker and real estate developer in Alabama.[140] He moved to Samoa the year before the court case, and no part of the surviving correspondence, of which there is much, leaves any confidence that Chambers adequately understood the complexities of the case. He did not understand the Samoan language or culture, despite living alongside Samoans for a year. This led to embarrassment. One night during the trial, for example, he found himself awakened at two o'clock when his house was surrounded by armed men. He only found

[140] "Wm. Lea Chambers," *The Successful American*, January 1902.

out two hours later, when he finally found an interpreter, that they were there to guard him.[141] Chambers, a wealthy Southern gentleman, banker, and Protestant likely had trouble developing relationships with Samoans.

When forced to make a decision, Chambers turned to those he trusted the most: the London Missionary Society (LMS). The LMS had long ties in Samoa, dating back to 1830, when John Williams landed on Savai'i. By the 1890s, the LMS was quite influential, especially after the former king, Laupepa, attended its school decades earlier. One of the primary theories in Samoa held that Chambers backed Tanumafili due to LMS influence. The German consulate, along with many others in Samoa, credited the LMS with having Chambers's ear and turning him against Mata'afa. I argue that a careful inspection of the LMS archives bears out the claims of those who saw the missionaries' fingerprints on the decision.

The LMS had a significant interest in preventing Mata'afa from obtaining political power. First, LMS missionaries in Samoa believed they were in a spiritual struggle with Catholics. Due to Mata'afa's Catholic background, the LMS missionaries thought it was in the interests of Samoans (their souls) that Mata'afa lose. For example, William Huckett, an LMS missionary, explained in an LMS report during the trial that "Mataafa fairly represents the Roman Catholic and anti-European element whereas Malietoa stands for Protestantism and the law as established by The Three Powers." He goes on to suggest that because Mata'afa "is so good a Roman Catholic," it "rouses naturally the suspicious [sic] of a British Protestant."[142] James Edward Newell, another LMS missionary, shared these prejudices, although he used a more sinister tone, opining that the effort to install Mata'afa was part of a global Catholic plot. Newell explained to the LMS that the Papal conspiracy was evidence that "the priests with us here as well as elsewhere throughout the world spare no effort and stop at nothing to retrieve the position they are losing throughout Christendom."[143]

---

[141] Chambers to Consuls. December 22, 1898. Enclosure 31. CD 76, December 27, 1889. Despatches from US Consuls in Apia, Samoa. Roll 25.

[142] William Huckett. Report of the Apia District, Samoa. December 26, 1898. Box 4, Folder 33. South Seas Reports. CWM-LMS. See also Newall to Thompson. December 22, 1898, Savaii. Box 4, Folder 33. South Seas Reports. CWM-LMS. By year's end, the LMS position had changed. The conflict had interrupted LMS life and instruction, and by December the LMS sought any solution to the conflict and welcomed the partition that would end the war. See Newell and Barradale. The Fifty-fifth Annual Report of the Malua Institution. December 31, 1898. Box 4, Folder 34. South Seas Reports. CWM-LMS.

[143] Newell to Thompson. December 23, 1898. Box 44B, Folder 7. South Seas Incoming Correspondence. CWM-LMS.

In the fight to win control over Samoan souls, there were serious perceived advantages to having an LMS-trained king. Malietoa Laupepa, Tanumafili's father, had attended LMS schools and services, and the missionaries believed he had helped the LMS gain adherents. More importantly, they worried that if Mata'afa was selected it would create a schism within the church. Most of Mata'afa's supporters were Protestants (most of Samoa was Protestant), and if Mata'afa won, those supporters might decide to leave LMS churches for other Protestant or Catholic missions.[144] They believed this potential schism was in fact Germany's motivation to back Mata'afa: Catholics plotted to elect Mata'afa, discrediting the LMS and making Samoa swing Catholic.[145]

Chambers's limitations provided an inroad for the LMS. To make sense of the case, Chambers needed a local "expert" – an intermediary – to help analyze complicated questions about succession.[146] He turned to Newell, of the London Missionary Society. Newell was closely tied to Tanumafili and his followers, had lived in Samoa for years, was fluent in the language, and understood Samoan politics and culture.[147] He also had significant experience working between the societies in his role as missionary. These are the signs of a socially skilled intermediary described in Chapter 1.

Newell used several of the strategies available to intermediaries to advance cooperation. He "explained" the kingship controversy to Chambers, translated the documents presented by the Mata'afa party – whose selection Newell opposed – and likely also relied on his knowledge of Samoan politics to help Chambers make sense of the shifting political ground.[148] Moreover, the LMS may have been able to present cooperation

---

[144] Huckett to Thompson. December 20, 1898, Box 44B, Folder 7. South Seas Incoming Correspondence. CWM-LMS; The Fifty-Fourth Annual Report of the Malua Institution, 1898. December 31, 1898. Box 4, Folder 33. South Seas Reports. CWM-LMS.

[145] Newell to Thompson. October 31, 1898, Box 44B, Folder 7. South Seas Incoming Correspondence. CWM-LMS.

[146] Newell to Thompson. December 23, 1898, Box 44B, Folder 7. South Seas Incoming Correspondence. CWM-LMS. The only other reference to an intermediary during the trial is a suggestion for a brief two-hour meeting with a German academic on theories of kingship in Samoa. It is unclear whether this meeting occurred. See Rose to Chambers. November 25, 1898. Enclosed in CD 71, November 29, 1899. Despatches from US Consuls in Apia, Samoa. Roll 25.

[147] Diary Entry December 4, 1898. Box 2. Newell Papers. CWM/LMS.

[148] Three of these translated documents have survived. See Samoan Chiefs to Chief Justice, December 6, 1898 (2 letters). Box 7, Folder 2. Newell Papers. CWM/LMS. See also Diary Entry December 8, 1898. Box 2. Newell Papers. CWM/LMS. Newell is described as an "expert" by the British consular staff. Morgan to Newell, January 11, 1899, Box 7, Folder 2. Newell Papers. CWM/LMS.

to Chambers in a way that made Samoan culture fit with Chambers's worldview. Chambers's critics described him as a partisan evangelical with a narrow outlook on the trial. Lloyd Osbourne, Stevenson's stepson, argued that Chambers had a long relationship with the LMS, having lived with them when he first reached Samoa a few years earlier. The LMS did not deny this association.[149] And, while there is no confirmatory evidence about Chambers's religious views, the charge that he was Protestant and cared deeply about religion was never denied in the many newspaper accounts that followed the decision. If Chambers was a "narrow-minded" protestant, then LMS endorsement of Tanumafili may have enhanced his trust in Tanumafili's party and made it appear there was a harmony of interests between the United States and Tanumafili.

There is clear evidence that Newell capitalized on the resources he gathered through his intermediary status to influence Chambers's decision-making. Not only did his meetings with Chambers provide opportunities to shape the decision, but the best evidence is that Newell was not shy about sharing LMS views with him. Newell passed rules that the LMS should not openly "meddle with Samoan politics in the way of public utterances on this rather ticklish subject," but the LMS archives show that LMS European missionaries, in private discussions with Chambers, and Samoan LMS Congregationalists, in private meetings with Samoan chiefs, discussed their support for Tanumafili.[150] In the controversy following Chambers's ruling, the LMS responded that they did not intervene directly in the war to support the Protestants.[151] The LMS was right. There was no *public* intervention in the war. Throughout the crisis, the LMS sought to distance itself from any direct involvement. They provided medical aid to the injured on both sides of the conflict, gave sanctuary to women and children regardless of whether they supported Mata'afa or Tanumafili, and issued a policy that missionaries who took up political work needed to resign their position from the society.[152] The LMS

---

[149] Lloyd Osbourne, "The Other Side of the Samoan Question," *The Independent* 51, no. 2637 (June 15, 1899): 1597–1601.

[150] Newell to Thompson. October 31, 1898, Box 44B, Folder 7. South Seas Incoming Correspondence. CWM-LMS.

[151] Newell to Thompson. December 23, 1898, Box 44B, Folder 7. South Seas Incoming Correspondence. CWM-LMS. Newell later denied that any LMS personnel discussed the case, besides his own translation of documents, which is manifestly untrue, as evidenced by his earlier correspondence. See Newell. Decennial Review of the Samoan Mission, 1891–1900. Box 6. Newell Papers. CWM/LMS.

[152] The Policy of the Society in Samoa (loose page accompanying "Let Samoa be Blessed"). Box 5. Newell Papers. CWM/LMS.

clearly did not want to encourage a religious war, especially when they were backing the unpopular candidate. There was, however, a clear gap between the LMS rules related to public support for Tanumafili, which was barred, and norms of providing private advice about Tanumafili's legal case and his qualifications. Perhaps most importantly, Newell met privately with Chambers in a long meeting on Christmas, three days before Chambers says he changed his mind about Mata'afa's eligibility.[153]

The most probable explanation, therefore, is that Chambers's decision to support Tanumafili was a product of missionary influence. Newell shared his views with Chambers during the trial, even before his long meeting on Christmas. Newell believed the case favored Tanumafili on its merits, and Mata'afa's case was constructed by "Samoan parasites and Romish priests."[154] Chambers had endless discussions with Newell and other LMS missionaries, and he likely trusted their advice because they were his intermediaries to Samoan society. There is no other compelling explanation for Chambers's decision. The legal rationale for his decision was absurd, if not stupid, and Chambers almost certainly knew that his judgment would spark a civil war. It is hard to find an interest, other than that of the LMS, that might be served by Chambers's decision.

In the context of this book, it's interesting to consider the primary defense made by the LMS against the charges of missionary influence.[155] The LMS claimed it was exonerated by the High Commission that the great powers sent to investigate the crisis in 1899.[156] The process by which the High Commission investigated the case provides another example of how LMS missionaries exploited the lack of direct personal relationships between westerners visiting Samoa and the Samoans themselves. The Commissioners knew less than Chambers about Samoan politics and culture. Bartlett Tripp, the American High Commissioner and later Head Commissioner, begins his account of his trip to Samoa by noting his surprise when he received a telegram asking him of his interest in the post. He did not know where the islands were or what issues might plague

---

[153] Diary entry, December 25, 1898. Box 2. Newell Papers. CWM/LMS.
[154] Huckett to Thompson. December 20, 1898, Box 44B, Folder 7. South Seas Incoming Correspondence. CWM-LMS.
[155] The first defense, considered earlier, was that the LMS made no public statement of support and treated the wounded from both parties. This defense responds to sinister charges – especially that the LMS refused medical aid to dying Catholics – that are clearly wrong. But, these charges are not at issue here because the LMS could aid the wounded while also trying to convince Chambers to side with Tanumafili.
[156] Newell. Decennial Review of the Samoan Mission, 1891–1900. Box 6. Newell Papers. CWM/LMS.

Samoan politics. He accepted, expecting to be given a month for study, but then received a second telegram asking him to be ready right away to leave for Washington and then Samoa. He recalls that his only comfort was that no one else he talked to knew anything about Samoa either. The only time they had to prepare was their time spent aboard ship.[157] In his account of the history of the kingship question, it is apparent that Tripp should have studied more diligently: he does not understand the history of Samoan politics or culture, and he confuses extraordinarily important details, such as whether the "kingship" is hereditary, its origins, and its purpose.[158]

Unsurprisingly, the Commission turned to the LMS. Upon their arrival, Newell immediately volunteered his services to furnish the Commission with information, translations, and advice.[159] The Commission accepted, likely because they considered the LMS to be the real authorities on Samoan history and culture owing to their long history in the islands.[160] As a result, the unfortunate situation developed in which Newell was translator and adviser in an investigation that, in part, was intended to investigate Newell. Newell may also have befriended the commissioners. The tone of the correspondence between the British Commissioner, C.N.E. Elliott, and Newell is more of confidant than examiner.[161] They continued their correspondence for quite some time after Elliott left Samoa.[162] In short, the High Commission's investigation of Samoa repeated the problems produced by Chambers's decision, while providing the same opportunities for LMS influence.

Once the LMS missionaries educated and supported Tanumafili, and persuaded Chambers to side with him, an alliance between US and British naval officers was almost inevitable. In reaction to Chambers's ruling, Mata'afa's men stormed Mulinuu, capturing the courthouse and forcing

---

[157] Bartlett Tripp, *My Trip to Samoa* (Cedar Rapids, IA: Torch Press, 1911), 7–11.

[158] Ibid., 47–9. The notes from the first meeting also show confusion. See "Minutes of the First Formal Meeting of the Samoan High Commission." May 13, 1899. Scrap inside of Volume 1. Records Relating to the Samoan High Commission, Box 1 (Entry 811), RG 43, NARA II.

[159] Letter from CNE Elliott to Newell, May 8, 1899. Box 7, Folder 1. Newell Papers. CWM/LMS.

[160] Tripp, *My Trip to Samoa*.

[161] Letter from CNE Elliott to Newell, Apia, May 22, 1899. Box 7, Folder 1. Newell Papers. CWM/LMS; Letter from CNE Elliott to Newell, Apia, July 13, 1899. Box 7, Folder 1. Newell Papers. CWM/LMS; Letter from CNE Elliott to Newell, Apia, July 15, 1899. Box 7, Folder 1. Newell Papers. CWM/LMS.

[162] Letter from CNE Elliott to Newell, British Embassy, Washington, DC, November 5, 1899. Box 7, Folder 1. Newell Papers. CWM/LMS.

Chambers, Tanumafili, and the American and British consuls to flee to their ships in the harbor. The consuls and Tanumafili barely escaped with their lives as they were evacuated to ships off shore. An enraged Chambers promised to remain in Samoa "until this gross and outrageous insult is righted."[163] Three days later, Mata'afa's forces were in control of Apia and declared a Provisional Government. On January 4, facing the surge in Mata'afa's support, the Consuls agreed to provisionally recognize Mata'afa's Provisional Government, at least until orders arrived from the capitals. But, when the German consul closed the courthouse where Chamber's had issued his ruling, it was too much for Chambers. Chambers asked the Captain of the HMS *Porpoise* to reopen the courthouse, by force if necessary.

Over the next two months, the situation grew worse when Rear Admiral Albert Kautz arrived on the USS *Philadelphia*. Kautz's orders note that the Secretary of the Navy is "without detailed information" about what was sparking the revolution in Samoa, but Kautz was to "be governed by the General Act of Berlin" and to "act in concert with the majority of consular officers."[164] Kautz himself had no other source of detailed information about Samoan politics, which he readily confessed. In one remarkable incident, after Tanumafili's forces beheaded Mata'afa's men and carried one boy's head through the streets of Mulinuu, Kautz explained to the German Consul that having just arrived, he was learning "day to day" about Samoan politics and culture.[165] On Kautz's reading, his orders meant war to defend Tanumafili and Chambers, because Chambers was the ultimate authority over the election and the majority of the consuls supported Tanumafili. Worse, questioning Chambers meant undermining the rule of law.[166] Kautz quickly issued a proclamation, stating that Chambers's decision was final, and he hoped he did not

163 Despatch. William Lea Chambers. Undated. Box 8 (Folder related to Albert Kautz). August V. Kautz Papers. LC.
164 Long to Kautz. Undated. Notes for meeting. Undated. Box 8 (Folder related to Albert Kautz). August V. Kautz Papers. LC.
165 Kautz to Rose. March 30, 1899. Enclosure K. Kautz to Secretary of the Navy, March 31, 1899. In Kautz. *Report on Affairs in Samoa, March 6 to May 18, 1899*. Box 8 (Folder related to Albert Kautz). August V. Kautz Papers. LC. This note is in response to a complaint from Rose, the German Consul, that Tanumafili's forces were carrying heads through the streets of Mulinuu.
166 Notes for meeting. Undated. Enclosure B. Kautz to Secretary of the Navy, March 23, 1899. In Kautz. *Report on Affairs in Samoa, March 6 to May 18, 1899*. Box 8 (Folder related to Albert Kautz). August V. Kautz Papers. LC.

need to use military force to have the decision upheld.[167] Within a week, when Mata'afa and the German Consul refused to recognize Kautz's authority to impose a government, Kautz became less subtle, threatening to "drive them away with the guns of this ship and the English Men-of-War."[168] Kautz, though, did not limit himself to bombarding the shore. When Mata'afa moved inland, where the *Philadelphia*'s guns were no use, Kautz sent sailors ashore to hunt Mata'afa's men, and he began giving guns to Tanumafili's forces.

The civil war of 1899 continued until the High Commission arrived in April and finally put an end to the bloodshed. The three powers were fed up. Britain traded its rights in Samoa for German rights in Tonga and elsewhere, and the United States and Germany partitioned the islands, with Germany taking the majority of land and creating Western Samoa, and the United States taking the eastern islands, creating American Samoa.

CONCLUSION

The alliances formed between the United States and Samoans are different from many in this book. The cooperation between the United States and Samoa is difficult to document, uncertain in its origins, and moved through a wide variety of figures. It was also, in many ways, less consequential. An American surveying new US holdings around 1900 would likely think about the commercial importance of Hawaiian plantations, how Puerto Rico would guard approaches to the canal, or the burden of civilizing the Philippines. They might puzzle over what US policy in Cuba should look like over the next decade. They likely would not think much of Samoa. The three sets of alliances documented in this chapter certainly did not change the world, because the world does not change for Samoa.

Understanding Samoa, however, is important for understanding long-term trajectories in American foreign policy. In other nineteenth-century cases – the First Barbary War and the Philippines during the Spanish–American War – the United States decided to go to war and then searched for allies. Samoa is an example of a different kind of case. In Samoa, Washington decided not to fight, but was eventually dragged

---

[167] Kautz. O Le Talaiga. March 11, 1899. Enclosure C. Kautz to Secretary of the Navy, March 23, 1899. In Kautz. *Report on Affairs in Samoa, March 6 to May 18, 1899*. Box 8 (Folder related to Albert Kautz). August V. Kautz Papers. LC.

[168] Kautz to Mata'afa. March 15, 1899. Enclosure L. Kautz to Secretary of the Navy, March 23, 1899. In Kautz. *Report on Affairs in Samoa, March 6 to May 18, 1899*. Box 8 (Folder related to Albert Kautz). August V. Kautz Papers. LC.

into a shooting war against Mata'afa's forces, for reasons obscure in Washington, over islands that few cared about, and no one could find on a map.

The puzzle then is why the war occurred despite the low stakes. The answer is that the stakes were high for decision-makers on the Beach. For three decades, American and British agents, living at the intersection of Samoan and American society, played a deadly game with German agents in Apia. The prize for winning was control over Samoan commerce and churches. To win, they needed to enlist military support for the Samoans whom they supported. These agents used their niche between societies to broker cooperation. Steinberger formed the militia in the 1870s; Blacklock, Moors, and Leary brokered cooperation in the 1880s; and the LMS convinced the Chief Justice to support Tanumafili in the 1890s, prompting American and British naval and ground support in the islands. These decisions were made in Apia and not in Washington. Because these agents were positioned between societies, they were trusted by western governments and Samoans to understand the interests, capabilities, and culture of both sides. They used this position between societies to frame cooperation in ways that appeared to westerners and Samoans as fruitful, all the while realizing their personal interests in political power, business, and the fate of Polynesian souls. Read in this light, Samoa was a high-stakes case for decision-makers who had de facto control over American foreign policy, although these decision-makers lived about 7,000 miles from Washington.

6

Islands or Canned Goods

I know what I'd do if I was Mack," said Mr. Hennessy. "I'd hist a flag over th' Ph'lippeens, an' I'd take in th' whole lot iv thim."

"An' yet," said Mr. Dooley, "tis not more thin two months since ye larned whether they were islands or canned goods... Suppose ye was standin' at th' corner iv State Sthreet an' Archey R-road, wud ye know what car to take to get to th' Ph'lippeens? If yer son Packy was to ask ye where th' Ph'lippeens is, cud ye give im anny good idea whether they was in Rooshia or jus' west iv th' thracks?"

"Mebbe I cudden't," said Mr. Hennessy, haughtily, "but I'm f'r takin' thim in, annyhow."
– *Finley Peter Dunne, Mr. Dooley in Peace and in War, 1913, 43.*

In the 1890s, the United States found itself in a position to affect the fate of communities across the world. In Latin America, the United States had begun to form what modern scholars often describe as an empire, using military force and economic leverage to determine who ruled in Honduras, Nicaragua, Panama, and elsewhere.[1] Intervening in Latin American affairs often involved the processes described in this book. The United States formed alliances with local partners, such as Panamanian separatists fighting against the Columbian government.[2] This phenomenon was not

---

[1] Walter LaFeber, *Inevitable Revolutions: The United States in Central America* (New York: Norton, 1983), chap. 1. See also David Lake, *Hierarchy in International Relations* (Ithaca: Cornell University Press, 2009); David Lake, "Legitimating Power: The Domestic Politics of U.S. International Hierarchy," *International Security* 38, no. 2 (2013): 74–111.

[2] Charles D. Ameringer, "Philippe Bunau-Varilla: New Light on the Panama Canal Treaty," *The Hispanic American Historical Review* 46, no. 1 (1966): 28–52; Charles D. Ameringer,

limited to Latin America. Across the Pacific, the United States was forming alliances with local political leaders in Hawaii and Samoa to control
their political futures (see Chapter 5). The largest acquisitions happened
during the Spanish–American War, after which the United States found
itself in possession of Guam, the Philippines, and Puerto Rico, two of
which remain in American hands today.

I concentrate on the Philippines as an example of cooperation during
the Spanish–American War in this chapter. The war in the Philippines was
conducted by the US Navy, led by Admiral Dewey, in cooperation with a
rebel Philippine army led by Emilio Aguinaldo. Aguinaldo's forces, at first
allied with the United States, quickly became disenchanted as they discovered that the United States did not plan to secure their freedom. By early
1899, the war with Aguinaldo turned into the war against Aguinaldo,
and despite early American successes, the Philippine–American War
threatened to grow increasingly difficult and costly as the rebels shifted
from regular to irregular fighting. New allies were needed. Across the
islands, the US Army began to form alliances with local political and ethnic groups. These allies formed the nucleus of the first overseas American
colonial army, enlisting thousands of Filipinos as scouts, as police, and in
paramilitary units. This latter process is described in the Chapter 7.

The US commitment to the islands is a historical puzzle. The United
States, simply put, knew almost nothing about the islands. One could
perhaps exaggerate. One historian, for example, argues that the story
that President McKinley did not know the Philippines' location until
he consulted a globe is likely a myth.[3] Americans might know something about the islands because a decade earlier two large companies
had failed in the Philippines, the press ran occasional stories about the
islands, and its hemp was used in American agriculture for cordage.[4]
McKinley, therefore, may have been able to find the Philippines on a
globe (the record is unclear). Washington certainly had much more
information on the Philippines compared to other cases of conquest

"The Panama Canal Lobby of Philippe Bunau-Varilla and William Nelson Cromwell,"
The American Historical Review 68, no. 2 (1963): 346–63; David McCullough, *The Path
Between the Seas: The Creation of the Panama Canal, 1870–1914* (New York: Simon &
Schuster, 2001).
[3] Stuart Creighton Miller, *Benevolent Assimilation: The American Conquest of the
Philippines, 1899–1903* (New Haven: Yale University Press, 1982), 13.
[4] Peter Stanley, "The Forgotten Philippines, 1790–1946," in *American-East Asian
Relations: A Survey*, ed. Ernest R. May and James C. Thomson (Cambridge: Harvard
University Press, 1972), 291–316.

in the Spanish–American War, such as Guam, where a Warrant Officer asked on the expedition when the island was taken, "What about Guam and where is it anyway, and what do we want of it?"[5] Yet, in 1897, Washington had surprisingly little information about the group of islands where tens of thousands of American soldiers would soon find themselves caught in two bitter wars.

The structural hole between Washington and the Philippines created a situation in which intermediaries who navigated between societies were empowered to shape international politics. Specifically, in 1898, two American consuls, who had no tangible political connections in Washington and were explicitly denied the authority to negotiate with the Philippine rebels, took advantage of the structural hole between Washington and Asia to occupy the niche between societies. They used their "betweenness" to misrepresent Philippine and American interests, making cooperation possible despite substantial conflicts of interests. The alliance that resulted from their meddling helped the United States take the Philippines from Spain, and pay almost no cost to do so.

A NOTE ON BETWEENNESS AND METHODOLOGY

Before continuing with this chapter, it is important to note that it is different in kind from others. There are two distinct historical traditions that relate to questions of betweenness and political power. One agrees with this book, placing the blame for an alliance between the United States and Aguinaldo on the influence of two intermediaries who used a monopoly on information to manipulate the US Navy and the Philippine rebels into an alliance that was in neither's interest. Another disagrees, claiming that the Philippine rebels knew all along that the war with the United States would turn into a war against it. Almost every fact is disputed. Was there an alliance? Whose idea was the alliance? What role did intermediaries play? The specific historiographical questions focus on five sets of meetings that preceded Aguinaldo's return to the Philippines. The differences between historians relates to whether the meetings occurred, what was said at the meetings, and whether the meetings changed the attitudes of Filipinos toward the United States.

Rather than simply citing the historians that agree with my perspective, this chapter opts to litigate the evidence is detail. One reason for this decision is that otherwise this book might be accused of cherry picking

---

[5] In David F. Trask, *The War with Spain in 1898* (New York: Free Press, 1981), 385.

secondary accounts that suit its purposes.[6] The more important reason, however, is that many of the histories of the way only treat these meetings as the briefest of sideshows before weighing in on issues that happened once the United States and its allies turn their guns on one another. The debate about the meetings sets up rather than is the main point of the debate between historians. As I explain in the conclusion to the book, when political scientists turn to histories as evidence, they often cite specific historical claims that the writer who they are citing has not spent adequate time investigating. When a specific historical claim is not the main claim of the historian – when the specific claim is color, helps begin the history, or fills a missing piece to make the narrative work – then the evidence is often not as carefully described or weighed. The origins of US involvement with Aguinaldo is a case of this.

To approach this issue, therefore, requires turning fresh eyes on old evidence. This chapter described the debate about each of these meetings in detail. It examines all of the documents that historians have used, explaining why they corroborate the role of intermediaries. It also goes much further because the meetings are the sole subject of this chapter, rather than being color to get the story going. I searched through every record I could find, looking for evidence that corroborates or refutes the role of intermediaries. In doing so, it makes the case that treating betweenness seriously requires looking for evidence that describes what happens at the intersections of societies. The records of sailors, junior officers, ship logs, colonial newspapers, and more are required to build a fuller understanding of how politics happens where societies meet. This chapter therefore produces the most exhaustive effort to date to resolve this thorny historical controversy.

THE WAR WITH SPAIN

The war with Spain in the Philippines was won largely by Philippine allies. During the first month of the war, the US fleet, under George Dewey, won a decisive naval battle against a slow and poorly armed Spanish fleet at Manila Bay. But, Dewey could not capitalize on the victory to seize Manila. The US army was slowly being assembled in San Francisco and was months away from reaching the Philippines.

---

[6] Ian S. Lustick, "History, Historiography, and Political Science: Multiple Historical Records and the Problem of Selection Bias," *The American Political Science Review* 90, no. 3 (1996): 605–18.

When the first army units were being unloaded in the Philippines, the Spanish forces already faced a general uprising. Emilio Aguinaldo's Philippine army fought the Spanish, limiting their freedom of movement to Manila, and that city was besieged. On June 12, 1898, Aguinaldo declared Philippine independence, and on June 23 he organized a new government. By early July, as the first 2,000 American soldiers were being unloaded in Cavite, Aguinaldo had already retaken most of the Philippines and now planned on taking Manila. By July 25, when the majority of the American Army arrived, 70,000 people were holed up in Manila, running out of food, and fearing the inevitable insurgent assault. By this stage, the demoralized Spanish forces were looking for a way to surrender. They had no hope of holding out against either the Americans or Aguinaldo. The Spanish commanders, fearing the consequences of surrendering to Filipinos whom they had abused, asked if they might surrender to the United States. The United States and Spain made a deal: they staged a mock battle around Manila, with a promise of a Spanish surrender in exchange for excluding rebels from its streets.

Except for the Battle of Manila Bay, the United States simply did not need to fight in the Philippines, because Aguinaldo's forces did the fighting on its behalf. And, when the rebels tried to gain their reward – control of Manila – US forces barred their entry. Before long, the US turned its guns against Aguinaldo as it sought to end the rebellion against American rule in the Philippines.[7]

Many of the first generations of histories of the Spanish–American War treat the United States as the primary victors in the Philippines, forgetting the role played by the long-standing rebellion against Spanish rule. Henry Cabot Lodge's *The War with Spain* concludes that rebels "forgot they owed their position entirely to the American fleet, and that but for American war-ships the chiefs would have been vegetating in exile at Hong-kong, and their followers hewing wood and drawing water for the Spaniards, as of yore."[8] This dismissal of the Philippine contribution to the war is part of a larger pattern, in which US historians have often dismissed the notion that the Spanish empire was on the brink of collapse before the United States entered the war. Some historians now recognize

---

[7] This summary of the war is indebted to Brian McAllister Linn, *The Philippine War, 1899–1902* (Lawrence: University Press of Kansas, 2000), 22–25; Trask, *The War with Spain in 1898*, 401–22.

[8] Henry Cabot Lodge, *The War with Spain* (New York: Harper & Brothers, 1899), 199.

that the rebellion in Cuba had already inflicted thousands of causalities on the Spanish army; and by the time the United States landed in Cuba, Spain was unable to conduct offensive operations because of disease and poor morale.[9] This case for a specifically American victory was always harder to making in the Philippines because the US Army had barely made it to the Philippines when the war ended.[10] To understand how the United States won thus means understanding the alliance between the United States and Aguinaldo's forces.

The central question this part of the chapter asks is why Aguinaldo chose to cooperate with the United States. This question is important for debates about the Spanish–American War. At the end of 1897, Aguinaldo lived in exile in Hong Kong. By the following May, he was onboard the USS *McCulloch,* bound for the Philippines, to organize resistance against Spain. The alliance has always been somewhat puzzling. Why would Aguinaldo choose to cooperate with the United States to secure Philippine independence when, in retrospect, he traded one colonial power for another?

The answer, given by many historians and Aguinaldo himself, relates to intermediaries. Aguinaldo claimed that he thought the United States' official policy was support for the self-determination of the Philippines, and he formed this impression due to political promises made by Americans in Asia.[11] In light of Aguinaldo's revelations, the extent of intermediaries' influence is central to debates about imperialism during the war. Who made what promises to Aguinaldo? Did Admiral George Dewey, the hero of Manila Bay, intentionally mislead Aguinaldo? Or, were low-level American officials in Singapore and Hong Kong, who had no authority to negotiate with Aguinaldo, the source of political promises? Then again, was Aguinaldo simply lying in order to discredit the emerging American empire? In 1899 and 1900, these questions were central to Senate debates on the Philippines. At the time, "Dewey Mania" was

---

[9] Louis A. Perez, *The War of 1898: The United States and Cuba in History and Historiography* (Chapel Hill: University of North Carolina Press, 1998), 106. More generally see Ada Ferrer, *Insurgent Cuba: Race, Nation, and Revolution, 1868–1898* (Chapel Hill: University of North Carolina Press, 1999); Louis A. Pérez, *Cuba between Empires, 1878–1902* (Pittsburgh: University of Pittsburgh Press, 1983); Louis A. Pérez, *Army Politics in Cuba, 1898–1958* (Pittsburgh: University of Pittsburgh Press, 1976).

[10] Carlos Quirino, "The Spanish Colonial Army: 1878–98," *Philippine Studies* 36, no. 3 (1988): 381–6.

[11] The most famous statement of this position is in Emilio Aguinaldo, *True Version of the Philippine Revolution (1899)* (Whitefish, MT: Kessinger, 2010).

sweeping the United States: babies were named George, and their older siblings ate "Dewey Chewies."[12] If the newfound empire was founded on deception – if the United States had turned its guns against allies whom they had pledged would remain free – it might color the war and provide resources to Senate anti-imperialists who were already sympathetic to Aguinaldo. Senator George Hoar encapsulated this debate in brief, explaining to the country that we "treated them as allied and assured them of independence."[13]

Beyond its intrinsic political importance, the question of intermediaries' influence is also theoretically important. I argue that a handful of intermediaries who were explicitly denied the institutional authority to negotiate for the United States manipulated parties across a structural hole to secure cooperation. Focusing on these intermediaries is not novel, but it is contentious. New Left historians, such as Leon Wolff and Stanley Karnow, agree that a small group of Americans with no institutional authority shaped cooperation between the United States and Aguinaldo. The problem, as Brian McAllister Linn notes, is that these histories are partisan, owing, in Linn's words, to an "almost perverse insistence on treating the Philippines as an early Vietnam"; this renders their treatment of the historical record unreliable.[14] Conversely, another group of scholars, influenced by John R.M. Taylor's official history, are skeptical of the

---

[12] David Brody, *Visualizing American Empire: Orientalism and Imperialism in the Philippines* (Chicago: University of Chicago Press, 2010); William P. Leeman, "America's Admiral: George Dewey and American Culture in the Gilded Age," *Historian* 65, no. 3 (2003): 587–614; Bonnie M. Miller, *From Liberation to Conquest: The Visual and Popular Cultures of the Spanish–American War of 1898* (Amherst: University of Massachusetts Press, 2011), 247–53.

[13] George Frisbie Hoar, *The Conquest of the Philippines: Extracts from the Speech of Hon. George F. Hoar of Massachusetts in the United States Senate* (Washington, 1900), 2. More generally, see Robert Beisner, *Twelve Against Empire: The Anti-Imperialists, 1898–1900* (New York: McGraw-Hill, 1968), 160–1, 197–203; H. W. Brands, *Bound to Empire: The United States and the Philippines* (New York: Oxford University Press, 1992), 20–35; Adam Cooke, "'An Unpardonable Bit of Folly and Impertinence': Charles Francis Adams Jr., American Anti-Imperialists, and the Philippines," *The New England Quarterly* 83, no. 2 (2010): 313–38; Michael Patrick Cullinane, *Liberty and American Anti-Imperialism: 1898–1909* (New York: Palgrave Macmillan, 2012); E. Berkeley Tompkins, *Anti-Imperialism in the United States: The Great Debate, 1890–1920* (Philadelphia: University of Pennsylvania Press, 1970).

[14] Linn, *The Philippine War*, 401. See Stanley Karnow, *In Our Name: America's Empire in the Philippines* (New York: Ballantine Books, 1989); Leon Wolff, *Little Brown Brother: America's Forgotten Bid for Empire Which Cost 250,000 Lives* (New York: Longman, 1970).

influence of any of the agents I discuss at length.[15] Taylor, like the New Left histories, appears to prejudge conclusions, creating issues with document selection and analysis. Both sides of the debate treat the influence of these intermediaries as a sideshow, however dramatic, before tackling broader questions. By focusing specifically on the recruitment of Aguinaldo, and turning to the original documents to litigate the intermediaries' motives and influence, I provide the most detailed, contemporary treatment of the question, relying on evidence that has been overlooked in earlier historical work. This comes at the expense of presenting a simple narrative, which can be found in earlier work such as Karnow and Wolff.

The first part of this section discusses the extent of US political knowledge of the Philippines, showing that a structural hole existed. The second part examines the nature of US–Philippine security cooperation, arguing that it was more extensive than some historians allow and merits the term "alliance." The final section, which is the crucial causal argument, traces the recruitment of Aguinaldo during the final months of 1897 and the early months of 1898, following Aguinaldo as he moved around Asia. In this part, I show that two intermediaries promoted cooperation by manipulating information across a structural hole.

The Structural Hole

The US relationship with the Philippines before the Spanish–American War was limited, producing a structural hole between Manila and Washington. In Chapter 1, I describe four observable implications for the existence of a structural hole. One observable implication is that the parties are unaware of one another. Before the Spanish–American War, the US government had almost no knowledge of their future cooperation partners in the Philippines, and actors with institutional authority frequently lamented their lack of knowledge. Commodore George Dewey, who commanded the fleet that was to engage the Spanish off Manila Bay, remarked that "at that time the Philippines were to us a *terra incognita.*"[16] When he was given the Pacific Command, the documents he received from his predecessor contained two sentences about the Philippines: "The newspapers have contained accounts, for some time

---

[15] John R.M. Taylor, *The Philippine Insurrection Against the United States*, vol. 1 (Pasay City, Philippines: Eugenio Lopez Foundation, 1971).

[16] George Dewey, *Autobiography of George Dewey: Admiral of the Navy* (New York: Scribner, 1913), 175.

past, of a rebellion in progress in the Philippine Islands. No official information has been received in relation thereto, and no information of any sort that shows American interests to be affected."[17] Moreover, there was no one to consult. No US navy ship had been to the Philippines in years, and the most recent official report was dated 1876.[18] The only American official in Manila was Oscar Williams, an overworked consul, who was not only tasked with protecting US property during the run up to the war (a difficult job), but was also the primary source for all intelligence information to the US military. A close look at this consular correspondence shows he likely had no or almost no contact with the Philippine rebels. When Dewey wrote to Williams in February 1898, shortly before the Battle of Manila Bay, that he was "without definite information regarding the Philippines and our relations with them," he meant he had almost no information about the colony or its politics.

Dewey's personal knowledge of the Philippines, and Asia in general, was even more scant. One early biographer credits Dewey's trip aboard the *Juniata* in the early 1880s as useful, because "he studied the situation with care and acquired information of immense importance ten years later."[19] Another biographer suggests that Dewey's two years of experience in Asia led "the administration to choose him for a much more important mission in those waters sixteen years later."[20] If Dewey had formed personal relationships during his travels in Asia, there would be no structural hole: an agent with institutional authority, Dewey, would have direct ties to elites in Asia. Despite the claims of many early Dewey enthusiasts, Dewey had never been to Asia, and especially not to the Philippines. Not only did the *Juniata* never make it to the Philippines, but Dewey did not make it to Asia: he left the *Juniata* in Malta during the first leg of the trip.[21] Dewey was no Asia expert – claims to the contrary come from hagiographies for a war hero, not serious, scholastic texts.

---

[17] McNair to Dewey. December 31, 1897. Area 10 File, Navy, M625 R362, NARA.
[18] Dewey, *Autobiography of George Dewey*, 175.
[19] William Lawrence, *A Concise Life of Admiral George Dewey* (Boston: J.F. Murphy, 1899), 40. See also Henry Williams, *Taking Manila or In the Philippines with Dewey* (New York: Hurst, 1899), 42.
[20] Rossiter Johnson, *The Hero of Manila: Dewey on the Mississippi and the Pacific* (New York: D. Appleton, 1899), 113.
[21] Dewey, *Autobiography of George Dewey: Admiral of the Navy*, 153–5. The *Juniata's* deck logs show that many stories about its trip are inaccurate; especially that it circumnavigated the globe. In fact, the *Juniata* never crossed the Pacific, sailing from New York to Japan via the Suez Canal, and then returning by sailing west. See Entries in *Juniata*, Volumes 28–33. Logs of US Naval Ships, 1801–1915, Logs of Ships and Stations, 1801–1946, RG 24, NARA.

A second observable implication for the existence of a structural hole is a poor communications infrastructure. If communicating with a community is costly and difficult, then interpersonal relations are unlikely to form. Before and during the war, the rebels and Washington had no direct line of communications, because there was no physical infrastructure between Washington and rebel-controlled areas throughout the Philippines. The difficulties newspapers had are illustrative. During the opening days of the war in Asia, newspapers competed to find the latest news out of Hong Kong or Manila. The only three correspondents were with Dewey in Manila Bay, a two-day sail from the telegraph line at Hong Kong and therefore from making headlines in Americans newspapers.[22] Owing to the poor communication network, according to Charles Brown's close analysis of war reporting, newspapers made stories up while they waited for more definitive news. The accurate news that papers finally gathered about Dewey's victory came from stories originating in Madrid via London, not correspondents in Asia.[23] The situation in Manila Bay, however, was much better than it had been earlier in the decade – at least three correspondents were near the Philippines. Before 1898, there was no reliable reporting. The *Washington Post*, a newspaper policymakers in Washington were likely to read, contained thirty stories referencing "Philippines" in 1896, and only twenty-eight in 1897, the years preceding the war when news may have been useful for US policymakers. A close examination of the reporting reveals how little reliable information was available. Of the thirty stories published in 1896, only four were more than brief summaries, and most relied on reporting from Hong Kong, Japan, Singapore, or Spain; no story leaves one with confidence that any reporter had ever spoken to a rebel. The situation was the same for the influential Hearst papers, which sent correspondents only after the war began.[24]

---

[22] There was a telegraph in Manila, but Dewey cut the cable, and then did not send a ship back to Hong Kong for five days because it was needed in the Philippines. Therefore, it took about a week for the reporters to be able to report the victory. Charles Brown, *The Correspondents' War: Journalists in the Spanish–American War* (New York: Scribner, 1967), 194.

[23] Ibid., 182–4.

[24] Christopher A. Vaughan, "The 'discovery' of the Philippines by the U.S. Press, 1898–1902," *Historian* 57, no. 2 (1995): 303–14. Telegram. Hearst to R. Wildman. May 14, 1898 (date difficult to read). Folder 3, Box 1. Wildman Papers. LC; and Telegram. Hearst to R. Wildman. November (Unclear), 1899. Folder 5, Box 1. Wildman Papers. LC. Consistent with the argument of this book, newspapers turned to intermediaries to broker information, and in fact turned to the same individual who Aguinaldo turned to and

The relationship between Washington and Manila is therefore a clear example of a structural hole. No one knew Aguinaldo, expected to cooperate with him, or had reliable information about his intentions. Similarly, Aguinaldo did not know the American government's policy with respect to the Philippines (if there was a policy), know or trust an American official, and likely had never considered the possibility of working with American forces. Moreover, the war made communication even more difficult, because Dewey cut the telegraph line to isolate the Spanish in Manila.

The existence of this structural hole creates political power for individuals between societies. Those who have contacts on both sides of the Pacific – even if only through weak ties – become the only agents capable of brokering cooperation. They can use this betweenness to advance their own parochial interests.

Was There an Alliance?

Before turning to the recruitment of Aguinaldo, I first need to establish that cooperation in the Philippines counts as cooperation with a non-state ally. One historical controversy about the Spanish–American War is whether there was ever an alliance between the United States and Aguinaldo. David Sibley, for example, reaches the conclusion that "technically, the Americans and the insurgents were allies against the Spanish," whereas David Trask intentionally does not call the collaboration an alliance, instead emphasizing its limited nature.[25] Before addressing the origins of security cooperation, I therefore briefly discuss whether there was indeed security cooperation, to show that the case counts as an example of a non-state ally.

The Philippine forces clearly regarded the United States as an ally. The manifesto that Aguinaldo handed out to Philippine rebels when the American fleet neared Manila was called *Mga Kababayan* (Countrymen),

---

is described later. Wildman is likely the source that Brown cannot identify for the Hearst newspapers. The *Journal* would not list him because it was inappropriate for the Consul to have a paid position with a newspaper. See Williams to Wildman. July 25, 1898. Folder 3, Box 1. Wildman Papers. LC. Over time, Wildman would develop a network to report. Telegram. Hearst to R. Wildman. May 8, 1899. Folder 4, Box 1. Wildman Papers. LC. Telegram; Hearst to R. Wildman. May 22, 1899. Folder 4, Box 1. Wildman Papers. LC. This secret relationship furnished the bit of accurate news described by Brown.

[25] David Silbey, *A War of Frontier and Empire: The Philippine-America War, 1899–1902* (New York: Hill and Wang, 2007), 46; Trask, *The War with Spain in 1898*, 402–10.

but was translated into English as "American Allies." The English translation captures its meaning better. It promised coordination between American and Filipino forces: Filipinos would operate on land while Dewey fought from sea. It asked Filipinos to rally to the American flag because the Navy was pledged to help.[26] During the Spanish–American War, Filipino rebels counted on American help, predicted that it would be forthcoming, and aligned themselves with what they believed to be promised political rewards.

From the American perspective, there was an alliance in substance if not in form. The only reason this question is contentious is because official American policy held that there was no alliance. The Secretary of the Navy telegraphed Dewey in May 1898: "It is desirable as far as possible and consistent for your success and safety not to have political alliance with the insurgents or any faction in the islands that would incur liability to maintain their cause in the future."[27] Dewey responded that he had "entered into no alliance with the insurgents or with any faction."[28] Despite the official policy emanating from Washington, there are significant reasons to count cooperation as an alliance. During the war, the United States and its Filipino partners engaged in joint operations and planning intended to aggregate their resources against a common political enemy. Dewey again is clear. After hearing Dewey's pledge that there was no alliance, the Secretary of the Navy followed up, asking about any "conferences, relations or co-operations military or otherwise" that Dewey had with Aguinaldo.[29] Dewey responded with quite a list. He had transported the exiled leaders, helped them land, protected their forces as they rallied to the leaders, and armed them with captured Spanish guns. Moreover, Dewey remarked, "I have given him to understand that I consider insurgents as friends, being opposed to a common enemy."[30] Dewey realized that cooperation could yield political and strategic gains, making the cooperation an alliance in all but name.

---

[26] Pratt to Day, May 20, 1898. CD 223. Despatches from US Consuls, Singapore. M464, R14, NARA II.

[27] Telegram (114). SECNAV to Dewey. May 26, 1898. Folder 2, Box 52. Dewey Papers. LC.

[28] Telegram (120). Dewey to SECNAV. June 3, 1898. Folder 2, Box 52. Dewey Papers. LC.

[29] Telegram (129). SECNAV to Dewey. June 14 1898. Folder 2, Box 52. Dewey Papers. LC.

[30] Telegram (134). Dewey to SECNAV. June 23, 1898. Folder 2, Box 52. Dewey Papers. LC. On captured Spanish arms, see Dewey to Officer of the Guard, May 7, 1898. Pratt to Dewey. April 15, 1898. Area 10 File, Navy, M625, R363, NARA,

Recruiting Aguinaldo

Why did the United States and Filipino rebels choose to cooperate? The debate about how Aguinaldo was recruited – who, if anyone, made political promises to Aguinaldo – is crucial for the argument of the book. One interpretation popular with imperialists in the United States, favored by David Trask, is that Aguinaldo cooperated with the United States knowing there was a sharp divergence between American policy and Philippine aspirations.[31] In this view, which is similar to the structural determinism alternative explanation outlined in Chapter 1, Aguinaldo cooperated with the United States against the immediate enemy in Spain, knowing that future conflict with the United States was likely. A second view, advanced by New Left and many historians from the Philippines, is that American agents knowingly misled Aguinaldo into cooperating with the United States.[32] This view, elaborated below, is consistent with the argument of the book: American agents used their position between societies to frame cooperation for the Philippines in a way that was consistent with Filipino aspirations for post-war independence.

The argument of this chapter is that American agents seized on the structural hole between the United States and the Philippines to manipulate Washington and the Hong Kong junta into supporting cooperation. In contrast to Trask and others, I agree with the New Left historians that at least Pratt and Wildman led the United States and the Philippine rebels to reach a deal. This view posits that betweenness was central to political power. Against the New Left historians, I suggest it is unlikely these intermediaries sought to intentionally mislead Aguinaldo to secure commercial interests or establish a colony in the Philippines. Instead, these intermediaries, although they wanted a colony in the Philippines, did not believe the United States would assume a colonial role. Their skepticism that the United States would assume the White Man's Burden led them to make political predictions and offer assurances that likely were read as political promises by Aguinaldo and the junta. In the absence of direct contact – because there was a structural hole between Washington and Hong Kong – these predictions secured cooperation, as Philippine leaders likely took them as statements of policy.

---

[31] Trask, *The War with Spain in 1898*. See also Taylor, *The Philippine Insurrection Against the United States*.

[32] Miller, *Benevolent Assimilation*; Silbey, *A War of Frontier and Empire: The Philippine–America War, 1899–1902*.

To demonstrate this argument, this chapter follows Aguinaldo on his trip into exile from the Philippines in 1898, to Hong Kong, then to Singapore on his way to Europe, then back to Hong Kong, and finally his return to the Philippines. At each stop he met one or more US agents. I follow the diplomatic record to show how Aguinaldo's confidence in America's role in the post-war world was shaped over time.

Early Meetings in Hong Kong

The first intermediary who met with the Philippine junta was Rounsevelle Wildman. Wildman was appointed as Consul to Hong Kong in 1897 and reached the city on September 11, 1897.[33] About three weeks after Wildman's arrival, Felipe Agoncillo, Aguinaldo's friend, wrote to Wildman asking for a meeting.[34] Agoncillo referred to himself in this letter as a representative of the "provisional revolutionary government" in the Philippines. Wildman reported to the State Department that he had accepted this proposal and had begun to have a set of secret meetings with Agoncillo. He noted that Agoncillo proposed "an alliance offensive and defensive with the United States, when it declares war on Spain," and Agoncillo asked for American arms in the interim, to be paid for after independence.[35]

These meetings did not end in an alliance. The start of the war with Spain was months away, the United States did not have a fixed policy toward the Philippines in the event of a war, and Aguinaldo had not even reached Hong Kong yet. These meetings, however, provide a number of important clues to figuring out the later record of the Pratt–Wildman–Aguinaldo talks.

First, the talks left Wildman in a brokerage position between Washington and the Philippine junta. In many ways, Wildman was a model intermediary. He had weak ties to the Philippine rebels, formed by a string of sporadic talks over a period of a few months in Hong Kong between 1897 and 1898. He also had only weak ties to Washington, where there is little record of any political influence. He also did not have the institutional authority to negotiate on behalf of the United States. The State Department made it clear that Wildman was not to accept the proposal, and that he should terminate his conversations with Agoncillo

33 Wildman to Day, September 11, 1897. CD 8. Despatches from US Consuls, Hong Kong, M 108 R19, NARA II.
34 Agoncillo to Wildman, October 2, 1897. Folder 3, Box 1. Wildman Papers. LC.
35 Wildman to Day, November 8, 1897. CD 19. Despatches from US Consuls, Hong Kong, M 108 R19, NARA II.

immediately. Wildman's interference was neither proper nor wanted. Therefore, his influence was premised strictly on his structural niche between societies. As the only representative of the United States with whom Agoncillo was meeting, Wildman's decisions mattered.

Moreover, the content of the meetings matter because they contain implicit assumptions that the United States would work to secure Philippine independence. When Wildman wrote to the State Department in November, he acted as if the United States had already recognized the rebel government: "I have been called upon several times by Mr. F Agoncilla [sic] Foreign Agent and High Commissioner etc. of the New Republic of the Philippines." He then implied that the government was legally constituted: "Mr. Agoncilla holds a Commission signed by the President, Members of Cabinet, and General-in-Chief of the Republic of the Philippines empowering him absolutely with power to conclude treaties with foreign governments."[36] These exchanges show that Wildman recognized, and believed that the United States would soon recognize, the Philippines as an independent sovereign state.

Why would Wildman endorse Philippine independence in 1897? And, what incentives did Wildman have to broker cooperation between Philippine rebels and the US government? There are two popular explanations. First, Wildman may have intended to profit financially, perhaps from commercial projects in the Philippines after Spanish rule ended. While this explanation would be consistent with the argument of this book, the evidence is underwhelming because Wildman had no clear financial interests in colonization. In none of his personal or diplomatic correspondence does he spend much time discussing commercial matters, and there are no records of commercial ventures started or supported by Wildman himself. The absence of this evidence is remarkable. Compare Wildman to his friend and correspondent who was the Consul to Siam.[37] From Siam, the Consul frequently wrote to American industrialists, highlighting the benefits of trade with Siam, and he would highlight commercial opportunities in the Philippines through the lens of American commercial interests.[38] Wildman, by contrast, rarely mentioned commerce,

---

[36] Wildman to Day, November 8, 1897. CD 19. Despatches from US Consuls, Hong Kong, M 108 R19, NARA II.

[37] On their relationship, see, e.g., Wildman to Barrett. January 15, 1898. Folder 2, Box 17. Barrett Papers, LC.

[38] Barrett to Smith, September 11, 1895. Cor. File April 1895–Mar. 1896, 191–2. Box 3. Barrett Papers, LC; Barrett to Motter. October 4, 1895. Cor. File April 1895–Mar. 1896,

seemingly paying as little attention as possible to his consular duties.[39]

The balance of the evidence suggests that Wildman likely sought to promote cooperation because he believed it was in the interests of the United States as well as the Philippines. To understand why Wildman would believe that cooperation was important requires understanding Wildman's worldview. Wildman was perhaps best known as an author of romantic, Kipling-esque stories related to empire.[40] His fiction provides important clues about his motives. Wildman's short stories show him to be an enthusiastic imperialist of a certain sort. Wildman depicts people of different races, the Malays in particular, as innately intelligent and capable of civilization, although trapped in superstition and dogma.[41] British rule, as Wildman repeatedly describes it, civilized the natives, who in turn lavished attention on their imperial civilizers. His writings romanticize the British agents. The Dutch and Spanish model, in contrast, tended to abuse rather than uplift natives, because they denied native peoples tutelage and did not hold out the promise of independence. The benefits of British imperialism, therefore, included not just the direct benefits of becoming more civilized, but also the indirect

---

239–43. Box 3. Barrett Papers, LC; Notes. "The Nicaraguan Canal a National Necessity." Undated. Cor. File Aug. 1896–Aug. 1897, 341–60. Box 3. Barrett Papers, LC; Bridges to Barrett. May 5, 1898. Folder 2, Box 17. Barrett Papers, LC. See also Salvatore Prisco III, *John Barrett: Progressive Era Diplomat: A Study of a Commercial Expansionist, 1887–1920* (University of Alabama Press, 1973).

[39] Another possibility, which is also consistent with the argument of this book, is that Wildman promoted cooperation in order to defraud the junta of money. The origins of this argument relate to events in 1898. Before leaving for Manila the following year, Aguinaldo left Wildman money to purchase arms for the insurgents. Wildman neither provided the shipment of arms nor returned the funds. Wildman therefore may have stolen the funds given in 1898 and 1899. See Teodoro Agoncillo, *Malalos: The Crisis of the Republic* (Quezon City: University of the Philippines, 1960), 154–5. This explanation for his decision making in 1897 is unlikely. The plan he recommended in 1897 asked for arms first and then money delivered years later, after independence. If executed, it would have left Wildman with no money. The 1897 plan for cooperation contains no apparent financial gain for Wildman, and therefore he had no opportunities for fraud in 1897.

[40] Wildman had been the editor of *Overland Magazine*, providing him a platform to disseminate his work. See Frank L. Mott, *A History of American Magazines, 1865–1885* (Cambridge: Harvard University Press, 1966), 402–9. His ideas are not necessarily original and the writing is neither wonderful nor awful – Kipling, who is writing of the same themes in the same period, is better – but literary criticism need not detain us here.

[41] Rounsevelle Wildman, "A New Year's Day in Malaya," *Overland Monthly* 26 (1896): 76–80; Rounsevelle Wildman, "Malayan Child Life," *Overland Monthly* 26 (1896): 270–6. See also Wildman to Moore, July 18, 1898. CD 63. Despatches from US Consuls, Hong Kong, M 108 R19, NARA II.

benefits of avoiding the worst excesses of imperialism.[42] Wildman identified American political culture as providing the same benefits as British.[43] This helps make sense of his correspondence with the State Department (described later), where he both laments Spanish rule, claiming that the Filipinos should be independent of Spain, and describes US imperialism as improving the islands.[44]

Two crucial points can be drawn from Wildman's fiction. First, Wildman's promotion of cooperation was consistent with his worldview. He believed that white rule – by Britain or America – would uplift the Philippines, whereas Spanish rule would make it worse.[45] Despite Wildman's hopes that the United States would pick up the White Man's Burden, he did not predict it would do so. No one living in Hong Kong in 1897 would have likely predicted an American colony in the Philippines in about a year.[46] Therefore, Wildman likely believed US support was in Philippine interests, because it would eliminate Spanish influences that prevented their cultural development – and the alliance would benefit the United States in its imminent war against Spain.

More importantly, Wildman sensationalizes agents who work between societies. His stories provide dramatic descriptions of agents of colonization who seize on structural niches to effect change. These figures were not only moral forces of nature, but also lived lives of adventure. He may have wanted to emulate the British heroes in his stories.

---

[42] See especially the discussions of James Brookes, the "White Rajah of Borneo" and Abu Baker of Johor, especially the final paragraph. Rounsevelle Wildman, *Tales of the Malayan Coast: From Penang to the Philippines* (Hong Kong: Lothrop, 1899), 292.

[43] In "The Simple Story of a Tailor Made Coat," Wildman begins a story with a reporter on a train from Jersey City to Washington who is surprised to discover that "the train was as cosmopolitan as the country. I could scarcely mention any phase of civilization or barbarism (so long as I stopped short of the Cannibals) which is not represented." Yet, Wildman is quick to observe that while they have strange manners and costumes, soon "these men will vote and make our laws, often more wisely than the legitimate sons of the soil; or that awkward red-faced woman may be the mother of a youth our country shall be proud to own and honor." Rounsevelle Wildman, "The Simple Story of a Tailor-Made Overcoat," *Overland Monthly* 27 (1896): 530.

[44] Wildman to Moore, July 18, 1898. CD 63. Despatches from US Consuls, Hong Kong, M 108 R19, NARA II.

[45] A set of brief biographies of Philippine leaders in his papers describes them in terms that reflect his short stories. These biographies appear to be the raw material for another set of political stories. Notes, Undated. Folder 1–2, Box 1. Wildman Papers. LC. See also his characterization of Philippine leaders. Wildman to Moore, July 18, 1898. CD 63. Despatches from US Consuls, Hong Kong, M108 R19, NARA II.

[46] I present evidence later that Wildman believed colonization unlikely.

Did Wildman, at these early meetings, suggest that the United States was willing to form an alliance in order to secure Filipino cooperation in the coming war? There is no evidence of an explicit political promise, but Wildman almost certainly discussed cooperation as if American support for Philippine independence was a certainty. Agoncillo told Wildman that he was negotiating on behalf of the "Republic of the Philippines." By engaging in negotiations with the rebels under these terms, Wildman would have acknowledged that, whether or not an alliance was forthcoming, discussions related to it would be between the recognized government of Filipinos and the United States. By taking recognition of independence for granted, Wildman would have made it appear that American and Philippine interests were aligned.

The Edward Wood Meetings

Wildman's meetings with Agoncillo occurred before either Dewey or Aguinaldo had arrived in Hong Kong. In the coming months, first Dewey with the fleet, and then Aguinaldo came to the city. When Aguinaldo first arrived, others besides Wildman first reached out to Aguinaldo. Aguinaldo recalled that when he reached Hong Kong, "some people came to me and in the name of the Commander of the U.S.S. *Petrel* asked for a conference in compliance with the wishes of Admiral Dewey. I had some interviews with the above-mentioned Commander, *i.e.*, during the evening of the 16th March and 6th April, during which the Commander urged me to return to the Philippines to renew hostilities against the Spaniards with the object of gaining our independence, and he assured me of the assistance of the United States in the event of war between the United States and Spain." When Aguinaldo asked the Commander of the *Petrel*, Edward Wood, about the post-war status of the Philippines, Wood responded, "*The United States is a great and rich nation and needs no colonies.*"[47] When Aguinaldo asked for the agreement in writing, Wood referred him to Dewey. But before Dewey could respond either way, Aguinaldo ended the negotiations because of a lawsuit with another Filipino in exile that forced him to flee on April 7.[48]

The meetings with Wood highlight critical observable implications for my argument. In the spring of 1898, Aguinaldo and his allies worried

---

[47] Aguinaldo, *True Version of the Philippine Revolution*, 6–7; Emilio Aguinaldo, *Second Look at America* (New York: R. Speller, 1957), 31.

[48] At some point during this period, Dewey himself may have met with junta members. George Dewey, "*Was There a Deal with Aguinaldo?*," ed. Henry Graff (Boston: Little, Brown and Company, 1969), 2.

about two problems facing cooperation with the United States. The first problem relates to conflicts of interest: Would the United States respect Philippine independence? On Aguinaldo's account, Wood and Hall articulated US policy, likely without authorization from Dewey and certainly without authorization from Washington, which made it appear the United States and the Philippines had a harmony of interests due to the American lack of interest in colonizing the Philippines. The second problem relates to mistrust: Aguinaldo, simply put, did not trust Hall and Wood. He asked for a deal to be written down, with direct authorization from those with institutional authority in the United States (e.g., Dewey). Unable to get a written assurance and fearing a lawsuit, Aguinaldo fled, refusing to cooperate. If these meetings occurred, then they are a crucial part of the story, because they highlight the two central issues that later intermediaries would need to negotiate: conflicts of interest and mistrust.

Aguinaldo's account of the visit with Wood has invited starkly different accounts by historians. Many historians favor Aguinaldo's account, retelling his story without looking for further confirmation.[49] In the closest analysis, in contrast, Trask denies that Wood played any role, arguing that there is "no evidence to confirm this story," and that "it is highly probable that the rebel leader misrepresented their content as a part of an effort to account for the decline in friendly relations" that occurred later. Considering skeptics' objections to the content, and even occurrence, of the *Petrel* meetings is important. If one can show that Aguinaldo lied about the meetings, then it undermines Aguinaldo's credibility regarding the influence of Dewey, Pratt, and Wildman discussed later.

Given Trask's skepticism, it is reasonable to inquire about whether these meetings occurred. There is significantly more evidence than Trask allows about Wood's meetings with the Filipino junta. R.V. Hall, who was aboard the *Petrel*, recalls that he was collecting intelligence on Manila Bay for the US fleet when he was put in touch with the junta through a jeweler named Mr. Levy. Hall does not record the details of what was said, but he explains that Wood met with the Filipinos on Dewey's order, writing that after a few initial meetings, Commander Wood went to Dewey's flagship and returned with orders to "go back and find out if they wanted to go back to the Philippines, how many men they could muster and what arms they would need." Hall notes the need to build trust, as Aguinaldo thought that Mr. Levy, the Hong Kong merchant, might be a Spanish

---

[49] See for example Agoncillo, *Malalos*, 121–2; Wolff, *Little Brown Brother*, 46–47.

spy.[50] The concern about spies is consistent with Aguinaldo's thought process described later in this section: the junta had concerns about Spanish agents trying to discredit the rebellion during March and April 1898.[51]

Beyond first-hand reports by participants on both sides, there is also more circumstantial evidence. Dewey exercised his fleet often during March and April 1898, and if the meeting dates cited by Aguinaldo occurred on a day reserved for fleet exercises, then the meeting likely did not occur. But, the *Petrel*'s logs show that the dates of meetings correspond to days when the *Petrel* was in harbor, distilling water, making meetings plausible.[52] Moreover, if the key source on the American side, R.V. Hall, was aboard the *Petrel* and never left ship in the period preceding the meeting, then he could not have met Mr. Levy or Aguinaldo. But, there is clear evidence that on March 12, only a few days before Aguinaldo's first meeting with Wood, Hall was not on board.[53] Hall's account is the only testimony that survives, and the most careful evaluation of the circumstantial evidence paints Hall's and Aguinaldo's accounts of the meetings as plausible.

Trask's second argument is that Aguinaldo's account of the *Petrel* meetings is not credible because if Aguinaldo believed the United States would support the war effort, then he would not have fled Hong Kong for Europe. Trask concludes that this shows Aguinaldo was more concerned with money than politics, and therefore the account of Wood's promises is unlikely. Trask's conclusions, based on Taylor's partisan account, are unsatisfactory.[54] The historical record shows that greed is insufficient to explain Aguinaldo's behavior. After he fled from Hong Kong, Aguinaldo went to Singapore where he learned the war had begun. If money and not politics guided Aguinaldo, he should have continued on to Europe with the junta's funds; instead, he returned to fight. Moreover, Aguinaldo gives a reasonable explanation in his accounts: he feared that Spanish agents

---

[50] Hall. Memorandum for Admiral Dewey Relating to Interviews with Junta in Hong Kong. Enclosure in Hall to Caldwell, February 9, 1900. Box 11, Folder 4. Dewey Papers. LC.

[51] Ronald H. Spector, *Admiral of the New Empire: The Life and Career of George Dewey* (Baton Rouge: Louisiana State University Press, 1974), 85–86.

[52] Entry for March 16 and April 6, 1898. Volume 18. *Petrel* (PG-2). Logs of US Naval Ships, 1801–1915, Logs of Ships and Stations, 1801–1946, RG 24, NARA.

[53] On March 12, the *Olympia* signaled to the *Petrel* for Hall to make repairs on the flagship, to which the *Petrel* responded that he was not on board. See Entry for March 12, 1898. Volume 18. *Petrel* (PG-2). Logs of US Naval Ships, 1801–1915, Logs of Ships and Stations, 1801–1946, RG 24. NARA. I assume the officer listed R.J. Hall in the log of officers is really R.V. Hall.

[54] Taylor, *The Philippine Insurrection Against the United States*, 1: 91–8.

were behind the lawsuits and were trying to sap political and financial support from the revolution.[55] Therefore, fleeing was the only rational response to support the revolution. Trask and Taylor provide no evidence to undermine this account.

In sum, there is no substantive reason to doubt Aguinaldo's account of the meetings. In fact, a review of the evidence shows a consistency between Aguinaldo's account of the meetings and Hall's account, as do ship movements and Hall's presence in Hong Kong. Therefore, in the absence of any contrary evidence, the meetings likely occurred and there is no reason to doubt that Hall and Wood led Aguinaldo to believe that the United States did not anticipate annexing the islands. Like Wildman's assertions that the United States would recognize the junta, this prediction would have seemed a slam dunk in early 1898 from aboard ship near Hong Kong.

The Hall and Wood meetings are important. They clearly show the extent of the structural hole between the junta and the United States. There were so few people capable of bridging the structural hole that a jewel merchant, who may have been a Spanish spy, was necessary to put the Navy in touch with Aguinaldo, and those meetings failed. No agent was yet trusted to bridge the gap between societies. The Hall and Wood meetings also show that Aguinaldo would not cooperate until two problems were resolved. The first was mistrust. Aguinaldo did not trust Hall and Wood to keep the promise of post-war independence. The irregularity of the meetings combined with their refusal to provide a written assurance meant Aguinaldo did not believe them. There also needed to be a war. Hall's and Wood's pledges were for US support *if* there was a war with Spain. Aguinaldo, hounded by lawsuits, could not comfortably wait in Hong Kong for the war to finally begin. The situation would change, however, while he was sailing to Singapore, the first stop on his way to Europe.

Singapore

Aguinaldo arrived in Singapore on April 21, the same day President McKinley asked the Congress to declare war on Spain. He intended to make a brief stop there on his way to Europe. Five days later, Aguinaldo left to return to Hong Kong instead. During the interim days, Aguinaldo

---

[55] Hall also recalls suspicion of foreign agents. See Hall. Memorandum for Admiral Dewey Relating to Interviews with Junta in Hong Kong. Enclosure in Hall to Caldwell, February 9, 1900. Dewey Papers. LC. Box 11, Folder

reports that he believed he had a reliable promise from the United States that if he cooperated in the coming Spanish–American War, the Philippines would be independent after the war. What happened? Did decision-makers in Washington change their policy to ensure post-war independence? Or did agents on the margins find a way to provide assurances to Aguinaldo that the United States would respect Filipino independence after the war?

Aguinaldo arrived in Singapore with a small entourage, traveling incognito. About two days after he arrived, Howard Bray, an English businessman who worked in the Philippines, met with E. Spencer Pratt, the US Consul General of Singapore, to tell him Aguinaldo had arrived. E. Spencer Pratt is the second intermediary who shaped Aguinaldo's thinking. I contend that Aguinaldo's meetings with Pratt likely shaped his decision-making, leading him to believe that the United States was a trustworthy ally, and its post-war aims were consistent with his own.

Pratt and Bray arranged to meet Aguinaldo the following morning at "the Mansion," a local inn. Like everything else in the run up to the war in the Philippines, what was said at the Mansion is disputed, but the following facts are clear. The meeting was attended only by Pratt, Aguinaldo, Aguinaldo's assistant, and Bray who acted as interpreter. Pratt and Aguinaldo agreed that if Dewey wanted Aguinaldo to return, then Aguinaldo should go back to Hong Kong. Pratt telegraphed Dewey that Aguinaldo was ready to cooperate, to which Dewey replied that Aguinaldo should return as soon as possible. Aguinaldo left on April 26, traveling under an assumed identity back to Hong Kong.[56] The next day, Pratt telegraphed the State Department that a deal had been struck: Aguinaldo would return to Hong Kong to "arrange cooperation" between Dewey and the insurgents near Manila.[57]

An enduring historical question is who said what at the Mansion that led Aguinaldo to change his mind. One possibility, suggested by supporters of American involvement in the Philippines, is that Bray, who served as translator for the meeting, engineered cooperation by mistranslating Pratt and Aguinaldo's conversation in such a way that Pratt appeared to be making political promises to Aguinaldo.[58] If Bray told Aguinaldo

---

[56] Pratt to Day, April 28, 1898. CD 212. Despatches from US Consuls, Singapore. M464, R14, NARA II.

[57] Telegram. Pratt to Secretary of State. April 27, 1898. Despatches from US Consuls, Singapore. M464, R14, NARA II.

[58] The most sophisticated version, giving an entertaining account of the supposed cover-up by Bray, is in Dean Conant Worcester, *The Philippines Past and Present* (New York: Macmillan, 1921).

that Pratt promised Philippine independence on behalf of the United States, then this assurance may have been sufficient for him to return to Hong Kong to cooperate with Dewey. This account is consistent with the argument of this book. If Pratt had no experience with Philippine insurgents, did not speak the language, and did not understand their interests, then he likely turned to a trusted intermediary to help him negotiate with Aguinaldo. There is clear evidence that Pratt trusted Bray, in part because of his knowledge of the Philippines.[59] Furthermore, Bray had an incentive to misrepresent Pratt's position: Bray was promised that if Aguinaldo's insurgency won, then he would have a position in the new government. Under this hypothesis, Bray used his social skill and weak ties to the United States and the Philippines to engineer cooperation by explaining parties' interests and establishing trust. If true, it makes the argument of this book in miniature. It is almost certainly not true however.

Pratt, not Bray, likely played the role of intermediary. Pratt provided Aguinaldo with reassurances that the United States did not intend to colonize the Philippines. This is Aguinaldo's view. Aguinaldo recounts that when he went to Singapore, Pratt explained that the US and Philippine interests were aligned. According to Aguinaldo, Pratt told him that the agreement he sought from Dewey had arrived via telegram, and the United States would at least "recognize the Independence of the Philippines under the protection of the United States Navy." Pratt also tried to build trust. Pratt told Aguinaldo there was no need for a formal agreement because the pledges of the Admiral and Consul were the "equivalent to the most solemn pledge that their verbal promises and assurance would be fulfilled to the letter."[60] In *A Second Look at America,* Aguinaldo explains that Pratt reassured him of American intentions by citing existing US policy: "You need not have any worry about America. The American Congress and President have just made a solemn declaration disclaiming any desire to possess Cuba and promising to leave the country to the Cubans... As in Cuba, so in the Philippines. Even more so, if possible; Cuba is at our door while the Philippines is

---

[59] Bray later wrote to Dewey, rightly, that he had offered Pratt "services which at least time were considered invaluable because no other persons possessed the unique knowledge required, or if they did it was not available." Bray to Dewey. May 21, 1900. Box 11, Folder 4. Dewey Papers. LC.

[60] Aguinaldo, *True Version of the Philippine Revolution,* 10.

10,000 miles away."[61] Howard Bray described the same political promises as Aguinaldo.[62]

Pratt was likely more responsible than Bray. The only other person
whom Aguinaldo spoke with in depth during his Singapore visit was the
editor for the Singapore Free Press, W.G. St. Clair. St. Clair reported the
same conversation: Aguinaldo asked for only temporary US protection
until the Philippines formed a stable government; and he expected the
US government would grant these terms. The important clue concerning Pratt's role is that Pratt forwarded the story that detailed his negotiations with Aguinaldo to the State Department without comment. His
non-comment matters. If Pratt did not make political pledges, he likely
would have commented on a story that he chose to forward in which his
political pledges are discussed.[63]

The clearest evidence of Pratt's role comes from after the fact. Recall
that one incentive for intermediaries to promote cooperation is that it
enhances their self-esteem. Pratt demonstrates how being at the center of
events can be exciting. In the year or two before the Spanish–American
War broke out, Pratt had been occupied with normal consular duties: he
reported on currency issues and the prospects for growing American
bicycle sales. Once Aguinaldo arrived, his correspondence changed. As
Leon Wolff puts it, "What fun ... Mr. Pratt was having in Singapore!
He had never known that diplomacy could be so intriguing and that
he was so talented at it."[64] When Aguinaldo's arrival in the Philippines
was reported in the Singapore papers, Pratt gloated to the State
Department: "Considering the enthusiastic manner General Aguinaldo
had been received by the natives and the confidence with which he
already appears to have inspired [in] Admiral Dewey, it will be admitted,
I think, that I did not overrate his importance and that I have materially

[61] Aguinaldo, *Second Look at America*, 34.
[62] See Howard Bray. "The Fate of the Philippines." June 8, 1898. *Singapore Free Press*.
    Enclosure 2. Pratt to Day, June 8, 1898. CD 228. Despatches from US Consuls, Singapore.
    M464, R14, NARA II.
[63] Pratt to Day, May 5, 1898. CD 217. Despatches from US Consuls, Singapore. M464,
    R14, NARA II. Pratt often commented on forwarded news accounts to explain them to
    the State Department. In addition, the charge of mistranslation is difficult to swallow
    with no evidence to support it. Although Pratt was not fluent in Spanish, he was fluent
    in French and English and likely spoke some Spanish. I find it unlikely that Bray could
    have engaged in so drastic a mistranslation of Pratt's meaning, while doing simultaneous
    translation, without Pratt becoming suspicious.
[64] Wolff, *Little Brown Brother*, 51.

assisted the cause of the United States in the Philippines in securing his cooperation." He goes on to criticize Wildman and perhaps Dewey in Hong Kong by explaining that he had no idea why they let Aguinaldo leave Hong Kong.[65] Pratt, in short, took credit for recruiting Aguinaldo.

Then there were the parties. On June 8, the Filipinos in Singapore arranged to have a 31-piece band play for Pratt, before a Philippine leader gave a speech praising Pratt for forming the alliance between Aguinaldo and Dewey. After Pratt gave his own speech thanking them, they all began to toast: "Hurrah for General Aguinaldo" and "Hurrah for the Republic of the Philippines!" Wolff tells the story well. Pratt then "walked up and down the room waving an American flag, then presented it to the Filipinos. More toasts were drunk to America, Dewey, Aguinaldo, and to Mr. Pratt himself. The band played again. At last the celebration ended, leaving the consul in a state of euphoria."[66] This desire to find oneself at the center of attention, described as an esteem benefit in Chapter 1, can be a powerful incentive to broker cooperation.

Pratt's descriptions of these parties also provide clear evidence that Pratt, and not Bray, played the critical role. An excited Pratt forwarded the articles about the parties to the State Department, promising to send translations of the addresses as soon as they were available. Before he could send translations, however, the State Department finally gave a verdict on his negotiations: "Avoid unauthorized negotiations with the Filipino insurgents." Unbeknownst to Pratt, the United States was beginning to rethink its policy concerning the Philippines, although only a few in the government, and none in the administration, had made statements in support of annexation.[67] Pratt responded, "No intention negotiate; left that Dewey: who desired Aguinaldo come."[68] The State Department was too late. By the time their message reached Pratt, not only had Aguinaldo left Singapore, but he had left Hong Kong and was taking ground quickly against Spanish forces.

By the time Aguinaldo left Singapore, he had begun to trust that the United States had no interest in colonizing the Philippines. In his final

[65] Pratt to Day, June 2, 1898. CD 225. Despatches from US Consuls, Singapore. M464, R14, NARA II.

[66] Enclosure 1 and 2. Pratt to Day, June 9, 1898. CD 129. Despatches from US Consuls, Singapore. M464, R14, NARA II; and Wolff, *Little Brown Brother*, 53.

[67] Ibid., 63.

[68] Pratt to Moore, June, 20, 1898. CD 235. Despatches from US Consuls, Singapore. M464, R14, NARA II. Telegram. Pratt to Secretary of State. June 19, 1898. Despatches from US Consuls, Singapore. M464, R14, NARA II. Pratt was full of excuses. See Pratt to Moore. June 27, 1898. CD 236. Despatches from US Consuls, Singapore. M464, R14, NARA II. See also Moore to Secretary of State. June 22, 1898. Despatches from US Consuls, Singapore. M464, R14, NARA II.

meeting before leaving for Hong Kong, Aguinaldo told Pratt that he hoped the United States would briefly establish a protectorate, while Aguinaldo set up an independent government.[69] In other words, whereas a month earlier in Hong Kong, Aguinaldo worried that the United States would not respect Philippine independence (during the Wood meetings), now Aguinaldo worried that the United States cared so little about the Philippines that it would not help Aguinaldo establish a stable government. Aguinaldo's views of American interests had fundamentally changed. The balance of evidence indicates that Aguinaldo, traveling incognito, spoke with very few people, but Pratt was engaged in backroom conversations with him. The evidence suggests that the source of Aguinaldo's new information must have been Pratt.

If Pratt found colonization unlikely, then a political reassurance – the United States does not need or want colonies – would simply be a statement of what he believed to be American policy. From Singapore in April, it probably looked extraordinarily unlikely that Washington would want to colonize the Philippines. After all, the war was only a few days old, Manila Bay was still controlled by the Spanish, and the majority of the American war effort focused on Cuba. At the time, Washington had no designs to control the Philippines after the war. Not until June is there talk in Singapore forwarded in the consular papers about US annexation, and then it is a hope and not a prediction. Pratt thought colonization desirable, but he worried the US would not take the necessary steps.[70] Pratt later came part of the way to giving this explanation himself. When interviewed after his return to the United States, Pratt explained that at the time, he did not know the post-war US plans. But, he found the Filipinos to be capable of self-government, he thought Aguinaldo was a mature leader, and he believed the US policy of cooperation had meant "tacit recognition" for the Filipino cause.[71] In short, the view from Singapore was different from the view at the White House: Pratt probably believed everything he said was simply an expression of US policy, even though he was not authorized to say it. Aguinaldo's decision to

---

[69] Pratt to Day, April 30, 1898. CD 213. Despatches from US Consuls, Singapore. M464, R14, NARA II.

[70] Pratt to Day, June 8, 1898. CD 228. Despatches from US Consuls, Singapore. M464, R14, NARA II.

[71] "Pratt Denies that Any Pledges to Aguinaldo Came from Him." Singapore Free Press. January 19, 1900. See also "Why Aguinaldo Resisted." May 22, 1901. Singapore Free Press. Pratt, however, continued to make the claim, which the consular correspondence disproves, that he had no political discussions with Aguinaldo and others.

return to Hong Kong was thus likely triggered by reassurances that the United States would cooperate after the war, because he was led to believe the Americans and Filipinos had a harmony of interests with respect to Philippine independence.[72]

The Return to Hong Kong and then Manila

When Aguinaldo left Singapore, he believed he was en route to Hong Kong to renew his meetings with the US fleet, but this time he would be hosted by Dewey instead of Wood. When he arrived, he was surprised to learn that Dewey had already left to fight at the Battle of Manila Bay. Instead, he received a note from Wildman, asking for another meeting. His first meeting with Wildman, he reported to the Hong Kong junta, was "unsatisfactory" because Wildman did not believe that Dewey would sign a written document. Aguinaldo thought this meant there would be no arms for the insurgency, so he asked for the junta's endorsement to travel to the Philippines and meet with Dewey directly.[73] Aguinaldo, however, did not travel directly to Manila Bay to meet with Dewey. He had to wait several weeks for the *McCulloch* to transport him.

During the interim, he continued to meet with Wildman. Wildman's talks with Agoncillo in 1897 left him in a position where he had a trusted relationship with the junta. As Wildman put it, "I have the absolute confidence of Aguinaldo and his leaders, and am closely in touch with their affairs."[74] Wildman continued to build this good will, showing that the United States intended to cooperate with the rebels and he "enthusiastically" took the lead in helping the Filipinos procure weapons.[75] In

[72] One objection to this interpretation comes from Dewey himself, who later dismissed Pratt's information as not "of much value," and wrote that Pratt "seemed to be a sort of busybody there and interfering with other people's business." Dewey, "Was There a Deal with Aguinaldo?" 7. Dewey was being dishonest. Pratt's intelligence was important owing to Singapore's status as a neutral port and location on Spanish shipping and mail routes. Pratt to Day, March 31, 1898. CD 198. Despatches from US Consuls, Singapore. M464, R14, NARA II; Pratt to Day, April 20, 1898. CD 207. Despatches from US Consuls, Singapore. M464, R14, NARA II; Pratt to Dewey. April 15, 1898. Area 10 File, Navy, M625, R363; Pratt to Dewey. April 22, 1898. Area 10 File, Navy, M625, R363; Pratt to Day, May 13, 1898. Pratt to Dewey. April 15, 1898. Area 10 File, Navy, M625, R363, NARA. Dewey responded, more than once, thanking Pratt for the intelligence, requesting more.

[73] Agoncillo, *Malalos*, 131–3.

[74] Letter. Wildman to Porter. October 13, 1898. Folder 3, Box 1. Wildman Papers. LC. Wildman asked that this not be placed on file.

[75] Aguinaldo, *Second Look at America*, 35–6. Aguinaldo to Wildman. May 27, 1898. Folder 3, Box 1. Wildman Papers. LC.

Aguinaldo's account, Wildman reiterated Pratt's predictions that the United States would respect Philippine independence because it had no interest in the islands. To do so, like Pratt, he cited the example of the Teller Amendment, which promised the recognition of an independent Cuba.[76]

These reassurances were not American policy, but they did not require Wildman to misrepresent his understanding of the American position with respect to colonization. Wildman may have been explaining or predicting American foreign policy more than making promises. For example, Wildman wrote to Aguinaldo in July, "Do not forget that the United States undertook this war for the sole purpose of relieving the Cubans from their cruelties under which they were suffering, not for the love of conquest or the hope of gain. They are actuated by precisely the same feelings toward the Philippines."[77] His correspondence to the State Department reveals that he genuinely believed the United States would not colonize the Philippines, but instead return them to Spain. He regretted this fact. He wrote an unsolicited letter to the State Department, protesting America's lack of interest in annexation: "If the United States decides not to retain the Philippine Islands, it's ten million people will demand independence, and the attempt of any foreign nation to obtain territory or coaling stations will be resisted with the same spirit which they fought the Spaniards."[78] Wildman, therefore, likely explained American reluctance to colonize the Philippines to Aguinaldo in such a way that it depicted a harmony of interests between the future allies and provided reassurances of American intentions.

When Aguinaldo left for the Philippines, he believed the US consular officers had provided substantial reassurances about the future policy of the United States toward the Philippines. Citing evidence of American foreign policy tradition, the Philippines small economy, and US policy toward Cuba, as well as being armed with American-procured weapons, Aguinaldo had gained enough confidence to return to the Philippines.

Alternative Explanation: Dewey as Broker?
One explanation that is historically complementary but paints an alternative theoretical logic is that Dewey himself misled Aguinaldo. As

---

[76] Ibid.
[77] In Agoncillo, *Malalos*, 153.
[78] Wildman to Moore. July 18, 1898. CD 63. Despatches from US Consuls, Hong Kong, M108 R19, NARA II.

Commander of the fleet, Dewey, who was under orders to avoid cooperation with Aguinaldo, had more institutional authority than did Pratt
and Wildman. Aguinaldo himself claims that he had Dewey's explicit
promise. Was Dewey responsible?

The controversy over Dewey's role is tied to Aguinaldo's arrival in the
Philippines on May 19. He and Dewey have two conversations aboard
the *Olympia* on May 19 and May 20. Aguinaldo recalls that during the
first meeting, his first question to Dewey was whether Dewey had sent a
telegram to Pratt regarding Aguinaldo; Dewey replied that he had. Dewey
would go on to say that the United States had "come to the Philippines
to free the Filipinos from the yoke of Spain," and that "America was
exceedingly well off as regards territory, revenue, and resources and
needed no colonies." Therefore, Dewey posited, "there was no reason
for me to entertain any doubts whatever about the recognition of the
Independence of the Philippines by the United States." The following
morning, Aguinaldo followed up at a second meeting, saying that many
still distrusted American assurances. Dewey replied that he thought they
should act as "friends and allies," and "the United States would unques-
tionably recognize the Independence of the people of the Philippines."[79]
Dewey denies making any promises. In Dewey's account of their meeting,
he told Aguinaldo, "Well, now, go ashore there, we have got our force at
the arsenal at Cavite, go shore and start your army." Aguinaldo returned,
Dewey claims, a few hours later, saying, "'I want to leave here; I want
to go to Japan.' I said, 'Don't give it up, Don Emilio.' I wanted his help,
you know. I said, 'Don't give it up.'"[80] Dewey would go on to say that "it
never entered my head that he wanted independence."[81]

Is there evidence to support Dewey's claims he did not know that
Aguinaldo, and the Philippine rebels, desired independence? There is circumstantial evidence on both sides of this question. On the one hand,
the Hong Kong junta made no secret of its political ambitions. Dewey
forwarded political documents in which the US policy was described as
"to secure the liberation" of the Philippines, and Dewey himself found
the Philippines "capable of self-government."[82] Dewey himself sent word
to the United States that he believed the Philippines were capable of self-
government, presumably implying that this was something they might

---

[79] Aguinaldo, *Second Look at America*, 38–9.
[80] Dewey, "Was There a Deal with Aguinaldo?," 3.
[81] Ibid., 9.
[82] Aguinaldo. "My Beloved Fellow Countrymen." May 24, 1898. Area 10 File, Navy, 625
R363, NARA. Aguinaldo. "Filippinos." Area 10 File, Navy, M625 R636, NARA.

want. On the other hand, Teodoro Agoncillo, who has done the most to unearth these discussions, concludes that the circumstantial evidence against Aguinaldo's version is strong because of inconsistencies between Aguinaldo's summary of his meetings and behavior.[83]

One conclusion we can reach is that Dewey likely had a confused understanding of Aguinaldo's intentions, produced perhaps by the fog of war or his parochial understanding of Philippine politics. In short, the best evidence is that Dewey was a dunce. Dewey's Senate testimony shows someone who had not thought through the major implications of cooperation with Aguinaldo, even years later. For example, at one point, Dewey explains that "I had in my mind an illustration furnished by the Civil War, and the only friends we had in the South were the negroes, and we made use of them; they assisted us on many occasions. I had that in mind; I said these people were our friends, and we have come here and they will help us just as exactly as the negroes helped us in the Civil War." Senator Patterson pointed out the obvious: slaves were "expecting their freedom" to which Dewey replied, "The Filipinos were slaves, too." The implication was obvious, if it had been reasoned through. The Filipinos wanted their freedom, just like those enslaved in the American South, and Dewey should have known that. Therefore, supporting Aguinaldo meant an implicit political promise. By all accounts, though, Dewey was not one to reason through ideas. Dewey cut it short: "they wanted to get rid of the Spaniard; I do not think they looked much beyond that."[84]

CONCLUSION

Before the start of the twentieth century, the Spanish–American War was the largest war fought against a European power. It led to the largest overseas land acquisitions in American history. It also turned the United States into a more traditional imperial power.

This chapter, through a detailed, step-by-step examination of evidence, shows that betweenness is central to the story about the origins of empire. The United States did not do the majority of the fighting against the Spanish; that was done by Philippine rebels. These rebels only fought because of the machination of the agents who filled the structural hole between the Philippines and Washington. These agents – Wildman and Pratt in particular – used their monopoly on information crossing borders

---

[83] Agoncillo, *Malalos*, 134–5.
[84] Dewey, "Was There a Deal with Aguinaldo?"

to inadvertently make cooperation appear useful to Philippine interests. Interestingly, politics in Washington is wholly unimportant for explaining cooperation. US interests and policy simply never mattered in the field. Instead, the agents between societies – Wildman and Pratt – were the source of cooperation.

This created America's largest colony in US history, and also created one of its bloodiest wars. Pratt and Wildman were certainly right that Aguinaldo could play a decisive role in the war. However, they wrongly predicted that the United States would not occupy the Philippines after the war. As a result, the end of the war saw a Philippine Army expecting independence, sitting only a few miles from the army that would ultimately deny them that independence. In 1899, the war with Aguinaldo turned into a war against him. Chapter 7 shows how betweenness explains new alliances that needed to form as the Spanish–American War gave way to the Philippine–American War.

7

The Daredevil and his Porter

When the United States fought Spain in the Philippines, it relied on a rebel army to do most of the fighting on the ground. Chapter 6 describes the politics of that alliance. The rebels presumed that the United States would respect Philippine sovereignty after the war. As US post-war aims clarified, and it became obvious the United States did not intend to grant the Philippines its independence, war became inevitable. By 1899, fighting broke out around Manila, spreading quickly to the countryside in Luzon, and from there to much of the rest of the Philippines. The Philippine–American War, or the Philippine Insurrection, as it has come to be known, was the first, and perhaps only, overseas American colonial war.[1]

The United States made a large military commitment to put down the insurrection, eventually sending more than 70,000 personnel. Most of the support for American personnel, however, was recruited in the Philippines and not in the United States. In the early days of the war, when the number of US Army personnel did not exceed 25,000 soldiers, the Quartermaster employed 132,000 native laborers, hundreds of thousands of Chinese porters, and at least several hundred Chinese and Philippine intelligence agents.[2] These numbers probably grew.

This chapter describes how cooperation emerged between the United States and a diverse group of Filipinos who volunteered to join companies of scouts for the United States. The first company was formed

---

[1] Miller, *Benevolent Assimilation*; Brian McAllister Linn, *The U.S. Army and Counterinsurgency in the Philippine War, 1899–1902* (Chapel Hill: UNC Press, 1989); Linn, *The Philippine War*; Wolff, *Little Brown Brother*.
[2] Linn, *The Philippine War*, 127.

in September 1899, drawn from Macabebe. Within a few months, three more companies were raised in Macabebe, and from there, the phenomena spread, eventually leading to the employment of about 15,000 Philippine personnel.

The Philippine contribution to the effort to put down the insurrection was essential. American understanding of the Philippines, especially outside Manila, was at best rudimentary at the outbreak of the war. Most American maps excluded many towns and villages and left out important features such as swamps and rivers. Most American soldiers did not speak Spanish, Tagalog, or any other language necessary to conduct counterinsurgency operations. They were wholly unprepared to fight the largest overseas war of American history up to that point. Native scouts, by contrast, knew the land well, allowing them to aid military planning and track enemy units. They spoke local languages, understood local politics, and performed a myriad of other functions. They made immeasurable contributions to the war effort.

The examples most often cited by American soldiers was their ability to tell an insurgent from a civilian. In the later part of the war, the US military was often frustrated because after a fight, insurgents would hide their weapons, change their clothes, and pretend to be a civilian friend of the United States ("amigos"). Philippine scouts, unlike American soldiers, could often distinguish between insurgents and civilians, providing a crucial resource against irregular forces.[3]

These Philippine companies were also important for shoring up political support for the war at home. The war became increasingly controversial as it bore on into 1901 and 1902. News of atrocities committed by American soldiers, the rising cost of the war, and the continued resistance of Philippine insurgents created heated debates on Capitol Hill about whether the war was legitimate and worth continued investment. The war's supporters used the participation of native military forces as a signal that US rule was accepted and therefore legitimate. These native forces were even put on display at the 1904 World's Fair, along with the band, to showcase the benefits of American colonial rule in the Philippines.[4] As

---

[3] Charles H. Franklin, *History of the Philippine Scouts, 1899–1934* (Ft. Humphreys, DC: Historical Section, Army War College, 1935); Clayton D. Laurie, "The Philippine Scouts: America's Colonial Army, 1899–1913," *Philippine Studies* 37, no. 2 (1989): 174–91; James Richard Woolard, *The Philippine Scouts: The Development of America's Colonial Army* (Dissertation, The Ohio State University, 1975).

[4] Jose D. Fermin, Maria Socorro I. Diokno, and Elynia S. Mabanglo, "1904 World's Fair: The Filipino Experience," *The Contemporary Pacific* 26, no. 1 (2014); Paul Kramer,

Mary Talusan explains, the Scouts were "effective propaganda, demonstrating to critics at home the benefits of American rule and projecting both to expansionists and antiimperialists the eventuality of the Filipinos becoming willing collaborators in the colonial enterprise."[5] An added benefit was that recruitment of Filipinos was cheap, helping to shift the burden away from American taxpayers and thus defuse charges levied by anti-imperialists.[6]

The question I ask relates to the recruitment of the scouts and the constabulary forces who later became scouts. When the war began, many Filipinos wanted to cooperate with the United States; others decided early in the conflict that an alliance with the United States was in their best interest. Yet, high-ranking American military officials did not trust Filipinos. Many in Washington and in the officer corps suspected that arming Filipinos would lead to more insurrection; they feared they would turn their guns on the United States or commit atrocities against other Filipinos. This mistrust prevented effective social ties from forming between high ranking military officials and the leaders of potential collaborating groups. In addition, fractured lines of communication created structural holes between high-ranking officers who made decisions about US strategy and Philippine groups throughout the islands who sought to cooperate with the United States.

Into this structural hole stepped agents who formed social relationships across borders: collaborators or low-ranking US officers. These individuals had useful experiences that placed them between societies, allowing them to see opportunities for collaboration that those in command could not see. Official Washington looked upon these intermediaries as curiosities. Representative I.P. Wanger described Matthew Batson, the first intermediary described in this chapter, that as "one of the biggest daredevils that the army has produced."[7] These "daredevils" secured cooperation with local forces by relying on personal connections and

---

"Making Concessions: Race and Empire Revisited at the Philippine Exposition, St. Louis, 1901–1905," *Radical History Review* 1999, no. 73 (1999): 75–114; Benito Manalo Vergara, *Displaying Filipinos: Photography and Colonialism in Early 20th Century Philippines* (Quezon City: University of the Philippines Press, 1995).

[5] Mary Talusan, "Music, Race, and Imperialism: The Philippine Constabulary Band at the 1904 St. Louis World's Fair," *Philippine Studies* 52, no. 4 (2004): 511.

[6] Laurie, "The Philippine Scouts," 190.

[7] Jesse Baten to Wanger. March 5, 1900. Folder 2, Box 1. Batson Papers, AHEC. See also Letter to Elkins and Scott. Mary 8, 1900. Folder 2, Box 1. Batson Papers, AHEC.

social skill. Their relationships with Filipinos were colorful and bizarre to US officials, whose racist blinders made Filipinos seem an exotic, dangerous animal to fight alongside.

The Philippines are an important case for a theory of betweenness. The war is substantively important because of the unusually high stakes for an American war in the nineteenth century. The United States sent around 70,000 troops to the Philippines to rule over a population of several million, and they did not leave for decades. Moreover, elements of the case make the Philippines important for showing the generalizability of a theory of intermediaries. In the other overseas cases discussed in this book, such as the First Barbary War, institutional authority for policymaking was held in Washington, making the existence of structural holes more likely because of geographic distance. The Philippines was different. Washington continued to play a role, but institutional authority literally traveled to the Philippines, as important political and military elites gained authority to administer the newfound possession. Geographic distances shortened, but the influence of betweenness remained. This chapter traces how structural holes emerged in the Philippines, even within a small geographic space, allowing for intermediaries to use their influence to broker cooperation with diverse political and ethnic groups in the islands. This presents, in short, a different context where a theory of structural holes is "least-likely," and it provides a fruitful comparison to Samoa (Chapter 5), where the presence of structural holes is "most-likely."[8]

STRUCTURAL HOLES

The relationship between the United States and independent Philippine groups in late 1898 and 1899 was characterized by a structural hole. Perhaps surprisingly, locating 70,000 American troops in the Philippines did not immediately eliminate the structural holes between Americans with institutional authority and local commanders throughout the islands. To understand why requires a bit of background about the islands at the turn of the twentieth century.

The Philippines are 7,000 islands, with more than 100,000 square miles of land. Many of these islands, such as Luzon, Samar, and Leyte, are divided into sections by nearly impenetrable mountain ranges and dense forests, creating distinct regions that are connected primarily by water

---

[8] On least likely cases, see John Gerring, *Case Study Research: Principles and Practices* (Cambridge: Cambridge University Press, 2007).

routes. The climate did not improve the situation, with a long monsoon season and prevalent tropical diseases preventing much travel beyond isolated outposts. The political and cultural climate of the Philippines likely contributed to the creation of structural holes. Luzon alone had five major linguistic groups, alongside dozens of more minor languages; groups on the other islands spoke many more languages. These features of the Philippines presented a challenge for a limited American force of about 70,000 soldiers to rule a population of 7,000,000.[9]

The Philippine human and natural geography led to a design for military occupation that ensured the opening of structural holes. Specific details are outlined in the cases discussed later; however, an overview is warranted to assess features held in common across the cases. The first consequence of the political, geographic, linguistic, and ethnic makeup of the Philippines was that many in the United States, and even most Americans in the Philippines, were unaware of opportunities for cooperation. American military and political elites often had not heard of, had prejudiced opinions of, or did not understand the politics of local groups in these diverse settings. Moreover, their response to the Philippine geography created an infrastructure that ensured poor communication across the islands. Faced with distinct theatres, the US commander, General Elwell Stephen Otis, dispersed his forces around the islands, often leaving small garrisons (typically one company) in isolated regions with little available support. As Brian Macalister Linn, who has written extensively about US military operations in the Philippines, explains, "The dispersal of American ground forces under Otis isolated many soldiers from direct supervision; in some areas orders from Manila took months to arrive and communications from provincial commanders could be delayed for weeks." A disconnect thus developed between local commanders who had extensive knowledge of political groups in their regions and those with the authority to draft and approve plans for cooperation. Linn underscores this dynamic: "Garrisoning also gave the troops extensive service in one region and allowed them to develop broad social contacts among the populace. This local knowledge was so important that Brig. Gen. Frederick Funston states that in the Philippines, 'the efficiency of a company depends largely on [its] knowledge of the people in the vicinity, and the country itself, which can be acquired only after some time.'"[10]

---

[9] Timothy Deady, "Lessons from a Successful Counterinsurgency: The Philippines, 1899–1902," *Parameters* 35, no. 1 (2005): 53–68; Linn, *The U.S. Army and Counterinsurgency in the Philippine War, 1899–1902*; Linn, *The Philippine War*.

[10] Linn, *The U.S. Army and Counterinsurgency in the Philippine War, 1899–1902*, 22.

Mistrust by American military officials' also contributed to the formation of a structural hole. There are several reasons why American military elites tended to discount the potential Philippine contribution to the war. One reason was that Dewey had armed Aguinaldo, and clearly that had been a strategic blunder, creating a once bitten, twice shy attitude among some military officers with reference to arming new Filipino groups. In the case of the Macabebe, discussed later, Otis was "afraid they would, if armed, turn traitors." Moreover, a preponderance of evidence shows that American prejudices against Filipinos conditioned their decision-making. At least some military elites viewed the Philippine War as a race war, referred to Filipinos as "gugus" or "niggers," and discounted the intellectual and political abilities of Filipinos, leading them to discount the prospects for cooperation.[11]

The crucial point is that there was limited contact between the military elites and many independent Filipino political groups throughout the islands. These problems, which regardless of occupation strategy were likely to be significant, were compounded by the decision to spread American troops into isolated outposts with no reliable means of communication. And, when military officials were brought into contact with groups who wanted to cooperate with the United States, a negative affect made American officials discount their pledges and promises. Due to these three factors, a structural hole developed between Filipinos throughout the islands and American decision-makers who had the institutional authority to make decisions.

Into this breach between American and Philippine societies stepped low-level American officers and their Philippine friends. Personal relationships formed in the field between American soldiers and those they met while stationed in the country led to extensive practices of collaboration upon which the colonial army would eventually be founded.

---

[11] Many historians, until recently, adopted the view that the American public, politicians, and army largely saw the Philippines through a racial lens, which affected American decision-making. Brands, *Bound to Empire*; Paul A. Kramer, *Blood of Government: Race, Empire, the United States, and the Philippines: Race, Empire, the United States, and the Philippines* (Chapel Hill: University of North Carolina Press, 2006); Miller, *Benevolent Assimilation*; Mark D. Van Elis, "Assuming the White Man's Burden: The Seizure of the Philippines, 1898–1902," *Philippine Studies* 43, no. 4 (1995): 607–22. Recent work by Linn questions the effects of racism, acknowledging that it mattered, although perhaps not as much as earlier generations of scholars found. Linn, *The U.S. Army and Counterinsurgency in the Philippine War, 1899–1902*; Linn, *The Philippine War*.

RECRUITING THE MACABEBE

The first episode of recorded cooperation on a large-scale was recruitment of the Macabebe Scouts. The Macabebe Scouts are historically important. They were effective soldiers in the Philippine–American War. The Macabebe were familiar with the terrain, spoke the local languages, could easily distinguish friend from foe in an irregular conflict, and were particularly good at scouting by canoe. All of these skills were invaluable.[12] Most memorably, an elaborate plan hatched by Frederick Funston employed the Macabebe Scouts to capture Aguinaldo by pretending that the Macabebe had captured Funston so as to avoid rebel pickets.[13] Their advocates – especially Matthew Batson, the first leader of the Philippine Calvary, and General Henry Lawton – would often describe the Macabebe as being as valuable as two Americans, but for half the price of one. The Macabebe Scouts also created a powerful demonstration effect: their success aided other officers' efforts to convince often skeptical high-level officers that Filipino cooperation was important for counterinsurgency efforts.[14] It was also a relationship that would last. Philippine units, which began with the Macabebe, would fight the Japanese during the Second World War.[15]

The question I ask is about the origins of cooperation between the Macabebes and the US military. Despite significant attention to the Macabebe's military contributions, there is comparatively little attention to how they were recruited. Many Macabebes were soldiers in the Spanish Army, fighting against the rebels since at least 1896. When the Spanish left the islands, the Macabebes sought to take up arms on behalf of the United States. Otis, the military governor of the Philippines, along with many other officers, found it a dangerous idea. They doubted that the Macabebes could be trusted. If their weapons were not turned on American soldiers, they might be turned on innocent Tagalog civilians.[16] Therefore, for much of 1899, the American policy was not to cooperate, despite the Macabebes' expressed interest. They were employed at the botanical gardens in Manila rather than as soldiers in the field.[17]

---

[12] United States Philippine Commission, *Annual Report of the Philippine Commission, 1901* (Washington, DC: GPO, 1901), 77–90.

[13] For a more dramatic account, see David H. Bain, *Sitting in Darkness: Americans in the Philippines* (Boston: Houghton Mifflin Harcourt, 1984).

[14] Woolard, "The Philippine Scouts."

[15] Edward Coffman, "Batson of the Philippine Scouts," *Parameters* 7, no. 3 (1977): 72.

[16] Matthew Batson to Florence Batson. September 17, 1899. Folder 3, Box 2. Batson Papers; Batson to AG. July 16, 1899. Box 3286. AGO 468092, RG 94. NARA.

[17] Woolard, "The Philippine Scouts."

In late 1899, the US position shifted dramatically. By the end of the year, the US government began forming Macabebe Companies in earnest. The first was recruited in September 1899, with three more to follow in the succeeding two months. Why did the United States trust the Macabebes by the end of the year enough to recruit and arm 500 soldiers?

Whose Idea?

What was the role of betweenness in recruiting the Macabebe? The heart of this question relates to the origins of a plan, authored by Lieutenant Matthew A. Batson, calling for the formation of the first Macabebe Company. There are two possible sources for the Batson plan. One prevailing view is that the decision to cooperate with the Macabebes was the result of a top-down decision, in which agents with significant institutional authority encouraged Batson to set down a plan. I am setting my argument against that furnished by Charles Franklin, who adopts this elite-driven account.[18] Franklin, who wrote an early history of the scouts, argues that General Henry Lawton, an agent with significant institutional authority owing to his position in the Eighth Corps, asked Batson to write and submit his plan.

If the top-down view is accurate, then understanding the role of intermediaries is not helpful for describing the case. High-ranking officers on this view, sensing the limits of US forces, began searching for allies. Betweenness is not central to the story.

The evidence for Franklin's account is underwhelming. The first piece of evidence comes from a letter written the following year to Batson by Clarence Edwards. Edwards writes that "General Lawton from the moment he landed in Manila until his death placed great importance and faith in the necessity and usefulness of native troops as auxiliaries for our army in the Philippines. He initiated and secured the employment of the Macabebes which resulted in the organization of one company called 'Batson's Macabebe Scouts,' and that successful experience gained him the necessary authority to organized a second, then a third, fourth, and a fifth company."[19] A close examination shows that the letter is a political ploy. In March 1900, Batson intended to enlarge the numbers of Macabebes, forming a regiment. As described later, this expansion was opposed the military governor of the Philippines. Edwards writes

---

[18] Franklin, *History of the Philippine Scouts, 1899–1934*.
[19] Edwards to Batson. March 24, 1900. AGO 317492, Box 2106. RG 94, NARA.

to Batson in the introduction to the letter that he intends this letter to be used to drum up support for Batson's plan. Lawton had recently died on the battlefield, a hero to many. By framing the Macabebes as Lawton's project, the scouts would have drawn significant support.

The second piece of evidence for a top-down process is the list of endorsements for Batson's plan. The endorsements, Franklin claims, show high-level support in the military, and therefore are evidence of high-level planning, particularly by Lawton. Franklin overstates the case. Lawton, whom Franklin claims spearheaded the plan, chose not to comment on the plan but simply wrote "Approved." Among the officers who did comment, there was no consensus. One officer found it so off-putting that he wrote, "A great hesitation is felt in placing arms in the hands of these people because of the anticipated action of revenge they might inflict on the Tagalos." General Arthur Macarthur, who would later become the Military Governor of the Philippines, challenged the claim that the Macabebe would commit revenge killings. After all, he argued, the Macabebe were already armed and they had yet to use their arms to commit excesses against surrounding towns. Macarthur, however, also gives caution, writing that this may only be due to their precarious position, surrounded by enemies without evidence of US assistance. Once armed, in other words, they might commit atrocities. At best, the endorsements show hesitant acceptance of the plan and not significant high-level support.[20]

Betweenness is central to the story in ways Franklin does not appreciate. Batson – the author of the plan – crafted the idea on his own. This section describes Batson's time in the Philippines, showing how his personal connections to his porter, Jacinto, created a network tie across societies that let him bridge the structural hole, conceive of the plan, and recruit the soldiers necessary for it to be successful.

In his letters home to his wife, Batson diagnosed two problems with winning the war. The first problem was simply not enough men. As he explained to his wife, "We have about 30,000 men here now. I have on the wall a map of Luzon about four feet long and three feet wide. On this map I can cover with my thumb all the territory held by these 30,000 men, and yet it keeps us scraping all the time."[21] The second problem was

---

[20] Batson to AG. July 16, 1899. Box 3286. AGO 468092, RG 94. NARA.
[21] Matthew Batson to Florence Batson. June 18, 1899. Folder 3, Box 2. Batson Papers, AHEC; see also Matthew Batson to Florence Batson. June 15, 1899. Folder 3, Box 2. Batson Papers, AHEC.

that the army's racism, war crimes, and general character would prevent pacification. He wrote that the "conduct of the Volunteers has been such that it could only irritate the inhabitants. Some things are too scandalous to write... We will never conquer these people so long as such conduct is tolerated. The Volunteer outposts will see some natives – they hear a shot, and then they turn loose and fire on everything they see – man, woman, or child. They then report that they have been attacked by Insurgents, and have driven them off with great loss to the Insurgents." The Regulars he found better, because they were content to kill chickens and steal food, and therefore they had not, "so far as I know, gone as far to desecrate Churches and burial places in search of loot." He was particularly concerned that Filipinos would be outraged when Volunteers "take their images of Christ and their Saints and dress them up in ridiculous garbs and generally insult their religion, and Christianity in general," asking "how can they look upon us as other than barbarians?"[22]

The solution, for Batson, was the recruitment of Filipinos. In June, he wrote, "There are two ways, in my opinion, that the rebellion can be put down and only two ways." The first was to occupy all of Luzon and garrison every town, with at least 100,000 men left in the Philippines indefinitely. This option "will not be used because the United States will never vote a suitable Army." Instead, alluding perhaps to the idea of the Macabebe Scouts: "The other method is to put confidence in the provinces that yield to our government, arm them and let them protect their provinces against the insurgents."[23]

Batson's placement on the front lines of the war provided social skill. He was one of many soldiers who placed American culture in perspective in his letters home, showing sensitivity to Philippine culture and an intolerance of much of American military practice and its "civilizing mission." He found the idea of civilizing Filipinos ironic, when in fact American Volunteers were burning towns and cracking open tombs to steal loot. He was astounded by the literacy rates in San Fernando, and wrote to his wife that "I find them an exceedingly interesting people – and when you hear of our people sending missionaries here tell them they had better put their missionaries to work in New York." Batson did not

<hr />

[22] Matthew Batson to Florence Batson. April 21, 1899. Folder 3, Box 2. Batson Papers, AHEC. See also the discussion of the sacking of Luna's sister's tomb in Matthew Batson to Florence Batson. May 21, 1899. Folder 3, Box 2. Batson Papers, AHEC.

[23] Matthew Batson to Florence Batson. June 15, 1899. Folder 3, Box 2. Batson Papers, AHEC.

trust reports of Filipino atrocities. He wrote, "I don't believe there has been an instance of this."[24]

The key source of social skill relevant to the Macabebe, however, came from a weak tie between Batson and the larger Macabebe community. In May, Batson had hired a Macabebe named Jacinto to cook and clean for him (his "boy" or "*muchado*"). Until May, and afterward when not referencing Jacinto, Batson's letters are cold and pessimistic. Jacinto, however, provided the exceptional moment of warmth. Batson's first mention of Jacinto to his wife relates, "He is a very nice little fellow and unusually bright. He does not understand Spanish or English but he <u>sabes</u> what I want pretty well."[25] By the next week, he wrote that Jacinto had become his "indespensible [sic] assistant," and they were "getting along famously together." Jacinto taught Batson some Kapampangan, and Jacinto learned some English. He thought Jacinto a quicker student than himself, although Batson had learned some basic Kapamangan, such as counting to a million.[26] Jacinto traveled with Batson for several months thereafter, and Batson always mentions him with a warm sincerity, describing how he would greet him with warm, dry clothes after a mission, or how they ate together.

Batson's experience with Jacinto provided a frame through which he interpreted a visit to the town of Macabebe, about a month before submitting the plan. In a letter home, he recalled that he was greeted warmly during his visit, ate dinner with 10,000 residents of the town, saw a fine elementary school, and the people were loyal and trustworthy. The crucial point, Batson underscored in his letter, is that in a town of 10,000 residents, no guard was placed on Batson. He was safe to eat with the Macabebes without fear of insurgent attacks. They hated the insurgents. Batson explained "The Spaniards were made prisoners of War but the Macabebes paid for their loyalty to Spain by having their heads chopped off." He laments that the United States had not already formed an alliance with the group: "When Aguinaldo decided to make War against the American troops he tried to get the Macabebes to join him, but, notwithstanding the fact that up to that time the Americans had treated the Insurgents as friends and the Macabebes as enemies, they refused to

[24] Matthew Batson to Florence Batson. May 21, 1899. Folder 3, Box 2. Batson Papers, AHEC.
[25] Matthew Batson to Florence Batson. May 13, 1899. Folder 3, Box 2. Batson Papers, AHEC.
[26] Matthew Batson to Florence Batson. May 21, 1899. Folder 3, Box 2. Batson Papers, AHEC.

join Aguinaldo. This placed them in a Pitiful condition. The Insurgents plundered them and the Americans ignored them. They did not have a rifle to defend themselves with. In fact they were completely helpless and defenscless [sic]."[27]

Batson had the social skills that most political elites lacked. He had spent time with the Macabebe and learned at least some of their language through daily interactions over several months. He also had recent experiences working with Cuban scouts in 1898 during the Santiago Campaign, and he may have drawn on these positive experiences brokering cooperation when framing cooperation for the US military.[28]

There is little doubt that Batson's relationship with Jacinto and his visit to Macabebe were the inspiration for the plan. It was submitted in July, one month after his visit to Macabebe, and two months after hiring and befriending Jacinto. Only after this tie formed could Batson, in his words, decide "in favor of organizing them and ... argued that we would have to do so before we would be able to put down the rebellion."[29] The operation, in other words, emerged by the ties between communities formed by the friendship between Batson, the daredevil, and his porter.

Selling Cooperation

Batson's informal relationship with the Macabebes provided the source of inspiration for cooperation. Once he formed the plan, however, he still needed to sell it to the army's commanders. There were three barriers. American military officials did not believe that the Macabebes would make a substantial military contribution, they mistrusted the Macabebes, and they imagined the Macabebes as a savage race, incapable of limiting violence toward civilians.

Batson worked hard to make the case that the Macabebes might make a substantial military contribution, describing the enterprise as an "experiment" that was "well worth trying." He first highlighted how Macabebe cooperation would aid the American war effort. In particular, he described the difficulty of American forces operating in the region, where rivers made travel nearly impossible for American troops. The Macabebe, in contrast, could travel by river in bancas (canoes) near high riverbanks

[27] Matthew Batson to Florence Batson. June 1, 1899. Folder 3, Box 2. Batson Papers, AHEC.
[28] Memorandum. "Reconnaissance Work Performed by me during the Santiago Campaign." Folder 4. Box 1. Batson Papers, AHEC.
[29] Matthew Batson to Florence Batson. September 17, 1899. Folder 3, Box 2. Batson Papers, AHEC.

FIGURE 7.1 Macabebe Scouts. Henry Lawton Papers, Library of Congress

that made them "invisible" to insurgents. If the United States chose to cooperate, the Macabebes would be useful scouts, defend American supply lines, and prevent telegraph lines from being cut (Figure 7.1).

Batson also capitalized on his direct experience with the Macabebes, which few officers had, to argue that they were trustworthy. He wrote that he had personally observed them "very closely for over two months" and was "firmly of the opinion that they would render loyal and faithful service." In particular, he argued that the Macabebe held a "friendly attitude" toward the occupation and had a "manifest desire to cooperate."[30]

Batson won approval to try his experiment, and in late 1899, the Macabebe Scouts scored some notable successes. Having decided that the experiment was working, Batson planned to expand the Scouts to a regiment. To do so, he needed to sell the expansion to a reluctant officer corps. In a March 1900 request to form a regiment of Macabebe, Batson

[30] Batson to AG. July 16, 1899. Box 3286. AGO 468092, RG 94. NARA.

notes that expansion was in the US interest, because the Macabebes were "fearless" and "impossible to ambush." He stresses that they can be trusted: "These soldiers under General Blanco were considered the best troops Spain had in the Philippines, and remained loyal to Spain until the sovereignty of the islands passed to United States, [sic] since which time they have been equally loyal to the United States. They have steadily refused to take part in any insurrectionary movement either as a tribe or individually. This has frequently cost them heavily both in lives and property."[31]

American military elites, especially Otis, were dubious about the value of Batson's plan to expand the Macabebe force. Otis cabled the Adjutant General at the War Department that he believed organizing further companies should "proceed slowly because trouble with MacAbebe [sic] Scouts who rob indiscriminately [sic] on opportunity." He concluded that "any native force now organized must be closely watched continuously."[32] There was some truth to allegations of Macabebe abuse. Macarthur, who endorsed the plan in July, had already begun to hear complaints about "depredation by armed Macabebes" by mid-September.[33] The Macabebe Scouts were court martialed for assault, rape, and other crimes; complaints were frequently forwarded to the individuals commanding Macabebe companies.[34] Yet, the reports of events that motivated Otis's bias were likely often political ploys by junior officers who were passed over for promotion when Batson and others gained prestige leading the scouts, or schemes by senior officers who wanted to delegitimize Batson's scouts so they might raise their own.[35] Paul Kramer argues this process of linking atrocities to the Macabebe was part of a larger pattern in which atrocities committed by American forces were blamed on the Macabebe.[36]

---

[31] Batson to AGWAR. March 23, 1900. AGO 317496, RG 94. NARA

[32] Cable. Otis to AGWAR. April 24, 1900. AGO 317496, RG 94. NARA. See also Otis to AGWAR. April 6, 1900. AGO 317496, RG 94. NARA.

[33] Macarthur to AG. September 19, 1899. Folder 5. Box 1. Batson Papers, AHEC.

[34] Charge and Specification against Scout Pedro Jiminez. February 2, 1900. Summary Court Cases, E 5812, RG 395; Edwards. Special Field Orders No. 30. December 6, 1899. Folder 4. Box 1. Batson Papers, AHEC; Edwards. Special Field Orders No. 32. December 8, 1899. Folder 4. Box 1. Batson Papers, AHEC; Major Commanding Third Infantry to Wilder, February 6, 1900. Letters. Entry 5807, RG 395, NARA.

[35] Letter to Francis H. Cameron. March 13, 1901. LR 1900–1901. Box 1. E 5815. RG 395; Munro to Batson. January 7, 1900. Folder 5. Box 1. Batson Papers, AHEC.

[36] Kramer, *Blood of Government*, 148–9. The specific claim is that the Macabebe were responsible because Americans were imitating them.

Batson himself, in at least one report, flips this argument on its head, suggesting that the Macabebes' reputation enhances American war aims. He reported, as he would throughout his career leading the Scouts, that the Macabebe were well-disciplined, perhaps more so than American Volunteers. But, the fear the Macabebe inspired got results. In his first report on Macabebe operations, only days after the Company was formed, he describes how the Macabebe were successful in finding arms at a town near Macabebe. As they approached the town in their bancas, insurgents with guns spotted them and began to flee. Batson reported that initially, their search of the town netted only one rifle and nine bolos, along with a revolver and some ammunition. Instead of being content with a few prisoners and one gun, Batson said, "I would not allow my soldiers to molest the people this time but that if he [the mayor] did not send in the other six rifles known to be held by them the next time I came I would permit [the Macabebe] to have their own way and that as a few Macabebes had recently been murdered in Minalin they would doubtless want to burn the town."[37] The mayor promised to hand in the rifles the next day.

In sum, Batson's structural position between the officer corps and the Macabebe community provided a crucial advantage in securing cooperation. His social skill, developed through his weak ties with the Macabebe community and experience brokering cooperation in Cuba, allowed Batson to see the structural hole that inhibited cooperation. He identified the Macabebes as cooperation partners, provided reassurances to the US military that they were trustworthy, framed cooperation as in both sides' interests, and mitigated cultural conflict that emerged because of the Macabebes' conduct on the battlefield.

COMPARISONS TO OTHER SCOUT COMPANIES

The recruitment of the Macabebe was only a first step toward the creation of Scout Companies throughout the islands. Eventually, more than fifty-three companies were recruited and deployed throughout the islands. Each company aided the American war effort in different ways. In this section I provide a brief assessment of the recruitment of two more companies.[38] Comparing the Macabebe to these other units is useful for understanding the power of betweenness.

---

[37] Batson to AG. September 13, 1899. Company LS. E 5804, RG 395. NARA.

[38] Moreover, the recruitment of local allies was not limited to scouts. Brian McAllister Linn documents, for example, the role played the *Guardia de Honor*, a religious sect, in

Before explaining what we learn from each unit, I need to describe why I focus on these cases. To learn about how these units were recruited, I spent an enormous amount of time in various archives. I would begin by reading all of the records left by the Army, including the company records, their officers' personnel files, and similar documents. These were often quite limited. Company records, for example, usually begin to be kept once a company is formed. They provide no backstory. The same problem is true for officers' records. Often, an officer is assigned to lead a unit once the unit is formed. I then searched military correspondence and personal papers, looking for the personnel who issues plans and recommendations. Using the bottom-up strategy described in Chapter 1, I concentrated my attention on the records of local commanders and others with whom the scout companies might come in contact with.

Despite spending an enormous amount of time searching for and reading the records of all of the Philippine units, only these two provide enough detail to understand how they were recruited. For all of the other cases, the Army records are simply too cursory to piece together a story. Recall that the Macabebe Scouts are one of the largest and most documented units in the war, and even their records are sparse. The units I describe in this chapter leave at best thin trails of evidence. Nevertheless, cautious, careful inference is possible for these two cases because the tidbits left in the archival record point to an interesting story that demonstrates how personal relationships in the field are important for forming alliances.

Lowe's Scouts

The first scout company that we are able to describe is Lowe's Scouts. At first glance, this unit appears to be a deviant case. John Gerring defines a deviant case as an instance that "by reference to some general understanding of a topic (either a specific theory or common sense), demonstrates a surprising value."[39] Unlike every other early case of the formation of scouts, Lowe's Scouts were a top-down creation.

Major General Henry Lawton planned the unit. Perhaps influenced by Batson's plan for recruiting Macabebe fighters, Lawton decided that

---

Northern Luzon, and how it was recruited by a single officer and operated against orders from the commanders of the Eighth Corps. Linn, *The U.S. Army and Counterinsurgency in the Philippine War, 1899–1902*. The Scouts, however, played perhaps the most important role during military operations.

[39] Gerring, *Case Study Research*, 105.

the employment of Tagalogs as scouts was essential to the war effort. After squabbling with Otis, Lawton was given the authority to enlist some Tagalogs as part of a scout company. The enlistment was qualitatively different from the Macabebe Company. The Macabebes Scouts were traditional enemies of the rebels, and they had earned the trust of Batson. The Taglogs, because they were of the same ethnic group as many rebels, were not trusted. Therefore, Lowe's Scouts was composed of a mix of Filipino and American troops, and the American troops were in part tasked with keeping an eye on the Filipinos.[40] Lowe's Scouts, from the perspective presented in Chapter 1, is surprising because Lawton, who commanded the Volunteers in the Philippines, had significant institutional authority.

The story of the creation of Lowe's scouts raises interesting questions that need careful assessment. The first question is why did Lawton support raising a company of scouts when others opposed it?

To understand Lawton's views on the scouts requires one to move back to an earlier point in his career. In the 1880s, Lawton was a captain in the Army, commanding a company of Apache Scouts looking for Geronimo. He was not yet a significant figure. The plan to raise the Apache Scouts was drafted by others, and others did the recruiting. Lawton largely followed orders to cooperate; he did not produce the orders.[41] Yet, Lawton's experience put him in almost daily contact with Apache Scouts for a period of many months. He learned they were valuable, often able to stay ahead of regular American units, and could move through "<u>awful</u> country."[42] Lawton was also fortunate enough to command Lt. Gatewood, who worked with the Apache Scouts to bring in Geronimo.[43] Lawton neither ordered the operation to capture Geronimo nor had the authority to negotiate terms. The terms were dictated to him by his commanding officer.[44] But, Lawton was lucky. By chance, he was on hand to accept Geronimo's surrender. The career rewards were enormous. The Apache Scouts who captured Geronimo indirectly advanced

---

[40] The Tagalog company was named after Captain Lowe, who was appointed to command it, although he left and later died before they took the field. The unit continued with his name. Edwards to Castner, December 15, 1900. E4945, Box 1341. RG 94, NARA.

[41] On intermediaries in the Apache Wars, see Grynaviski, "Brokering Cooperation."

[42] Emphasis in original. Lawton to Wife. July 21, 1886. Folder 7, Box 1. Lawton Papers, LC; On nearly daily contacts, see Lawton to Wife. July 7, 1886. Folder 6, Box 1. Lawton Papers, LC; and Lawton to Wife. August 1, 1886. Folder 7, Box 1. Lawton Papers, LC.

[43] Lawton to Wife. August 26, 1886. Folder 7, Box 1. Lawton Papers, LC.

[44] Miles to Lawton. August 31, 1886. Folder 8, Box 1. Lawton Papers, LC.

Lawton's career, as the public and political elites gave him much of the credit for the operation.

Recall that experience can help agents "see" structural holes, noticing opportunities for gains from cooperation that others cannot see. One way of interpreting Lawton's experiences with the Apache Scouts is that he learned that cooperation between communities may pay dividends. In other words, his experience working a project that was brokered by others let him "see" the structural hole in the Philippines.[45]

Even if Lawton could successfully see the structural hole, the perspective adopted in Chapter 1 suggests Lawton would not be skillful enough to close it. He did not know the language, was not bicultural, and there are no records that he spent much time with Filipinos. There is certainly no evidence that he developed close, personal connections to those he would recruit, as Batson did with Jacinto. A theory of betweenness implies that this dearth of social skill should make recruitment unsuccessful. The empirical record supports this view. The first efforts at raising Tagalog defectors were failures. As one officer recalled, "Three of four would be employed, who would remain for a day or two and then disappear." Only after some effort and several weeks of work were twenty scouts hired.[46]

Within-case variation points to the role of intermediaries. Captain Lowe, whose name was given to the company, left the company and died before it mustered into service. His successor had recently arrived from Alaska. He had no understanding of Philippine politics. Under him, no scouts were recruited except those few who would join for a day and then leave. Eventually, a local police chief was employed. The police officer, who was from the Philippines, had some more success, finding twenty scouts. While the evidence is limited, one can surmise that the recruiters social ties to the local society helped build support for the unit.[47] Even that was insufficient to create a full-strength company.

In short, the history of Lowe's Scouts is consistent with the argument of this book. Lawton, who in 1886 found himself thrust into a

---

[45] Unfortunately, the best sources of evidence concerning Lawton's thinking were detailed letters that he wrote to his wife. As he explained in 1898, these letters would provide a written history of his efforts. Unfortunately, Lawton's wife accompanied him to the Philippines, making such letters (and historical insight) impossible to glean. See Notebook for Letters. June 15, 1898. Folder 2, Box 2. Lawton Papers, LC.

[46] Edwards to Castner, December 15, 1900. E4945, Box 1341. RG 94, NARA. I deduce several weeks from Castner's arrival to the first action. See Castner's Efficiency Report, 1899. E4945, Box 1341. RG 94, NARA; Castner's Efficiency Report, 1900. E4945, Box 1341. RG 94, NARA

[47] Edwards to Castner, December 15, 1900. E4945, Box 1341. RG 94, NARA.

position of brokerage between the US military and the Apache scouts, may have learned to "see" structural holes that prevented opportunities for cooperation. Yet, Lawton was unable to make good on the brokerage opportunity because he did not realize how important social skill is for recruiting allies. When recruitment slowly increased beyond a three or four Tagalogs, it was not due to efforts by US officers in charge of the situation, but rather attributable to a Police Chief who likely had some kind of tie with the community in which he recruited. The only surviving evidence shows that Lowe's Scouts are a deviant case because an agent with institutional authority ordered cooperation, but this deviant case supports rather than undermines the main claims of the book. Lawton's experience with the Apache let him see a structural hole, but being able to see it does not mean one can form a bridge between communities. Instead, agents need that quality of betweenness – biligualism, bicultural, and experience brokering relations – that allows for successful cooperation. Lawton had none of these qualities, so he failed.

Leyte Scouts

The third case I discuss is the Leyte Scouts. I chose the Leyte Scouts to maximize the differences between the cases. The Leyte Scouts were recruited on the island of Samar in the Visayas, southeast of Luzon. They came from a different theatre of operations than the Macabebe and Lowe's Scouts. The differences in theatre are important. Whereas most combat operations took place on Luzon, the principle island in the Philippines, American forces also had to pacify Filipinos in the islands to the south. In this theatre, American forces fought on a group of smaller islands and had little contact with Luzon or one another. The recruitment of the Leyte Scouts from Samar is representative of an overall pattern in this theatre. Many units, such as the Lepanto, Panay, and Sepanto Scouts, came from regions that contributed a single or a few companies. In the case considered here, only two companies were raised in 1900, providing an example of these small-scale, local recruitment efforts.

Despite their small size, however, they made an important contribution to the war effort. Specifically, the Leyte Scouts were used in the operation to capture Lukbán, the rebel leader on Leyte and Samar, effectively ending the war on those islands.[48] Peter Traub of the Fifth Calvary wrote

---

[48] Donald Chaput, "The Founding of the Leyte Scouts," *Leyte-Samar Studies* 9 (1975): 5–10.

that capturing Lukbán "without the aid of these native troops, would have been absolutely impossible."[49]

In April 1900, American forces in Samar found themselves in a difficult position. Like much of the Philippines outside of Luzon, Samar was not a priority.[50] Major Henry T. Allen, who commanded the sub-district of Samar, had too few men (two small battalions) to occupy an island of 5,200 square miles. Allen's orders were to concentrate on opening two ports to restart trade. Not content with guarding the ports, Allen wanted to engage in a broader campaign. He garrisoned positions throughout Samar, and he sent out small squads of six to eight men to scout or act as couriers.[51] Violence in March and April significantly increased American casualties, especially at Catubig where 600 insurgents trapped 31 soldiers in a church, killing 19 and wounding 5. Allen began to question his ability to pacify the island, writing, "My old motto that man is preeminently a fighting animal is again fully verified, and I doubt whether you or I live to see the peaceful status here that many believe imminent."[52]

Allen's position vis-à-vis district headquarters highlights how the American strategy of deploying forces created structural holes. Writing to Headquarters on the same day as the fighting in Catubig began, Allen explained that poor communications and logistics had created an inability to pass even basic information around the islands. Samar had no roads and few trails, leaving isolated detachments on one side of the islands unable to communicate with the other side of the island. There was no regular boat service or telegraph line to contact Headquarters. At best, his only means of communication was "chance transportation to Iloilo" where the Headquarters was located.[53]

The formation of the Leyte Scouts occurred against this backdrop. At some point in January or February, a small expedition was sent to the east coast of Leyte, and eight soldiers were left to garrison the town of Tacloban. Shortly thereafter, the town experienced a large attack, estimated to be as large as 707 insurgents. The Presidente of Brongan (which is on Samar) and his followers came to the soldiers' aid along with many Chinese. The eight soldiers, with about one hundred of their allies in

[49] Peter Traub, "The Island of Samar and the Capture of Lukbon," *Journal of the Military Service Institution of the United States* 33 (1903): 372.
[50] Linn, *The Philippine War*, 233.
[51] Allen to AG, March 31, 1900. Folder 1, Box 32. Allen Papers, LC; ibid., 231–3.
[52] Allen to Woodbury, March 26, 1900. Box 30, LS (26). Allen Papers, LC.
[53] Allen to AG, April 15, 1900. Box 30, LS (26). Allen Papers, LC.

Tacloban, sought to escape by rowboat. One of the boats was captured, and three Americans were captured and likely killed.[54]

These eight soldiers, cut off from any assistance or communication with Allen, who in turn was more or less cut off from regular communication with department headquarters, led to the formation of the Leyte Scouts.[55] When the Presidente of Borongan fled to Allen's Headquarters in Catbalogan with the five surviving soldiers, he did not arrive alone. He brought his family, some of whom had served with the Spanish, as well as his police force. He offered his services to Allen "anywhere at any time" to fight the insurrectionists. The family had a price on their head, likely because they had collaborated with the Spanish and were now collaborating with the Americans. Allen points out that "the entire family is keen to avenge itself on the insurgents." Allen recommended that they form a Visayan Company. Without authorization, he armed them with rifles, provided them with rations, and harbored them near his headquarters.[56] His superiors at first resisted, and Allen worked to persuade them that the scouts were trustworthy and could make valuable contributions to the war effort.[57]

These scouts served as the nucleus for the Leyte Scouts. Shortly after receiving authorization to form the Provincial Police of Samar, which was the Leyte Scouts first name, Allen recruited twenty men. Even these twenty scouts made a difference, helping a small force of American troops seize and destroy the insurgent stronghold on Samar nicknamed "The Center." They also carried the American wounded back down mountain trails that were so difficult to traverse they needed to walk on all fours.[58] By August, they had been relocated to Leyte, and on September 1, forty-eight enlisted in the First Company of Leyte Scouts, stationed in Dulag, Leyte.[59] This group grew to a nearly full strength company by the following year, and it spread across Leyte, garrisoning towns.[60] Juan Sulse, the

---

54 Allen to AG, March 31, 1900. Folder 1, Box 32. Allen Papers, LC

55 On how garrisons in northern towns could not communicate with Allen, see Allen to AG, April 30, 1900. Box 30, LS (26). Allen Papers, LC.

56 Allen to AG, March 31, 1900. Folder 1, Box 32. Allen Papers, LC; Allen to AG, April 15, 1900. Box 30, LS (26). Allen Papers, LC.

57 Chaput, "The Founding of the Leyte Scouts," 6.

58 Allen to AG, May 21, 1900. Folder 1, Box 32. Allen Papers, LC.

59 Gasser to Post Adjutant, August 20, 1900. Company LS. E 5785, RG 395, NARA; Gasser to Post Adjutant, September 1, 1900. Company LS. E 5785, RG 395, NARA; Oath Book, September 1, 1900. E5790, RG 395, NARA.

60 Gasser to AAG, June 15, 1901. Company LS. E5785, RG 395, NARA; Oath Book, September 1, 1900. E5790, RG 395, NARA.

son of the Borongan Presidente who had fled to Catbalogan and was one of the men who carried Americans back from The Center, remained their Chief of Scouts.[61]

Although the historical record leaves more gaps than it fills, one can draw two conclusions from the case of the Leyte Scouts. The first is that local intermediaries mattered: personal relationships helped the United States recruit scouts. Without these personal relationships, which created weak ties to fill structural holes between small numbers of soldiers and a town leader during an ambush, cooperation may have never occurred. Moreover, the original enlistment papers show that most recruits were from Borongan, and most had been referred either by the Borongan leader, who fled to Allen with the five soldiers, or his son Sulse.[62] Moreover, we know that local commanders made decisions in the field without authorization, presenting and framing schemes for cooperation to headquarters after local recruits had already been armed and provisioned.

CONCLUSION

The experience of the United States in the Philippine–American War bears out the two central arguments of this book. The first argument is that the United States depended extensively on non-state allies to conduct its most important military operations. The Macabebe captured Aguinaldo, and the Leyte Scouts captured Lukbán, effectively ending the insurgency on Leyte and Samar. In other areas these allies were equally important. The Guardia de Honor, a religious sect in Northern Luzon, formed an alliance with local American commanders and gave the United States the first intelligence information about how the rebels operated, allowing for successful counterintelligence operations. Throughout the islands, the Philippine Calvary and Constabulary came to play roles on par with American forces as their numbers grew along with the funding available from Washington.

To understand the origins of America's colonial army requires appreciating the power of betweenness. The personal relationship between Batson and Jacinto, or the meetings between Allen and Sulse, created trust between parties and explained mutual interests to the parties in ways that made cooperation likely. The best evidence indicates that this

---

[61] Gasser to AG. September, 26, 1901. Company LS. E5785, RG 395, NARA;
[62] See the Enlistment Cards. Leyte Scouts Miscellaneous Papers, 1900–1901. E5789, RG 395. NARA.

bridging role was necessary for the formation of trust and the mutual realization of mutual interests in cooperation. The case of Lowe's Scouts provides more evidence for the causal relationship. When Lawton, an agent with significant institutional influence in the American military but little knowledge of the Philippines, tried to erect his own Company, the recruitment was slow and largely ineffective. I argue that Lawton's lack of social skills may have played an important role.

One important conclusion drawn from this chapter relates to the nature of US imperialism. The Philippines became the case where the United States came closest to acting as a traditional European imperial power, taking and holding the Philippines for decades. For traditional colonial powers, local collaboration was important for colonial rule and is often treated as a defining feature of imperialism.[63] In many of these states, such as the British in India, official policy called for the creation and recruitment of colonial armies. Formal policies drove informal empire.

Like the British, the United States also had a network of collaborators. By 1902, the United States had adopted the same policy with an institutionalized relationship with Philippine military units who conducted much of the remaining counterinsurgency and policing operations. Unlike the British, in the US case it was agents on the periphery who agitated for that relationship. These intermediaries – Pratt and Wildman, and Batson and Allen – seized on their position between the United States and the Philippines to build trust and interest in Washington and the Philippines for cooperation in a period where few thought it was in their interests. If local collaboration is a defining feature of empire, then these were empire's architects.

---

[63] Daniel H. Nexon and Thomas Wright, "What's at Stake in the American Empire Debate," *The American Political Science Review* 101, no. 2 (2007): 253–71; Ronald Robinson, "Non-European Foundations of European Imperialism: Sketch for a Theory of Collaboration," in *Studies in the Theory of Imperialism*, ed. Owen and Sutcliffe (London: Longman, 1972), 117–42. See also John Gerring, Daniel Ziblatt, Johan Van Gorp, and Julián Arévalo, "An Institutional Theory of Direct and Indirect Rule," *World Politics* 63, no. 3 (2011): 377–433; Mahmood Mamdani, *Citizen and Subject: Contemporary Africa and the Legacy of Late Colonialism* (Princeton: Princeton University Press, 1996).

8

Joe and the Sheikh

During the Iraq War, the US Army sought out local allies to help in its fight against Iraqi insurgents. One officer developed a briefing that summarized how to recruit fighters in Anbar Province. The PowerPoint presentation, which used stick figures, began "This is an American soldier... We'll call him Joe. Joe wants to win in Al Anbar. But sometimes it seems like other people don't share that idea. How can Joe win in Al Anbar? By fighting insurgents." The problem was that "Poor Joe can't tell the terrorist from the good Iraqis." Patriquin continued that for the operation to be successful, they needed a breakthrough. If one Sheik recruited locals to become a police force, then that "sheik brings more sheikhs, more sheikhs bring more men. Joe realizes that if he'd done this three years ago, maybe his wife would be happier."[1] Patriquin's logic is the same as that presented in Chapter 1. The United States military needs non-state allies to prosecute its wars successfully. To gain those allies requires closing structural holes between the United States and local communities (by winning the first sheik). Once that structural hole is closed, cooperation becomes possible.

Anbar Province is not unique. The central problems discussed in contemporary security debates are not so different from the problems facing decision-makers two hundred years ago. Great powers continue to need the aid of irregular forces to fight against other great powers, as well as to win counterinsurgency wars. Great power conflicts, such as World War II and the Cold War, contained moments where competition over

[1] Thomas E. Ricks, *The Gamble: General Petraeus and the American Military Adventure in Iraq* (New York: Penguin, 2009), 68.

non-state allies mattered dramatically for local outcomes. Today, the wars in Afghanistan and Iraq see the United States intensely searching for new allies to help manage growing insurgencies. To recruit and secure these allies requires bridge building, or finding and cultivating relationships.

The central argument of this chapter is that intermediaries and non-state allies continue to be relevant in a modern, globalized world. In developing this argument, I set it against a skeptical view. One might believe that global information technologies close structural holes, the size of the modern army diminishes the importance of non-state allies, and foreign policy institutions are now mature enough that people without institutional influence will likely matter less. In short, I have successfully shown the complicated pathways by which individuals achieved agency in global politics in the past, but are those pathways closed today? If so, agency among ordinary individuals would be rarer – or at least would follow other pathways – than has historically been the case. Against these suspicions, I present the empirical case that non-state allies continue to dominate foreign policy discussions, structural holes continue to exist between the government and those allies, and intermediaries often close those holes.

I develop this chapter in three steps. First, I review three objections to the continued relevance of this book in the modern era, showing that theoretically these objections are wanting. Second, I evaluate three cases: Albania in World War II, cooperation with the Northern Alliance in the earliest phases of the war in Afghanistan, and Special Forces operations that occurred in the following years. In each case, the theory presented in Chapter 1 shows the importance of intermediaries in shaping contemporary global politics. The last section steps back from the focus on non-state allies to think through how the theory presented in Chapter 1 extends to larger questions of diplomatic history: it shows how the logic of brokerage and structural holes helps us gain leverage on the broader question of how diplomacy is undertaken.

THREE REASONS THE MODERN WORLD IS DIFFERENT

A skeptic might view the evidence presented in the first six chapters of this book as interesting but irrelevant to the modern world. The argument of Chapter 1 – that individuals who have little institutional authority but have experience working between societies can gain agency in international politics – may make sense in cases such as the Philippines or

Samoa but not today. In this section, I review three reasons for skepticism that network structure and intermediaries still matter for world politics.

The Emergence of a Modern Army

The first concern is whether non-state allies continue to be important today. Intermediaries may be important in a world where armies are small and the stakes in war are low, but the modern army and the scale and scope of modern warfare renders non-state allies less important. In the event of a future war against China or North Korea, fighting is likely to occur in the air or on the sea, and fighting on land will occur between large, mechanized armies.

The claim that non-state allies do not matter in great power conflicts is simply wrong. The largest wars the United States has fought – against Germany and Japan in World War II, for example – included significant activities by non-state allies. During World War II, the allies depended on non-state actors for a variety of missions, including fighting behind enemy lines, collecting intelligence, blowing up bridges, and sabotaging enemy supply lines. Some of these Partisan groups were significant in size. The Yugoslav Partisans, for example, comprised nearly one million people by the end of World War II. To combat them, Germany deployed 15 divisions of German troops and 100,000 native troops.[2] One can find historical precedents for the importance of non-state allies in great power wars. Napoleon had to expend incredible resources fighting Partisans in Spain, for example; and more recently, the United States and the Soviet Union relied on non-state actors in prosecuting the Cold War in Africa and Asia.[3] In each of these great power conflicts, significant attention was paid to how to engineer resistance behind enemy lines in order to harass and intimidate enemy forces.

---

[2] Patrick K. O'Donnell, *Operatives, Spies, and Saboteurs: The Unkownn Story of the Men and Women of World War II's OSS* (New York: Free Press, 2004), 101. On these missions, see Franklin Lindsay, *Beacons in the Night: With the OSS and Tito's Partisans in Wartime Yugoslavia* (Stanford: Stanford University Press, 1996).

[3] Charles J. Esdaile, *Fighting Napoleon: Guerrillas, Bandits, and Adventurers in Spain 1808–1814* (New Haven: Yale University Press, 2004); Carl Schmitt, *Theory of the Partisan: Intermediate Commentary on the Concept of the Political,* trans. G.L. Ulmen (New York: Telos Press Publishing, 2007). To be clear, I am referring to non-state allies, or militias or rebels not associated with a state, who are fighting primarily for political reasons. This is distinct from the mercenary armies that were often important in medieval warfare, and the guerilla armies associated with states in Europe and Asia, such as Soviet partisans fighting against the Nazis.

Moreover, small wars, not global conflicts between great powers, dominate American foreign policy, and explaining success and failure in these small wars is central to understanding American power.[4] In these wars, the contribution of non-state allies continues to matter. In Afghanistan, the early fighting and dying was done largely by the Northern Alliance, removing the need for the United States to deploy large numbers of conventional forces in the war's early days.[5] In Iraq, militias allied with the United States government in Anbar Province – the Sons of Iraq – are often credited with drastically reducing violence. In Libya, NATO coordinated with rebel groups on the ground in the overthrow of Muammar Qaddafi. In performing these operations, US non-state allies are important because they reduce the cost of American operations, enhance intelligence gathering capabilities, and strengthen American warfighting capabilities.

To show concretely how these non-state allies continue to matter, the second half of this chapter describes World War II and Afghanistan. World War II is an appropriate case to test whether non-state allies matter in a global war, because it is the largest war fought between professional armies in world history. By showing that non-state allies affect wars of that scale, one can be comfortable believing non-state allies will matter in future conflicts. I chose Afghanistan because it is an example of modern, small wars.

Structural Holes in a Globalized World

The second concern is whether structural holes are likely to exist in the modern era. A critic might point out that the world in the eighteenth and nineteenth centuries was different in kind from the modern world, because today we are interconnected. Globalization, trade, the Internet, telephones, text messaging, and other communications media suggest that structural holes are unlikely to form. If no structural holes form, then intermediaries cannot be politically relevant.

Structural holes, however, are more common than this objection allows. Consider the argument for information technology. One observable implication of a structural hole as described in Chapter 1 is the absence of direct communications. Due to telephones and email, however,

---

[4] Max Boot, *The Savage Wars of Peace: Small Wars and the Rise of American Power* (New York: Basic Books, 2002).

[5] Richard B. Andres, Craig Wills, and Thomas E. Griffith, "Winning with Allies: The Strategic Value of the Afghan Model," *International Security* 30, no. 3 (2006): 124–60.

communication is much easier today than it was 200 years ago. Do email and Internet chat rooms close structural holes?

Structural holes exist even in the face of seeming interconnectivity. Empirically, many studies show that structural holes can be found even in industries with the highest levels of technology, such as corporate America, the Italian TV production industry, and the open software industry.[6] Workers in these industries have access to email and cell phones; yet, structural holes form because there are impediments to social ties beyond access to communications technologies. Employees from two corporations working on similar projects may be unaware of each other, because they are "trapped" within the institutionalized ties of their own organization. Without opportunities to meet and interact with individuals from other firms, ties across corporations cannot form. Social structure – competition between firms – might also discourage employees from meeting and interacting with people from other firms. Second, social structures are dynamic. A new start-up might enter the marketplace, with employees from different industries. In its earliest phases, this new "hub" may have few connections to existing firms in the marketplace. A liability of newness, as some sociologists refer to it, emerges due to the absence of social ties for the new firm.[7] Furthermore, problems related to homophily – the clustering together of similar individuals – may deter interactions between individuals who are not alike.[8] In short, structural holes can emerge in diverse social settings, regardless of technology. The absence of communications technologies likely encourages structural holes, but the presence of these technologies is insufficient to close them.

Within the context of the continued dependence of the United States on non-state allies, there are three reasons why structural holes may continue to form in a globalized world. These reasons mirror many of the problems highlighted by sociologists. First, structural holes are likely to form when regions suddenly become important. The United States government pays

---

[6] Ronald Burt, Robin M. Hogarth, and Claude Michaud, "The Social Capital of French and American Managers," *Organization Science* 11, no. 2 (March 1, 2000): 123–47; Yong Tan, Vijay Mookerjee, and Param Singh, "Social Capital, Structural Holes and Team Composition: Collaborative Networks of the Open Source Software Community," *ICIS 2007 Proceedings*, 2007, Paper 155; Akbar Zaheer and Giuseppe Soda, "Network Evolution: The Origins of Structural Holes," *Administrative Science Quarterly* 54, no. 1 (2009): 1–31.

[7] The seminal statement is Arthur L. Stinchcombe, "Social Structure and Organizations," in *Handbook of Organizations*, ed. J.G. March (Chicago: Rand McNally, 1965), 142–93.

[8] For a review, see Miller McPherson, Lynn Smith-Lovin, and James M. Cook, "Birds of a Feather: Homophily in Social Networks," *Annual Review of Sociology* 27 (2001): 415–44.

active attention to live war zones, but it typically spends fewer resources on areas with no active conflict. In such areas, political information is more limited, encouraging the formation of structural holes. As the allies moved across Burma to launch offensives against Japan in World War II, for example, new regions of the world suddenly became important; small ethnic groups in the hills of Burma with which the United States had little previous interaction garnered high level of attention as they were effective soldiers against Japanese occupiers. Similarly, the United States paid little attention to Afghanistan during the 1990s as the communist threat to the country faded. This inattention proved problematic in 2000 and 2001 when the United States tried to rekindle former relationships in the war against the Taliban.[9] This is similar to instances in which individuals' routinized ties within a firm prevent the creation of connections to new firms with which they have not historically done business.

Second, new potential non-state allies emerge who face the same liability of newness as new firms in a market. In Syria, for example, the Carter Center has tracked the emergence of more than 7,000 new armed groups since the conflict began a few years ago.[10] During the Libyan civil war, at least 236 revolutionary brigades formed to fight against Qaddafi, in addition to other armed groups. More formed in the post-war years.[11] Similar patterns are found in areas where state control over territory is weak, with a large number of fighting forces forming in Afghanistan, Congo, and Sudan, for example. These new rebel groups and militias are dynamic. To enhance their power, these groups often form alliances; in other instances they splinter. In addition, interpersonal ties can be severed as leaders are killed or displaced, as occurred with the leaders in the Anbar Awakening in Iraq who first cooperated with US forces.[12] The entry of new groups, dynamic alliance structures between those groups, and changes in group leadership will likely produce structural holes: government agents may not know or have a relationship with new political agents in changing landscapes abroad. Instead, brokers within these

---

9 These cases are reviewed in the next section.
10 Tim Wallace, Maher Samaan, Sergio Peçanha, K.K. Rebecca Lai, Karen Yourish, Sarah Almukhtar, Jeremy White, Larry Buchanan, and Josh Keller, "Varied Rebel Groups Make Up the Opposition." *New York Times*. September 30, 2015. www.nytimes.com/interactive/2015/09/30/world/middleeast/syria-control-map-isis-rebels-airstrikes.html (accessed October 2, 2017).
11 Brian McQuinn, "After the Fall: Libya's Evolving Armed Groups," *Small Arms Survey* (Geneva: Graduate Institution of International and Development Studies, 2012).
12 John A. McCary, "The Anbar Awakening: An Alliance of Incentives," *The Washington Quarterly* 32, no. 1 (2009): 43–59.

societies, I expect, help identify and broker relations between foreign governments and new political actors in-country.

Finally, war itself can produce structural holes in ways not explored by sociologists. War is a significant shock to social systems, often disrupting social relationships that bridge structural holes during peacetime. When a war breaks out, it is often followed by the expulsion of diplomats, the relocation of businesses, and the closing of travel. If any of these means were previously used to pass information across borders, then there is an increased likelihood that a structural hole forms. For example, World War II created a structural hole, separating Indochina from the West. Before the war, France had a colonial presence in the region, but, as Jane Hamilton-Merritt explains, "Under Japanese occupation, French Indochina was cut off from the West, resulting in an intelligence void that crippled allied military planning to liberate the area."[13] The French wanted to reestablish intelligence operations in the region, and they also wanted to press for an indigenous resistance movement. Maurice Gauthier, the leader of the team they parachuted into French Indochina, had never been to the region and did not know anything about the groups who lived there. Once he arrived, he met with the Provincial French Garrison and made contact with a police inspector. The inspector suggested they work with the Hmong. To make contact with the Hmong, whom Gauthier had never heard of before, he contacted a "crusty former French Legionnaire with a checkered past" who had married a woman from the area.[14] These weak ties were sufficient to promote cooperation.[15]

Analogously, war often disrupts parties' ability to communicate. During World War II, telegraph and telephone lines were often cut, which meant the United States could not talk to its non-state allies abroad. The United States' efforts to recruit Thai fighters during the war, for example, included daring missions whose primary purpose was simply to get a radio to the right people in Thailand.[16] Little has changed. In the run up to the war in Afghanistan, establishing communications with Taliban commanders required finding ways to sneak satellite telephones into the country

---

[13] Jane Hamilton-Merritt, *Tragic Mountains: The Hmong, the Americans, and the Secret Wars for Laos, 1942–1992* (Bloomington: Indiana University Press, 1993), 22.

[14] Ibid., 27.

[15] Ibid., 34–5; Paul Hillmer, *A People's History of the Hmong* (St. Paul: Minnesota Historical Society, 2010), 52.

[16] E. Bruce Reynolds, *Thailand's Secret War: OSS, SOE and the Free Thai Underground During World War II* (New York: Cambridge University Press, 2005).

to make contact.[17] Wartime communication disruption encourages structural holes, because it is difficult for parties to identify groups with whom to cooperate. In addition, the creation of new political groups, described earlier, may magnify communication problems, because great powers are frequently out of touch with changing dynamics on the ground.

Similarly, wars can encourage structural holes because insecurity prevents the formation of social ties. US combat operations in Ramadi (Iraq) suffered in the early part of the war because local tribal leaders and others were afraid to talk to US personnel, for fear that they would be targeted; those who considered cooperation were assassinated.[18] The same dynamic frequently occurred in Afghanistan, where elders who were on the verge of cooperating with US forces often received "night letters" threatening them and their families.[19] When potential collaborators are targeted, it encourages the growth of structural holes: former brokers are killed and new brokers are deterred from filling structural holes.

To show how structural holes can form in the modern world, I concentrate on two different kinds of cases. First, I describe relationships during World War II with Communist Partisans in Albania. If the presence of large groups in a world of instantaneous communication should close structural holes, then the large Partisan army in Albania during that era should be a good test case. Second, I examine cooperation with the Northern Alliance in Afghanistan as a more modern example, showing how structural holes can form in an era of globalization with high levels of information technology.

The Growth of the National Security Bureaucracy

The third concern is whether the figures who fill these structural holes are likely to be intermediaries. A critic might argue that executive restructuring in the United States has led to a decline in the influence of agents with little institutional power. One change that might affect social structure is the growth of the bureaucracy. The United States has more professional

---

[17] Robert Grenier, *88 Days To Kandahar: A CIA Diary* (New York: Simon & Schuster, 2015), 54.

[18] Ricks, *The Gamble*, 63–4.

[19] MSG D. Berry, "Establishing a Special Forces Firebase," in *Long Hard Road: NCO Experiences in Afghanistan and Iraq* (Fort Bliss, TX: US Army Sergeants Major Academy, 2007), 59–62; Linda Robinson, *One Hundred Victories: Special Ops and the Future of American Warfare* (New York: Public Affairs, 2013), 55.

agents than ever before. In 1807, the State Department had fewer than a dozen employees; today, the Foreign Service has 13,000 employees, the Civil Service has 11,000, and the State Department has 45,000 additional staff at overseas posts.[20] Moreover, the military and intelligence agencies have people dedicated to working with non-state allies. With the government awash in agents who are tasked with building personal relationships overseas, what role do intermediaries have?

A second change is the professionalization of diplomacy. In the nineteenth century, diplomacy was conducted by amateurs. The *New York Daily Herald* summarized the US Foreign Service in 1857, noting, "Diplomacy is the sewer through which flows the scum and refuse of the political puddle. A man not fit to stay at home is just the man to send abroad."[21] Beginning in the 1890s, the US government professionalized its diplomatic corps, creating the modern, professional American diplomat.[22] In the modern world, a critic might believe that these professional agents – who are clearly agents of the executive branch – are more likely to play a role than are missionaries, escaped prisoners, or former slaves. Professional bureaucrats, endowed with institutional power as part of government reforms a century ago, are therefore the more likely actors to broker cooperation.

Two empirical observations may undo the confidence that institutionalized agents have control over American foreign policy. When the United States was collecting intelligence about Iraqi Weapons of Mass Destruction – an enormously important mission – did it rely on intelligence produced by agents on the ground in Iraq to provide the "eyewitness account of these mobile production facilities" that Colin Powell described in his speech in front of the United Nations? No. Bob Drogin, summarizing the US intelligence in Iraq, writes, "they may as well scribble the Latin *hic sunt dracones* on the map: Here be dragons."[23] The primary source in Powell's speech was Rafid Ahmed Alwan al-Janabi, nicknamed Curveball by his handlers. Alwan had worked at a television

[20] U.S. State Department. "Mission." https://careers.state.gov/learn/what-we-do/mission (accessed May 10, 2016).

[21] Harry W. Kopp and Charles A. Gillespie, *Career Diplomacy: Life and Work in the U.S. Foreign Service* (Washington, DC: Georgetown University Press, 2011), 11.

[22] Henry Mattox, *The Twilight of Amateur Diplomacy: The American Foreign Service and Its Senior Officers in the 1890s* (Kent: Kent State University Press, 1989); Salvatore Prisco, "A Note on the Training of Professional American Diplomats, 1899," *Diplomacy & Statecraft* 3, no. 1 (1992): 143–6.

[23] Bob Drogin, *Curveball: Spies, Lies, and the Con Man Who Caused a War* (New York: Random House, 2007), 49.

production company in Baghdad and was wanted by the government for theft. He fled to Germany, where he claimed to have worked for Rihab Rashid Taha ("Dr. Germ"), building mobile labs for biological weapons. In exchange for information, the German government granted him asylum. Alwan's intelligence became the key evidence presented to the public and the international community.[24] Did Alwan have strong ties to the US or Iraqi governments? No. He had no ties. How many Americans met Curveball? Exactly one.[25] He traded on his position between communities, and a supposed monopoly on information, to get asylum and money from the German government. Despite hundreds of thousands of US government employees, the media, and foreign agents all providing intelligence, Alwan, a corrupt Iraqi trying to get asylum, produced the "intelligence" on which the war turned.

A second observation is that the US military now understands the basic logic of structural holes and intermediaries for forming contemporary alliances. The *U.S. Army/Marine Corps Counterinsurgency Field Manual* explains that insurgents "hold a distinct advantage in their level of local knowledge. They speak the language, move easily within the society, and are more likely to understand the population's interests." To win, therefore, requires "immersion in the people and their lives to achieve victory."[26] The logic mirrors that presented in Chapter 1. If American soldiers understand and can appeal to locals, then cooperation with American forces is more likely. David Kilcullen, in his influential "Twenty-Eight Articles," explains this argument in more depth. He suggests that winning "hearts and minds" requires a network logic: "once you have settled into your sector, your key task is to build trusted networks" composed of "local allies, community leaders, local security forces, NGOs and other friendly or neutral non-state actors in your area and the media." He suggests that if one is successful at winning allies in one village, then one should leverage that to understand that village's social relationships to other villages by seeing "why they trade, intermarry, or do business with." This requires, most importantly, social skill. Kilcullen believes

---

[24] Drogin, *Curveball*; Robert Jervis, *Why Intelligence Fails: Lessons from the Iranian Revolution and the Iraq War* (Ithaca: Cornell University Press, 2010), 123–55.

[25] Select Committee on Intelligence, U.S. Senate. July 7, 2004. *Report on the U.S. Intelligence Community's Prewar Intelligence Assessments on Iraq.* The National Security Archives, George Washington University. http://nsarchive.gwu.edu/NSAEBB/NSAEBB234/SSCI_phaseI_excerpt.pdf (accessed October 2, 2017).

[26] U.S. Army and Marine Corps, *The New U.S. Army/Marine Corps Counterinsurgency Field Manual* (Chicago: University Of Chicago Press, 2007), 1–24.

that officers with rank will likely not have these social skills: "someone with people skills and a 'feel' for the environment will do better than a political science graduate."[27] Contemporary memoirs bear out the inverse relationship between command and social skill. Soldiers in the field rarely cite the commander as brokering relationships with local allies. One Special Forces soldier who spent several tours in Afghanistan explained that "[j]ust placing U.S. and Afghan soldiers at an outpost and conducting their presence patrols and occasionally bantering with locals" is ineffective if a person does not have "in-depth knowledge of tribal structure, alliances, and feuds" to assess credibility and identify biases.[28] Breakthroughs often happened through doctors or interpreters – people without institutional influence but who met with and won the trust of locals – not at military commanders' once-a-month meetings with political elites. In the second half of this chapter, I concentrate on interpreters as intermediaries between American forces and Afghan society.

In the contemporary era, if structural holes continue to exist, then intermediaries can continue to play an important role in international politics. Earlier I showed that the emergence of new groups, wartime disruption of diplomatic and intelligence ties in dangerous regions of the world, and the creation of new hotspots that have previously received little attention suggest there are and will continue to be political groups around the world who do not have trusted, interpersonal ties with agents with institutional influence in the centers of political power. In these circumstances, intermediaries, like Curveball, are likely to surface. Moreover, we reflectively understand the continued importance of intermediaries. Today, intelligence agencies search out people who have access to political information that the organizations do not presently have, looking for people with ties to terrorist groups, militias, and rebels abroad. These figures occasionally become famous, like Alwan or Ahmed Chalabi. More often, they probably do not. Until the full archival record is produced and we know who shaped information behind the scenes, we will not be able to identify who they are. But, that does not mean they are not there, working to broker cooperation across societies.

Ultimately, the test of whether weak ties continue to matter for security cooperation is an empirical question. To test the role of figures with

---

[27] David Kilcullen, "Twenty-Eight Articles': Fundamentals of a Company-Level Counterinsurgency," *Military Review* 86, no. 3 (2006): 103–8.

[28] In H. John Poole, *Expeditionary Eagles: Outmaneuvering the Taliban* (Emerald Isle, NC: Posterity Press, 2010), 223.

institutional authority requires closely examining modern cases to see if intermediaries played the same role post-1900. Testing this argument in the contemporary record is more difficult than testing for the presence of structural holes, for reasons outlined later. Yet, I examine several different kinds of cases to identify the full scope of intermediaries' potential roles in the modern world.

THREE MODERN EXAMPLES

World War II and Afghanistan show the continued role of social structure on the battlefield. I chose these two wars because of how drastically different the US commitment was. During World War II, more than twelve million Americans fought; in Afghanistan in 2003, with Iraq taking the most significant military assets, about 10,000 US soldiers were on the ground. I concentrate on the US alliance with Albanian rebels during World War II, cooperation with the Northern Alliance in 2001–2002, and the reliance on translators in Afghanistan afterwards. These three episodes, in different ways, show that structural holes remain central to security politics, intermediaries continue to broker important deals across borders, and non-state allies continue to do much of the fighting necessary for the extension of US power.

A Note on Method

Before turning to these cases, I first want to describe the differences in the approach taken in this chapter from earlier chapters. In the previous chapters, I used extensive archival research to engage in process tracing, comparative analysis, and counterfactual analysis to show the causal powers of intermediaries. For historical cases, following the trail of information through the archives is difficult but possible. This chapter posed more difficulty because of limitations to contemporary evidence. For contemporary events, I need to rely much more heavily on accounts by journalists and memoirs than on direct historical evidence.

The liabilities of using this contemporary evidence are enormous. First, the majority of high-profile books on Afghanistan and Iraq emphasize debates in the White House, especially during the Bush administration. The central aim of these books is to analyze decisions made by political elites, placing blame on some and heaping laurels on others. If history is prologue to the future, this book shows that contemporaneous accounts bias the political record toward a focus on political elites to whom reporters have access or from whom publishers solicit memoirs, and away from the contributions made by agents without institutional authority.[29] Clues about these latter figures usually emerge from the archival record, where one can track the circulation of information through longer chains of correspondence. Second, too many accounts of these recent wars are written with an eye to drama and sales rather than for historical comp leteness. Memoirs are often coauthored by screenwriters, and hagiographies are written by reporters who depended on their hero for access.[30] The tendency of these books to focus on creating heroes and villains produces bias.

Most importantly, few of these books provide the necessary details about the individuals who are most likely candidates for intermediaries. In one telling example, Robert Grenier, a former CIA Station Chief, describes an Afghan-American from Houston named "Akbar" who helped broker a relationship between Taliban commanders and the CIA. Apparently, Akbar helped develop a relationship because he wanted to profit if sanctions were lifted through commercial ties. He is described in a few sentences, and then the CIA's role is developed at great length.[31] For a book about the politics around figures like Akbar, we need to wait for fuller evidence.

Therefore, the evidence upon which this chapter rests is more tentative. One reason I selected the Albania case (described below) is that it is comparatively well documented. The two cases in Afghanistan are more problematic. A careful review of memoirs and documents clearly shows the presence of structural holes and the importance of social skill. Yet, a full and reliable account of the origins of cooperation with disparate elements of Afghan society that speaks to more general issues is not yet available. This chapter tries to pick up promising threads in the story of

---

[29] Even the records from World War II may contain bias. Richard Breitman, a historian who has worked extensively in the OSS records, notes that classification rules and missing documents mean we know little about foreign agents and informers working for the OSS during the war. Richard Breitman, "Research in OSS Records: One Historian's Concerns," in *The Secrets War: The Office of Strategic Services in World War II* (Washington, DC: National Archives and Records Administration, 1992), 105–6.

[30] The most influential screenwriter has been Ralph Pezullo, who coauthored *Jawbreaker, Inside Seal Team Six,* and *Zero Footprint.* Unfortunately, political scientists have relied on these works, especially Jawbreaker, to draw larger conclusions about the nature of contemporary intelligence and the need for reform without noting the potential problems that come from having a fiction writer as a coauthor.

[31] Grenier, *88 Days to Kandahar,* 51–4.

the war, while acknowledging that more reliable historical evidence is needed.

World War II

If one wants to test whether non-state allies matter in modern wars characterized by large armies, there is no better instance than World War II. The war was one of the largest in human history. Much of the war turned on aircraft carriers, the atomic bomb, and the modern use of tanks. Yet, even in a war of this scope and scale, non-state allies mattered. I chose the case of the Albanian Partisans from Europe to show that non-state allies are important in great power war. By selecting a smaller non-state ally, I show how even relatively small groups can contribute to broader war efforts (thus constituting a "hard case" for the importance of non-state allies). Moreover, since this book is about American foreign policy, I concentrate on Albania because the United States had a significant role in recruiting, supplying, and working with Albanian groups.[32] I then analyze the case to show that structural holes affected cooperation, and bridges were supplied by intermediaries.[33]

Albania

In 1939, Italy invaded Albania as a prelude to the invasion of Greece. Albania had significant geostrategic significance. In addition to being a pathway to Greece and a satellite for Italy, its coast also watched the Straits of Otranto, which controlled the Adriatic.[34] As Italy assumed power in Albania, a resistance formed, composed principally of three groups: the communist Partisans, the conservative Balli Kombëtar (BK, or National Front), and a group led by Major Abaz Kupi, who supported the restoration of King Zog. In 1944, British policymakers concluded that the Partisans alone had pinned down two and a half German divisions, killing more than six thousand and occupying a key evacuation route from Greece.[35] The problem for the allies was that while these groups

---

[32] In other cases, such as Yugoslavia, the British dominated decision-making. See Lindsay, *Beacons in the Night.*

[33] Elsewhere I describe the recruitment of groups around Burma using the same perspective. See Eric Grynaviski, "Brokering Cooperation."

[34] Gani Manelli, "Partisan Politics in World War II Albania: The Struggle for Power, 1939–1944," *East European Quarterly* 40, no. 3 (2006): 335–6.

[35] Bernd J. Fischer, "Abaz Kupi and British Intelligence in Albania, 1943–4," in *Eastern Europe and the West*, ed. John Morison (New York: St. Martin's Press, 1992), 135.

fought tenaciously against first Italian and then German forces, they also fought amongst themselves for control over Albania. In short, in 1943, Albania was erupting into a three-sided civil war, as well as a war against Nazi occupation.

To understand the growing US role in Albania requires understanding the process by which Hoxha met allied officers. When the first British mission parachuted into Greece, headed for Albania, the civil war had not yet begun. Kupi's Zogite forces allied with the BK and communists against the Germans, although relations were tense. Kupi had a relationship with the British. With British backing, he put together a united movement in 1942, arranging to work with anti-Zogist groups.[36] When the British Special Operations Executive (SOE) mission entered Albania in 1943 to cooperate, it intended to focus on aiding Kupi's fight against Germany and Italy. The problem was that the coalition was breaking down: the Communists, led by Enver Hoxha, had become the dominant political force in Albania and were the most effective resistance against Germany.

The British were largely unaware of the internal political situation in Albania, as the war had caused a clear structural hole between London and Albania. The way in which the structural hole formed illustrates some of the dynamics described above about why structural holes are likely to form during wartime. First, the war generated new groups with which the British had little contact. British intelligence services had some ties to northern Albania, where forces loyal to King Zog fought, but the center of political power was shifting to the south, where the most significant resistance would be recruited. The formation of these new parties in the south meant the opening of a structural hole. Second, the war severed social relationships. Agents working through Athens and Belgrade were displaced when Germany conquered Greece and Yugoslavia. This disrupted the route via which intelligence tended to travel. Moreover, the war eliminated effective communication. In 1941 and 1942, British intelligence gathering was limited to collecting stories from individuals who traveled out of Albania.[37]

The first British mission into Albania arrived in 1943. Major Billy McLean, Captain David Smiley, and Lieutenant Gavin Duffy – three SOE officers – landed in Greece and snuck into Macedonia, carrying machine

[36] Ibid., 129–31.
[37] Reginald Hibbert, *Albania' National Liberation Struggle: The Bitter Victory* (Pinter: London, 1991), 42–9.

guns and bags of gold. Their mission was to find someone (anyone) to fight the Germans and Italians, and they probably planned to aid the pro-Zog forces, in part, because they were unaware of the relative strength of the Partisans.[38] To succeed, the British mission sent to Albania needed to find a way to close the structural hole between London and Albania. It was ill-equipped to do so, however, due to a lack of social skill. Because of the poor intelligence, the mission had no preexisting knowledge of Partisan politics and very limited understanding of Albanian politics in general.[39] They also did not speak the language and had to communicate with local guides with limited French.[40] Even though British officers had been in the country since the spring of 1943, by the end of that year "a firm grasp of the resistance and political scene still eluded both SOE and the Foreign Office."[41]

Moreover, the Partisans did not trust the British team, making them ineffective in closing the structural hole between London and Albania. British agents engaged in unilateral operations, refusing to coordinate with the Partisans. In one example, David Smiley blew up the bridge that Hoxha's Partisans intended to use to escape from a German offensive; the shattered Partisan bridge almost led to Hoxha's capture.[42] These kinds of errors contributed to mistrust. In addition, the British government's policy was to aid any group fighting the Germans. Therefore, it provided aid to Kupi's pro-Zog forces, in addition to the Partisans. From the Partisan perspective, the British decision to aid groups who contributed little to the fight against Germany was evidence of British interest in preventing Hoxha from assuming power after the war.[43] At one point, this suspicion of British collusion with Kupi led Hoxha to threaten to arrest British officers. The policy of helping all parties – engineered by the British agent McLean – was likely the result of his failure to understand the politics on the ground in the country.

Whereas the relationship with the British was limited and inspired mistrust, Hoxha's relationship with the American team was friendlier. The American team was composed of individuals who, in the language

---

[38] Peter Lucas, *The OSS in World War II Albania: Covert Operations and Collaboration with Communist Partisans* (Jefferson: McFarland, 2007), 27.

[39] David Smiley, *Albanian Assignment* (London: Hogarth Press, 1984), 28–9.

[40] Roderick Bailey, "OSS-SOE Relations, Albania 1943–44.," *Intelligence & National Security* 15, no. 2 (2000): 32–3.

[41] Ibid., 28. See also Hibbert, *Albania' National Liberation Struggle*, 22–3.

[42] Lucas, *The OSS in World War II Albania*, 48.

[43] Hibbert, *Albania' National Liberation Struggle*, 139–42.

of Chapter 1, are best described as intermediaries because they had weak ties across borders. The head of the Albania desk was Harry Fultz, who shortly before the war was involved in special education in Illinois. Fultz understood Albania because he helped run a vocational school in Tirana from 1922 until 1933. Many of the partisans had been students in Fultz's school.[44] In addition, the OSS sent Thomas Stefan. Stefan's parents had moved to the United States from Albania, opened a grocery store, and helped Stefan attend college. To support himself, Stefan was a busboy before the war; he had no political influence.[45] Other agents would later arrive with similar skill sets. These individuals had a tremendous amount of social skill and influence stemming from their connections across societies; but they did not have significant institutional authority.

This OSS team became the primary mechanism through which the United States and the British learned of the politics of Albanian groups and decided whom to back. The OSS team had two assets that helped them. The first was Stefan's language skills. When Stefan met Hoxha in April 1944, he formed a relationship that would prove significant for the alliance; this relationship developed, in part, due to Stefan's social skill. According to Peter Lucas, who has written the only comprehensive history of the OSS mission, "Hoxha probably extended his hand in friendship to Stefan because Stefan's parents were from Albania. And not only could Stefan speak Albanian, he spoke in Hoxha's own Tosk dialect."[46] Apart from Stefan, no other American or British agent had access to Partisan decision-making. According to Nick Kuckich, another OSS agent in Albania, "It seemed like Tom could go up and talk with Hoxha any time. In fact he never had to call him in advance. Tom had a good, strong, personal relationship with Hoxha. Very strong."[47]

Stefan became the most important bridge for political information between the allies and the Partisans. Stefan was the only foreign agent invited to the Congress of Përmet (May 1944), in which Hoxha was installed as the leader of Communist forces. In addition, he met frequently with and helped Hoxha understand US policy. These close contacts led Stefan to recommend a set of policies likely to make cooperation more successful. Specifically, he recommended that the allies stop sending

---

[44] Lucas, *The OSS in World War II Albania*, 63–4.
[45] Ibid., 80–2.
[46] Ibid., 87.
[47] Ibid., 91.

weapons to the Partisans' rivals within Albania, and he recommended focusing exclusively on supporting the Partisans.[48]

Reflexive evidence also indicates the importance of Stefan as a bridge between communities: Stefan's information became so important that the British developed a clever plan to have Stefan route it through them rather than through American agents. The British convinced him to destroy his American radio during a German attack. This meant that Stefan needed to use the British radio to communicate to the allied commands. British agents working in Albania intercepted Stefan's reports and claimed them as their own.[49] Stefan's intelligence precipitated a policy shift. Stefan's reports of growing Communist strength and the unwillingness of their political opponents to fight made cooperation with Hoxha more desirable. All of this political intelligence appears to have trafficked across Stefan. His monopoly on information crossing borders provided him political influence that far exceeded his institutional power.

Over time, the alliance that formed between the Partisans and the allies was heavily conditioned by Stefan's reports, because Stefan managed to play the role of intermediary, closing the structural hole between Albania and Washington. Through Stefan – a trusted intermediary – Hoxha was able to cultivate a western alliance that excluded his rivals, helping him gain weapons, support, and marginalize his political opponents.

ANALYSIS. The experience of the OSS in Albania confirms the central argument of this chapter. First, the war produced a structural hole in an era of instantaneous communications. Despite the existence of the radio, there was a dearth of interpersonal relationships between the allies and the most significant Partisan group in Albania; not only did the war disrupt former relationships, but the Partisans were politically unimportant before the war. Second, the individuals who closed the hole were not professional diplomats. They were low-level government agents who were effective because they had linguistic skills and came from bicultural backgrounds. Third, these intermediaries shaped allied communications in a way that made cooperation with the Communist Partisans more effective and more likely.

The Albanian mission provides two sources of leverage to test causal arguments. First, it provides a unique opportunity to test the influence of social skill because of the differences in the composition of the American

---

[48] Ibid., 94–103.
[49] Lucas, *The OSS in World War II Albania.*

and British teams. Recall that British agents preceded American agents into Albania by several months. Those British agents, however, failed to understand the situation and shape an effective alliance with the Partisans. Their lack of social skill, in fact, contributed to mistrust. US agents, who had significantly more social skill, effectively closed the structural hole, in part by simply being able to understand and appeal to Albanian interests.

Moreover, this case allows us to test alternative explanations. Material explanations would suggest that the United States formed alliances to enhance its ability to fight the Nazis. Material factors might explain why *an* alliance forms, but not *which* alliance might fom when there are several competing factions to choose from. In Albania, for example, the United States had to choose between competing factions in the country's civil war. One OSS agent noted that being forced to choose between them was crazy: "I know this sounds monstrously stupid; so be it: the Albania of January, 1944, is politically absurd and monstrously stupid."[50] Supporting Kupi, the BK, or the Partisans made sense in terms of balancing against German power; the key question was which groups the intermediary would suggest. This decision was enormously consequential. The allies chose to back the Communist party, contributing to the Communists seizing power after the war. Albanian cooperation also casts doubt on ideological explanations. Recall that some International Relations scholars believe that similar ideologies help support cooperation. In the case of Albania, however, the western allies supported a Communist group against the more pro-western forces led by Kupi. Ideological similarities do not explain alliance choices here.

To explain alliance-making in Albania, one must turn to the agent who navigated between Albania and the allies. Stefan – and perhaps a few agents alongside him – used their comparative social skill to recruit and sustain Hoxha. Stefan's decision to support Hoxha – not broader, structural factors – explains alliance decision-making in Albania.

Afghanistan

The second case I focus on is the US war in Afghanistan. I describe two phases of the war. The first part relates to the early phase of the war, especially in late 2001 when the United States cooperated with the Northern Alliance. How did the deal with the Northern Alliance form? The second part describes operations that occurred later in the war, especially in

---

[50] Ibid., 56.

2003 and 2004. During this period, the United States military sought new allies to pacify significant portions of Afghanistan. What role did social structure have in producing cooperation between isolated commands in the field and local allies?

The Northern Alliance

The United States entered Afghanistan after the September 11 terrorist attacks. The CIA, however, had already been present in the region for at least four years. Since the spring, plans had been underway to arm the Northern Alliance to fight against the Taliban. Those plans were approved on September 4, a week before the September 11 attacks.[51] When the war began, this relationship with the Northern Alliance proved enormously useful during the ground war. Fighting a large-scale conventional war was not a good option: it would take a long time to deploy US assets, risked a potential quagmire, and was expensive. The presence of the Northern Alliance, however, allowed the initial phases of the war to begin immediately and cheaply. The United States inserted Special Operations Forces to work alongside the Northern Alliance. Using air power combined with Afghan fighters, the Northern Alliance achieved quick success on the battlefield.[52]

At first glance, one might say that strong ties mattered, because there was no structural hole between the US government and the Northern Alliance. President Bush would later say, "I was impressed by their [the CIA's] knowledge of the area. We've had assets there for a long period of time. They had worked, had been thinking through things."[53] Bush's comment suggests there was no structural hole between the United States government and the Northern Alliance. Instead, there was a close, durable institutional relationship that was activated to secure the Northern

---

[51] Bob Woodward, *Bush at War* (New York: Simon and Schuster, 2003), 35–6, 51.

[52] There are two views about the effectiveness of the Northern Alliance. On view gives more of a role to American airpower, showing that airpower combined with local spotters, including the Northern Alliance, was sufficient for victory. Andres, Wills, and Griffith, "Winning with Allies"; Richard Andres, "The Afghan Model in Northern Iraq," *Journal of Strategic Studies* 29, no. 3 (2006): 395–422. A second view gives more credit to the well-trained Northern Alliance forces who could succeed on the ground when the Taliban forces began to disperse and use terrain to avoid airpower. Stephen Biddle, "Afghanistan and the Future of Warfare," *Foreign Affairs* 82, no. 2 (2003): 31–46; Stephen Biddle, "Allies, Airpower, and Modern Warfare: The Afghan Model in Afghanistan and Iraq," *International Security* 30, no. 3 (2006): 161–76.

[53] Woodward, *Bush at War*, 53.

Alliance's help. Did far-sighted agents have long-standing relationships that led to cooperation with an alliance?

In reality, the social relationship between the United States and the Northern Alliance in the summer and fall of 2001 appears to have been thin at best. Gary Schroen, who wrote a memoir about being the CIA agent tasked to recruit the Northern Alliance, provides the best description. During the 1990s, "We had no embassy in Afghanistan. No CIA personnel were there – I certainly could attest to that. Islamabad did a little reporting on Afghan issues but focused on narcotics-related affairs."[54] The structural hole between Washington and Afghanistan illustrates two of the themes presented earlier in this chapter. First, low-priority areas received little attention, producing structural holes. During the war against the Soviet Union, the United States paid attention to Afghanistan. After the Soviet Union withdrew, US attention turned elsewhere. In addition, the rise of the Taliban further disrupted the American relationship, as it became difficult for the United States to operate within the country. A structural hole therefore formed between the Northern Alliance and the US government. Furthermore, even though the war occurred in 2001, Afghanistan lacked the kind of infrastructure necessary for information technology to close structural holes. As the CIA Station Chief in Islamabad explained, "Afghanistan at this point had no cell phone system, no international phone service of any kind outside of a handful of government-controlled lines into Pakistan, and no independent media. The country was nearly opaque to the outside world."[55]

The United States began to pay attention to Afghanistan again after the 1998 Cole bombing. In 2000, a CIA team conducted a mission in Afghanistan. This mission intended to provide support to the Northern Alliance against a planned Taliban offensive. The CIA sent agents whom they thought would make the most effective use of existing social relationships. But these agents scored low in the criteria we would expect to show social skill. The Northern Alliance had one person who spoke English, and the CIA team had one Farsi-speaking officer to deploy.[56] The team was quickly withdrawn. After September 11, the CIA again deployed this team alongside the Northern Alliance as part of the war

---

[54] Gary C. Schroen, *First In: An Insider's Account of How the CIA Spearheaded the War on Terror in Afghanistan* (New York: Ballantine Books, 2006), 53. See also Gary Bernstein and Ralph Pezzullo, *Jawbreaker: The Attack on Bin Laden and Al-Qaeda: A Personal Account by the CIA's Key Field Commander* (New York: Crown Publishers, 2005), 44.

[55] Grenier, *88 Days to Kandahar*, 120.

[56] Bernstein and Pezzullo, *Jawbreaker*, 43–4.

against the Taliban. This team, followed by a larger commitment, fought hand in hand with the Northern Alliance.

How did the structural hole that existed between 1990 and 1998 close? Until a few days before September 11, Ahmad Shah Massoud was the leader of the Northern Alliance. To explain how the structural hole closed requires understanding how the CIA formed a close relationship with Massoud. During the 1980s, Massoud cooperated with the United States in the war against the Soviet Union. But, with the withdrawal of US agents from Afghanistan, Massoud had few contacts. As the United States withdrew, some of its operatives relocated to Pakistan. In Pakistan, Gary Schroen, a CIA officer, developed a relationship with Masood Khalili, an adviser to Massoud. When Schroen met Khalili, his aim was to find a broker to help him make contact with Mujahedin commanders through-out Afghanistan. At that time, the United States rarely had direct access to the Mujahedin, because the Pakistanis were trying to funnel support to their allies within Afghanistan. Schroen and Khalili developed a close friendship, and even though Schroen did not meet Massoud during the period, "the goodwill, trust, and confidence that Khalili had in me was transferred to Masood, something that would serve me, and the CIA, well in the future."[57]

Ties that developed between Schroen and Khalili developed into a bridge, making cooperation possible. Schroen describes how his rela-tionship with Khalili developed into a close friendship. After Khalili was arrested and asked to leave Pakistan, he came to the United States to lobby for support for the Afghan government. Schroen also left Pakistan. Khalili and Schroen began to socialize, meeting in nor-thern Virginia. Schroen recalls that there was no "official aspect" to their relationship; they met once a month, usually for lunch, becom-ing much closer friends.[58] Schroen was later sent to Islamabad again and witnessed the rise of Taliban power. In 1996, he reached out to Khalili, who was then in India, asking for a meeting with Massoud. Massoud agreed, and they met with Khalili serving as translator. In the middle of the night, they began to iron out terms for US assistance to the Northern Alliance, focusing on the capture of bin Laden. Schroen claims that these meetings – engineered because of his close personal relationship with Khalili – were the foundation for the alliance with the Northern Alliance in 2001: "In hindsight, this was an extraordinarily

---

[57] Schroen, *First In*, 50.
[58] Ibid., 52.

significant meeting. The door to future cooperation with Masood and the Northern Alliance was again open. This proved critical in making it possible for my team to enter Afghanistan on 26 September 2001 to a warm, friendly welcome from the Northern Alliance leadership." He continues, "That relationship and trust were the key elements in allowing the U.S. government to have the strategic base and the strong local allies necessary to bring down maximum force onto the main body of Taliban and al-Qa'ida fighters at exactly the correct place and time, resulting in a rapid, decisive victory on the battlefield and in ridding Afghanistan of Taliban suppression." [59]

ANALYSIS. The social structure of diplomacy between the United States and the Afghan government before the rise of the Taliban affected cooperation. If Schroen's account is correct, then even though Massoud was a political elite within the Afghan government in the early 1990s, he had few formal relationships with figures with institutional power within the United States. In fact, Massoud distrusted American officials who had abandoned him after the Soviets withdrew from the region. To close the structural hole created by governmental inattention required an informal relationship. Schroen's relationship with Khalili – characterized more as a friendship than anything else – provided the opportunity to close the structural hole between Langley and Afghanistan.

One feature of this case is that both Khalili and Schroen had institutional power. Khalili was a diplomat and Schroen was a CIA agent, and in 1996, a relatively high-ranking agent. This appears to undermine the logic presented in Chapter 1, where a central claim is that relations are rarely brokered by the institutionally powerful. Instead, perhaps the growth of the modern national security apparatus led the United States to rely more on official agents rather than intermediaries who have little institutional authority. I would, however, offer a countervailing view. Afghanistan was a crucial theatre in the Cold War during the 1980s, and American agents had many strong relationships with mujahedeen commanders during the war. The Northern Alliance should therefore be a case in which thick institutional ties explained cooperation a decade later. Yet, the strong ties between the Afghan fighters allied with the United States against the Soviets rapidly weakened in the late 1980s, as the United States reduced its commitment to Afghanistan. In the end, the US relationship with the Northern Alliance hung on a thin thread of lunches

[59] Ibid., 63–4.

that took place in Virginia between two people who had no institutional authority to broker a deal.[60] While they had strong ties to one another and their governments – so the theory presented in Chapter 1 technically does not capture the case – it is uncanny how informal relationships brokered the structural hole between the United States and the Northern Alliance. In short, in a powerful sense, the lack of strong, direct ties to explain cooperation presents compelling evidence of the resurgence of structural holes and the importance of brokerage in international politics.

Moreover, the relationship between the Northern Alliance and Washington was not exceptional during that first phase of the war. Throughout the early months of the war, the United States depended on local allies about whom they knew little. Their relationships were brokered through relationships with other local allies, in a confusing social structure whose identification is beyond this book. To fight in Tora Bora, the United States relied on the Eastern Alliance, made up of Pashtun warlords. The CIA needed a personal relationship with the Eastern Alliance to initially secure their cooperation. According to Gary Bernstein, the CIA agent tasked with helping the Northern Alliance, the logic closely mirrors this book: "We were in search of allies... They [the Northern Alliance] put me in contact with Babrak [Ali]. So that was the bridge to the other guys. And then Nuruddin [Zaman] shows up, but he had already made contact with the U.S. in Pakistan, and then he appears, just as we are doing this stuff. So we thought, okay – he has fighters too."[61] Weak ties and personal relationships were important.

After the Fall of the Taliban

After the swift offensives of the beginning of the war, US attention began to shift. In 2002 and 2003, as the United States withdrew forces from Afghanistan to fight in Iraq, it deployed small forces throughout Afghanistan to control large amounts of territory. Of the 10,000 US soldiers in Afghanistan, 8,000 were located in Bagram and Kandahar,

---

[60] Schroen's efforts were important because he was the only agent in the extant historical record with these ties. The CIA Station Chief in Islamabad, Robert Grenier, opposed working with the Northern Alliance in the beginning of the war. Instead, Grenier was working on a plan to turn Taliban commanders – a plan that had its origins in a Houston-based Afghan-American – one of a few "opportunists, operators, looking to develop unsavory contacts with an eye for the main chance" – who had put Grenier into contact with a few members of the Taliban leadership. Grenier, *88 Days to Kandahar*, 51–3.

[61] Yaniv Barzilai, *102 Days of War: How Osama Bin Laden, Al Qaeda & the Taliban Survived 2001* (Washington, DC: Potomac Books, 2013), 89.

leaving 2,000 to fight throughout the rest of the country. These 2,000 soldiers were spread far too thinly. For example, Captain Ronald Fry, who led a Special Forces Unit, described how he had fifteen men to control the Kunar and Nursitan Provinces, an area of operations that covered about 5,000 square miles, or the size of Connecticut.[62] This meant that close, productive relationships with the local population were essential for military success.

Soldiers' memoirs reveal the structural holes between these Special Operations teams and the local population. The first Special Forces units on the ground knew very little about Afghanistan. Although their mission was to recruit and work with local allies, they had no information about them. They were told "CIA analysts at Langley were working on it," so they relied on the Internet to learn about Afghanistan.[63] Later, they were given some old issues of *National Geographic* magazine and some Discovery Channel shows on VHS and told, "Consider it more intel." Eventually, they managed to convince the publisher of *The Bear Went Over the Mountain,* a book on the Soviet war, to send them copies of the book.[64] Their language skills also prevented Special Forces units from being able to work with locals. Even years later, American Special Forces Units would often describe their language skills as "bad,"[65] and many did not know any of the local languages, even after multiple deployments. References to soldiers or intelligence agents who speak Arabic are rare, people speaking Pashtu are very rare, and people speaking Dari fluently (the predominant language of the Northern Alliance) are almost non-existent in that first year.[66] One Special Forces Team, for example, designated to work in Asia, had members who could speak Korean, Laotian, Mandarin, and Thai. According to the team's commander, "In the rugged mountain reaches of Central Asia, our language expertise was doing us as much good as our Combat Diver badges."[67]

---

[62] Fry and Tuleja, *Hammerhead Six.*

[63] Doug Stanton, *Horse Soldiers: The Extraordinary Story of a Band of U.S. Soldiers Who Rode to Victory in Afghanistan* (New York: Scribner, 2009), 34.

[64] Ibid., 47.

[65] Rusty Bradley and Kevin Maurer, *Lions of Kandahar: The Story of a Fight Against All Odds* (New York: Bantham Books, 2011), 19.

[66] The only instance I can find of someone described as fluent in Dari is a CIA paramilitary officer. Stanton, *Horse Soldiers*, 7. On problems with Pashtu as well, see Saima Wahab, *In My Father's Country: An Afghan Woman Defies Her Fate* (New York: Crown Publishers, 2012), 77–8, 87.

[67] Fry and Tuleja, *Hammerhead Six,* 229.

In a situation where there is a structural hole between Special Forces teams and potential local allies, I expect cooperation will most likely be the product of intermediaries. To be successful, Special Forces units usually developed close relationships with their assigned interpreter, and soldiers recognized this dependence. Mitch Weiss and Kevin Maurer, two journalists who documented one Special Forces unit, wrote, "Soldiers – especially Special Forces – had to go into villages and deal with local leaders to restore services to shattered communities. They had to understand the intricacies of tribal culture and politics as well as identifying enemy from friendly groups. They had to spend time training the Afghan police and commandos. All were major keys to success, and in most cases, translators were critical to carrying out the missions."[68] These translators were intermediaries. In most cases, they were not political elites. Instead, they tended to be people driven by necessity into a quite dangerous occupation. These interpreters linked US Special Forces to local allies.

Translators' higher levels of social skill likely provided better understandings of who one might cooperate with and how to appeal to them, especially compared to soldiers who learned about a warzone through Wikipedia and old Discovery Channel programs. Although the politics of translators has escaped attention in International Relations studies, it is more pronounced in general studies of translation. In such cases, translators play several roles that fit the logic provided in Chapter 1. First, translators exert agency. They are often not "neutral" conveyors of meaning, but can alter or effect information as it traffics through them.[69] One way translators exert agency is by playing the role of gatekeepers.

---

[68] Mitch Weiss and Kevin Maurer, *No Way Out: The Story of Valor in the Mountains of Afghanistan* (New York: Berkley Caliber, 2012), 92. This same dependence is often noted in Iraq, although mistrust of interpreters in Iraq is more pronounced. See Vincente Rafael, "Translation in Wartime," *Public Culture* 19, no. 2 (2007): 239–46; Tom Peter, "An Iraqi Interpreter as Chronicler of the War," *Christian Science Monitor*, March 16, 2008. The lack of social skill was not limited to the military. Junior officers from the State Department and USAID were also lost. Robert M. Perito, "*U.S. Experience with Provincial Reconstruction Teams in Afghanistan: Lessons Identified*," Special Report 152 (Washington, DC: United States Institute of Peace, October 2005), 12.

[69] For a small group of these studies focusing on conflict situations, see Mona Baker, "Interpreters and Translators in the War Zone," *The Translator* 16, no. 2 (2010): 197–222; Jerry Palmer, "Interpreting and Translation for Western Media," in *Translating and Interpreting Conflict*, ed. Myriam Salama-Carr (Amsterdam: Rodopi, 2007), 13–40; Lawrence Wang-Chi Wong, "Translators and Interpreters During the Opium War Between Britain and China (1839–1842)," in *Translating and Interpreting Conflict*, ed. Myriam Salama-Carr (Amsterdam: Rodopi, 2007), 41–60. The more general literature emphasizing these themes is significant, and their findings well-established.

Translators are often tasked with seeking out meetings and sorting out problems. They are "fixers." Moreover, translators help defray cultural conflict. Translators helped build trust in Afghanistan by coaching US forces on how to behave with respect toward the local population; they also helped the local population understand American customs.[70] Translators can also exert agency by representing their clients directly in negotiations. Saima Wahab, who has written the most comprehensive first-person account of translating for the US military in Afghanistan, described how she was called on to make political speeches at events such as International Women's Day, where she became the representative of American customs and culture instead of a simple translator.[71] Most likely, translators in today's war zones act as intermediaries, assigned to help soldiers find and craft deals with local allies. They find partners, frame cooperation, and manipulate the teams to which they are assigned to support cooperation.

ANALYSIS. Translators are only one kind of modern intermediary that may be less visible in the contemporary record. Yet, two salient themes emerge from this brief analysis. First, social structure continues to matter on the battlefield. American Special Forces units, even those trained to immerse themselves in local cultures, cannot do so because of an absence of social skill. Therefore, they need to seek out socially skilled individuals to help broker deals across borders. Second, these socially skilled figures tend to be intermediaries. They become important because they fill the network position between locals and soldiers: not because they initially had any institutional influence. Furthermore, IR scholars would benefit from paying attention to agency in-between societies. In theory, translation can be "neutral" if a translator's job is to simply try to convey meaning, but translators are also useful "fixers" who arrange meetings and understand local politics. Translators likely convey options for locals and soldiers alike in bargaining, mitigating cultural conflict, and building trust.

One basic change not reviewed in this chapter is the increased recognition of the problems associated with social skill and network structure. This chapter briefly describes senior military officials' recognition of the importance of social skill for recruitment, as well as the problems engendered by insufficient social connections. Military doctrine

---

[70] Wahab, *In My Father's Country*, 246–9.
[71] Ibid., 105–8.

in counterinsurgency operations understandably struggles with changing social structures in the field and developing political connections to potential allies. This study of Afghanistan shows that soldiers, at the company or even individual level, face these same struggles. The recognition of these problems is not new. Special Forces units have been advising and training indigenous forces, including non-state allies, since the end of World War II. But the growing recognition of US personnel's lack of social skills and connections in certain areas is leading to some changes. The problem still exists, and structural holes remain; but, the United States government is now moving to more effectively monitor the intermediaries upon whom it relies. In Iraq and Afghanistan, for example, translators may earn their way to the United States if they successfully broker for units overseas.

The recognition that social structure matters may have several effects. Most importantly, increased recognition of the presence of structural holes may make it more likely that those holes will be closed. As I described in Chapter 1, social psychologists have found that individuals can be "trained" to see structural holes; similarly, the development of military training and doctrine that emphasizes the effects of structural holes may provide a mechanism to ensure that opportunities for brokerage are missed less often. Second, the military and intelligence services may now better appreciate the importance of social skill. This study of Afghanistan shows that the United States dedicated no resources to improving soldiers' understandings of Afghanistan, its culture, or its languages before September 11; I presume there was a substantial increase thereafter. If the government appreciates the role of social skill, agents with institutional influence would have more incentive to spend time learning about a region, so as to take the place of intermediaries more quickly than in past cases.

Yet, the empirical record should make us suspicious that military doctrine has fundamentally changed – to date, there is scant evidence that structural holes are closed or that the military is now filled with socially skilled individuals. Although the military recognized its poor understanding of Afghan society, it did not do much to fix the problem. One major response to the problem of limited understanding, for example, was the emergence of controversial Human Terrain Teams. Human Terrain Teams were designed to develop social scientific knowledge of theatres in which the United States conducts military operations, especially Afghanistan and Iraq.[72] These teams were to be composed of academics and other

---

[72] On the interesting aspects of Human Terrain Teams, see Jonathan Gilmore, "A Kinder,

experts with significant regional expertise. Their task was to produce ethnographies of war-torn regions that created the kind of in-depth understanding of society and culture necessary to develop social connections.

Did the Human Terrain program produce socially skilled individuals? The short answer is no. The training took place in the basement of a mini-mall in Kansas. The trainees often knew nothing about Afghanistan or Iraq. Some of the social scientists who were trained and later deployed in Iraq had done their field work on Latin America, American Indians, or Dumpster divers. Their training included basic course work in languages and research methods. Their final exercise, Weston Resolve, was to do an ethnography of the people living on the Kansas–Missouri border. Vanessa Gezari, a journalist who followed them on their training exercise, describes how they wandered around, interviewing "a young woman making smoothies at a local gym, a man on an exercise bike, mall walkers, college students, and people eating lunch at the food court on the nearby military base." As she watched them, Gezari realized that "whatever information they would be providing did not stem from any special knowledge of Iraqi or Afghan culture."[73] In the field, they were unsuccessful.[74] The experiences of the Human Terrain program shows that even if the military recognizes and attempts to establish the kinds of social skills necessary to ensure cooperation, it will often be ineffective if it selects individuals who do not have experience brokering cooperation across structural holes. These individuals are rare and unusual. They are not easy to produce.

CONCLUSION

This chapter shows that three key themes of this book continue to be relevant in the modern era. First, non-state allies continue to be important. In modern small wars, such as Afghanistan and Iraq, significant attention has been paid to recruiting and working with non-state allies. Furthermore, in the last great power war (World War II), the allies spent significant resources recruiting and retaining non-state allies in Europe

Gentler Counter-Terrorism Counterinsurgency, Human Security and the War on Terror," *Security Dialogue* 42, no. 1 (2011): 21–37; Maja Zehfuss, "Culturally Sensitive War? The Human Terrain System and the Seduction of Ethics," *Security Dialogue* 43, no. 2 (2012): 175–90.

73 Vanessa M. Gezari, *The Tender Soldier: A True Story of War and Sacrifice* (New York: Simon & Schuster, 2013), 164.

74 See also the assessment in Wahab, *In My Father's Country*, 278–85.

and Asia. Second, social structure remains essential to understanding the politics of alliance formation. The relationship between great powers and many non-state groups continues to be characterized by the presence of structural holes. Interpersonal ties between states and their allies are often limited, even in the modern world, during war. War severs social relationships, isolating non-state allies from potential patron states. Third, brokerage continues to be important. When structural holes are present, weak ties are effective at bridging.

The continued presence of structural holes and intermediaries' influence points to fundamental problems with contemporary security scholarship. IR scholars should move away from a focus on political elites in assessing current security policy, and toward a focus on new classes of agents. Too often, International Relations scholars interested in American foreign policy do not concentrate on agents outside of Washington. Yet, these individuals – presidents, Cabinet-level appointees, or military brass – often have little control and no knowledge over what is happening within warzones. Robert Grenier, the CIA Station Chief in Islamabad, complained, "Senior officials in Washington crave one thing: the illusion of control. Oh, yes, they get to issue policy pronouncement, and over time, they can nudge the ship of government policy roughly a few degrees in this direction or that. But for the most part, they are far removed from the actual work that is being done in their agencies, and they have little idea how it actually happens." The problem is distance: "Those in the upper reaches generally don't know the questions that have arisen, let alone the answers, and for the most part it doesn't matter: they attend their rounds of meetings and talk confidently to one another as though their actions had relevance."[75]

This chapter contends that Grenier understates the case. Principals in nations' capitals must depend on agents, such as Grenier, but those agents are powerless without weak ties to intermediaries – translators, middlemen, and others – who choose what information to pass onto them. Intermediaries function between societies and therefore are often not agents in any meaningful sense. Their ability to shape communication means that information reaches principals only after the politics of manipulation and gatekeeping have already occurred. Security scholars therefore need to focus on the intersections of societies, where politics starts, rather than in capitals, where it stops.

---

[75] Grenier, *88 Days to Kandahar*, 91.

Conclusion

Stories of missionaries, traders, and crooks are often seen as historical trivia by International Relations scholars. They are often treated as interesting anecdotes, worth a passing footnote in the history of a war, if they are described at all. Instead, the drama of international politics is thought to depend on great powers and great men.

The main aim of this book has been to undermine this view. One of the most potent forms of political power is the power of betweenness. This power can make historical figures who at first glance seem like oddballs central to the drama of international politics. When agents live at the intersections of societies, they help fill holes in global politics. They place potential cooperation partners in touch with one another. They also monopolize information across borders. Intermediaries can manipulate information, build trust, identify partners for cooperation, and manage identity politics in ways that make cooperation (or war) more likely. Their social skill – their ability to understand the worlds of both parties – allows them to appeal to parties' interests, identities, and beliefs in ways that make cooperation appear useful.

These engineers of cooperation have shaped American foreign policy for more than two centuries. During the American Revolution, a missionary managed to secure the cooperation of the Oneidas, providing a valuable ally in the fight for New York. The first American overseas adventures – the First Barbary War as well as the Spanish–American War – were examples of cases where intermediaries secured the valuable allies who did much of the fighting. The American Civil War saw thousands of American Indians fighting on both sides. Their services were secured by ordinary soldiers, prisoners, and traders.

The same pattern repeats in World War II and modern conflicts like Afghanistan and Iraq.

In making the case for intermediaries' power to shape cooperation, this book has shown that betweenness is a source of political power. The first chapters made the case using network theory. Individuals who are positioned between societies often have little institutional power. They are "intermediaries" as I defined them. Traditionally, we do not expect missionaries isolated overseas, traders with small amounts of capital in unimportant markets, or former slaves to shape history. Our theories of political power deny that they should. Why would individuals with so little institutional and material power matter? The answer this book provides is based on a structural analysis of international politics. The world is not as connected as we often depict it. If IR scholars think about the structure of international politics in interpersonal terms, then they may discover that it is filled with "structural holes." These structural holes are instances in which institutional actors do not have relationships with a specific group or community outside their borders. If particular communities have few interpersonal connections, then the individuals who fill these structural holes obtain significant political power. These intermediaries control the flow of information between societies, providing opportunities to manipulate parties to encourage war or peace.

Taking betweenness seriously is important for IR scholars. It points to new forms of political power, new questions about the history of American foreign policy, new places where politics occurs, and new ways to study politics. This conclusion explores each of these themes in turn.

BETWEENNESS AND POLITICAL POWER

What makes something (a state or a person) powerful? I lack the space here to provide a full account of how IR scholars understand power, because the debate is too multi-sided. Instead, I want to briefly make the case that betweenness is a novel form of power, underexplored in IR scholarship.

I use as my point of departure Michel Barnett and Raymond Duvall's recent exploration of the concept, because it offers itself as a comprehensive treatment. They show that traditional treatments of power in International Relations scholarship are premised on compulsory power. Power is that which allows a state to compel others to do what the state wants them to do. Usually, the emphasis in compulsory power is on strong agents who have more material resources, and therefore can coerce the weak to do what they want. Barnett and Duvall contrast this form of power with three others. The closest form to betweenness is structural power. Structural power refers to social relationships, including "the production and reproduction of internally related positions of super- and subordination, or domination, that actors occupy."[1] Master-slave social relations, for example, create differential capabilities for masters and slaves; so too do relationships of global capitalism create unequal material and social powers. The emphasis is on relationships that produce structural domination.[2]

Unlike other forms of power, betweenness does not depend on material or social domination. Agents' betweenness provides an advantage. It allows an agent to control information and ideas as they circulate through networks. This marks betweenness as different from other forms of power. Slaves, in Barnett and Duvall's account, are powerless. They can neither compel masters to do what they want, nor do they have a powerful position produced by social structures. Historically, however, slaves who occupy essential niches in networks (see the case of Cathcart in Chapter 3) have proved important. It is precisely this ability to make the weak strong that makes betweenness such an interesting feature of international politics. To appreciate it requires redrawing part of the ontology of international politics to include network-based approaches to understanding structure and agency.

Asking new questions about political power specifically related to betweenness has the potential to unlock new and interesting aspects of international politics. It may help us unpack questions about how groups or individuals with little institutional standing play an important role in international politics. This book continues in a tradition begun by historians and pursued by postcolonial and feminist scholars in IR scholarship, trying to show how individuals we normally do not associate with political power exercise influence in international politics.[3] Throughout this book, I made the case that we are simply wrong to ignore these

---

[1] Michael Barnett and Raymond Duvall, "Power in International Politics," *International Organization* 59, no. 1 (2005): 55.

[2] They are similar because they focus on relations. Structural power highlights relationships that produce capabilities. In this sense, the social system constrains and enables agents through the creation of relationships of super- and subordinate, just as social networks constrain and empower agents depending on their network position.

[3] Katharine Moon, *Sex Among Allies* (New York: Columbia University Press, 1997); Cynthia Enloe, *Bananas, Beaches and Bases* (Berkeley: University of California Press, 2000); J. Ann Tickner, *Gender in International Relations: Feminist Perspectives on Achieving Global Security* (New York: Columbia University Press, 1992).

figures. Their betweennness makes them interesting for many reasons. They are interesting, first, because they are simply neat figures in world history. Their travels between societies often read as adventure stories. Their exploits are filled with intrigue and careless blunder, clever diplomatic maneuvers and idiotic schemes, and of course lots of scandal. Figures empowered by betweenness are also interesting because they are historically important. One cannot adequately explain US expansion, the next section argues, without a theory that captures the work of US intermediaries around the globe. These intermediaries are the channels through which American influence travels abroad. They build bridges to the world in places where governments pay little official attention. And, they build national interests in remote regions that serve as the causes of war and expansion.

More broadly, betweenness may also help us understand how weaker powers obtain influence through their leaders' personal networks. Some scholars have used this idea to describe how the network positions of great powers and their leaders may enable them to obtain influence in international politics.[4] Yet small powers are especially interesting, as they often find themselves in important diplomatic positions. In the early 1970s, for example, Pakistan's president, Yahya Khan, used his position as a broker of relations between the Nixon White House and Mao's China to enhance his position as a US alliance partner. His ability to provide a bridge provided him a form of influence that far exceeded Pakistan's material capabilities.[5] Personal relationships that bridge structural holes, in other words, affect alliance politics, and small states' leaders may be well positioned to help form these relationships.

The same advantages of betweenness present in 1972 mattered in North America in 1772. Historians of North America often point to betweenness as a source of political power for Indian empires and republics during the colonial period. One source of influence for the Mohawks, for example, was their geographic position between settlers in New York and western nations. The Mohawks' ability to monopolize diplomacy and trade was central to the drama of American power before and during the American Revolution.[6]

---

[4] Stacy Goddard, "Brokering Change: Networks and Entrepreneurs in International Politics," *International Theory* 1, no. 2 (2009): 249–81.

[5] Gary Bass, *The Blood Telegram* (New York: Alfred Knopf, 2013).

[6] See especially Timothy Shannon, *Iroquois Diplomacy on the Early American Frontier* (New York: Viking, 2008). A fuller discussion is in Chapter 2.

Understanding betweenness may also us help us to understand the nature of diplomacy. In recent years, political scientists have returned to the study of diplomacy. This emerging body of work often emphasizes how diplomats are like brokers. James Der Derian's seminal work on diplomacy, for example, compares early diplomatic culture to "the bridges of medieval cities" that provided a "link between alien quarters."[7] This is important for understanding international society as a whole, because diplomats provide ties across states. Diplomacy, in Alan James's words, is "the communications system of international society" and "without it there could be no international society."[8] A theory of intermediaries points toward possible theories of diplomacy that emphasize the structural position of diplomats. Such an emphasis may lead to new questions about the conditions under which diplomats matter (when other relationships are scarce), who counts as a diplomat (anyone who fills the structural position), and the role of diplomacy in making the international system (closing holes between networks).

Weak individuals, weak powers, and diplomats are only three kinds of agents who may profit from social position. By taking network position seriously as a form of power, IR scholars may be able to follow other social sciences in unlocking new avenues to understanding agency and politics.

UNDERSTANDING AMERICA'S RISE

This book points toward a different story about the historical rise of the United States. IR scholars usually describe the expansion of the United States in a way that makes individuals' efforts unimportant. For example, some Realists describe international politics in such a way that security motives for expansion were hardwired into the international balance of power, making the move west and then abroad seem inevitable. Others point to economic motives. The United States needed land for settlers, markets for trade, or commodities for consumption, explaining the growth of American power. Still others stress American political culture, pointing to the ways ideas of race, empire, and liberty helped promote an image of the United States as a global power with global responsibilities. In all these narratives of the rise of American power, only powerful state

---

[7] James Der Derian, *On Diplomacy* (Oxford: Blackwell, 1987), 42. Der Derian's argument is quite different, but there are similarities at the margins regarding positionality.

[8] Alan James, "Diplomacy," *Review of International Studies* 19, no. 1 (1993): 95.

interests or ideas capable of capturing the imagination of a nation play a role. Agents between communities play little to no role.

These explanations of America's path to expansion are all partly right. The balance of power created opportunities to expand, commerce provided one motive (among many), and race provided a major justification. Yet, these explanations are historically inaccurate because they ignore the "pipes and prisms" of the social structure of international politics.[9] Information about the strategic value of territory, the value of its markets, and the "maturity" of its inhabitants came from agents who had the quality of betweenness this book describes.

Without a theory of intermediaries, one cannot explain *where* the United States expanded. Even if the balance of power or security politics explains why the United States went to the Philippines or Samoa, they cannot explain why the United States limited its territorial aspirations. For example, why intervene in the Philippines in 1898, but not make a play for the islands that became the modern day Mariana Islands, Micronesia, or Palau at the same time? These islands were Spanish possessions and should likely have been spoils of war.[10]

Betweenness helps explain the direction of imperial expansion. The historical record shows few agents who had experience in these territories agitating for commercial or strategic opportunities. For example, individuals testifying before Congress during the period pointed out that they simply did not know enough about the Marianas to make a judgment about whether they were important.[11] There were no social or economic connections between Washington and the islands, leaving an unclosed structural hole. Without intermediaries, expansion is unlikely because no one can or will make the case for war or empire.

Furthermore, without a theory of intermediaries, one cannot explain *how* the United States expanded. During the eighteenth and nineteenth centuries, the United States was not a great power. Yet, it competed globally beyond its weight class. It subdued the Philippines where Spain failed; it dealt a blow to Barbary piracy that European nations could not; and it conquered North America. The standard explanations for why western states outperform their rivals in these kinds of conflicts are premised on superior firepower and better-organized manpower. These

---

[9] Joel M. Podolny, "Networks as the Pipes and Prisms of the Market," *American Journal of Sociology* 107, no. 1 (2001): 33–60.

[10] Don A. Farrell, "The Partition of the Marianas: A Diplomatic History, 1898–1919," *ISLA: A Journal of Micronesian Studies* 2, no. 2 (1994): 273–301.

[11] Ibid.

explanations, however, fail to explain the rise of US power. Compared to European countries, the United States was militarily weak, yet it continually outperformed its European rivals.

To understand American power during requires understanding its social power. Military power's effectiveness is often limited. Paul MacDonald shows that British military power was in itself insufficient to conquer peripheral states. Distance and local resistance combined to make British arms ineffective against the large numbers of people British power wanted to conquer. More important than arms were allies. Local collaborators could provide intelligence, support, and manpower to subdue resistance. MacDonald refers to the ability to secure these collaborators as a form of social power that made imperialism possible.[12]

Like the British in India, the United States has relied on collaborators in almost every major war since its founding. These allies have often done more fighting than the US military, limiting the need to use blood and treasure to prosecute wars abroad. To understand how the United States expanded, therefore, requires understanding its social rather than military power. This is especially important because the United States was not the only power looking to develop these alliances. In most cases, the United States faced rivals who wanted to recruit the same indigenous forces. British and American agents courted Oneidas, the Union and Confederacy solicited Cherokees, and German and American firms pursued Samoan allies. Why did the United States win these contests for important allies so often?

Betweenness is essential to the story about why the United States had the social power necessary to secure indigenous collaborators. Unlike its European rivals, the United States often described itself as anti-imperial. In fact, at the exact moments when the United States tipped toward imperialism, intermediaries wielded a reputation for anti-imperialism as a weapon to win important allies. Promises of land and freedom were made to American Indians like the Oneidas and to foreign peoples like the Samoans and Filipinos. These intermediaries painted a picture in which the United States would liberate peoples and leave them to govern their own affairs. This message of ideological solidarity – coming from a non-European state of colonial origins – resonated across the world. These intermediaries were the spin masters who wove together an empire by promising that there would never be a empire.

---

[12] Paul MacDonald, *Networks of Domination* (New York: Oxford University Press, 2014). This is not limited to the British. See Klooster, *The Dutch Moment*.

By understanding where and how the United States expanded, we can also understand *why* it grew. Michael Doyle describes two explanations for why empires form. Metrocentric explanations concentrate on imperial powers' interests, and pericentric explanations focus on politics within the future imperial possession.[13] By contrast, a theory of betweenness points to the intercentric interests that motivate agents to connect the dots to make expansion possible.

The intercentric interests that drove the formation of ties across borders are not what we traditionally believe are the grist for great power expansion. One initial title for this project was *Pigs, Papists, and Pirates*. Expansion happened because of intermediaries' concerns about their pigs, their worry that Catholics would steal a march in the Pacific, and their umbrage after pirates insulted American honor. The case for Iraq, similarly, was premised on the seemingly trivial, parochial interests of individuals, such as Chalabi and Curveball. These intermediaries sold the Iraq War as a case of high politics upon which US national security depended, but in fact the war turned on their desire for a little bit of money, some power, or a passport. These are not high-minded national interests. They are petty and small. Only by appreciating the importance of intermediaries between American and the world can we see how so much depends on so little.

Appreciating the importance of intermediaries' interests and political power draws a different picture of the rise of the United States. America's rise to superpower status may have been inevitable, but the ways that power was channeled abroad was not a natural outgrowth of changes in the balance of power, American ideas of its place in the world, or the growth of American commerce. Instead, it depended on dynamic changes in the social structure of international politics. As American agents went abroad, they formed connections with new markets and new political actors. When these agents believed that war and conquest were necessary for their interests, they used their weak ties between societies to drive the United States forward. They were the essential piece of social fabric that tied a growing United States to the outside world.

SITES OF POLITICS

One issue this book has not yet addressed is the geographic sense of betweenness. In Chapter 1, I focused on betweenness in the social sense

---

[13] Michael W. Doyle, *Empires* (Ithaca: Cornell University Press, 1986).

of a person between two social networks. In addition to a sociological interpretation, betweenness has a geographic aspect. There are geographic zones – points of contact or borderlands – where people meet, trade, and fight. To create a social position between societies usually requires negotiating these complicated borderlands. Focusing on these geographic regions could revitalize IR scholarship by changing the physical sites at which we think politics takes place.

While I have not developed these geographic arguments as much as the social networks-based arguments, they are important. Many historians are interested in the idea that there are regions where peoples are brought into contact with one another over extended periods.[14] "Borderlands scholarship," a borderlands historian explains, "argues that where nations meet, there exists not just a frontier line but also a land, a region where identities, economies, languages, and what we call cultures create mestizo realities."[15] Agents who travel to the borders between societies often create communities where intermarriage, biculturalism, and trade become common. Richard White, for example, describes the Great Lakes region before the founding of the United States as a borderland, where cultural hybridity, trade, and intermarriage between French and Native Americans was common.[16] Other historians have investigated borderlands with the Spanish, Mexican-Americans, and other Indians. These borderlands often produced the figures I called intermediaries throughout this book.

IR scholars can learn much from borderlands historians. The most important lesson is that IR scholars often locate where international politics happens in the wrong place. Some borderlands historians would call much of what IR scholarship produces "centrist" narratives, because they locate the action in centers of political power.[17] Borderlands histories are a powerful reaction to these stories. First, borderlands are important

---

[14] Important conceptual work is in Herbert Eugene Bolton, *The Spanish Borderlands: A Chronicle of Old Florida and the Southwest* (New Haven: Yale University Press, 1921); Jeremy Adelman and Stephen Aron, "From Borderlands to Borders: Empires, Nation-States, and the Peoples in between in North American History," *The American Historical Review* 104, no. 3 (1999): 814–41; Pekka Hämäläinen and Samuel Truett, "On Borderlands," *The Journal of American History* 98, no. 2 (2011): 338–61.

[15] David A. Chang, "Borderlands in a World at Sea: Concow Indians, Native Hawaiians, and South Chinese in Indigenous, Global, and National Spaces," *Journal of American History* 98, no. 2 (2011): 385.

[16] Richard White, *The Middle Ground: Indians, Empires, and Republics in the Great Lakes Region, 1650–1815* (Cambridge: Cambridge University Press, 1991).

[17] Hämäläinen and Truett, "On Borderlands."

sites to understand international politics. Historians have shown that relations between great powers often played out in these borderlands contexts, where agents in the periphery made the important decisions that affected the outcomes of great power struggles. Centers of political power – in Washington or London, for example – had little control over or knowledge about how politics worked in borderlands contexts. Yet, the outcome of local power struggles could greatly affect trade, war, and settlement patterns. Second, this arena has different rules: social skill, hybridity, and identity become forms of power. To be successful did not simply require more material power; winning required western states to develop alliances with indigenous peoples. Trade goods (economic power) were important. But, so too was the development of effective intermediaries who had a kind of cultural hybridity that allowed them to identify with and appeal to diverse communities. As David Thelen explains, "since some people created borderlands to make war and others to make love, people on both sides placed high value on interpreters and brokers who could turn conflicts into problems to be solved."[18] Third, an emphasis on borderlands helps make seemingly marginal peoples important for the story of international politics. American Indians are central to the history of America's political development. Yet, scholars in American politics have systematically excluded that part of history from the canon of work on US politics.[19] Within IR, this is regrettable. Warring, settlement, and trade in the borderlands constitute the primary interactions the United States has had with other nations during its political history. Our understanding of how the United States expanded and became a great power needs to engage with the complicated politics occurring in these borderlands context. Without this engagement, we see only the smallest of slivers of US diplomatic history.

Borderlands scholarship, in sum, demonstrates that international politics often has little to do with what happens in nations' capitals or international organizations. Studies of traditional halls of power miss the most interesting and important events and patterns relevant to international politics throughout much of human history. If we do not look to borderlands, we are looking for international politics in the wrong places.

---

[18] David Thelen, "Of Audiences, Borderlands, and Comparisons: Toward the Internationalization of American History," *The Journal of American History* 79, no. 2 (1992): 439.

[19] Kennan Ferguson, "Why Does Political Science Hate American Indians?," *Perspectives on Politics* 14, no. 4 (2016): 1029–38.

IR scholars and sociologists have much to add to conversations with historians interested in borderlands. One of the primary contributions our field might make is to understand structural variations in power that matter for the exercise of agency by individuals in borderlands. Some borderland histories describe communities that are well populated. The US–Mexico border, for example, is composed of millions of people who intermarry, engage in trade, and so on. The area is a sea of brokers. Brokerage and hybridity are important for any individual to navigate the borderland, but they are such common characteristics that they do not have much explanatory power. Without structural holes, such socially skilled individuals have fewer opportunities to influence events. Other borderlands histories emphasize cases in which only a few individuals engage in trade or intermarry at sites where societies meet. In these cases, the few individuals who have the traits necessary for successful brokerage are more important. There is a significant theoretical difference between these kinds of sites. When there are a substantial number of brokers, institutional power may matter more, because stable, institutional structures are available to direct political power. When social skill is a rarer trait, individual brokers, and not institutional influence, may matter more.

Capturing these differences may require disentangling metaphors. For the cases described in this book, I prefer the term beach rather than borderland. In nineteenth-century Samoa, the Beach was the home of a comparatively small community of foreign agents, some of whom had the characteristics of cultural brokers (many did not). The Beach was a specific location where ships would dock, stay for a while, and then leave. It was also the location of political intrigue, where foreign agents would come to work with local collaborators to secure a favorable political climate for trade or annexation. In many ways, the Beach was a borderland. But, beaches and borderlands are different. Beaches are examples of borderlands that are not densely populated. There are few bicultural agents. Their scarcity empowers cultural brokers and gives them more influence than they might have in traditional borderlands regions. Their rarity provides influence.[20]

Understanding the interplay of borderlands histories and political science may make both better. By thinking differently about the social structure of the beach and borderlands, historians can think creatively

---

[20] Like borderlands, I mean this to be a broad metaphor: the beach refers to any location where communities interact and there are few cultural brokers able to make those interactions successful.

about how borderlands concepts help produce interesting histories in new regions of the world. The interplay of people, culture, and brokerage works differently depending on the social structure within the sites being studied. For political scientists, leaving the city and heading to the border would lead to new, interesting questions about culture and brokerage, providing opportunities to enrich our disciplinary vocabulary to include new sources of political influence and richer perspectives on international history.

PERSPECTIVE AND ARCHIVAL RESEARCH

The final contribution of this book concerns understanding the role of perspective in archival research. Specifically, this book describes an approach that shifts perspectives, moving from evidence describing political elites' understandings of international politics to looking through the eyes of intermediaries working on the intersections of societies. Concretely, this means analyzing different archival materials. In this section, I describe why this is so important for IR scholarship.

IR scholars tend to adopt one of two perspectives in their research. Realist security scholars typically rely on archival material that views international politics through the eyes of political elites, beginning their studies with memoirs, presidential papers, and histories or biographies written about these elites. The events these scholars focus on, the players they discuss, and the threats they are concerned with are those perceived from nations' capitals, usually far from the action of world politics. Moreover, when Realist security scholars engage with historians on issues of method, they usually turn to traditional diplomatic historians who share this emphasis.[21] The other school of thought most closely tied to history is the English School, which is interested in broad historical questions, for example, questions about different forms of global order.[22] They tend to use secondary sources to describe systems in broad ways. In doing so, they provide an omniscient perspective.[23] These histories escape the problem of perspective by being lofty and synthetic.

[21] For engagement with traditional historians, see, for example, the historians who contributed to Colin Elman and Miriam Fendius Elman, eds., *Bridges and Boundaries: Historians, Political Scientists, and the Study of International Relations* (Cambridge, MA: MIT Press, 2001).

[22] See, for example, Hedley Bull, *The Anarchical Society: A Study of Order in World Politics*, (New York: Columbia University Press, 2002).

[23] For recent work, see, for example, Christian Reus-Smit, "Reading History through Constructivist Eyes," *Millennium* 37, no. 2 (2008): 395–414; John M. Hobson and

Haber, Kennedy, and Krasner make an explicit plea for these kinds of traditional diplomatic history, especially the first kind. They first show that work outside of IR scholarship is moving away from relying on traditional sources and interpretations of the historical record. Whereas traditional diplomatic history emphasized Stalin and Churchill, the new histories emphasize people from the margins, such as women, the colonized, slaves, and so on. Concentrating on non-traditional perspectives, they believe, abandons the focus on international relations or diplomatic history properly understood. They believe that marginalized voices rarely speak to traditional questions, which are "the studies of elites, or rulers" or "foreign relations," and instead focus on the "internal character of American society." Concentrating on marginalized voices, they argue, produces bad scholarship. Non-traditional agents leave too few written records. Therefore, to concentrate on them means, in their words, "the historical discipline as a whole has disengaged somewhat from its traditional commitment to empirical evidence, and is making more room for ruminative argument in which the evidentiary gaps are filled by sometimes bold, though sometimes silly interpretive artifice."[24]

These arguments against incorporating a variety of perspectives in historical work are wrong-headed. IR scholarship concerns more than the world of elites and rulers. Exchanges of goods, information, or violence can occur between states or societies without rulers even being aware it is occurring (see the case of Samoa), and leaders' opinions or beliefs may not matter if decision-making is delegated, highly constrained, or overdetermined. Moreover, IR scholars are interested in the effects of foreign policy on people's lives. Feminist scholarship, for example, shows that understanding world politics through the eyes of marginalized groups is important for understanding policies' consequences for the people most dramatically affected.[25] If a key reason we care about politics is its influence on ordinary people's lives, we need to look through their eyes to understand the impact of others' decisions.

George Lawson, "What Is History in International Relations?," *Millennium* 37, no. 2 (2008): 415–35.

[24] Stephen H. Haber, David M. Kennedy, and Stephen D. Krasner, "Brothers under the Skin: Diplomatic History and International Relations," *International Security* 22, no. 1 (1997): 38–40.

[25] Enloe, *Bananas, Beaches and Bases*; Cynthia Enloe, *Maneuvers: The International Politics of Militarizing Women's Lives* (Berkeley: University of California Press, 2000); Caroline Kennedy-Pipe, "International History and International Relations Theory: A Dialogue beyond the Cold War," *International Affairs* 76, no. 4 (2000): 741–54.

This book has made an empirical case that focusing on elites' perspectives leads to distortions of the record of international politics. This is the most important argument this book advances. If "silly interpretive artifice" characterizes any body of work, it is that of the elites themselves. In the case of alliances with non-state allies, elites are often unaware of brewing conflicts. When they are aware, it is often because someone at the intersection of societies has brought the conflict to their attention (see, for example, the case of Samoa). Most elites do not know about or understand potential allies abroad (see, for example, the Philippines). When they are aware of these allies, they are culturally incapable of negotiating with them in ways that are sensitive to others' cultural, political, or religious beliefs (see the Pawnee and Oneidas). To seek out information, they turn to people at the fringes of political life; many of these figures are disreputable, untrustworthy, and take advantage of elites' limitations to pursue parochial agendas (see the case of Chalabi). Rulers and leaders are limited because their eyes rarely move beyond their desk or their office. The problems documented in this book with taking only political elites' perspective on world events are closely related to problems that have been articulated in other fields.

The key advantage to exploring wider ranges of perspectives is that it provides for better empirical inquiry. Unlike Subaltern Studies that concentrate on marginalized individuals, this book concentrates on the perspective of people navigating between societies.[26] Intermediaries who cross borders have a different perspective on cooperation and conflict. They witness events on the ground as they unfold, they know what information is passed between societies, and their biculturalism and bilingualism help us understand what diverse agents make of a situation. They may be the people who report a state's foreign policy to peoples abroad,

[26] Subaltern Studies also pursues a bottom-up approach, and therefore I want to differentiate my view from that important perspective. Itoften describes how emphasizing the perspective of "others," for example, social and economic classes harmedby colonialism, is important. This view is right to point to the importance of adding perspectives to our histories of international politics in order to understand the effects of and causes for political and social domination. However, for IR scholars, even this is insufficient. To understand the politics of the relationship between core and periphery requires adding a third perspective: the agents between oppressor and oppressed who orchestrate relations between them. On Subaltern perspectives in IR, see Mohammed Ayoob, "Inequality and Theorizing in International Relations: The Case for Subaltern Realism," *International Studies Review* 4, no. 3 (2002): 27–48; Giorgio Shani, "Toward a Post-Western IR: The Umma, Khalsa Panth, and Critical International Relations Theory," *International Studies Review* 10, no. 4 (2008): 722–34.

and their explanations of how they communicated with others, and what others' reactions were, may be central to understanding important events in world politics. As such, intermediaries are perhaps the best-placed agents at many sites for understanding the politics of international relations. They are the eyewitnesses to history.

Studying international history through the eyes of intermediaries has three advantages that other approaches to multiplying historical perspectives may miss. First, intermediaries, for the reasons given above, are the best-placed agents to directly observe the transmissions across borders that are critical themes in IR scholarship, such as the transmission of goods or information. Second, intermediaries provide ground-level reports of events of interest in international politics. When doing archival work, IR scholars frequently suggest that one should look to newspapers to understand context.[27] Intermediaries are even better. Intermediaries, first, may be the agents whom newspapers turn to in order to gather information (see the case of Wildman in the Philippines). By focusing on intermediaries themselves, researchers can go directly to the source, and skip past the middle man, the international news. Newspapers also present fractured records: limited space in a newspaper leads to sporadic reporting. Intermediaries' personal papers may be better places to follow a story as it unfolds. Finally, intermediaries leave paper trails. One well-known problem with Subaltern Studies is that the voiceless rarely leave archival materials that directly report what they thought or did. When papers are available, they are organized and written from the colonial perspective. Intermediaries, in my experience, often leave some trail in the archival record, written by their own hand: they typically leave sufficient evidence with which to work. We are not confronting the more radical cases of historical silence, and therefore we do not need to read against the grain within the sources to understand the record.[28]

In moving beyond traditional sources, IR scholars should also move beyond our reliance on narrative history. Most of the historians who are widely read by political scientists are narrative historians. These historians piece together stories of politics, and these stories are usually organized in ways that produce some form of

---

[27] Deborah Welch Larson, "Sources and Methods in Cold War History: The Need for a New Theory-Based Archival Approach," in *Bridges and Boundaries: Historians, Political Scientists, and the Study of International Relations*, ed. Colin Elman and Miriam Fendius Elman (Cambridge, MA: MIT Press, 2001), 327–50.

[28] On historical silence, see Michel-Rolp Troullot, *Silencing the Past: Power and the Production of History* (Boston: Beacon Press, 1995).

drama.[29] Political scientists often note that relying on historians creates problems, especially in cases in which different narratives provide strikingly different answers to the same questions.[30] The question I want to ask is whether the reliance on narratives produced by historians is itself a problem. Historians who emphasize narrative are often limited because they are missing pieces of the story, making stringing a narrative together difficult. This is especially a problem when studying marginalized peoples. For example, it is difficult to tell a narrative about the recruitment of American Indians, because we do not have first-hand accounts of what it was like to recruit, what was said to potential enlistees (except for snippets), and how recruiters were received. Unit histories, pension papers, and other sources, however, provide better evidence about what American Indians did after joining. Therefore, the best histories narrate Indian service rather than recruitment, because their service is comparatively well documented.[31] Narrative histories thus often ignore parts of the archival record that do not fit with the story they are telling, or their stories have large gaps due to a lack of documents.

IR scholars' approach to history does not require the narrative approach that characterizes a significant portion of diplomatic and military history. Unlike narrative historians, we can take the surviving records and see if the pieces of the story we have are consistent with a broader theory. In the case of recruitment of Native Americans, we know who the recruiters were, we have information about their backgrounds, and we have records from officers describing their importance; we can use this evidence to make inferences about the importance of social skill by comparing recruiters' successes and examining officers' reports. Such an approach, however, requires moving beyond a reliance on narrative secondary sources. If IR scholars are willing to do the work to return to primary source documents, they will find a wealth of evidence left behind by narratively trained historians, which did not fit into their stories, awaiting discovery and use by political scientists.

---

[29] Hayden White, *Metahistory: The Historical Imagination in Nineteenth-Century Europe* (Baltimore: John Hopkins University Press, 1975).

[30] Ian S. Lustick, "History, Historiography, and Political Science: Multiple Historical Records and the Problem of Selection Bias," *The American Political Science Review* 90, no. 3 (1996): 605–18.

[31] See, for example, Laurence Hauptman, *Between Two Fires: American Indians in the Civil War* (New York: Free Press, 1995).

If IR scholarship is to undergo a revolution in qualitative methods, especially in archival work, it needs to more closely consider the problems with archival research. Usually, the best work on archival methods discusses selection bias, the distinction between primary and secondary sources, and sometimes differences in hard and soft sources.[32] These are helpful conversations. Yet, as a discipline we are far behind in our understanding of how to exploit the vast evidentiary legacy that has been left to us. We are not taking seriously path-breaking work in other fields that has opened vistas on world politics by dramatically expanding what kinds sources are consulted and which viewpoints are described and used as evidence. If IR scholars continue to hitch our horse solely to traditional diplomatic history, we will find ourselves unable to participate in the broader conversations across the social sciences and humanities about history, evidence, and world politics.

THE FUTURE OF SOCIAL STRUCTURE

One of the most important implications of this book is that the future will continue to have the same kinds of social structures as the past. Academics and pundits regularly point to the emergence of a united, globalized world in which distance has shrunk. Political scientists interested in globalization point to the reshaping of information, the economy, and society in ways in which mutual interdependence is increasingly a cornerstone feature of world politics. Keohane and Nye describe this as a world with "more interconnections" than ever before.[33] The primary reason is that communication is easier. Travel, technology, and interdependence have led to a change in the fundamental social structure of world politics. Sociologists such as Anthony Giddens believe that these changes have led to a situation in which face-to-face encounters are no longer necessary for the formation of social ties.[34]

One lesson from this book is that we should pause before overestimating the level of interconnectedness in global politics. Reducing drags on networks created by distance makes connections easier. It does not mean we are easily and directly connected to everyone else.

---

[32] Cameron Thies, "A Pragmatic Guide to Qualitative Historical Analysis in the Study of International Relations," *International Studies Perspectives* 3 (2002): 351–72.

[33] Robert O. Keohane and Joseph S. Nye, "Globalization: What's New? What's Not? (And So What?)," *Foreign Policy*, no. 118 (2000): 109.

[34] Anthony Giddens, *The Consequences of Modernity* (Cambridge: Polity, 1990), 21.

Ernest Cline's *Ready Player One* imagines a world in which everyone on the planet, disgusted with the real world, plays a virtual reality video game. They put on headsets and gloves, living in the game as much as possible. In this virtual world, communication between players is nearly costless. One can email, go to chat rooms, or use other in-game communication features that are free. To broadcast information across the world, a player can create a feed or blog that everyone else can see and read. As the novel develops, the reader discovers that forming social connections in this online world is as difficult as in the real world (if not more so). To make a connection requires you to spend (virtual) time with others, hang out with others, learn what makes them tick, and develop friendship and trust. Only then does a user develop the kind of social bonds that allow for the important episodes of cooperation that move the plot of the book forward. Communication and travel open possibilities, but they cannot reshape social structure as conceived in network language.[35]

Just like Cline's imagined virtual world, the modern global system is not well integrated. Structural holes remain. Afghanistan and Iraq underscore that in international politics, finding allies and developing trust with them is as difficult as ever. Wars, crises, and politics create holes in international social structures that need to be filled in order to create an interconnected global society. The world hangs together because of the individuals who plug the holes in international society. By understanding how their betweenness is central to this new global world, we will have better respect for the limits and sources of political power in the next century.

[35] Ernest Cline, *Ready Player One* (New York: Crown, 2011).

Collections and Government Documents Consulted

Government Record Groups

National Archives, Washington DC
   Record Group 24: Records of the Bureau of Naval Personnel
   Record Group 75: Records of the Bureau of Indian Affairs
   Record Group 94: Office of the Adjutant General
   Record Group 393: Records of United States Army Continental Commands,
      1821–1920
   Record Group 395: Records of US Army Overseas Operations and Commands,
      1898–1942
National Archives II, College Park, MD
   Record Group 43: Records of International Conferences, Commissions, and
      Expositions
   Record Group 59: General Records of the Department of State

Manuscript Collections

Carlisle, PA
   US Army Heritage and Education Center
   Matthew A. Batson Papers
Chapel Hill, NC
   Southern Historical Collection, The Wilson Library, University of North
      Carolina at Chapel Hill
   Wishart Family Papers, circa 1830–1999
Chicago, IL
   The Newberry Library
   Orville E. Babcock Papers
Clinton, NY
   Hamilton College Library Collections
   Samuel Kirkland Collection (Digital and Print)

Lincoln, NE
  Nebraska State Historical Society
  Frank North Papers
  Luther Hedden North Papers
London
  School of Advanced Studies, University of London
  Council for World Mission / London Missionary Society Archives
Newark, DE
  Special Collections at the Morris Library, University of Delaware.
  George Bates Papers
Washington, DC
  Library of Congress
    Henry T. Allen Papers
    John Barrett Papers
    Thomas F. Bayard Papers
    James L. Cathcart Papers
    George Dewey Papers
    August V. Kautz Papers
    Henry W. Lawton Papers
    Edward Preble Papers
    Rounsevelle and Edwin Wildman Papers

Governmental Published Sources

Annual Reports of the Commissioner of Indian Affairs.
Journals of the Continental Congress, 1774–1789.
Naval documents related to the United States wars with the Barbary powers.

Published Collections (Non-governmental)

John Adams

The Adams Family Correspondence, ed. L. H. Butterfield, Wendell D. Garrett, and
  Marjorie E. Sprague. Cambridge: Harvard University Press.
The Diary and Autobiography of John Adams, ed. L. H. Butterfield, Leonard C.
  Faber, and Wendell D. Garrett. Cambridge: Harvard University Press.
The Papers of John Adams.

Cherokees

Cherokee Cavaliers: Forty Years of Cherokee History as Told in the
  Correspondence of the Ridge-Watie-Boudinot Family (Norman: University
  of Oklahoma Press, 1939).
The Life of the Late Gen. William Eaton (Brookfield: Merriam & Co., 1813).

Peter Gansevoort, Jr.

David A. Ranzan and Matthew J. Hollis, eds., *Hero of Fort Schuyler: Selected Revolutionary War Correspondence of Brigadier General Peter Gansevoort, Jr.* (Jefferson, NC: McFarland, 2014).

Thomas Jefferson

The Papers of Thomas Jefferson, ed. Julian Boyd (Princeton: Princeton University Press, 1954).

Samuel Kirkland

Walter Pilkington, ed., *The Journals of Samuel Kirkland* (Clinton, New York: Hamilton College, 1980).

Pawnees

Richard Jensen, ed., *The Pawnee Mission Letters, 1834–1851* (Lincoln: University of Nebraska Press, 2010).

Chief John Ross

Papers of Chief John Ross, ed. Gary E. Moulton (Norman: University of Oklahoma Press, 1985).

William T. Sherman

Brooks Simpson and Jean Berlin, eds., *Sherman's Civil War: Selected Correspondence of William T. Sherman, 1860–1865* (Chapel Hill: University of North Carolina Press, 1999).

Index